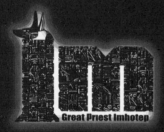

Great Priest Imhotep

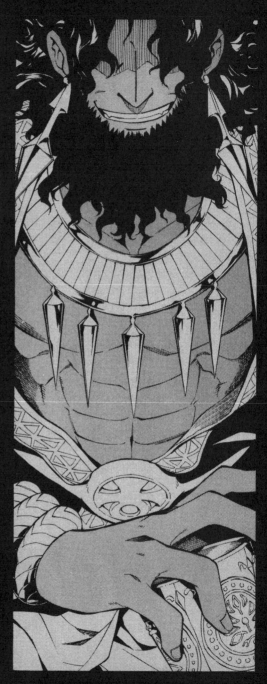

MAKOTO
MORISHITA

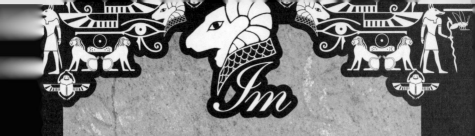

SCROLL **20**3 DRINK, LAUGH,
IT'S A TOAST

SCROLL **21**47 ASSALAMU☆EGYPT

SCROLL **22**93 THE SEED THAT HAS
YET TO SPROUT

SCROLL **23**135 SUN'S BUD,
HINOME

Great Priest Imhotep

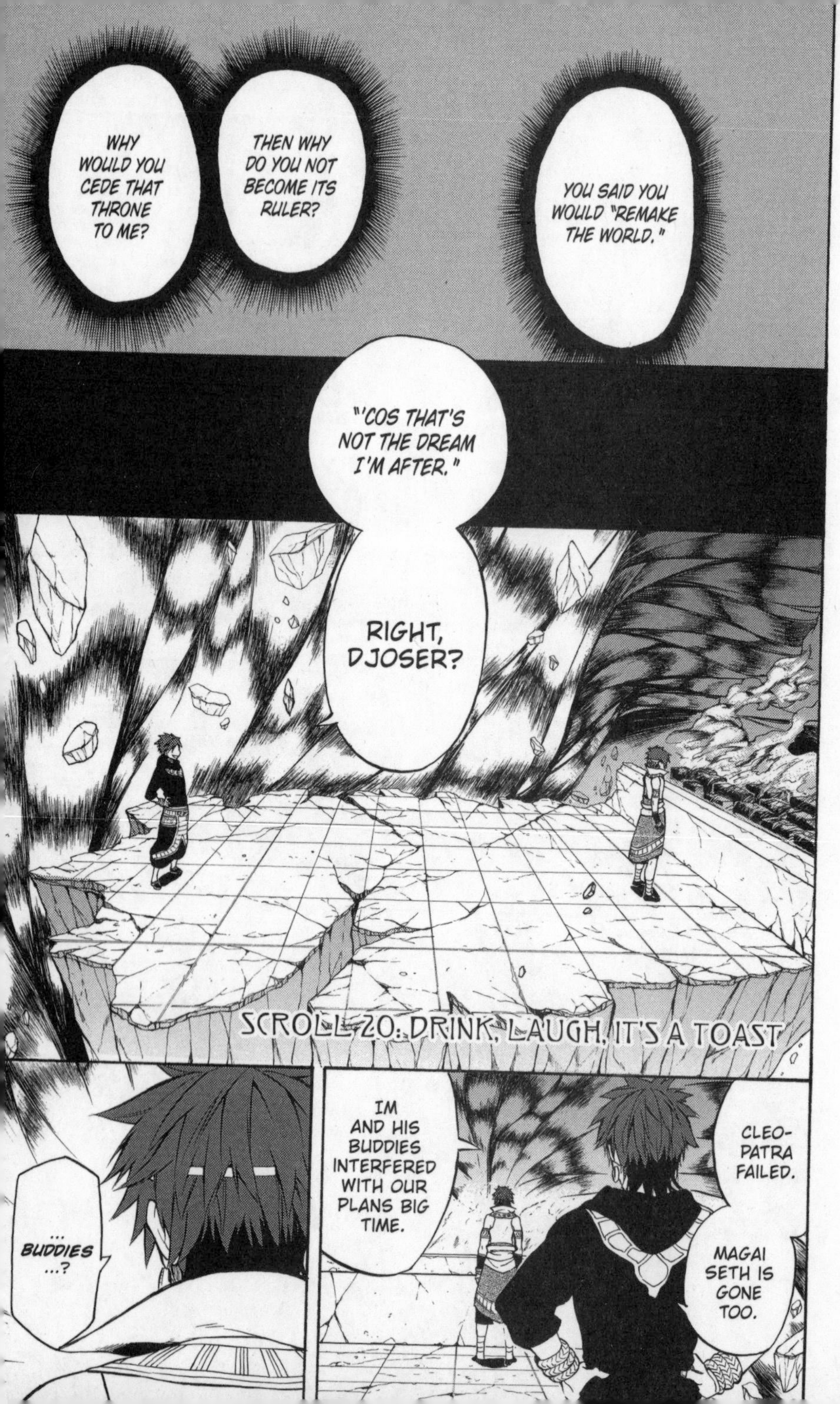
YOU SAID YOU WOULD "REMAKE THE WORLD."
THEN WHY DO YOU NOT BECOME ITS RULER?
WHY WOULD YOU CEDE THAT THRONE TO ME?
"'COS THAT'S NOT THE DREAM I'M AFTER."
RIGHT, DJOSER?
SCROLL 20: DRINK, LAUGH, IT'S A TOAST
CLEO-PATRA FAILED.
MAGAI SETH IS GONE TOO.
IM AND HIS BUDDIES INTERFERED WITH OUR PLANS BIG TIME.
...BUDDIES...?

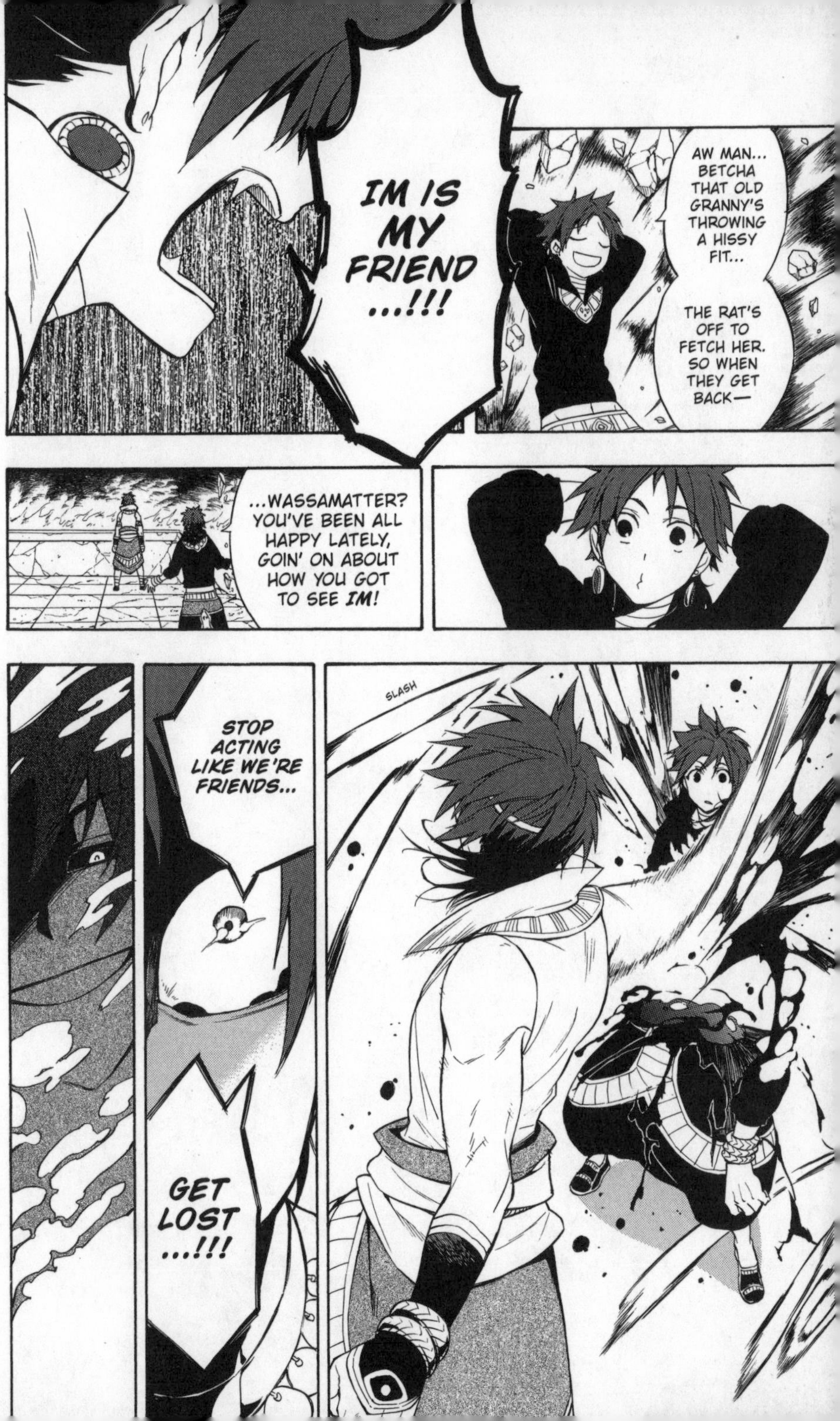
AW MAN... BETCHA THAT OLD GRANNY'S THROWING A HISSY FIT...
THE RAT'S OFF TO FETCH HER. SO WHEN THEY GET BACK—
IM IS MY FRIEND ...!!!
...WASSAMATTER? YOU'VE BEEN ALL HAPPY LATELY, GOIN' ON ABOUT HOW YOU GOT TO SEE IM!
SLASH
STOP ACTING LIKE WE'RE FRIENDS...
GET LOST ...!!!

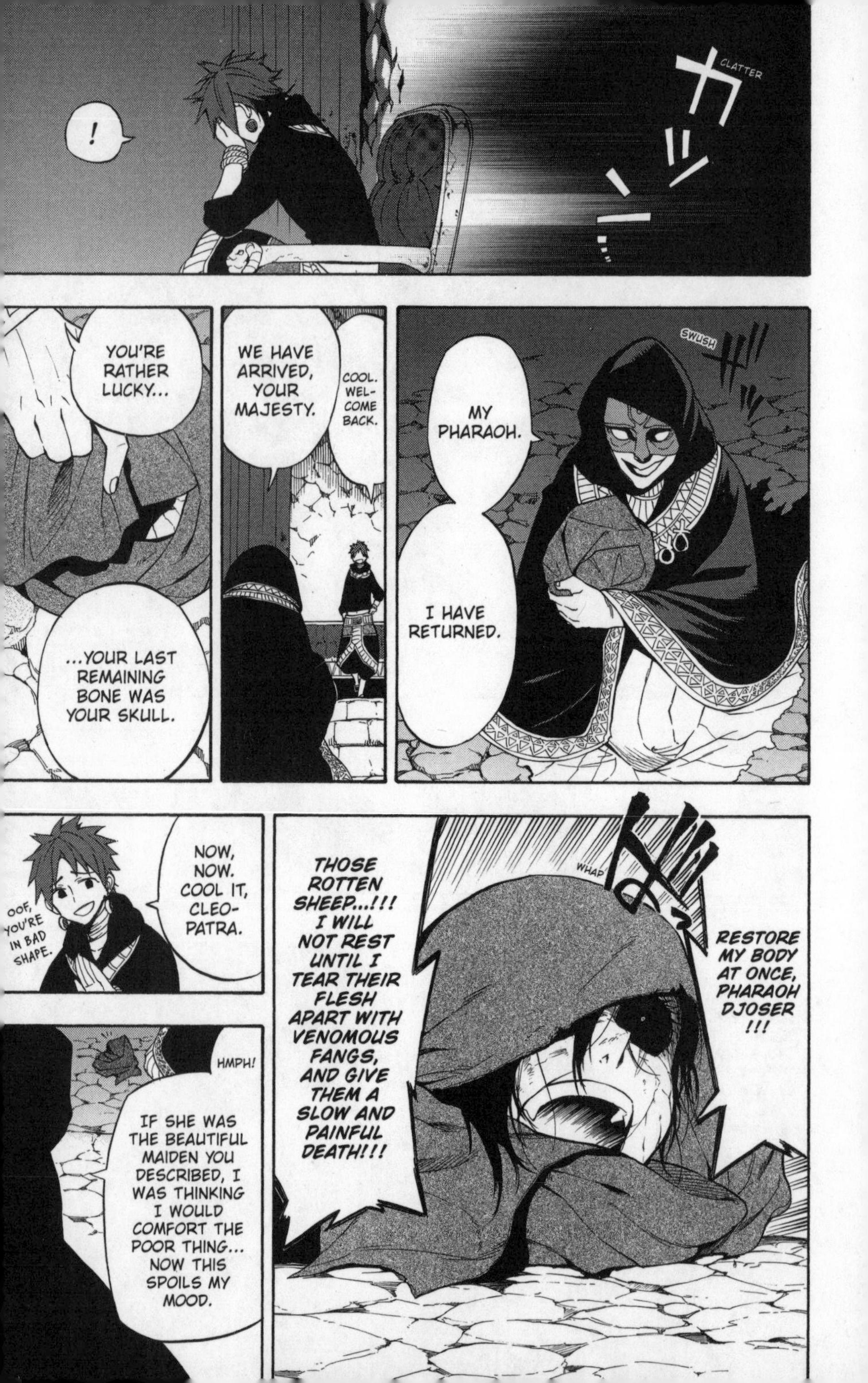
CLATTER
!
SWUSH
MY PHARAOH.
I HAVE RETURNED.
WE HAVE ARRIVED, YOUR MAJESTY.
COOL. WEL-COME BACK.
YOU'RE RATHER LUCKY...
...YOUR LAST REMAINING BONE WAS YOUR SKULL.
WHAP
RESTORE MY BODY AT ONCE, PHARAOH DJOSER!!!
THOSE ROTTEN SHEEP...!!! I WILL NOT REST UNTIL I TEAR THEIR FLESH APART WITH VENOMOUS FANGS, AND GIVE THEM A SLOW AND PAINFUL DEATH!!!
NOW, NOW. COOL IT, CLEO-PATRA.
OOF, YOU'RE IN BAD SHAPE.
HMPH!
IF SHE WAS THE BEAUTIFUL MAIDEN YOU DESCRIBED, I WAS THINKING I WOULD COMFORT THE POOR THING... NOW THIS SPOILS MY MOOD.

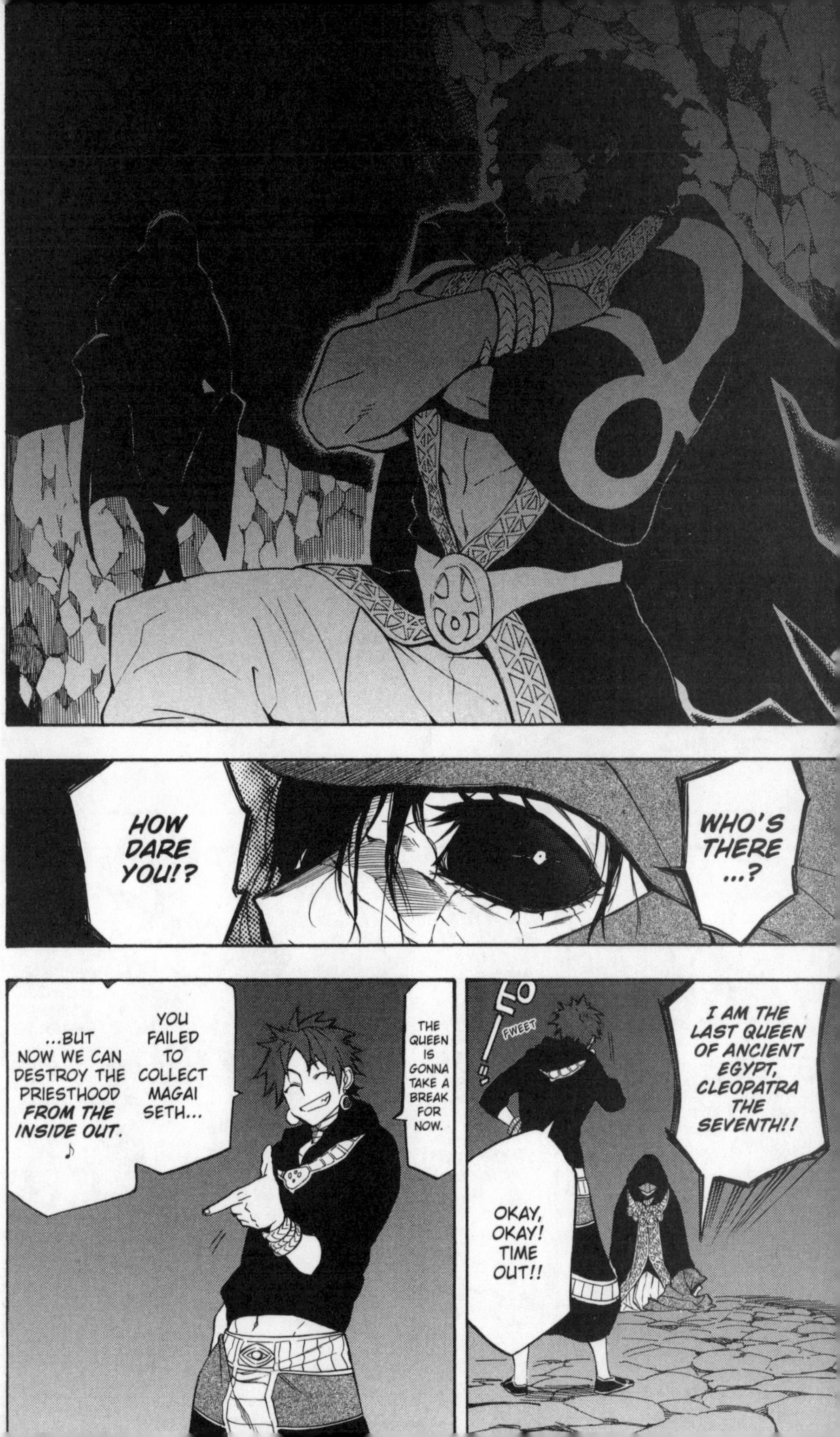
WHO'S THERE ...?
HOW DARE YOU!?
I AM THE LAST QUEEN OF ANCIENT EGYPT, CLEOPATRA THE SEVENTH!!
FWEET
OKAY, OKAY! TIME OUT!!
THE QUEEN IS GONNA TAKE A BREAK FOR NOW.
YOU FAILED TO COLLECT MAGAI SETH...
...BUT NOW WE CAN DESTROY THE PRIESTHOOD FROM THE INSIDE OUT. ♪

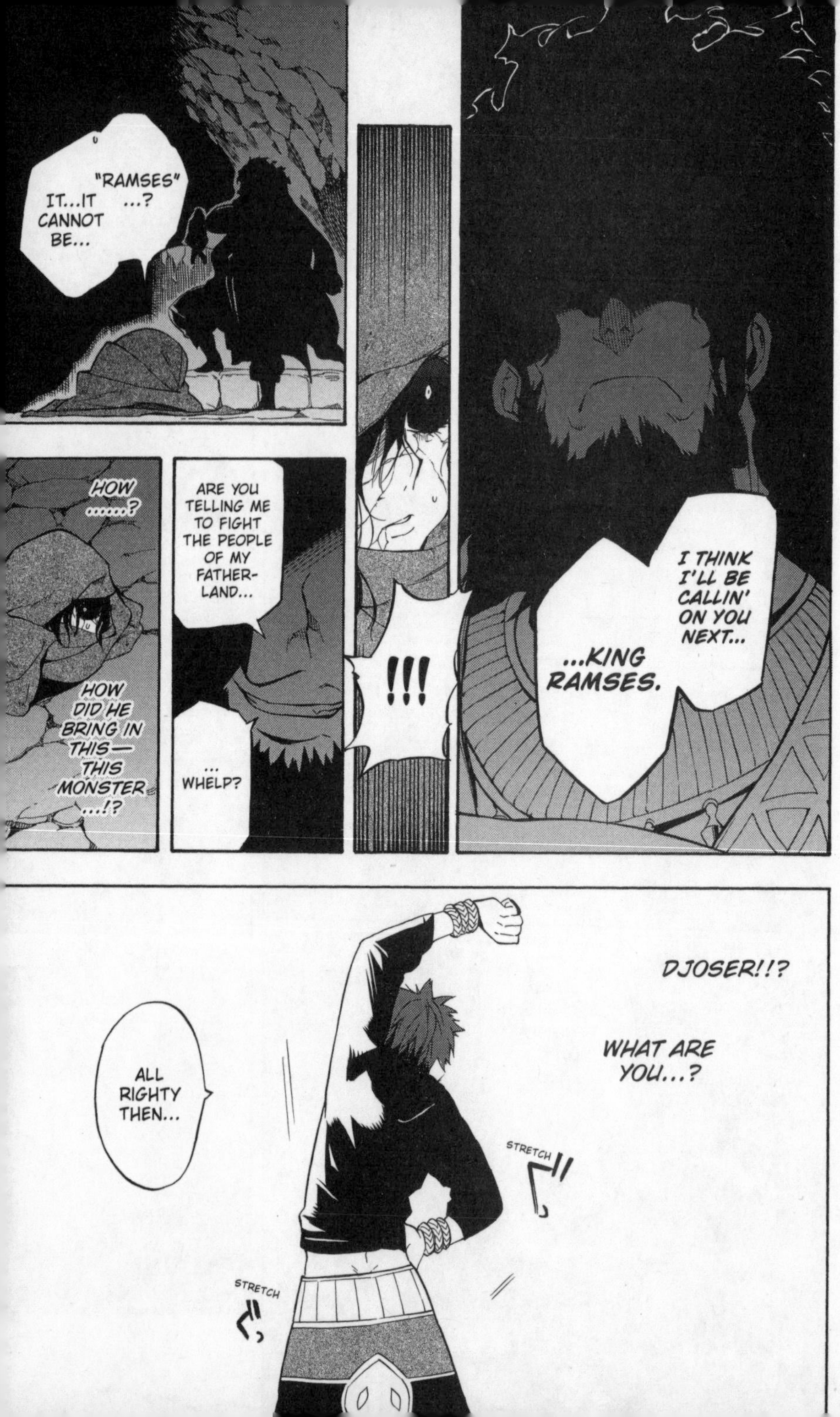
I THINK I'LL BE CALLIN' ON YOU NEXT...
...KING RAMSES.
"RAMSES" ...?
IT...IT CANNOT BE...
!!!
ARE YOU TELLING ME TO FIGHT THE PEOPLE OF MY FATHER-LAND...
... WHELP?
HOW ......?
HOW DID HE BRING IN THIS—THIS MONSTER ...!?
DJOSER!!?
WHAT ARE YOU...?
STRETCH
ALL RIGHTY THEN...
STRETCH

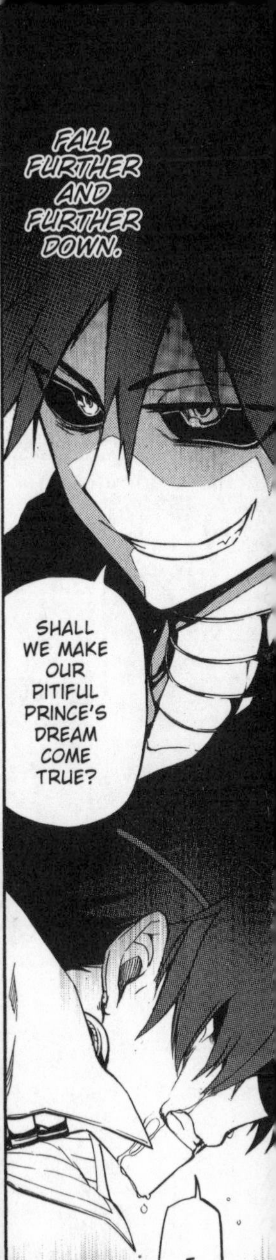
FALL FURTHER AND FURTHER DOWN.
SHALL WE MAKE OUR PITIFUL PRINCE'S DREAM COME TRUE?
...I...
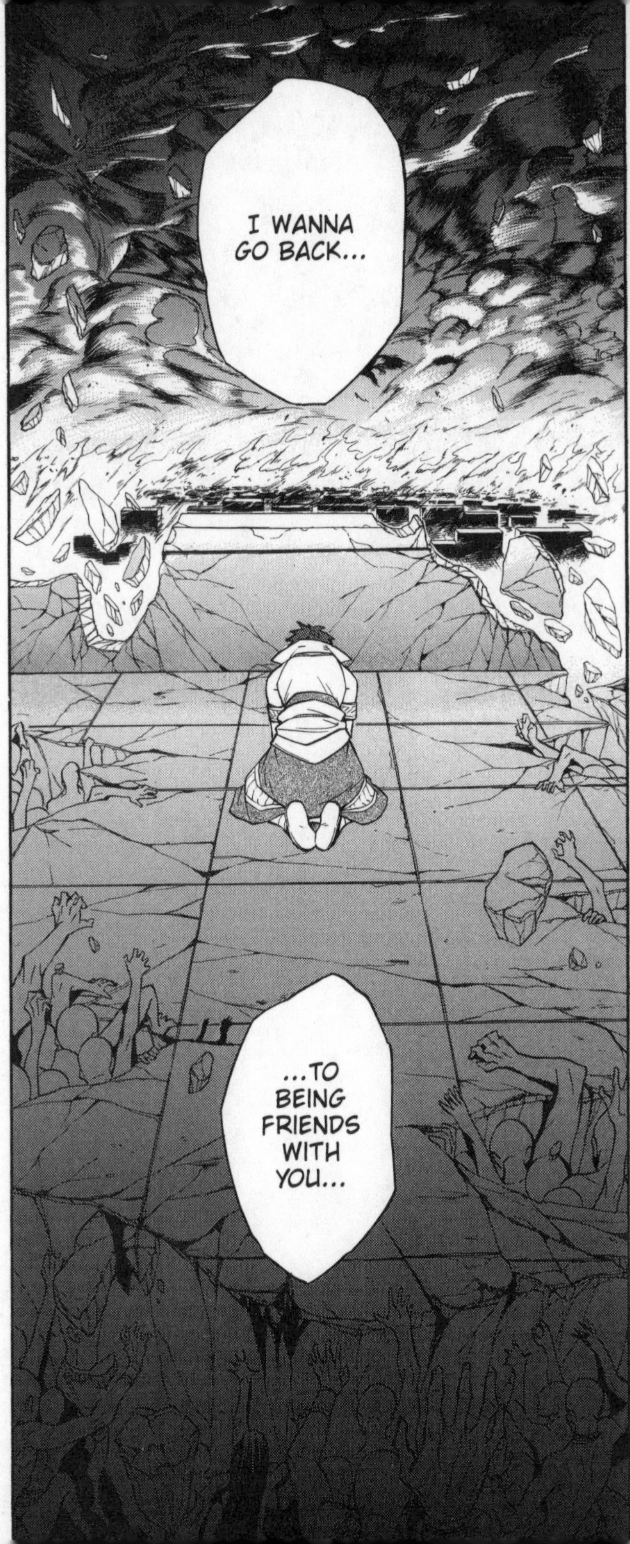
I WANNA GO BACK...
...TO BEING FRIENDS WITH YOU...

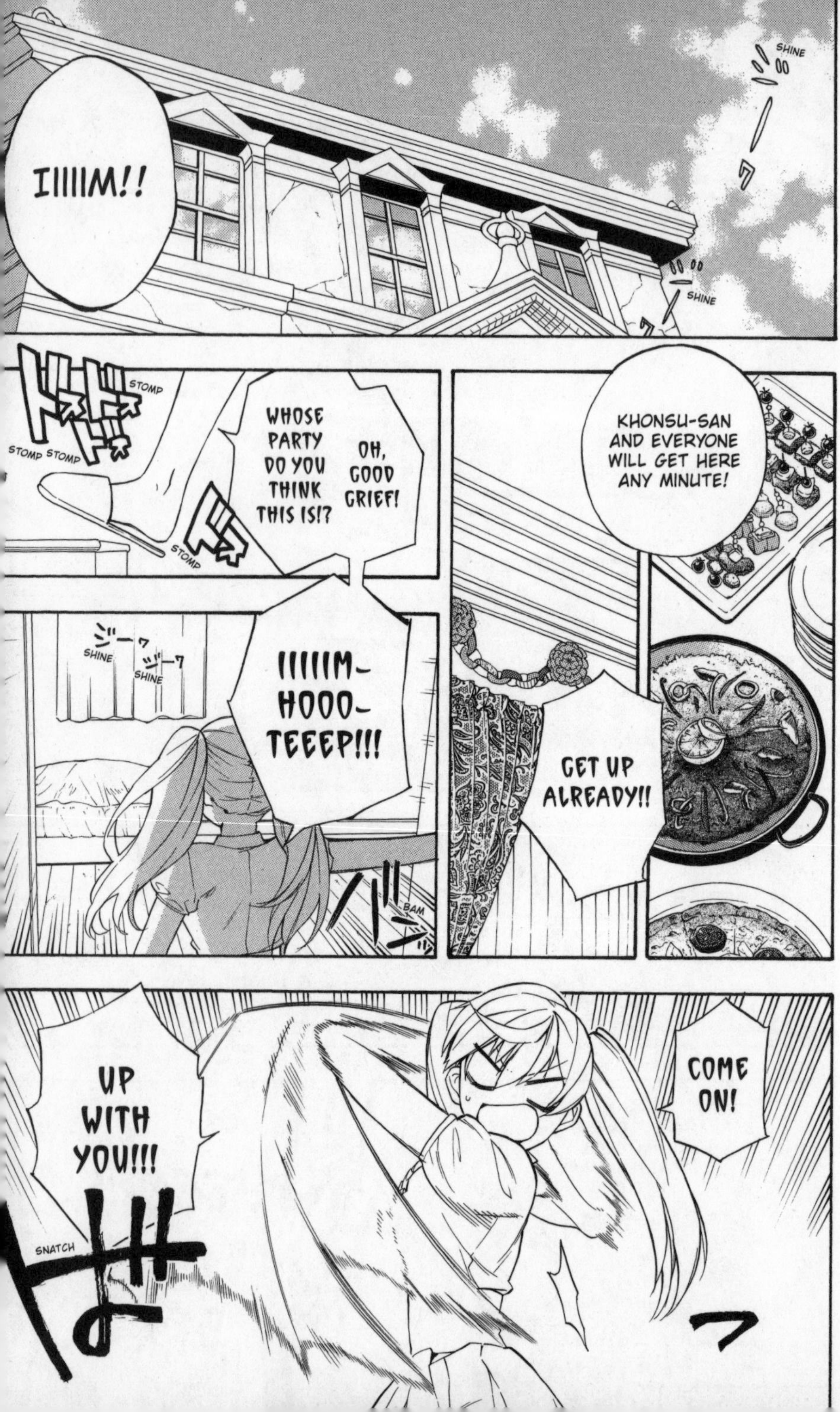
SHINE
SHINE
IIIIIM!!
KHONSU-SAN AND EVERYONE WILL GET HERE ANY MINUTE!
GET UP ALREADY!!
OH, GOOD GRIEF!
WHOSE PARTY DO YOU THINK THIS IS!?
STOMP
STOMP STOMP
STOMP
IIIIIM-HOOO-TEEEP!!!
SHINE
SHINE
BAM
COME ON!
UP WITH YOU!!!
SNATCH

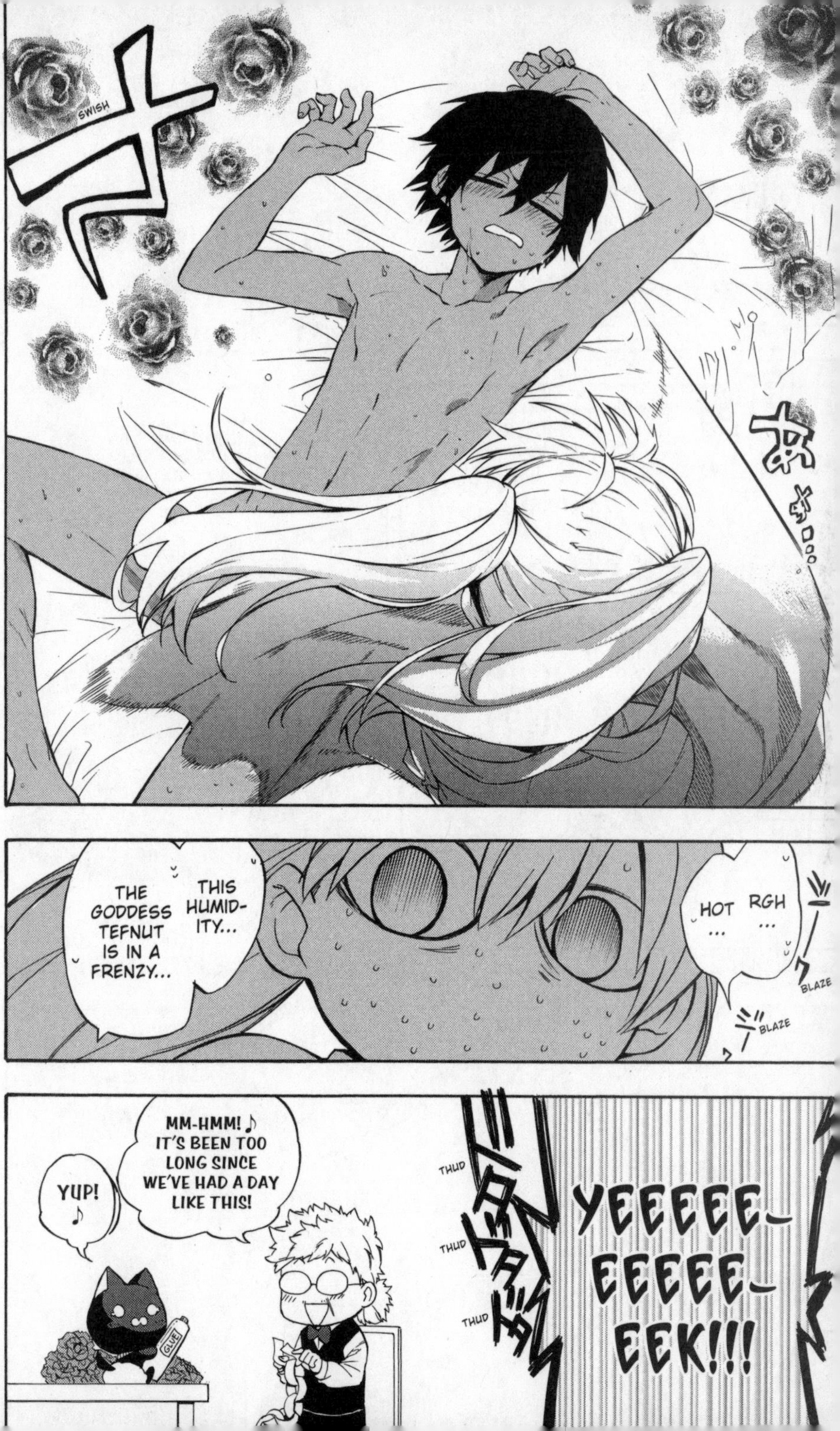
SWISH
RGH ...
HOT ...
BLAZE
BLAZE
THIS HUMIDITY...
THE GODDESS TEFNUT IS IN A FRENZY...
YEEEEE-EEEEE-EEK!!!
THUD
THUD
THUD
MM-HMM! ♪ IT'S BEEN TOO LONG SINCE WE'VE HAD A DAY LIKE THIS!
YUP! ♪
GLUE

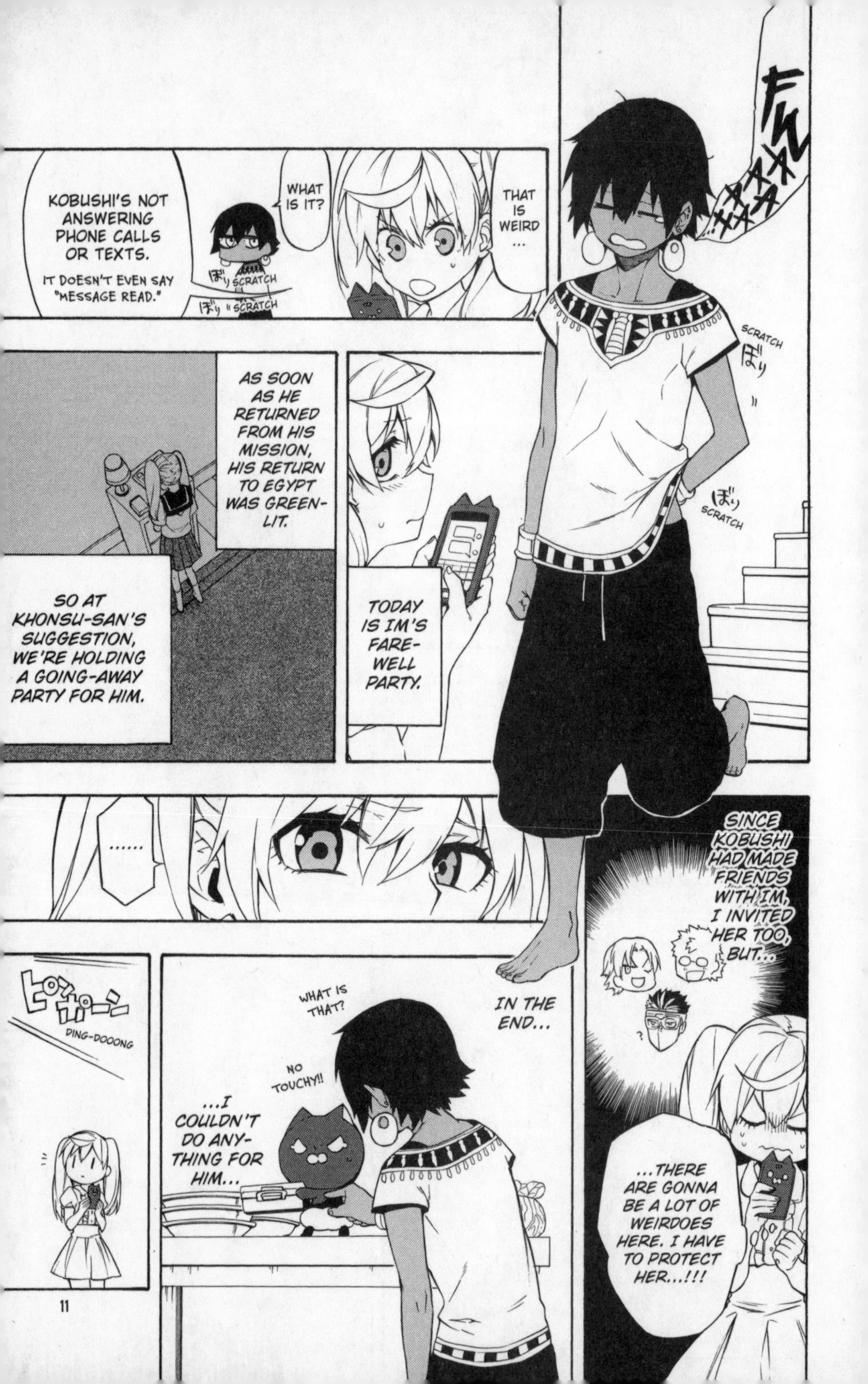
FWAAAAAAA
SCRATCH ぼり
ぼり SCRATCH
THAT IS WEIRD...
WHAT IS IT?
KOBUSHI'S NOT ANSWERING PHONE CALLS OR TEXTS.
IT DOESN'T EVEN SAY "MESSAGE READ."
ぼり SCRATCH
ぼり SCRATCH
TODAY IS IM'S FARE-WELL PARTY.
AS SOON AS HE RETURNED FROM HIS MISSION, HIS RETURN TO EGYPT WAS GREEN-LIT.
SO AT KHONSU-SAN'S SUGGESTION, WE'RE HOLDING A GOING-AWAY PARTY FOR HIM.
SINCE KOBUSHI HAD MADE FRIENDS WITH IM, I INVITED HER TOO, BUT...
...THERE ARE GONNA BE A LOT OF WEIRDOES HERE. I HAVE TO PROTECT HER...!!!
......
WHAT IS THAT?
NO TOUCHY!!
IN THE END...
...I COULDN'T DO ANY-THING FOR HIM...
ピンポーン
DING-DOOONG

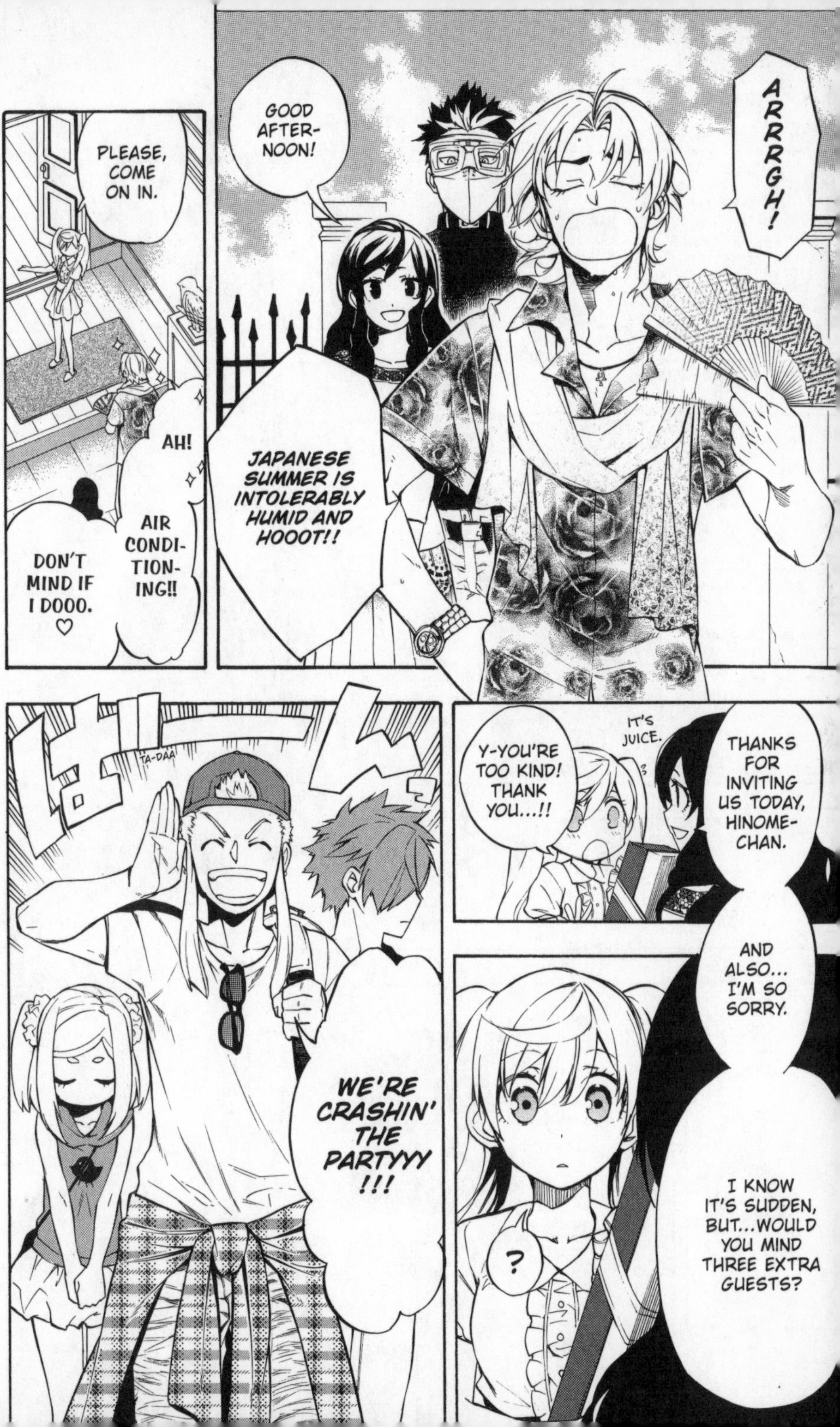
ARRRGH!
GOOD AFTER-NOON!
JAPANESE SUMMER IS INTOLERABLY HUMID AND HOOOT!!
PLEASE, COME ON IN.
AH!
AIR CONDI-TION-ING!!
DON'T MIND IF I DOOO. ♡
THANKS FOR INVITING US TODAY, HINOME-CHAN.
IT'S JUICE.
Y-YOU'RE TOO KIND! THANK YOU...!!
AND ALSO... I'M SO SORRY.
I KNOW IT'S SUDDEN, BUT...WOULD YOU MIND THREE EXTRA GUESTS?
?
TA-DAA
WE'RE CRASHIN' THE PARTYYY !!!

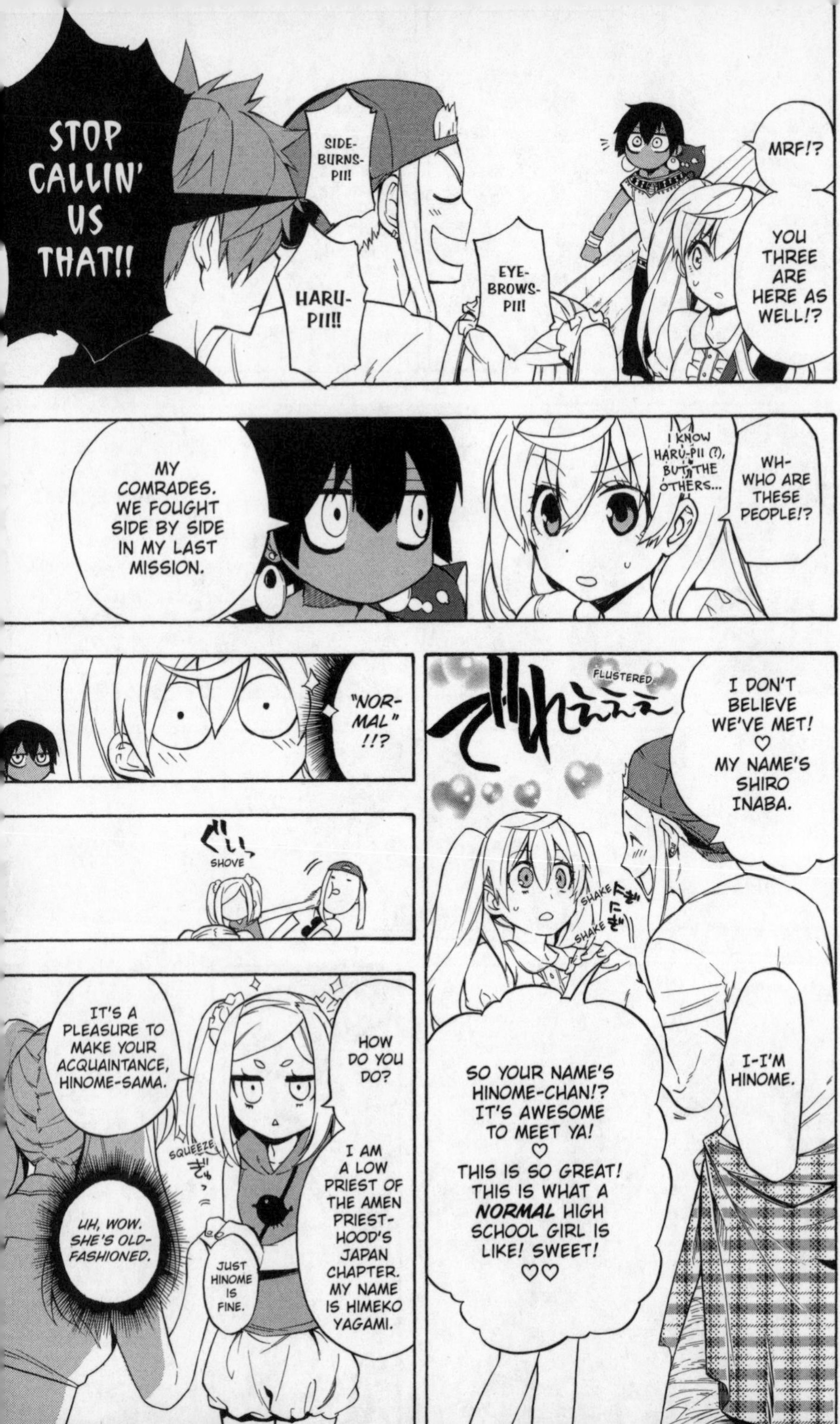
MRF!?
YOU THREE ARE HERE AS WELL!?
SIDE-BURNS-PII!
EYE-BROWS-PII!
HARU-PII!!
STOP CALLIN' US THAT!!
WH-WHO ARE THESE PEOPLE!?
I KNOW HARU-PII (?), BUT THE OTHERS...
MY COMRADES. WE FOUGHT SIDE BY SIDE IN MY LAST MISSION.
I DON'T BELIEVE WE'VE MET! ♡ MY NAME'S SHIRO INABA.
FLUSTERED
SHAKE
SHAKE
I-I'M HINOME.
SO YOUR NAME'S HINOME-CHAN!? IT'S AWESOME TO MEET YA! ♡ THIS IS SO GREAT! THIS IS WHAT A ***NORMAL*** HIGH SCHOOL GIRL IS LIKE! SWEET! ♡♡
"NOR-MAL" !!?
SHOVE
HOW DO YOU DO?
I AM A LOW PRIEST OF THE AMEN PRIEST-HOOD'S JAPAN CHAPTER. MY NAME IS HIMEKO YAGAMI.
IT'S A PLEASURE TO MAKE YOUR ACQUAINTANCE, HINOME-SAMA.
SQUEEZE
JUST HINOME IS FINE.
UH, WOW. SHE'S OLD-FASHIONED.

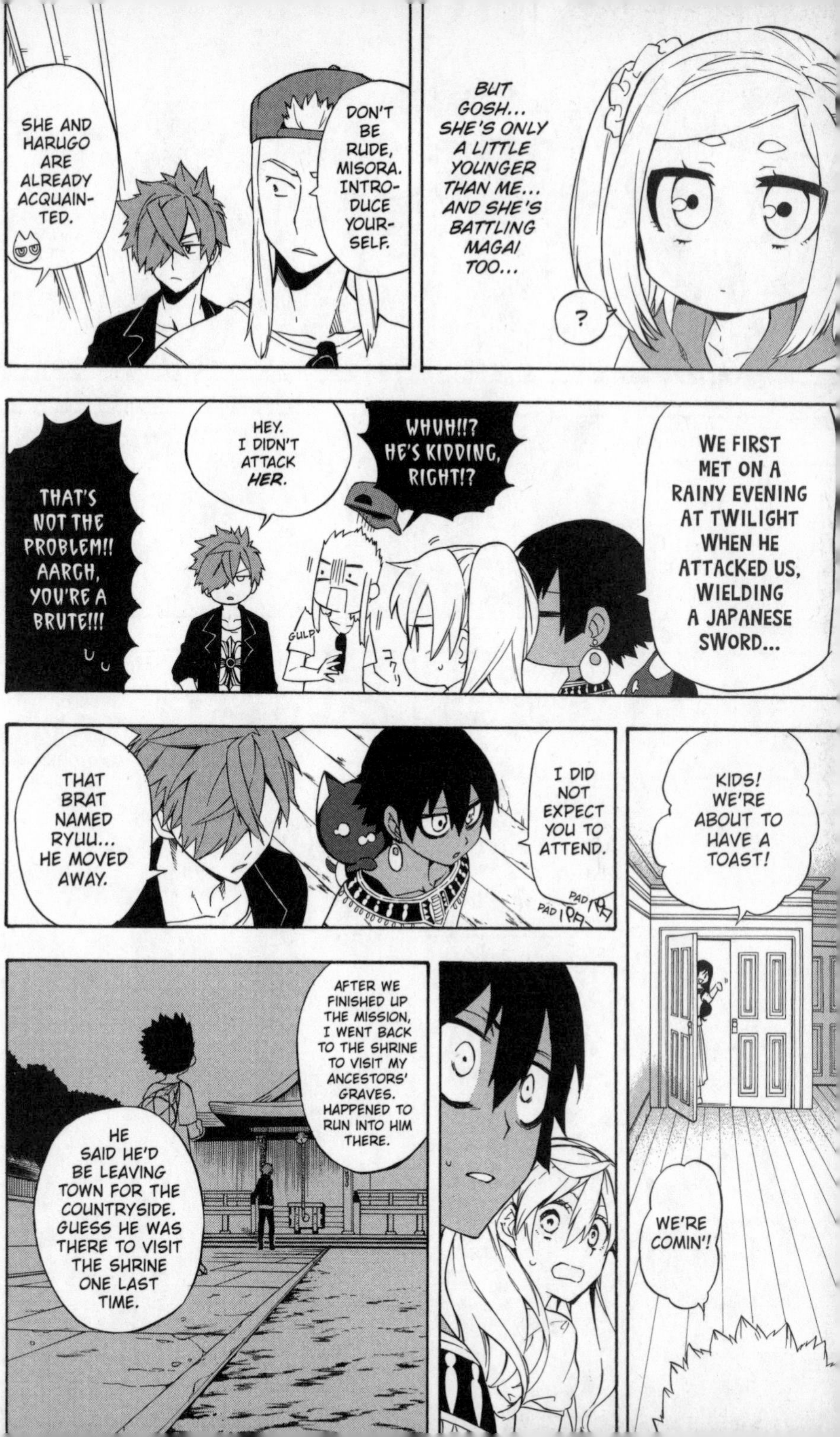
BUT GOSH... SHE'S ONLY A LITTLE YOUNGER THAN ME... AND SHE'S BATTLING MAGAI TOO...
?
DON'T BE RUDE, MISORA. INTRODUCE YOURSELF.
SHE AND HARUGO ARE ALREADY ACQUAINTED.
WE FIRST MET ON A RAINY EVENING AT TWILIGHT WHEN HE ATTACKED US, WIELDING A JAPANESE SWORD...
WHUH!!? HE'S KIDDING, RIGHT!?
HEY. I DIDN'T ATTACK *HER*.
THAT'S NOT THE PROBLEM!! AARGH, YOU'RE A BRUTE!!!
GULP
KIDS! WE'RE ABOUT TO HAVE A TOAST!
WE'RE COMIN'!
I DID NOT EXPECT YOU TO ATTEND.
PAD PAD
THAT BRAT NAMED RYUU... HE MOVED AWAY.
AFTER WE FINISHED UP THE MISSION, I WENT BACK TO THE SHRINE TO VISIT MY ANCESTORS' GRAVES. HAPPENED TO RUN INTO HIM THERE.
HE SAID HE'D BE LEAVING TOWN FOR THE COUNTRYSIDE. GUESS HE WAS THERE TO VISIT THE SHRINE ONE LAST TIME.

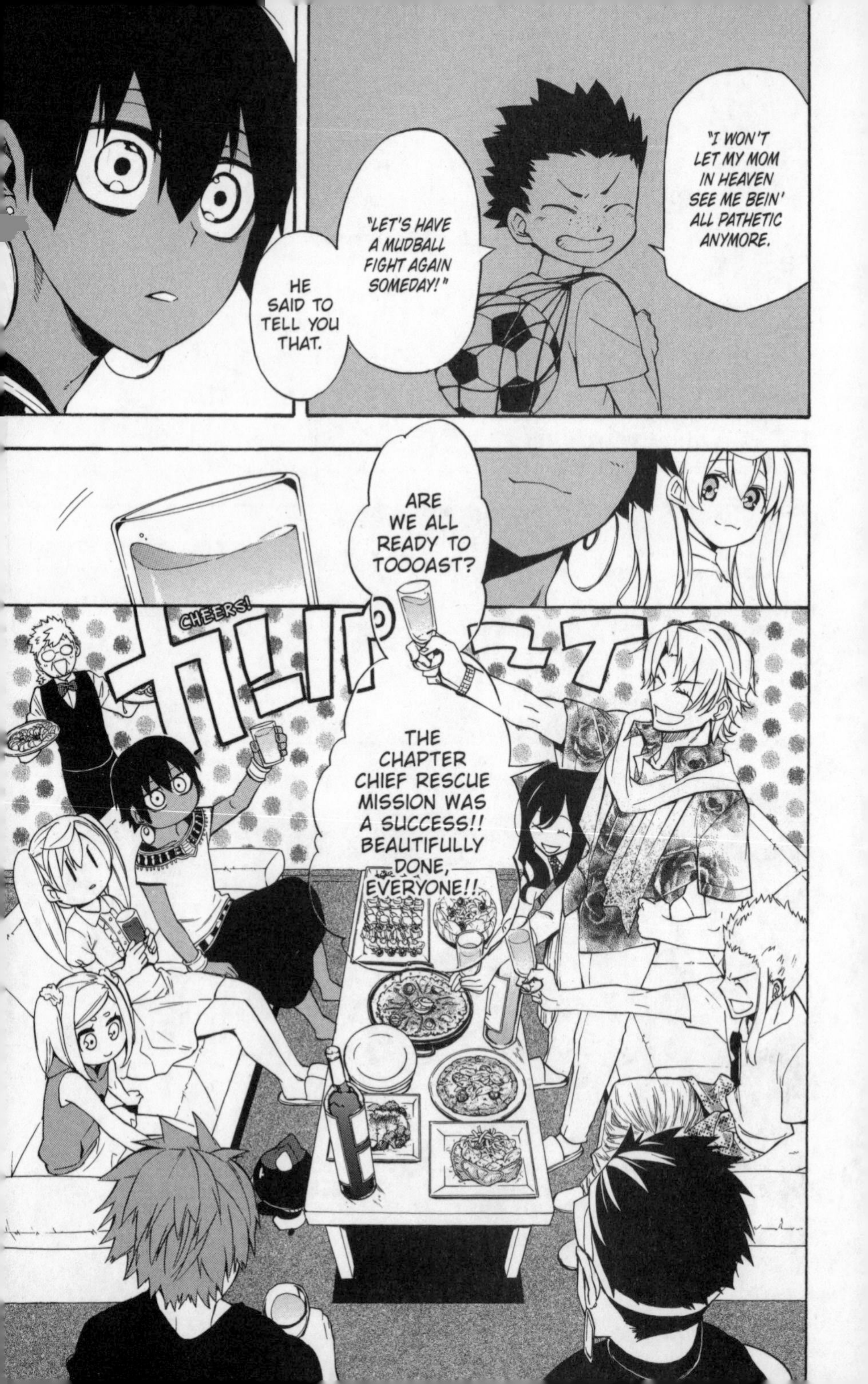
"I WON'T LET MY MOM IN HEAVEN SEE ME BEIN' ALL PATHETIC ANYMORE.
"LET'S HAVE A MUDBALL FIGHT AGAIN SOMEDAY!"
HE SAID TO TELL YOU THAT.
ARE WE ALL READY TO TOOOAST?
CHEERS!
THE CHAPTER CHIEF RESCUE MISSION WAS A SUCCESS!! BEAUTIFULLY DONE, EVERYONE!!

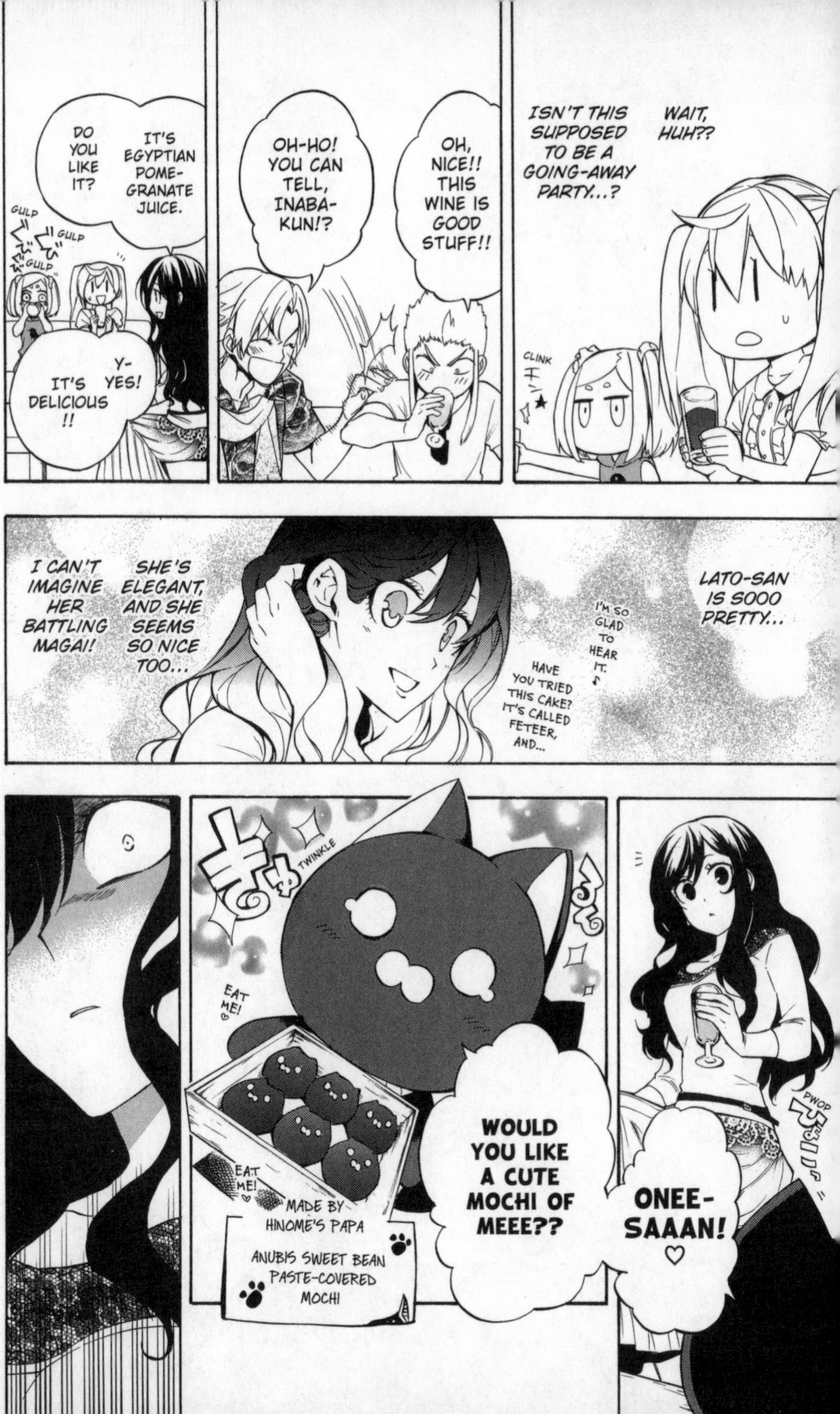
WAIT, HUH??
ISN'T THIS SUPPOSED TO BE A GOING-AWAY PARTY...?
CLINK
OH, NICE!! THIS WINE IS GOOD STUFF!!
OH-HO! YOU CAN TELL, INABA-KUN!?
IT'S EGYPTIAN POMEGRANATE JUICE.
DO YOU LIKE IT?
GULP
GULP
GULP
Y-YES! IT'S DELICIOUS!!
LATO-SAN IS SOOO PRETTY...
I'M SO GLAD TO HEAR IT. ♪
HAVE YOU TRIED THIS CAKE? IT'S CALLED FETEER, AND...
SHE'S ELEGANT, AND SHE SEEMS SO NICE TOO...
I CAN'T IMAGINE HER BATTLING MAGAI!
PWOP
ONEE-SAAAN! ♡
TWINKLE
EAT ME! ♡
WOULD YOU LIKE A CUTE MOCHI OF MEEE??
EAT ME! ♡
MADE BY HINOME'S PAPA
ANUBIS SWEET BEAN PASTE-COVERED MOCHI

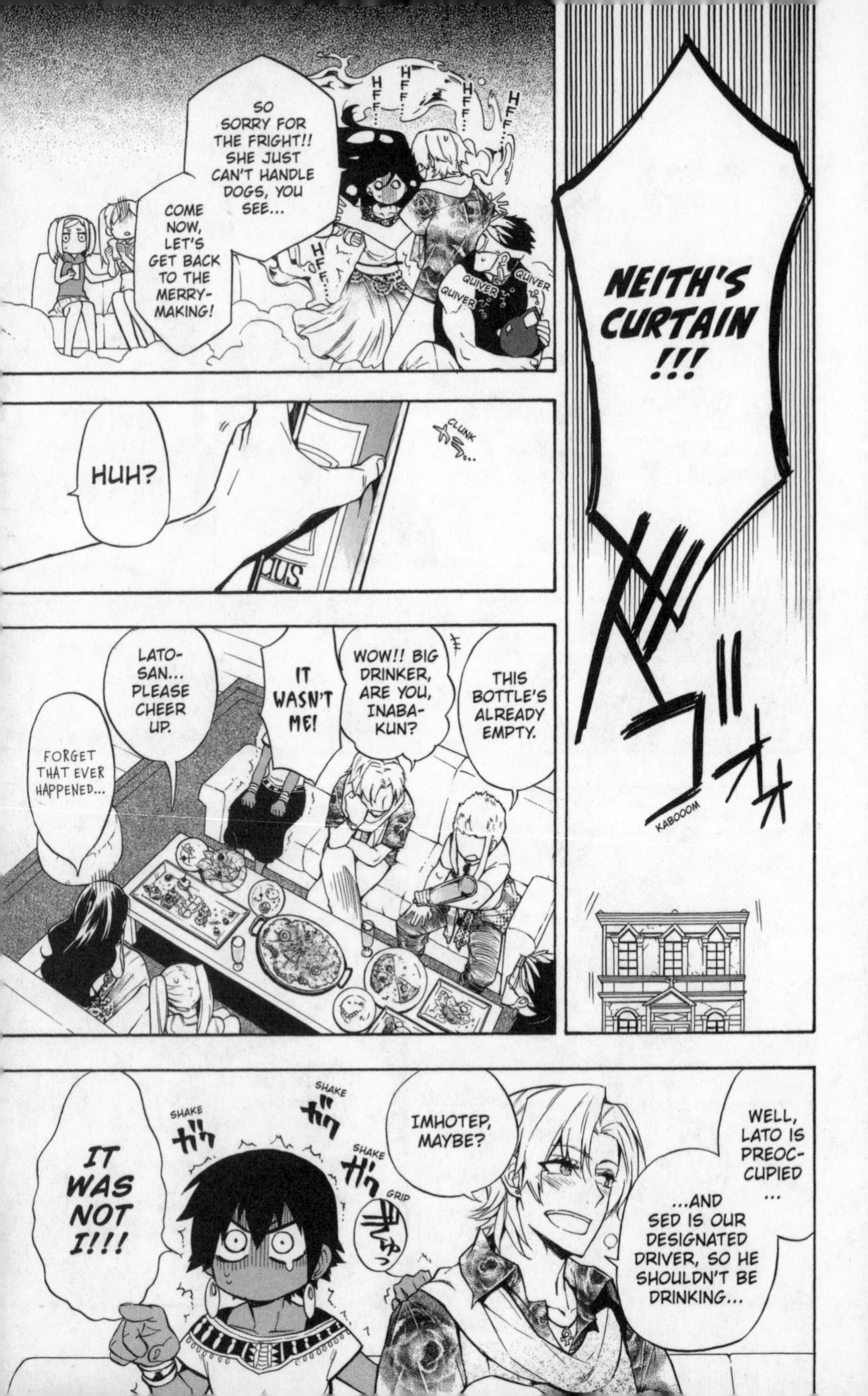
NEITH'S CURTAIN!!!
KABOOOM
HFF... HFF... HFF... HFF... HFF...
SO SORRY FOR THE FRIGHT!! SHE JUST CAN'T HANDLE DOGS, YOU SEE...
COME NOW, LET'S GET BACK TO THE MERRY-MAKING!
QUIVER QUIVER
CLUNK...
HUH?
THIS BOTTLE'S ALREADY EMPTY.
WOW!! BIG DRINKER, ARE YOU, INABA-KUN?
IT WASN'T ME!
LATO-SAN... PLEASE CHEER UP.
FORGET THAT EVER HAPPENED...
WELL, LATO IS PREOCCUPIED...
...AND SED IS OUR DESIGNATED DRIVER, SO HE SHOULDN'T BE DRINKING...
IMHOTEP, MAYBE?
SHAKE SHAKE SHAKE
GRIP
IT WAS NOT I!!!

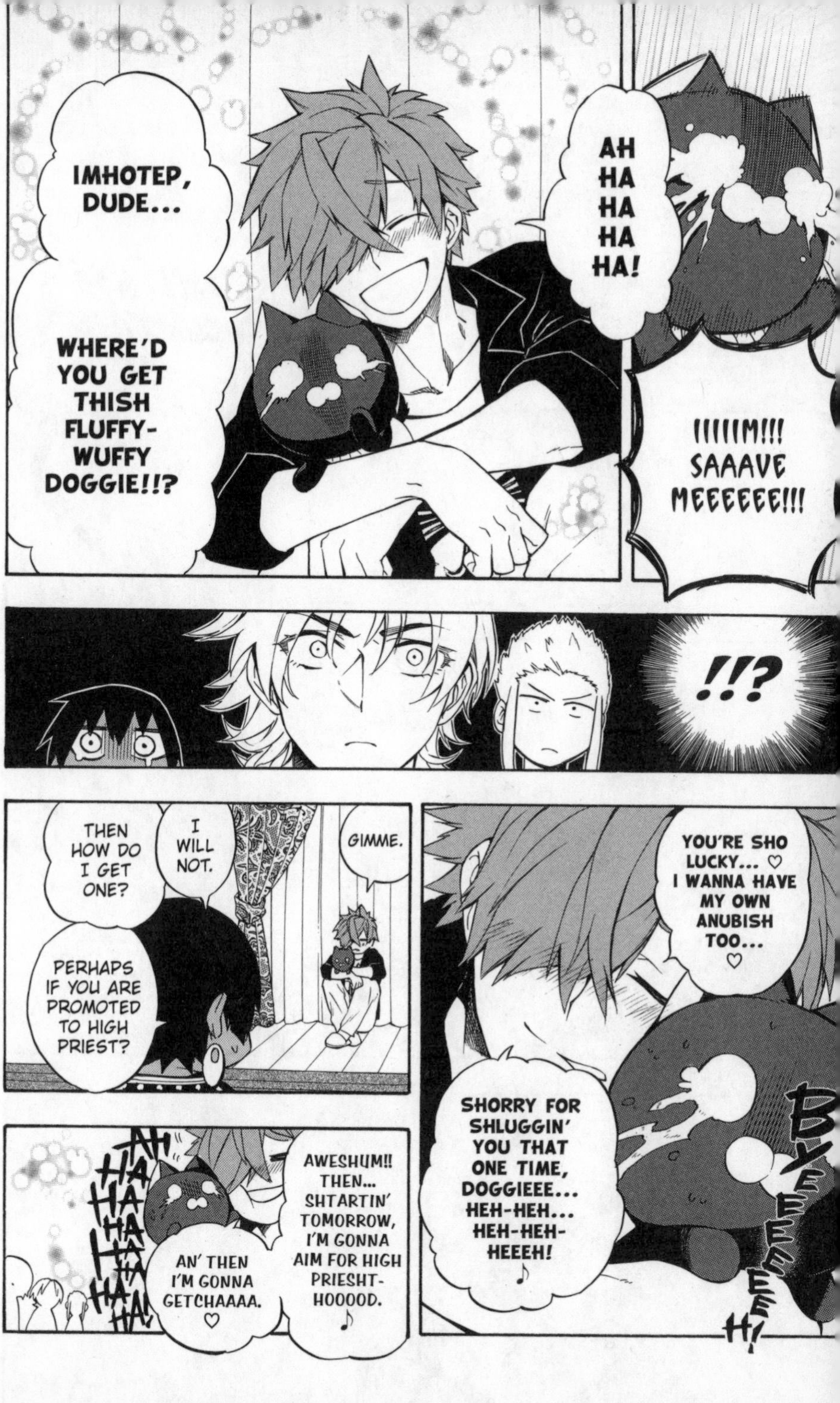
AH HA HA HA HA!
IIIIIIM!!! SAAAVE MEEEEEE!!!
IMHOTEP, DUDE...
WHERE'D YOU GET THISH FLUFFY-WUFFY DOGGIE!!?
!!?
YOU'RE SHO LUCKY... ♡ I WANNA HAVE MY OWN ANUBISH TOO... ♡
SHORRY FOR SHLUGGIN' YOU THAT ONE TIME, DOGGIEEE... HEH-HEH... HEH-HEH-HEEEH! ♪
BYEEEEEEEH!
GIMME.
I WILL NOT.
THEN HOW DO I GET ONE?
PERHAPS IF YOU ARE PROMOTED TO HIGH PRIEST?
AWESHUM!! THEN... SHTARTIN' TOMORROW, I'M GONNA AIM FOR HIGH PRIESHT-HOOOOD. ♪
AN' THEN I'M GONNA GETCHAAAA. ♡

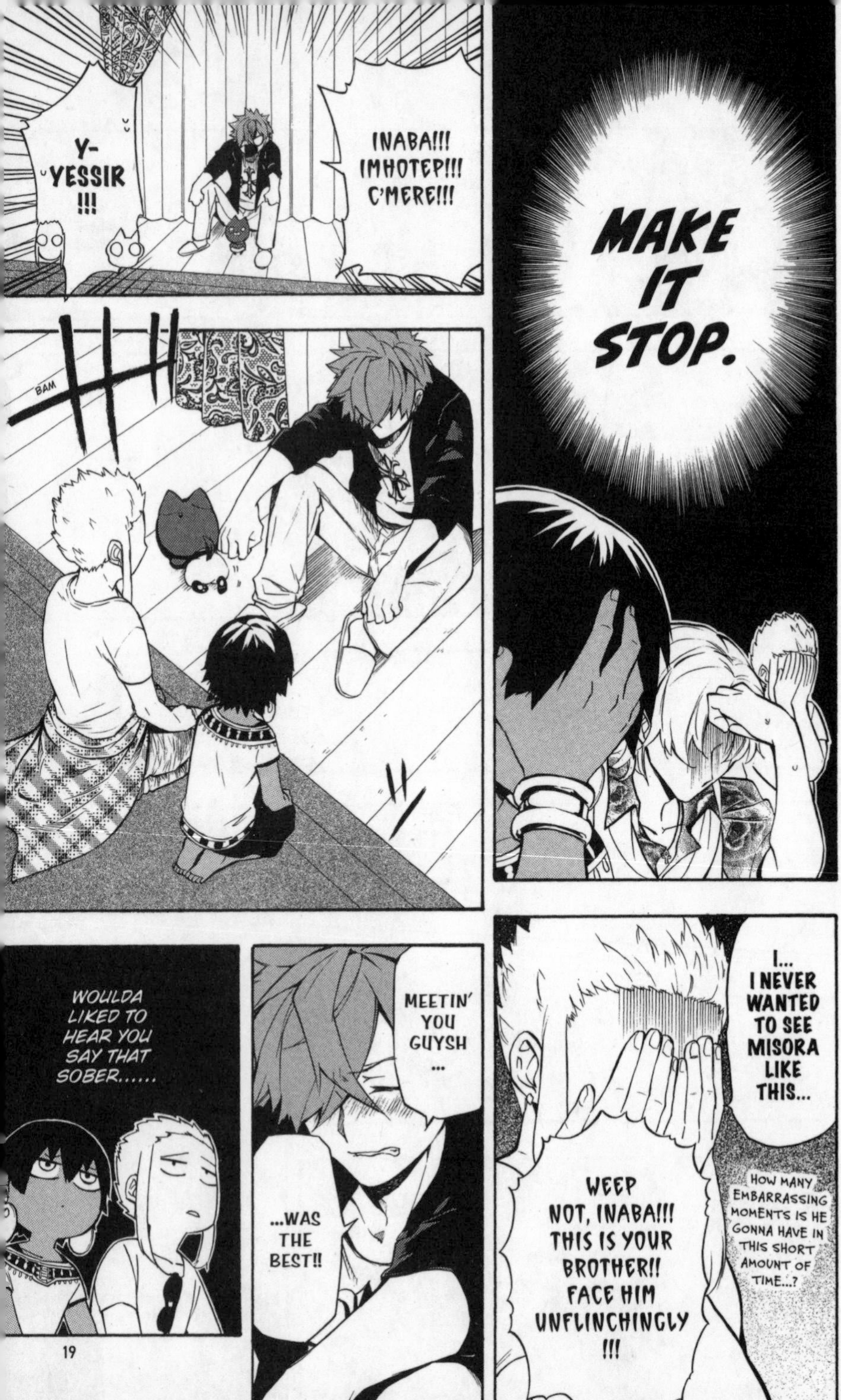
MAKE IT STOP.
INABA!!! IMHOTEP!!! C'MERE!!!
Y-YESSIR!!!
BAM
I... I NEVER WANTED TO SEE MISORA LIKE THIS...
WEEP NOT, INABA!!! THIS IS YOUR BROTHER!! FACE HIM UNFLINCHINGLY!!!
HOW MANY EMBARRASSING MOMENTS IS HE GONNA HAVE IN THIS SHORT AMOUNT OF TIME...?
MEETIN' YOU GUYSH...
...WAS THE BEST!!
WOULDA LIKED TO HEAR YOU SAY THAT SOBER......

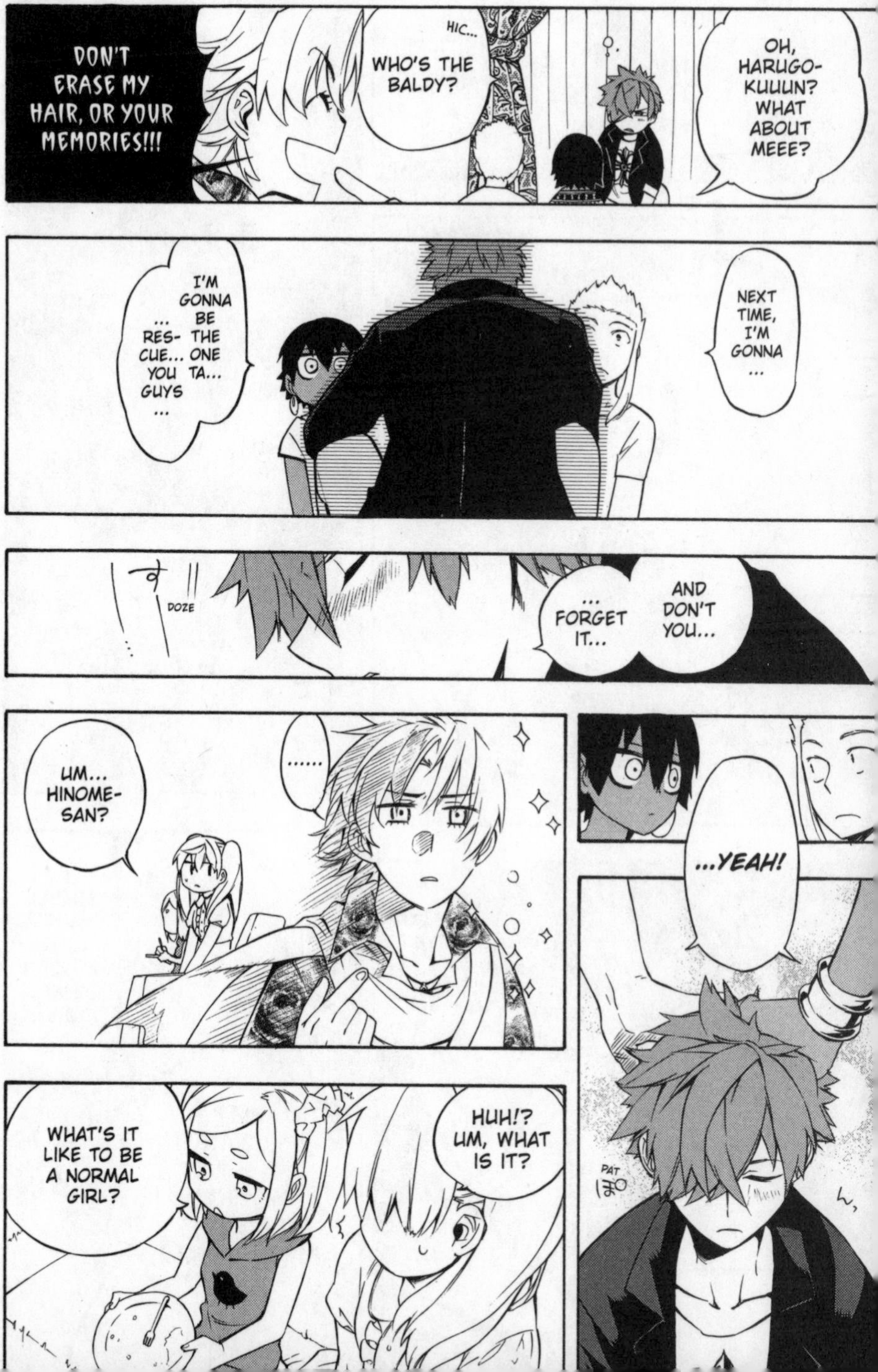
OH, HARUGO-KUUUN? WHAT ABOUT MEEE?
HIC...
WHO'S THE BALDY?
DON'T ERASE MY HAIR, OR YOUR MEMORIES!!!
NEXT TIME, I'M GONNA ...
I'M GONNA BE THE ONE TA...
...RES-CUE... YOU GUYS ...
AND DON'T YOU...
... FORGET IT...
す DOZE
...YEAH!
PAT ぽ
ん、
......
UM... HINOME-SAN?
HUH!? UM, WHAT IS IT?
WHAT'S IT LIKE TO BE A NORMAL GIRL?

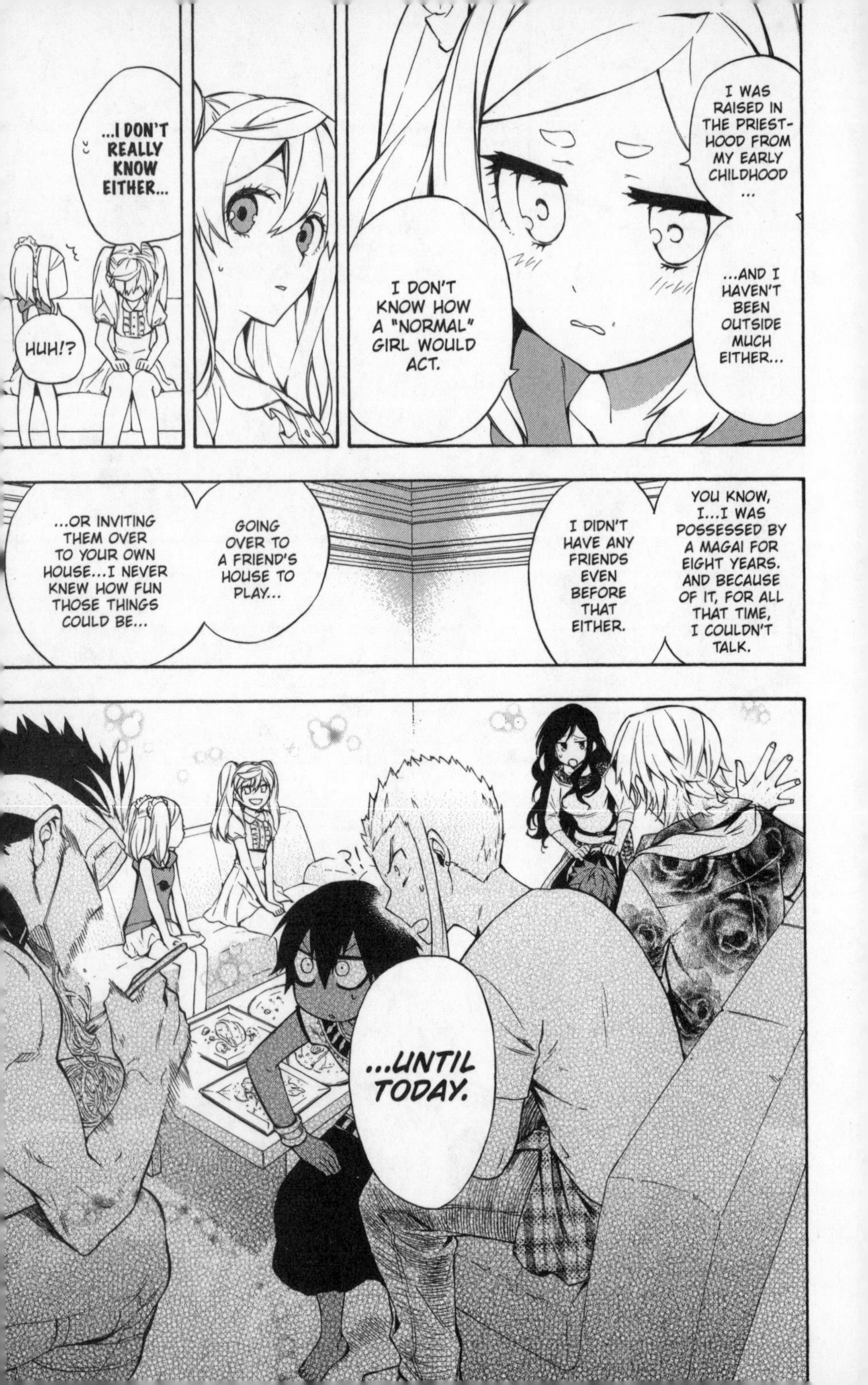
I WAS RAISED IN THE PRIEST-HOOD FROM MY EARLY CHILDHOOD ...
...AND I HAVEN'T BEEN OUTSIDE MUCH EITHER...
I DON'T KNOW HOW A "NORMAL" GIRL WOULD ACT.
...I DON'T REALLY KNOW EITHER...
HUH!?
YOU KNOW, I...I WAS POSSESSED BY A MAGAI FOR EIGHT YEARS. AND BECAUSE OF IT, FOR ALL THAT TIME, I COULDN'T TALK.
I DIDN'T HAVE ANY FRIENDS EVEN BEFORE THAT EITHER.
GOING OVER TO A FRIEND'S HOUSE TO PLAY...
...OR INVITING THEM OVER TO YOUR OWN HOUSE...I NEVER KNEW HOW FUN THOSE THINGS COULD BE...
?!
...UNTIL TODAY.

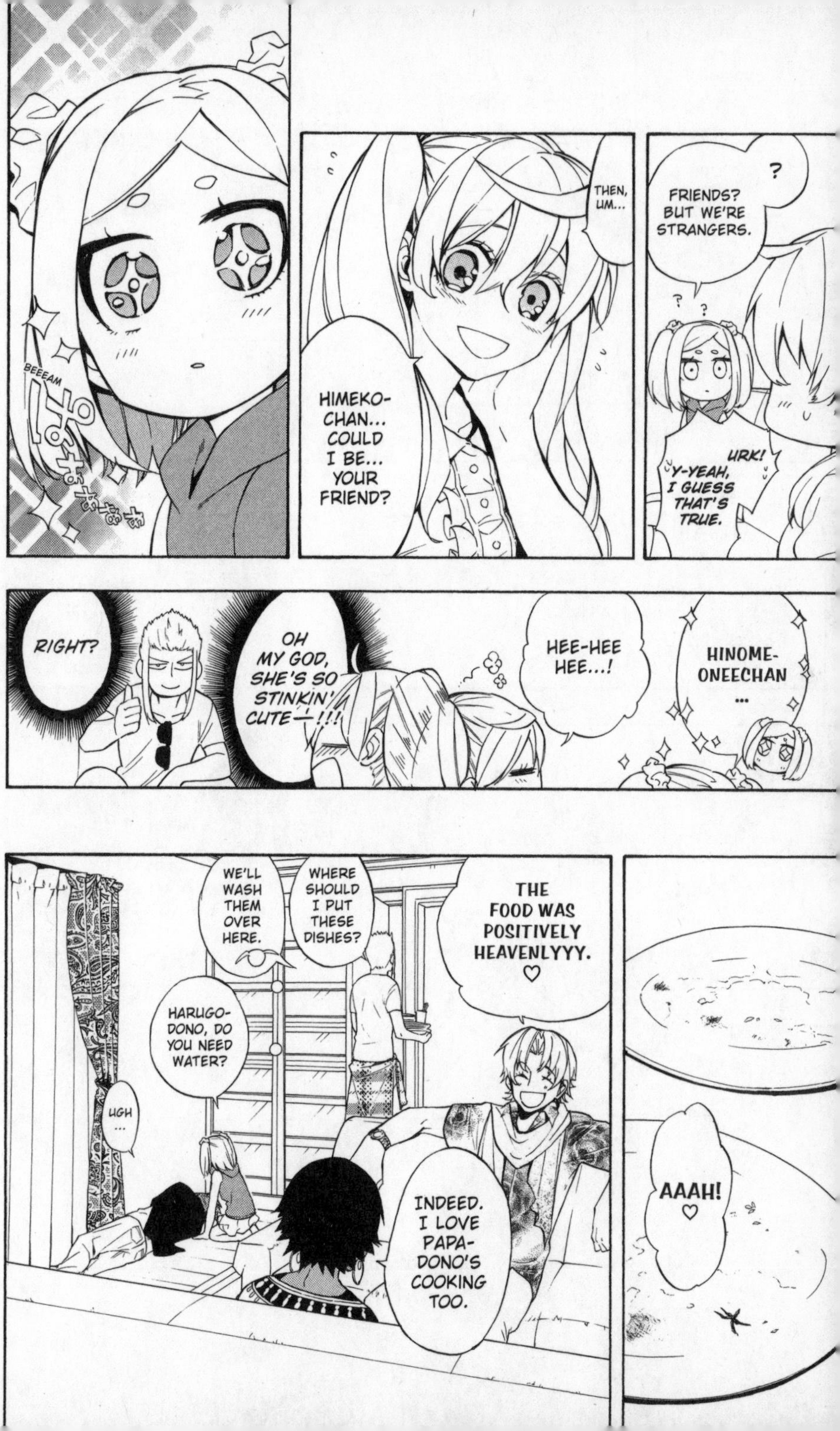
?
FRIENDS? BUT WE'RE STRANGERS.
URK! Y-YEAH, I GUESS THAT'S TRUE.
THEN, UM...
HIMEKO-CHAN... COULD I BE... YOUR FRIEND?
BEEEAM
HINOME-ONEECHAN ...
HEE-HEE HEE...!
OH MY GOD, SHE'S SO STINKIN' CUTE—!!!
RIGHT?
AAAH! ♡
THE FOOD WAS POSITIVELY HEAVENLYYY. ♡
WHERE SHOULD I PUT THESE DISHES?
WE'LL WASH THEM OVER HERE.
HARUGO-DONO, DO YOU NEED WATER?
UGH ...
INDEED. I LOVE PAPA-DONO'S COOKING TOO.

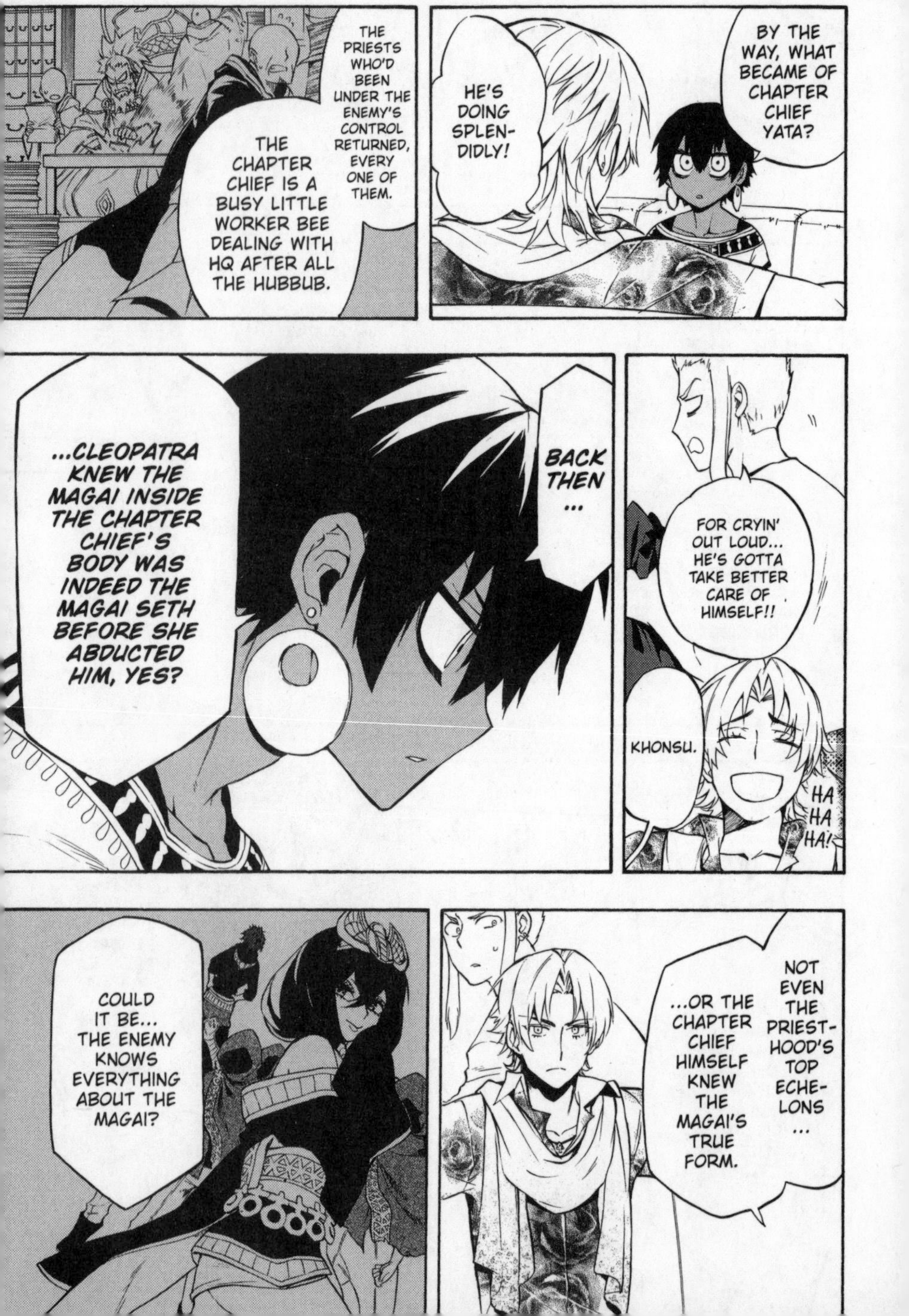
BY THE WAY, WHAT BECAME OF CHAPTER CHIEF YATA?
HE'S DOING SPLEN-DIDLY!
THE PRIESTS WHO'D BEEN UNDER THE ENEMY'S CONTROL RETURNED, EVERY ONE OF THEM.
THE CHAPTER CHIEF IS A BUSY LITTLE WORKER BEE DEALING WITH HQ AFTER ALL THE HUBBUB.
FOR CRYIN' OUT LOUD... HE'S GOTTA TAKE BETTER CARE OF HIMSELF!!
HA HA HA!
KHONSU.
BACK THEN...
...CLEOPATRA KNEW THE MAGAI INSIDE THE CHAPTER CHIEF'S BODY WAS INDEED THE MAGAI SETH BEFORE SHE ABDUCTED HIM, YES?
NOT EVEN THE PRIEST-HOOD'S TOP ECHE-LONS...
...OR THE CHAPTER CHIEF HIMSELF KNEW THE MAGAI'S TRUE FORM.
COULD IT BE... THE ENEMY KNOWS EVERYTHING ABOUT THE MAGAI?

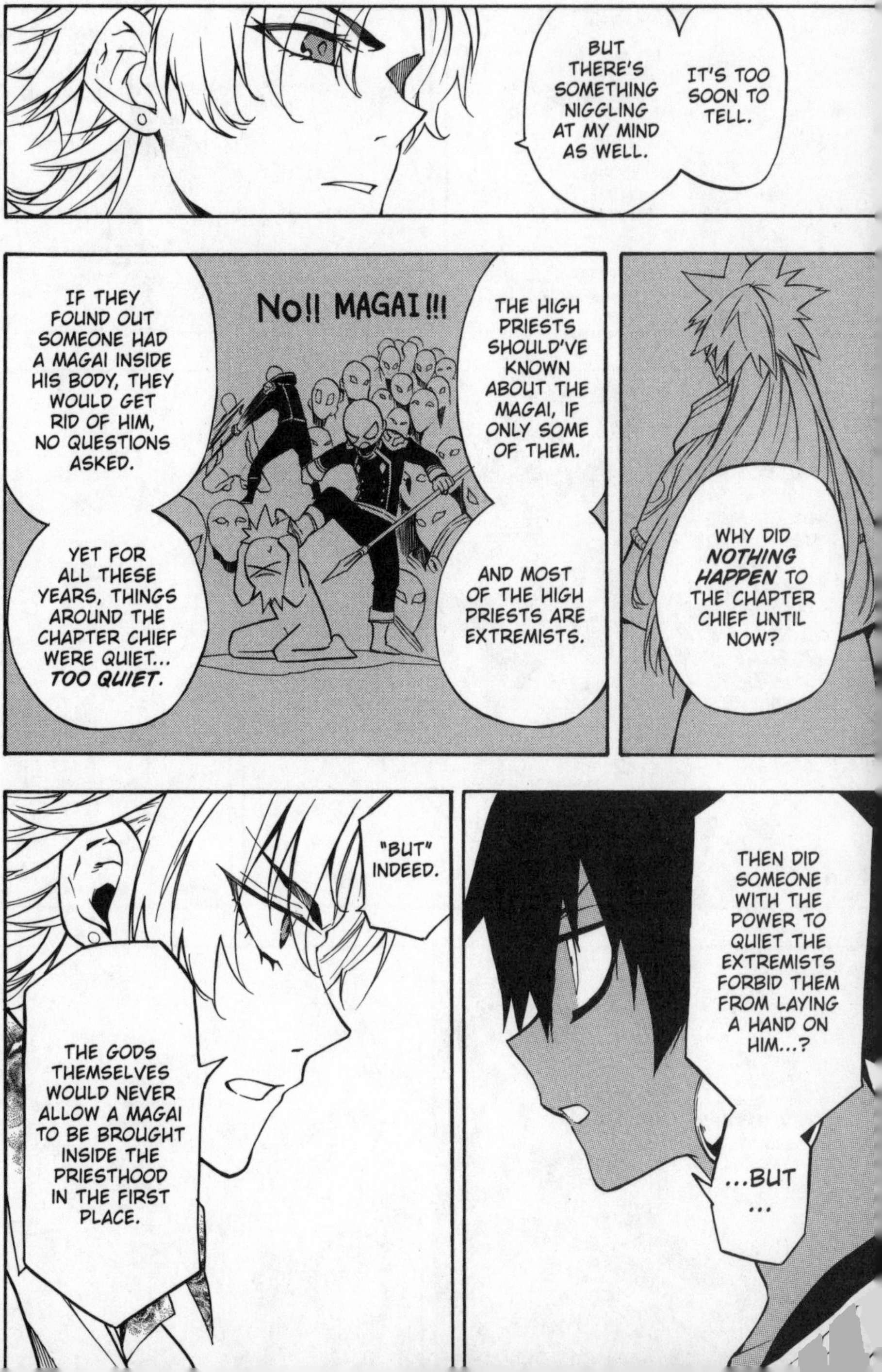
IT'S TOO SOON TO TELL.
BUT THERE'S SOMETHING NIGGLING AT MY MIND AS WELL.
WHY DID NOTHING HAPPEN TO THE CHAPTER CHIEF UNTIL NOW?
THE HIGH PRIESTS SHOULD'VE KNOWN ABOUT THE MAGAI, IF ONLY SOME OF THEM.
AND MOST OF THE HIGH PRIESTS ARE EXTREMISTS.
No!! MAGAI!!!
IF THEY FOUND OUT SOMEONE HAD A MAGAI INSIDE HIS BODY, THEY WOULD GET RID OF HIM, NO QUESTIONS ASKED.
YET FOR ALL THESE YEARS, THINGS AROUND THE CHAPTER CHIEF WERE QUIET... TOO QUIET.
THEN DID SOMEONE WITH THE POWER TO QUIET THE EXTREMISTS FORBID THEM FROM LAYING A HAND ON HIM...?
...BUT ...
"BUT" INDEED.
THE GODS THEMSELVES WOULD NEVER ALLOW A MAGAI TO BE BROUGHT INSIDE THE PRIESTHOOD IN THE FIRST PLACE.

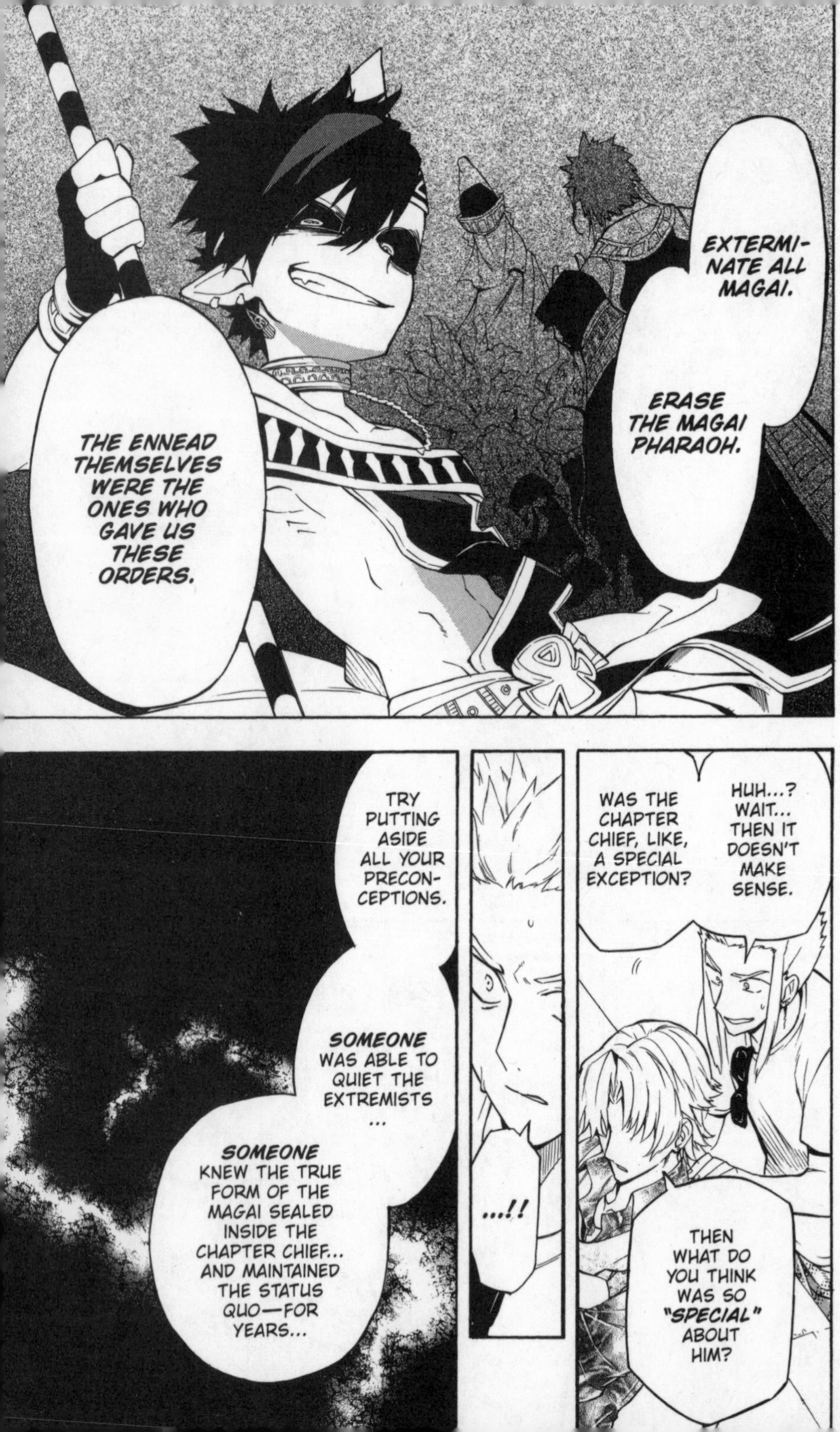
EXTERMINATE ALL MAGAI.
ERASE THE MAGAI PHARAOH.
THE ENNEAD THEMSELVES WERE THE ONES WHO GAVE US THESE ORDERS.
HUH...? WAIT... THEN IT DOESN'T MAKE SENSE.
WAS THE CHAPTER CHIEF, LIKE, A SPECIAL EXCEPTION?
THEN WHAT DO YOU THINK WAS SO "SPECIAL" ABOUT HIM?
...!!
TRY PUTTING ASIDE ALL YOUR PRECONCEPTIONS.
SOMEONE WAS ABLE TO QUIET THE EXTREMISTS...
SOMEONE KNEW THE TRUE FORM OF THE MAGAI SEALED INSIDE THE CHAPTER CHIEF... AND MAINTAINED THE STATUS QUO—FOR YEARS...

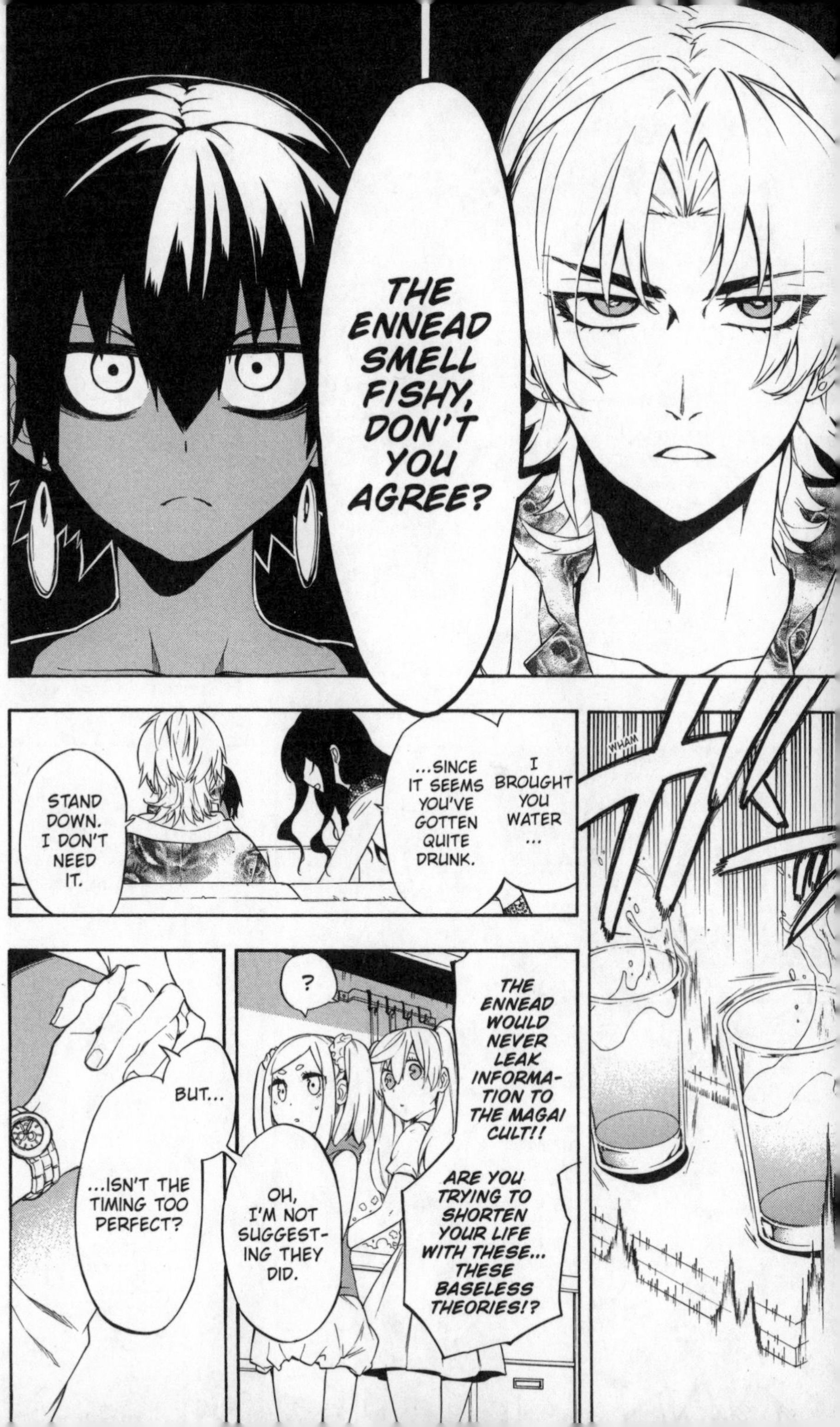
THE ENNEAD SMELL FISHY, DON'T YOU AGREE?
WHAM
I BROUGHT YOU WATER...
...SINCE IT SEEMS YOU'VE GOTTEN QUITE DRUNK.
STAND DOWN. I DON'T NEED IT.
THE ENNEAD WOULD NEVER LEAK INFORMATION TO THE MAGAI CULT!!
ARE YOU TRYING TO SHORTEN YOUR LIFE WITH THESE... THESE BASELESS THEORIES!?
?
OH, I'M NOT SUGGESTING THEY DID.
BUT...
...ISN'T THE TIMING TOO PERFECT?

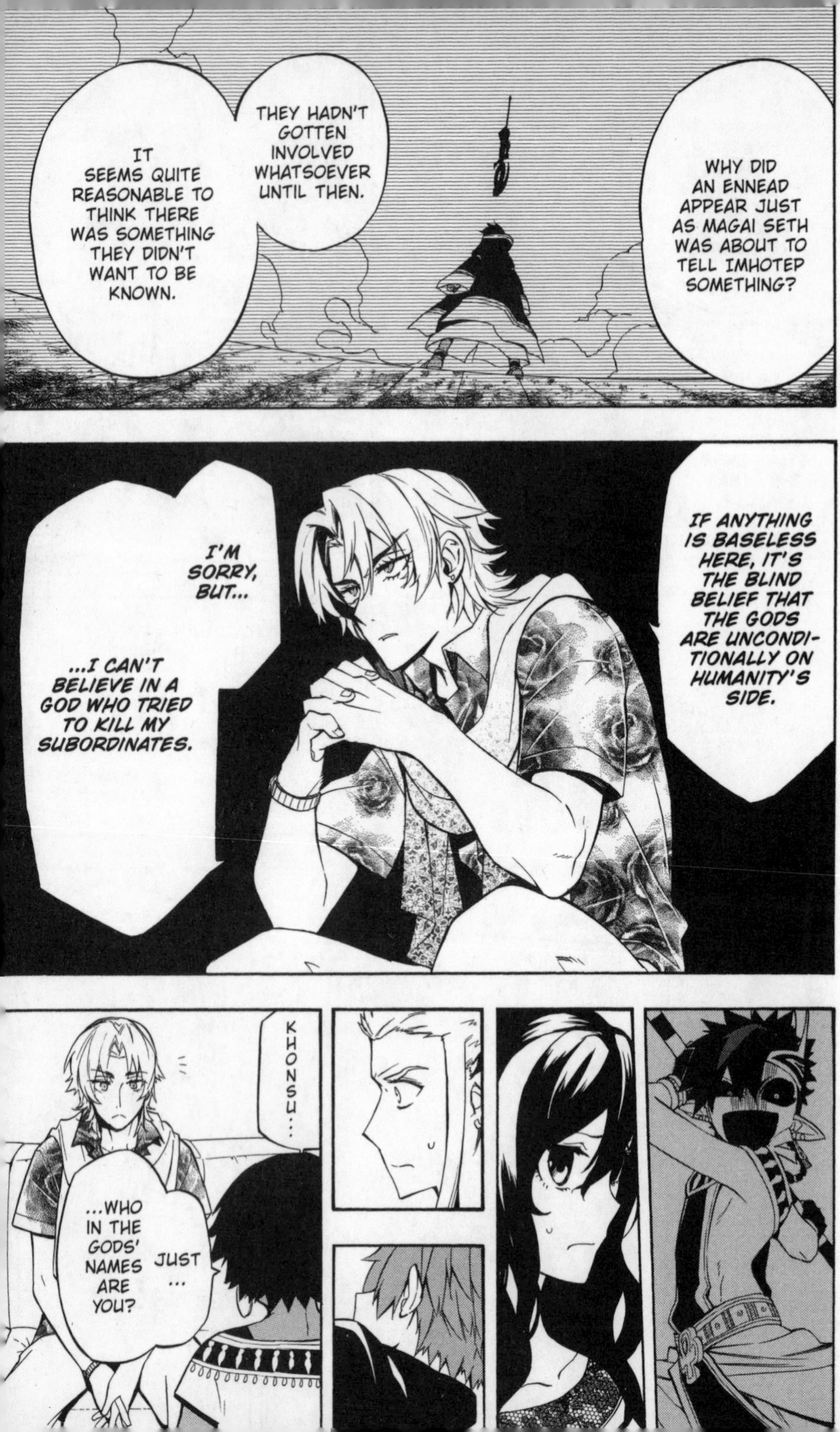
WHY DID AN ENNEAD APPEAR JUST AS MAGAI SETH WAS ABOUT TO TELL IMHOTEP SOMETHING?
THEY HADN'T GOTTEN INVOLVED WHATSOEVER UNTIL THEN.
IT SEEMS QUITE REASONABLE TO THINK THERE WAS SOMETHING THEY DIDN'T WANT TO BE KNOWN.
IF ANYTHING IS BASELESS HERE, IT'S THE BLIND BELIEF THAT THE GODS ARE UNCONDITIONALLY ON HUMANITY'S SIDE.
I'M SORRY, BUT...
...I CAN'T BELIEVE IN A GOD WHO TRIED TO KILL MY SUBORDINATES.
KHONSU...
...WHO IN THE GODS' NAMES JUST ... ARE YOU?

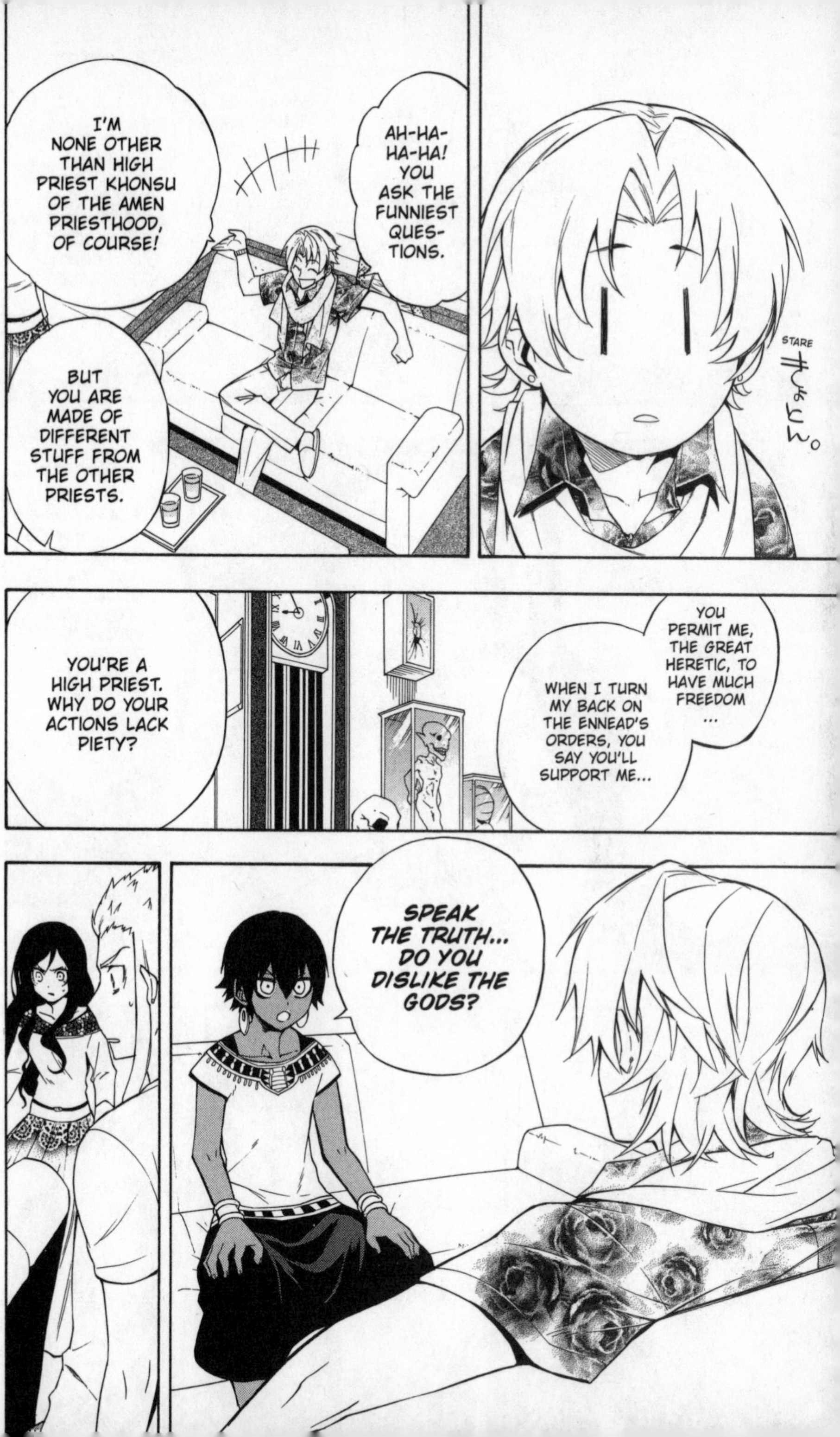
STARE
きょとん。
AH-HA-HA-HA! YOU ASK THE FUNNIEST QUES-TIONS.
I'M NONE OTHER THAN HIGH PRIEST KHONSU OF THE AMEN PRIESTHOOD, OF COURSE!
BUT YOU ARE MADE OF DIFFERENT STUFF FROM THE OTHER PRIESTS.
YOU PERMIT ME, THE GREAT HERETIC, TO HAVE MUCH FREEDOM ...
WHEN I TURN MY BACK ON THE ENNEAD'S ORDERS, YOU SAY YOU'LL SUPPORT ME...
YOU'RE A HIGH PRIEST. WHY DO YOUR ACTIONS LACK PIETY?
SPEAK THE TRUTH... DO YOU DISLIKE THE GODS?

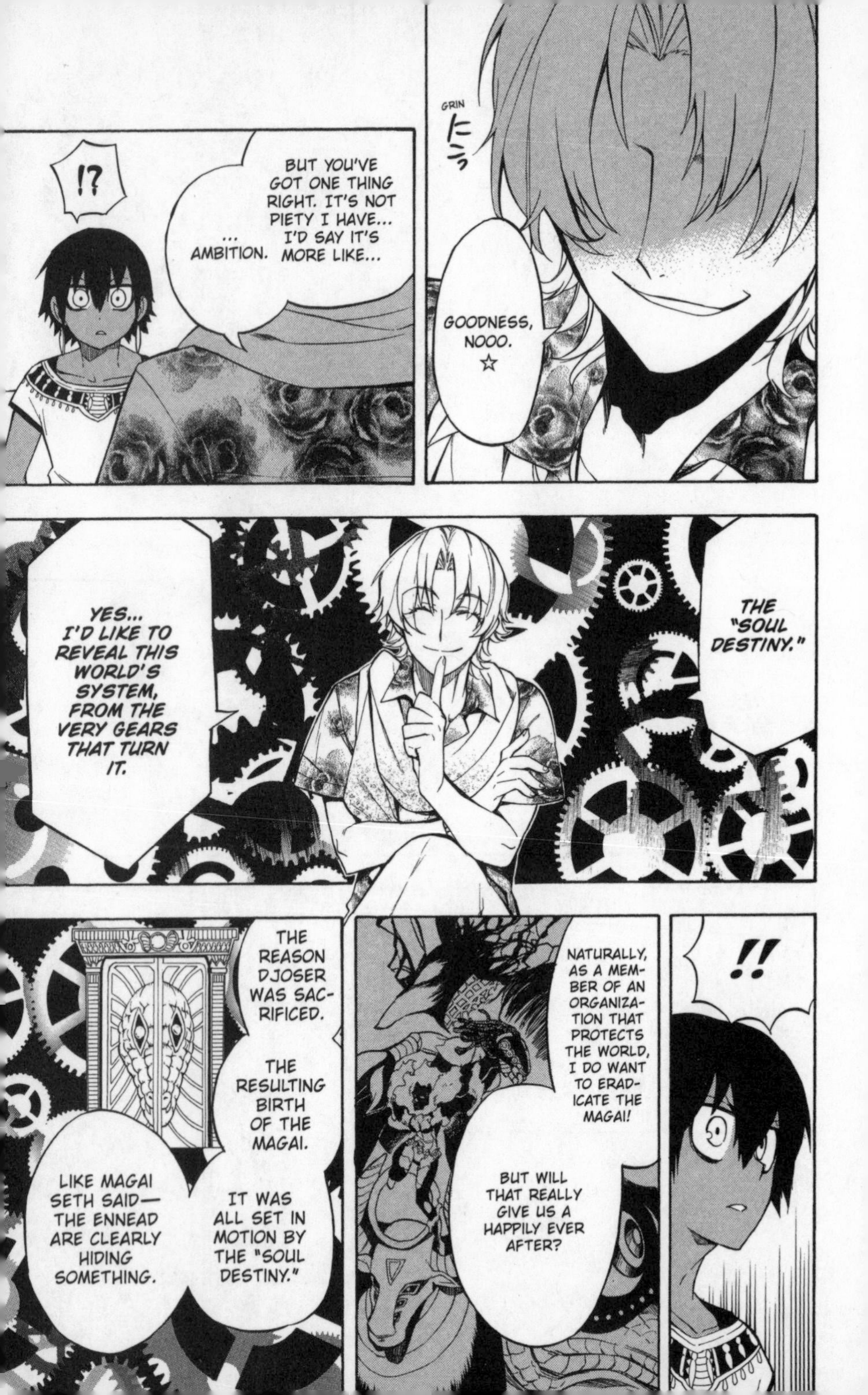
GRIN
GOODNESS, NOOO. ☆
!?
BUT YOU'VE GOT ONE THING RIGHT. IT'S NOT PIETY I HAVE... I'D SAY IT'S MORE LIKE...
... AMBITION.
YES... I'D LIKE TO REVEAL THIS WORLD'S SYSTEM, FROM THE VERY GEARS THAT TURN IT.
THE "SOUL DESTINY."
!!
NATURALLY, AS A MEMBER OF AN ORGANIZATION THAT PROTECTS THE WORLD, I DO WANT TO ERADICATE THE MAGAI!
BUT WILL THAT REALLY GIVE US A HAPPILY EVER AFTER?
THE REASON DJOSER WAS SACRIFICED.
THE RESULTING BIRTH OF THE MAGAI.
IT WAS ALL SET IN MOTION BY THE "SOUL DESTINY."
LIKE MAGAI SETH SAID— THE ENNEAD ARE CLEARLY HIDING SOMETHING.

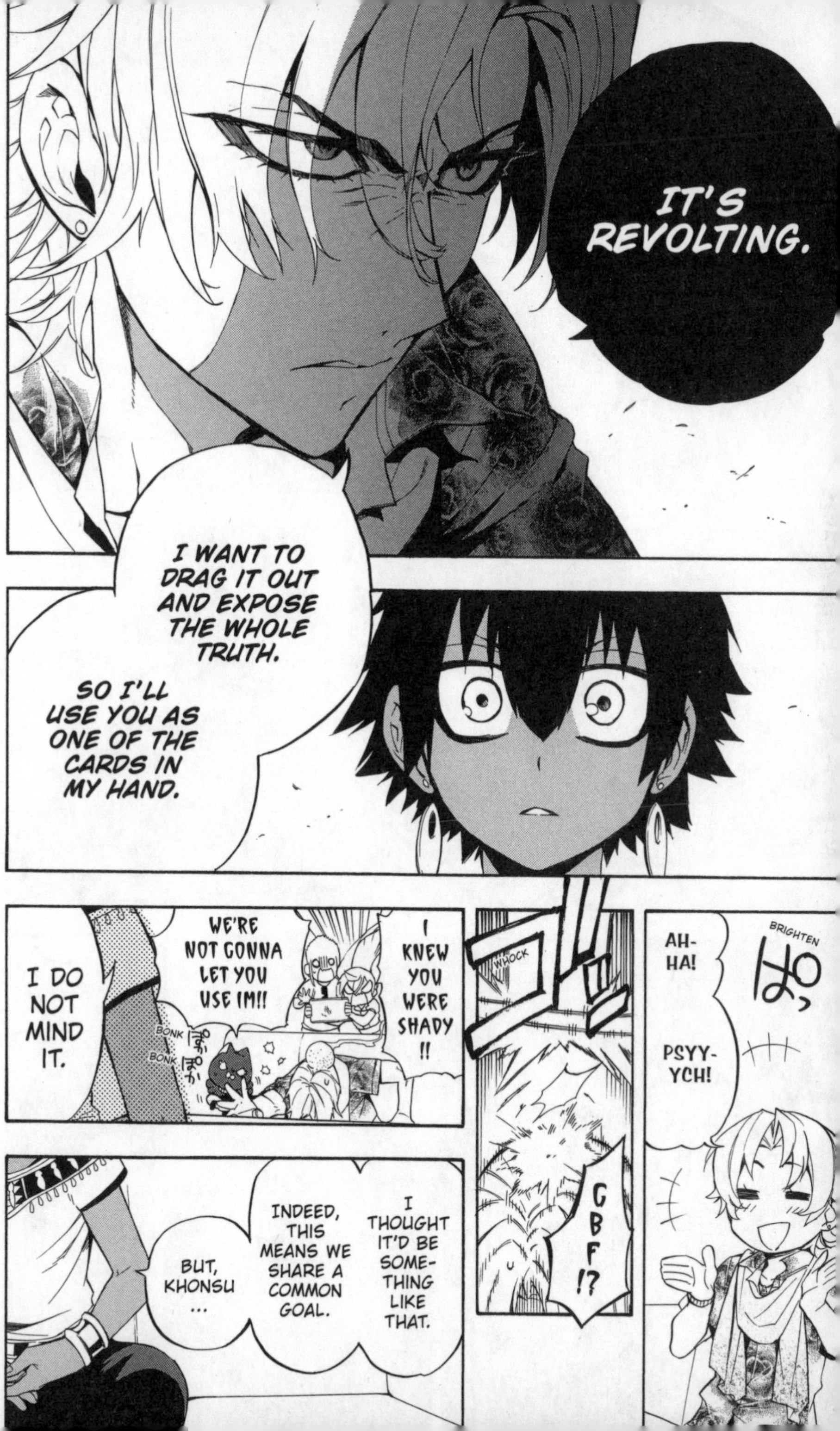
IT'S REVOLTING.
I WANT TO DRAG IT OUT AND EXPOSE THE WHOLE TRUTH.
SO I'LL USE YOU AS ONE OF THE CARDS IN MY HAND.
BRIGHTEN
ぱっ
AH-HA!
PSYY-YCH!
WHOCK
GBF!?
I KNEW YOU WERE SHADY!!
WE'RE NOT GONNA LET YOU USE IM!!
BONK
BONK
I DO NOT MIND IT.
I THOUGHT IT'D BE SOME-THING LIKE THAT.
INDEED, THIS MEANS WE SHARE A COMMON GOAL.
BUT, KHONSU...

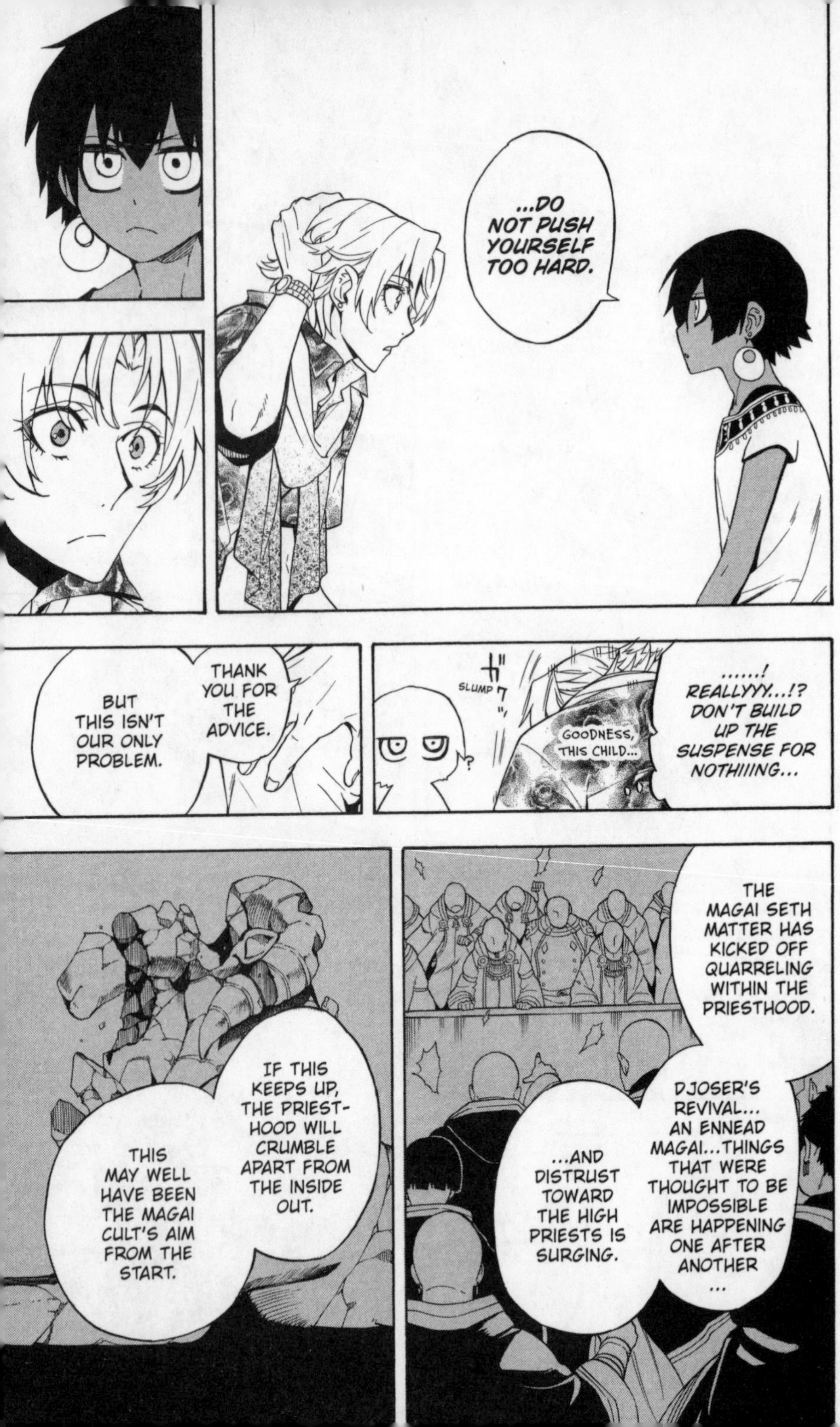
...DO NOT PUSH YOURSELF TOO HARD.
......! REALLYYY...!? DON'T BUILD UP THE SUSPENSE FOR NOTHIIIING...
GOODNESS, THIS CHILD...
SLUMP
THANK YOU FOR THE ADVICE.
BUT THIS ISN'T OUR ONLY PROBLEM.
THE MAGAI SETH MATTER HAS KICKED OFF QUARRELING WITHIN THE PRIESTHOOD.
DJOSER'S REVIVAL... AN ENNEAD MAGAI...THINGS THAT WERE THOUGHT TO BE IMPOSSIBLE ARE HAPPENING ONE AFTER ANOTHER...
...AND DISTRUST TOWARD THE HIGH PRIESTS IS SURGING.
IF THIS KEEPS UP, THE PRIEST-HOOD WILL CRUMBLE APART FROM THE INSIDE OUT.
THIS MAY WELL HAVE BEEN THE MAGAI CULT'S AIM FROM THE START.

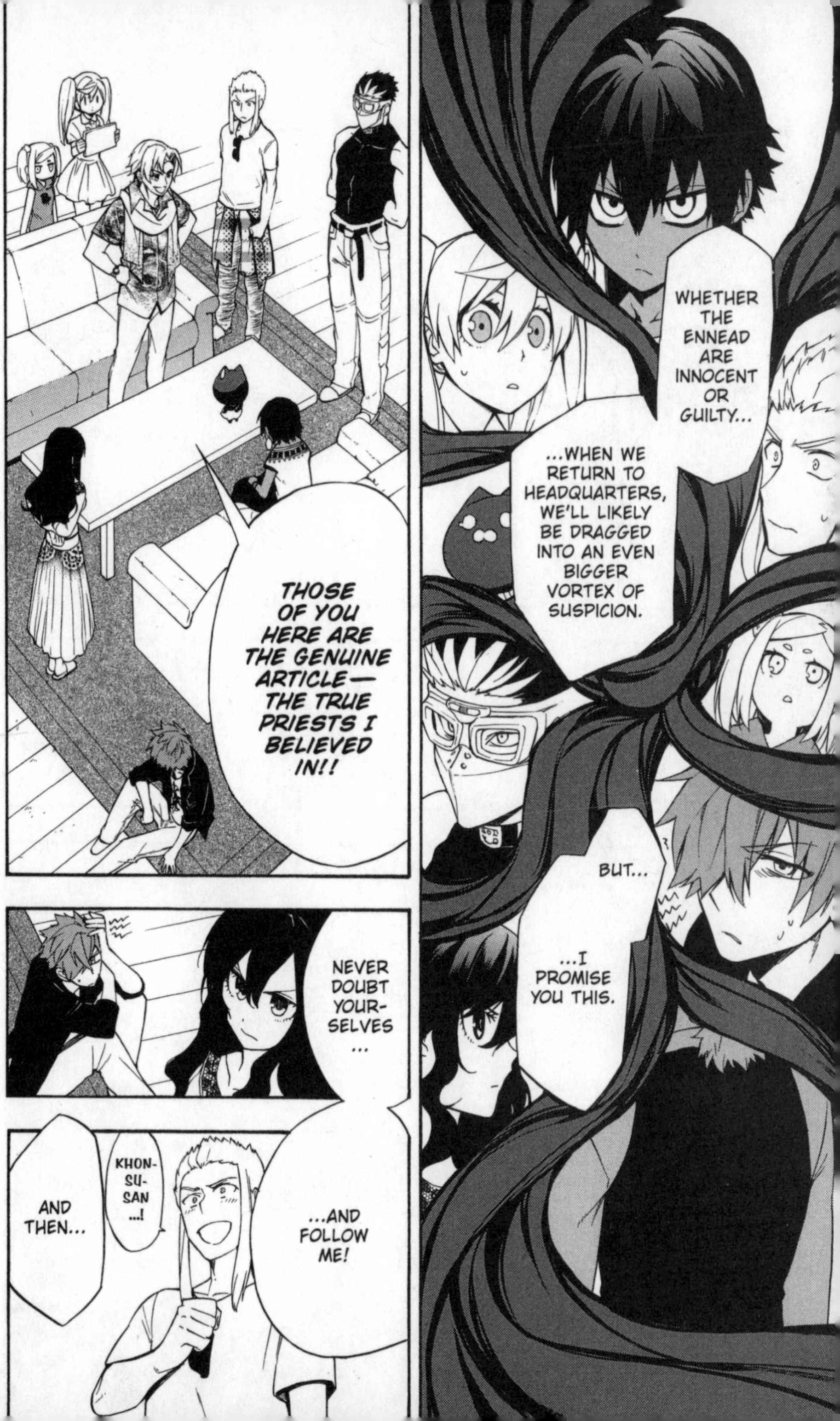
WHETHER THE ENNEAD ARE INNOCENT OR GUILTY...
...WHEN WE RETURN TO HEADQUARTERS, WE'LL LIKELY BE DRAGGED INTO AN EVEN BIGGER VORTEX OF SUSPICION.
BUT...
...I PROMISE YOU THIS.
THOSE OF YOU HERE ARE THE GENUINE ARTICLE—THE TRUE PRIESTS I BELIEVED IN!!
NEVER DOUBT YOURSELVES...
AND THEN...
...AND FOLLOW ME!
KHONSU-SAN...!

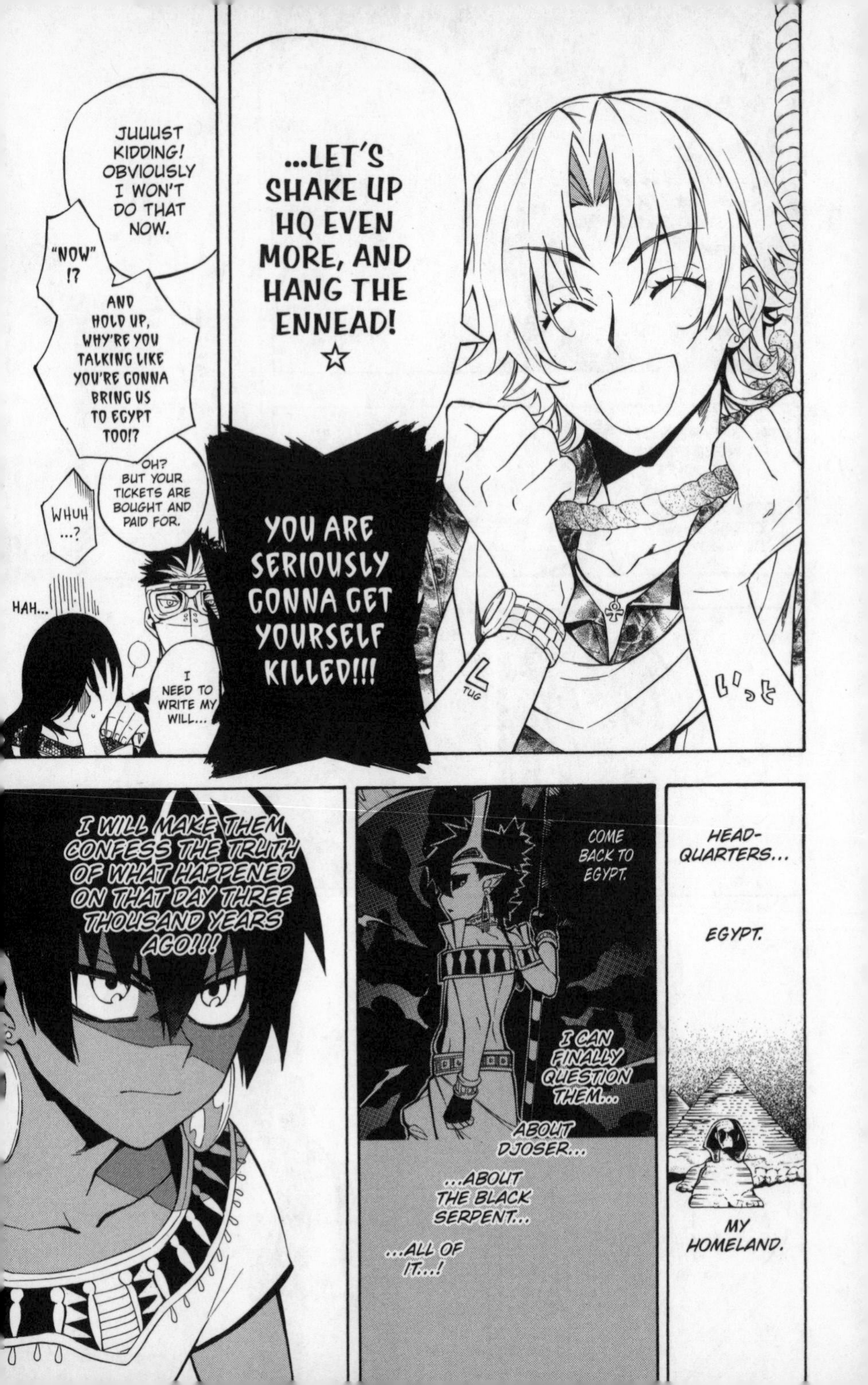
...LET'S SHAKE UP HQ EVEN MORE, AND HANG THE ENNEAD! ☆
TUG
JUUUST KIDDING! OBVIOUSLY I WON'T DO THAT NOW.
"NOW" !?
AND HOLD UP, WHY'RE YOU TALKING LIKE YOU'RE GONNA BRING US TO EGYPT TOO!?
OH? BUT YOUR TICKETS ARE BOUGHT AND PAID FOR.
WHUH ...?
YOU ARE SERIOUSLY GONNA GET YOURSELF KILLED!!!
I NEED TO WRITE MY WILL...
HAH...
HEAD-QUARTERS...
EGYPT.
MY HOMELAND.
COME BACK TO EGYPT.
I CAN FINALLY QUESTION THEM...
ABOUT DJOSER...
...ABOUT THE BLACK SERPENT...
...ALL OF IT...!
I WILL MAKE THEM CONFESS THE TRUTH OF WHAT HAPPENED ON THAT DAY THREE THOUSAND YEARS AGO!!!

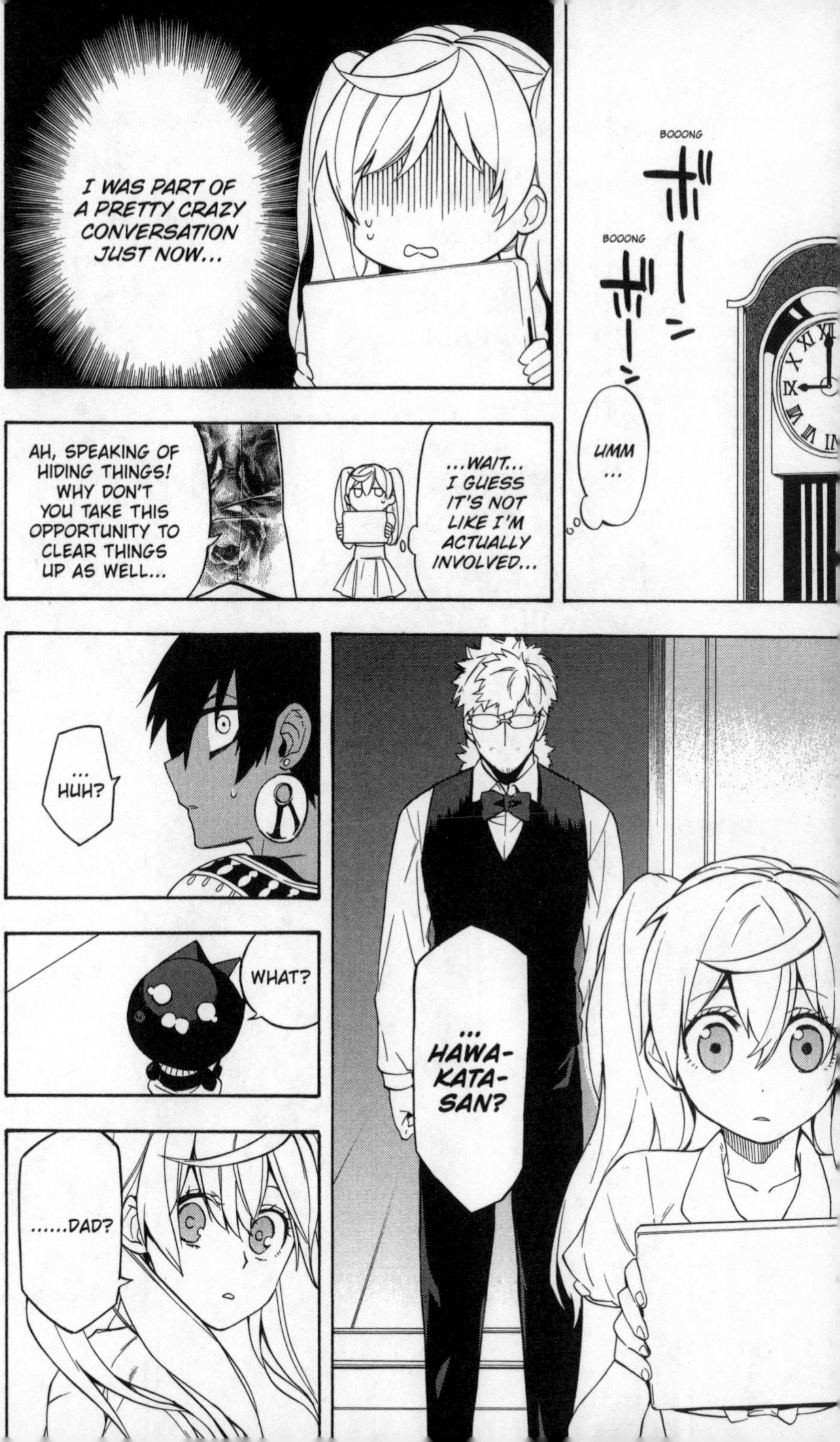
BOOONG
ボーン
BOOONG
ボーン
UMM ...
I WAS PART OF A PRETTY CRAZY CONVERSATION JUST NOW...
...WAIT... I GUESS IT'S NOT LIKE I'M ACTUALLY INVOLVED...
AH, SPEAKING OF HIDING THINGS! WHY DON'T YOU TAKE THIS OPPORTUNITY TO CLEAR THINGS UP AS WELL...
... HAWA-KATA-SAN?
... HUH?
WHAT?
......DAD?

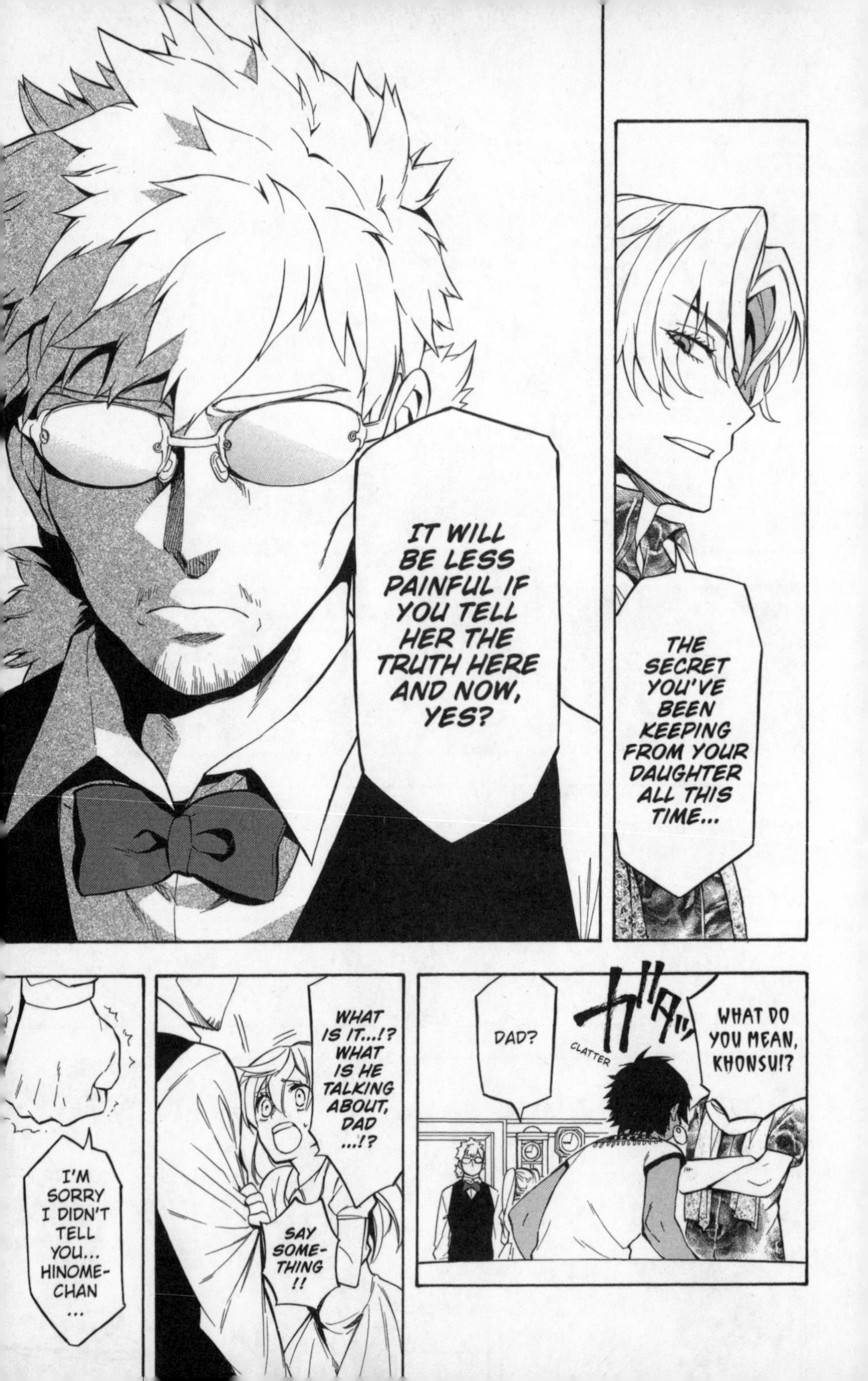
THE SECRET YOU'VE BEEN KEEPING FROM YOUR DAUGHTER ALL THIS TIME...
IT WILL BE LESS PAINFUL IF YOU TELL HER THE TRUTH HERE AND NOW, YES?
WHAT DO YOU MEAN, KHONSU!?
ガタッ
CLATTER
DAD?
WHAT IS IT...!? WHAT IS HE TALKING ABOUT, DAD ...!?
SAY SOME-THING!!
I'M SORRY I DIDN'T TELL YOU... HINOME-CHAN ...

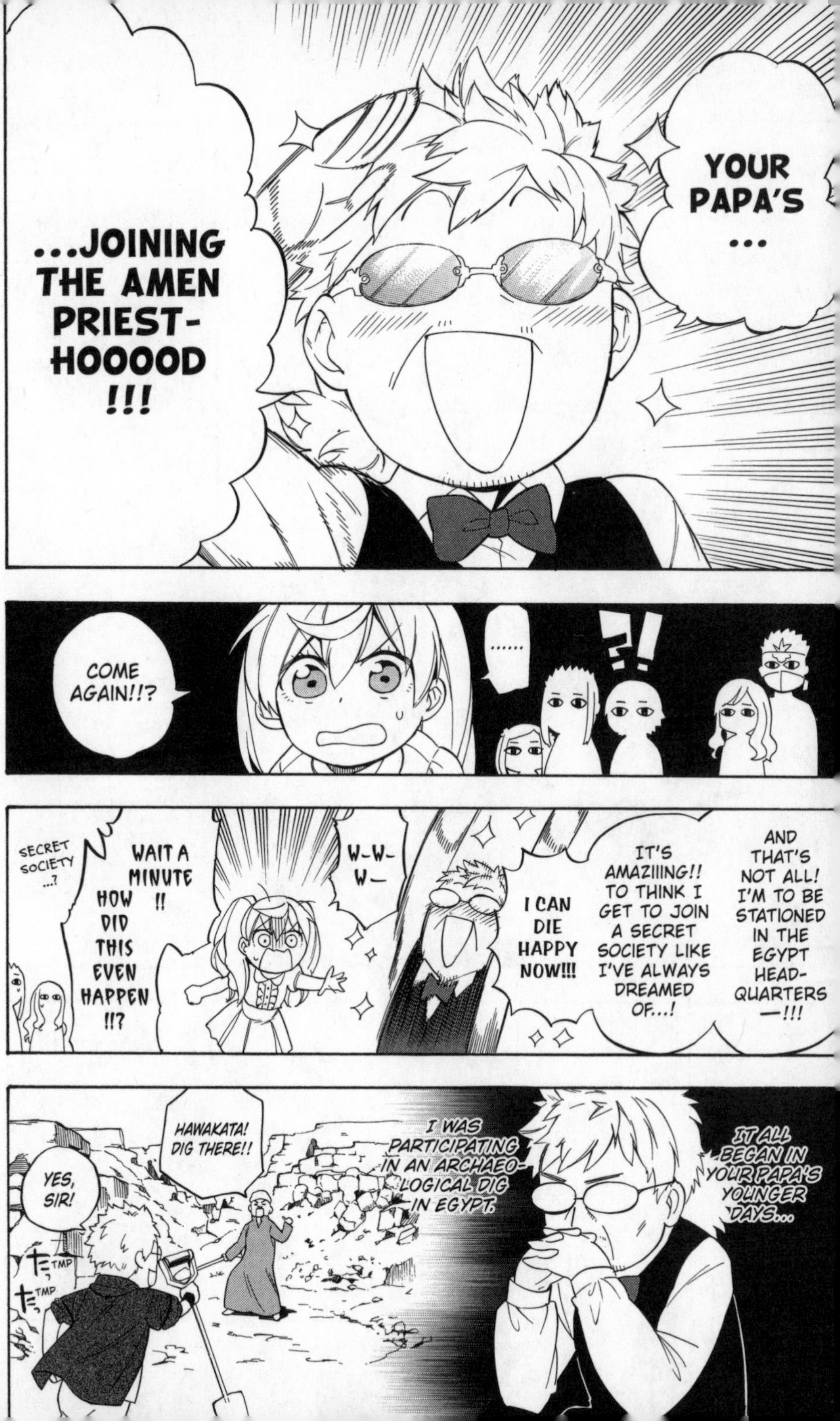
YOUR PAPA'S ...
...JOINING THE AMEN PRIEST-HOOOOD!!!
?!
......
COME AGAIN!!?
AND THAT'S NOT ALL! I'M TO BE STATIONED IN THE EGYPT HEAD-QUARTERS—!!!
IT'S AMAZIIING!! TO THINK I GET TO JOIN A SECRET SOCIETY LIKE I'VE ALWAYS DREAMED OF...!
I CAN DIE HAPPY NOW!!!
W-W-W—
WAIT A MINUTE!!
HOW DID THIS EVEN HAPPEN!!?
SECRET SOCIETY ...?
IT ALL BEGAN IN YOUR PAPA'S YOUNGER DAYS...
I WAS PARTICIPATING IN AN ARCHAEO-LOGICAL DIG IN EGYPT.
HAWAKATA! DIG THERE!!
YES, SIR!
TMP
TMP

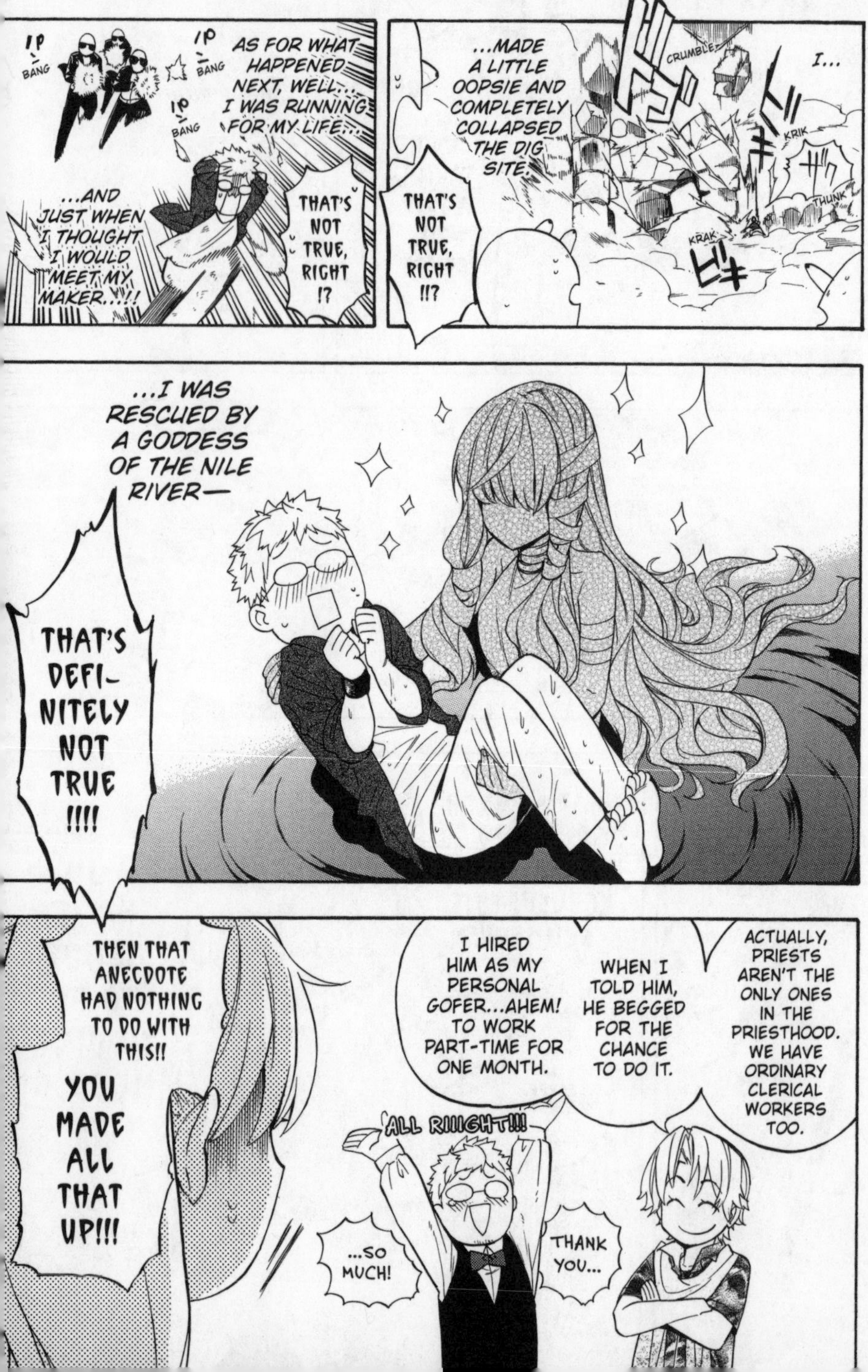
I...
...MADE A LITTLE OOPSIE AND COMPLETELY COLLAPSED THE DIG SITE.
CRUMBLE
KRIK
THUNK
KRAK
THAT'S NOT TRUE, RIGHT!!?
AS FOR WHAT HAPPENED NEXT, WELL... I WAS RUNNING FOR MY LIFE...
BANG
BANG
BANG
...AND JUST WHEN I THOUGHT I WOULD MEET MY MAKER...!!
THAT'S NOT TRUE, RIGHT!?
...I WAS RESCUED BY A GODDESS OF THE NILE RIVER—
THAT'S DEFI-NITELY NOT TRUE!!!!
ACTUALLY, PRIESTS AREN'T THE ONLY ONES IN THE PRIESTHOOD. WE HAVE ORDINARY CLERICAL WORKERS TOO.
WHEN I TOLD HIM, HE BEGGED FOR THE CHANCE TO DO IT.
I HIRED HIM AS MY PERSONAL GOFER...AHEM! TO WORK PART-TIME FOR ONE MONTH.
ALL RIIIGHT!!!
THANK YOU...
...SO MUCH!
THEN THAT ANECDOTE HAD NOTHING TO DO WITH THIS!!
YOU MADE ALL THAT UP!!!

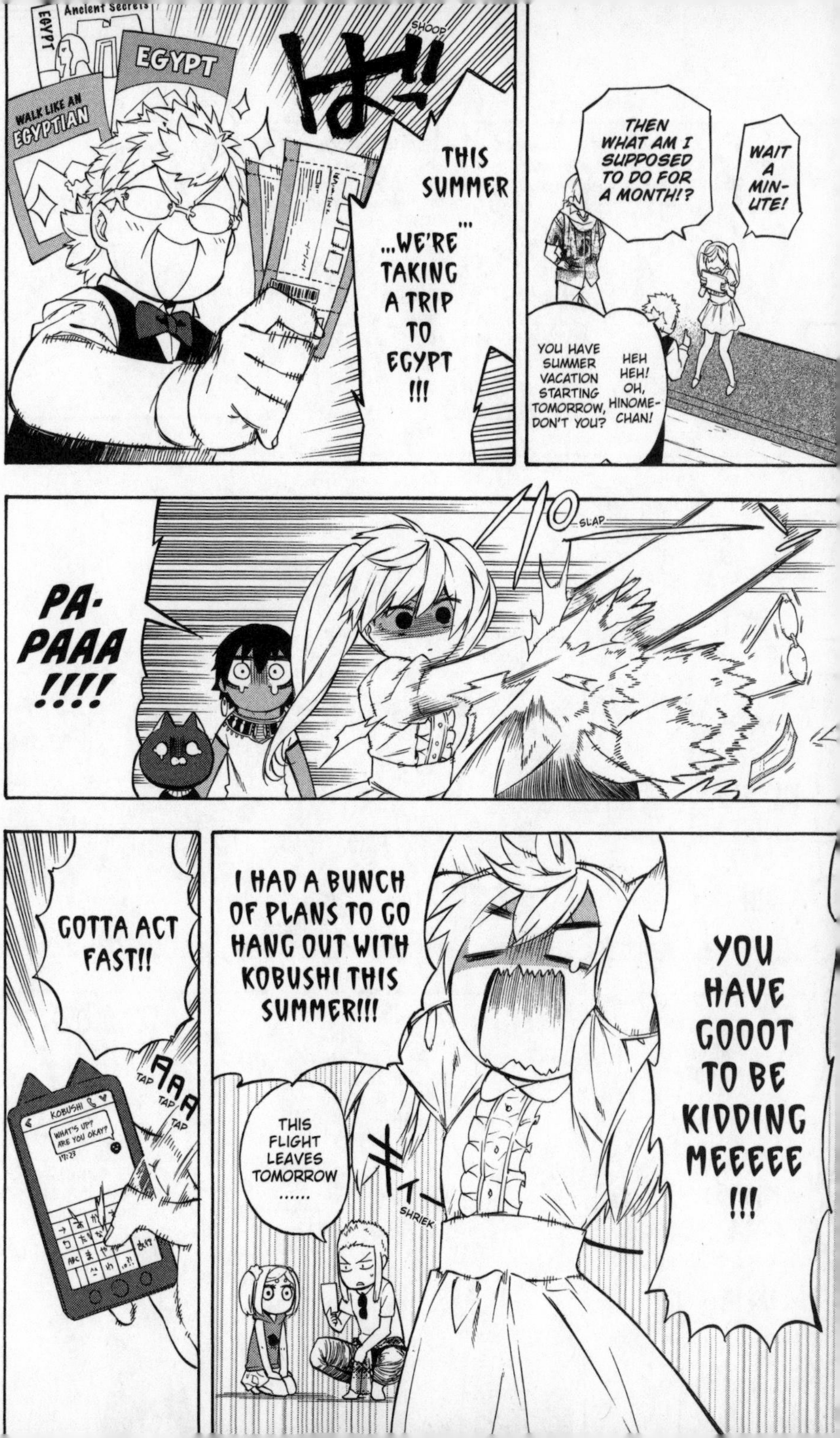
WAIT A MINUTE!
THEN WHAT AM I SUPPOSED TO DO FOR A MONTH!?
HEH HEH! OH, HINOME-CHAN!
YOU HAVE SUMMER VACATION STARTING TOMORROW, DON'T YOU?
SHOOP
THIS SUMMER
...WE'RE TAKING A TRIP TO EGYPT!!!
Ancient Secrets
EGYPT
EGYPT
WALK LIKE AN EGYPTIAN
SLAP
PA-PAAA!!!!
YOU HAVE GOOOT TO BE KIDDING MEEEEE!!!
I HAD A BUNCH OF PLANS TO GO HANG OUT WITH KOBUSHI THIS SUMMER!!!
SHRIEK
THIS FLIGHT LEAVES TOMORROW......
GOTTA ACT FAST!!
AAA
TAP
TAP
TAP
KOBUSHI
WHAT'S UP? ARE YOU OKAY?
17:23

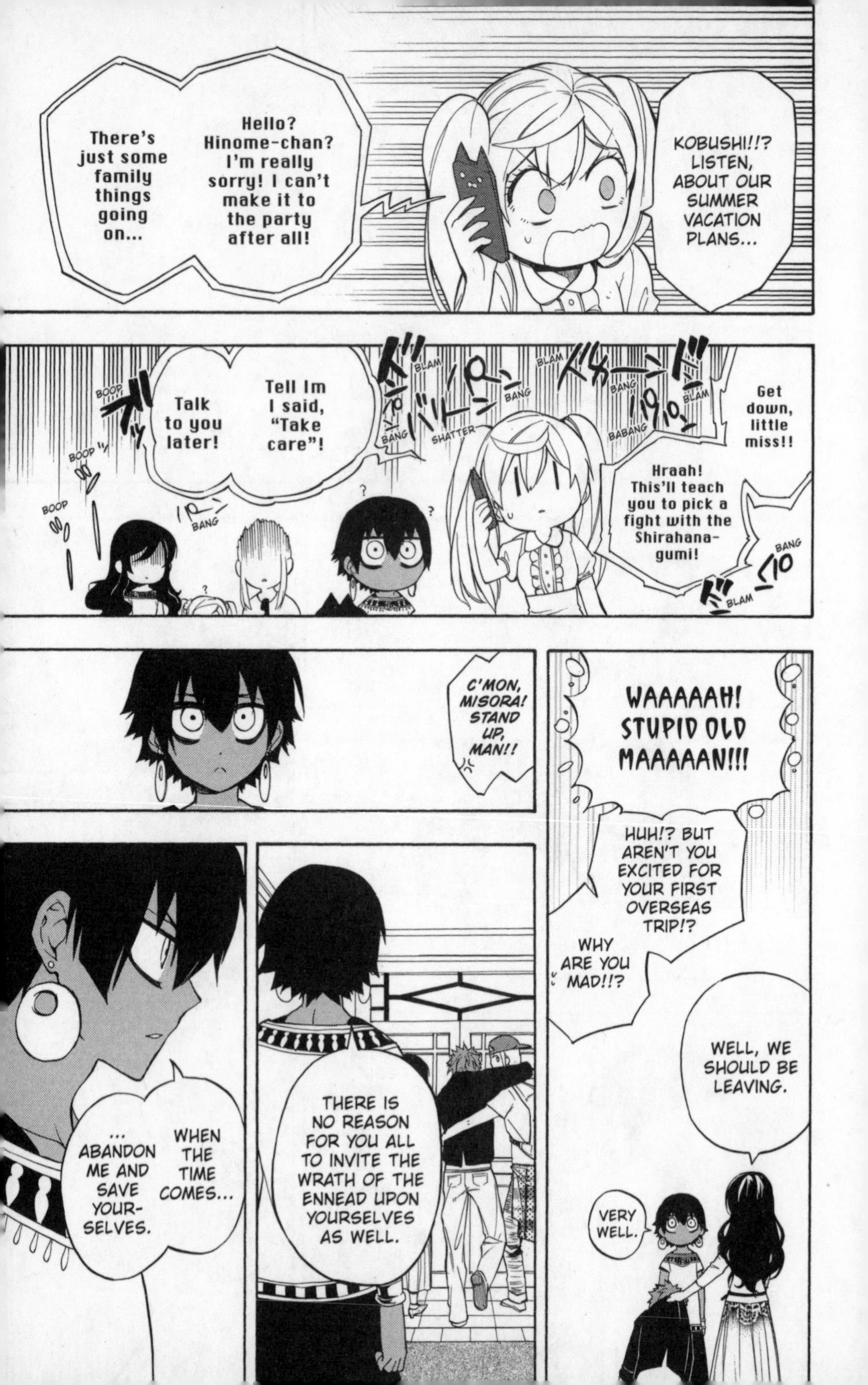
KOBUSHI!!? LISTEN, ABOUT OUR SUMMER VACATION PLANS...
Hello? Hinome-chan? I'm really sorry! I can't make it to the party after all!
There's just some family things going on...
Get down, little miss!!
BLAM
BANG
BLAM
BABANG
BANG
SHATTER
BANG
BLAM
Hraah! This'll teach you to pick a fight with the Shirahana-gumi!
BANG
BLAM
Tell Im I said, "Take care"!
Talk to you later!
BANG
BOOP
BOOP
BOOP
WAAAAAH! STUPID OLD MAAAAAN!!!
HUH!? BUT AREN'T YOU EXCITED FOR YOUR FIRST OVERSEAS TRIP!?
WHY ARE YOU MAD!!?
WELL, WE SHOULD BE LEAVING.
VERY WELL.
C'MON, MISORA! STAND UP, MAN!!
THERE IS NO REASON FOR YOU ALL TO INVITE THE WRATH OF THE ENNEAD UPON YOURSELVES AS WELL.
WHEN THE TIME COMES...
...ABANDON ME AND SAVE YOURSELVES.

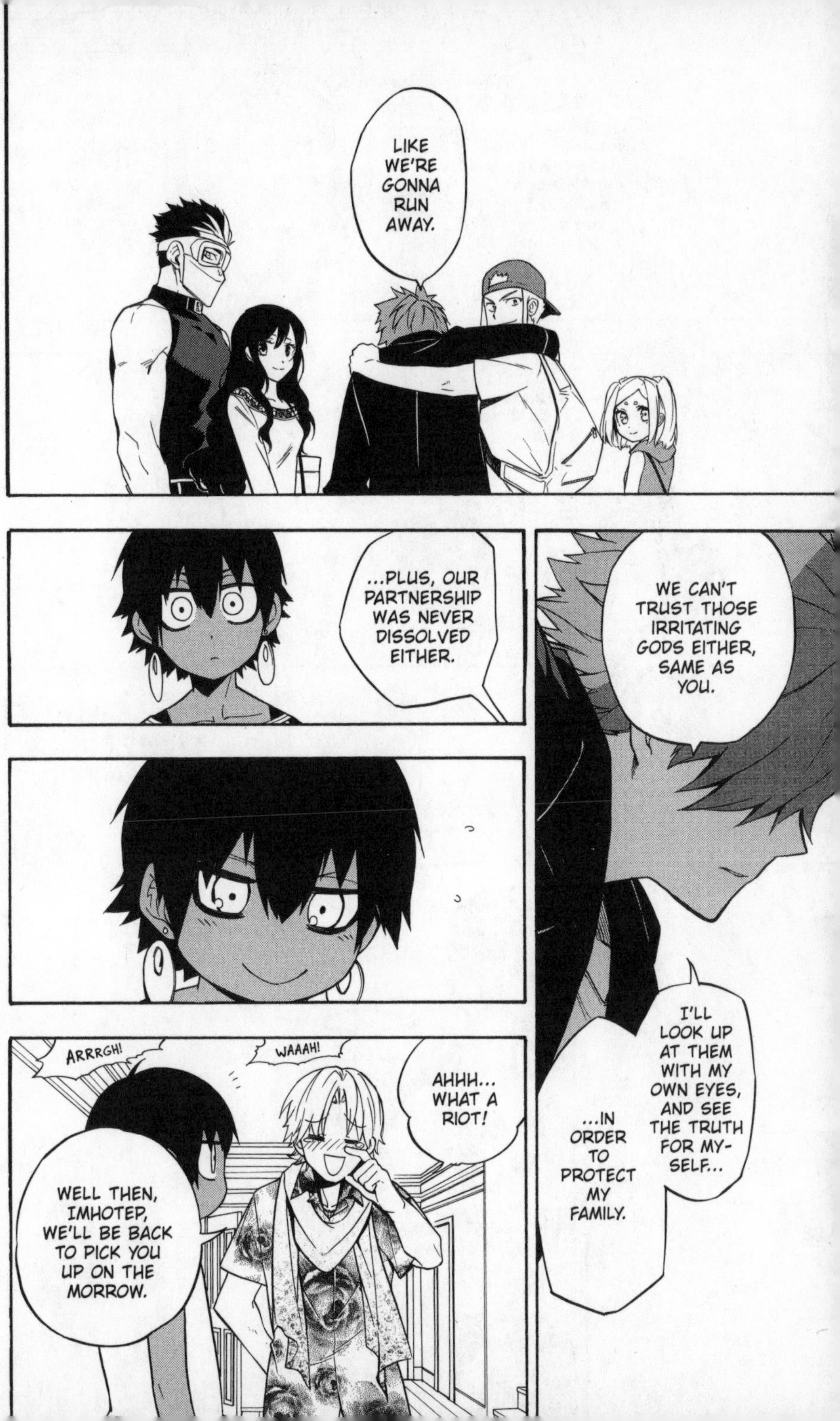

LIKE WE'RE GONNA RUN AWAY.
WE CAN'T TRUST THOSE IRRITATING GODS EITHER, SAME AS YOU.
I'LL LOOK UP AT THEM WITH MY OWN EYES, AND SEE THE TRUTH FOR MY-SELF...
...IN ORDER TO PROTECT MY FAMILY.
...PLUS, OUR PARTNERSHIP WAS NEVER DISSOLVED EITHER.
AHHH... WHAT A RIOT!
WAAAH!
ARRRGH!
WELL THEN, IMHOTEP, WE'LL BE BACK TO PICK YOU UP ON THE MORROW.

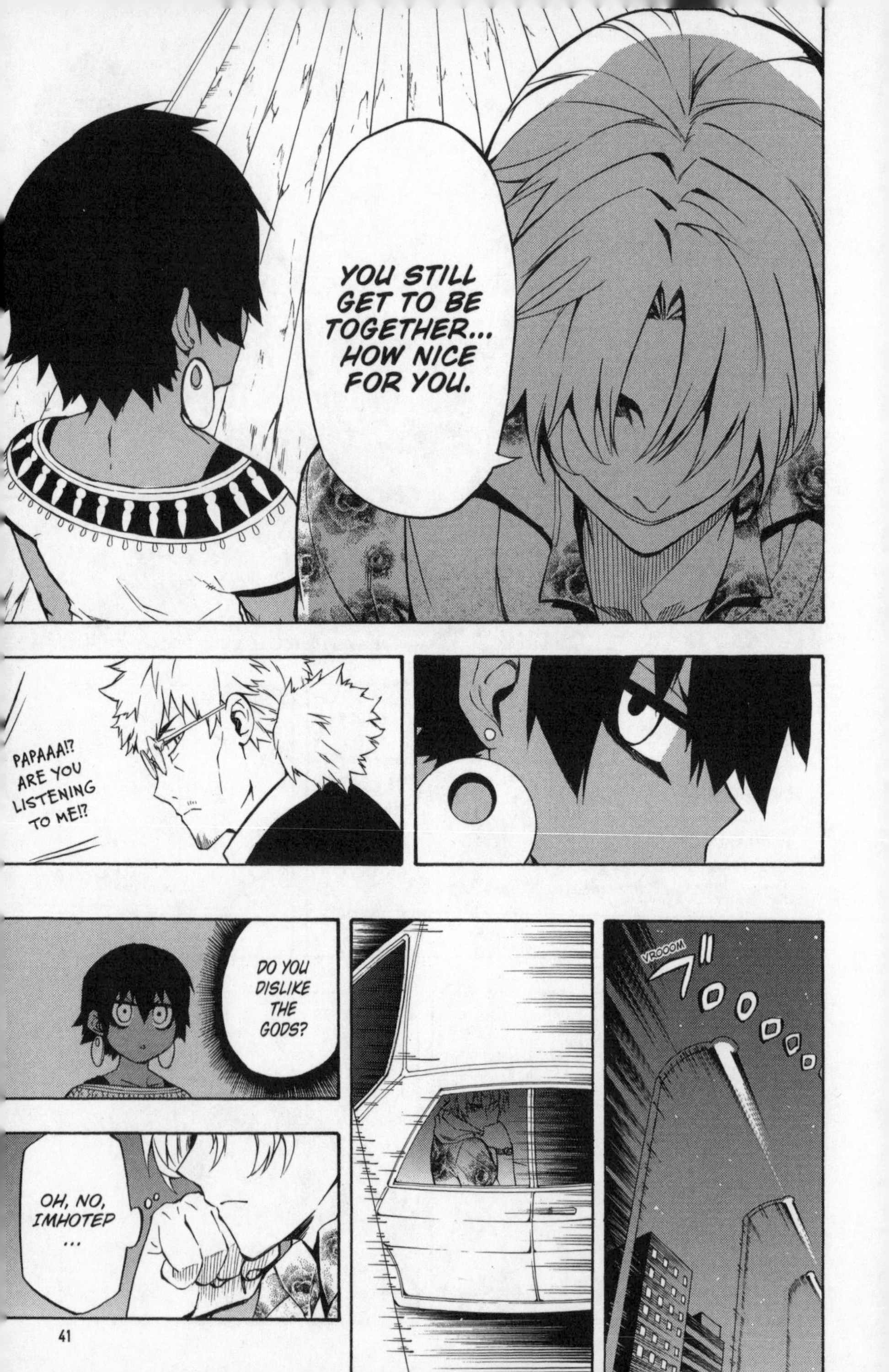

YOU STILL GET TO BE TOGETHER... HOW NICE FOR YOU.
PAPAAA!? ARE YOU LISTENING TO ME!?
VROOOM
DO YOU DISLIKE THE GODS?
OH, NO, IMHOTEP ...

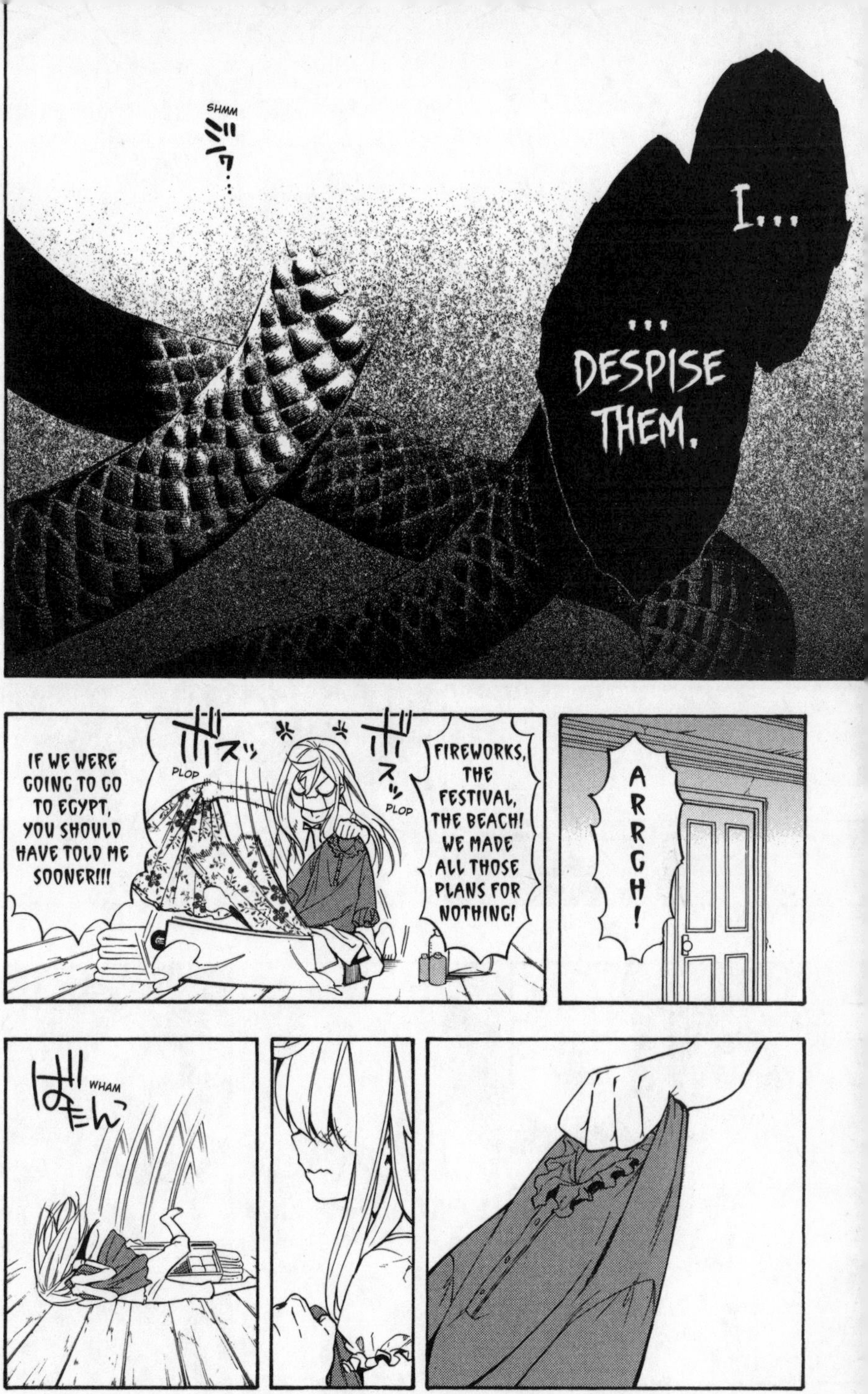
ジワ…
SHMM
I...
...DESPISE THEM.
ARRGH!
FIREWORKS, THE FESTIVAL, THE BEACH! WE MADE ALL THOSE PLANS FOR NOTHING!
ボスッ
PLOP
ボスッ
PLOP
IF WE WERE GOING TO GO TO EGYPT, YOU SHOULD HAVE TOLD ME SOONER!!!
ぱたん
WHAM

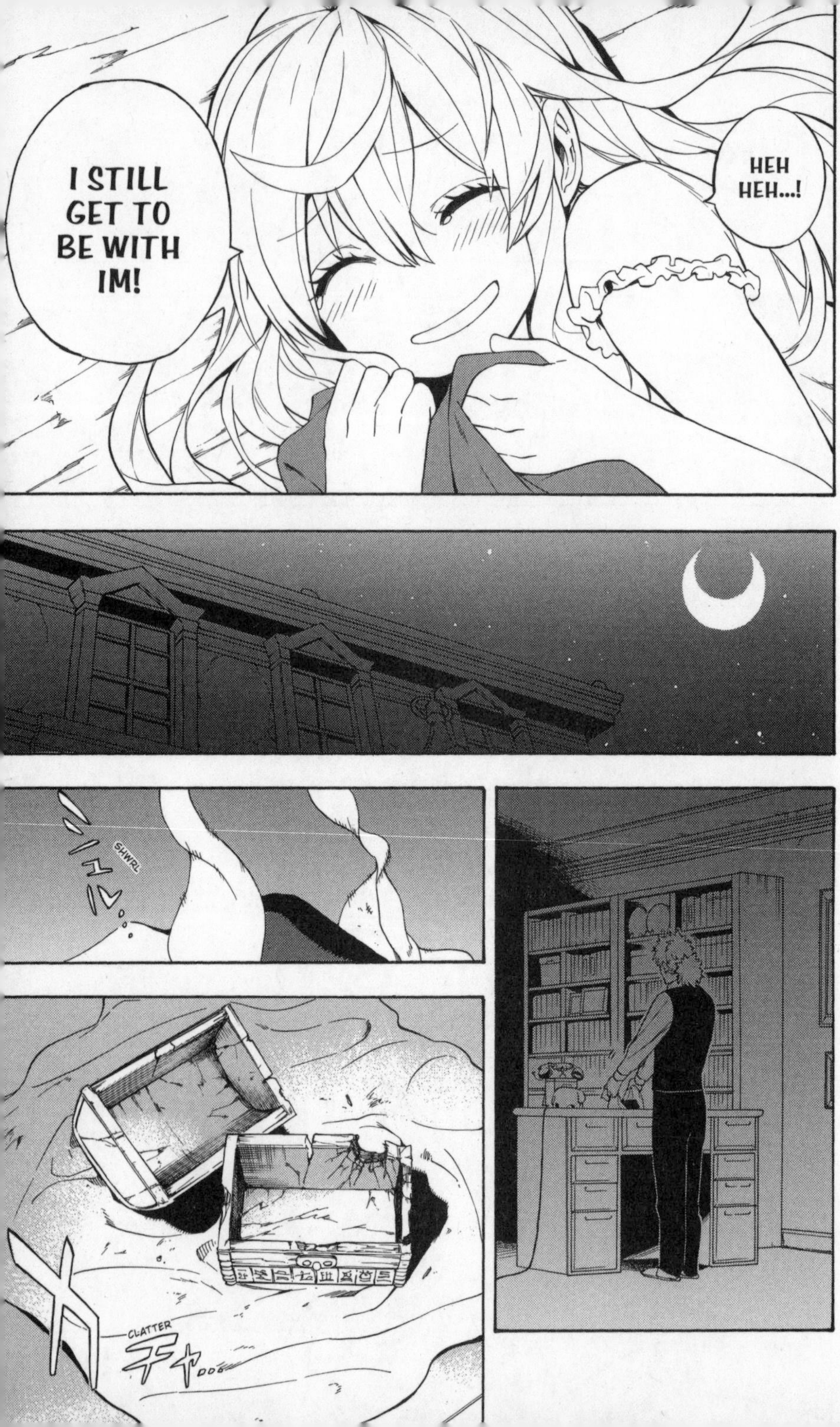

HEH HEH...!
I STILL GET TO BE WITH IM!
シュル...
SHWRL
カチャ...
CLATTER

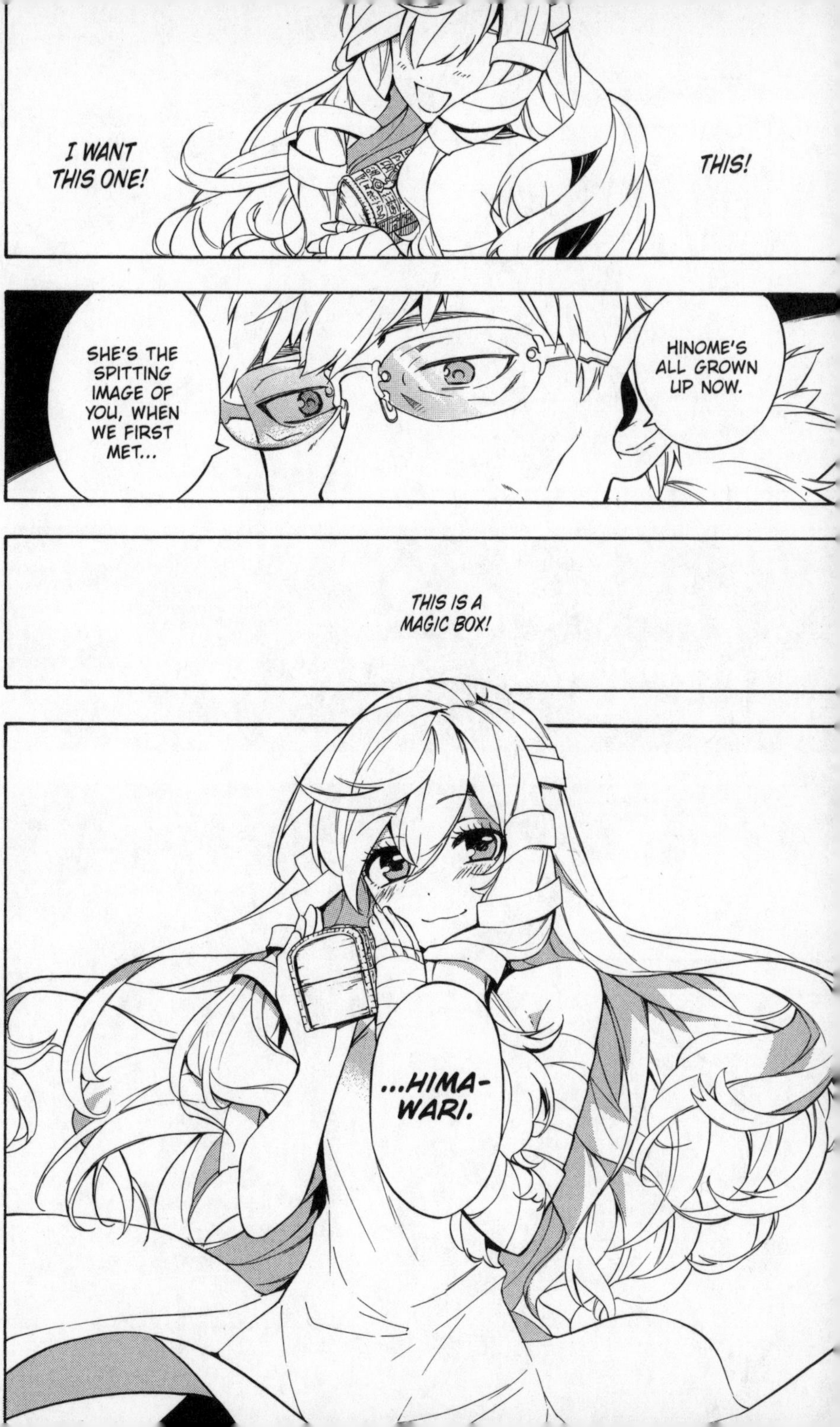
THIS!
I WANT THIS ONE!
HINOME'S ALL GROWN UP NOW.
SHE'S THE SPITTING IMAGE OF YOU, WHEN WE FIRST MET...
THIS IS A MAGIC BOX!
...HIMA-WARI.

AFTER VOLUME 5, CHAPTER 19

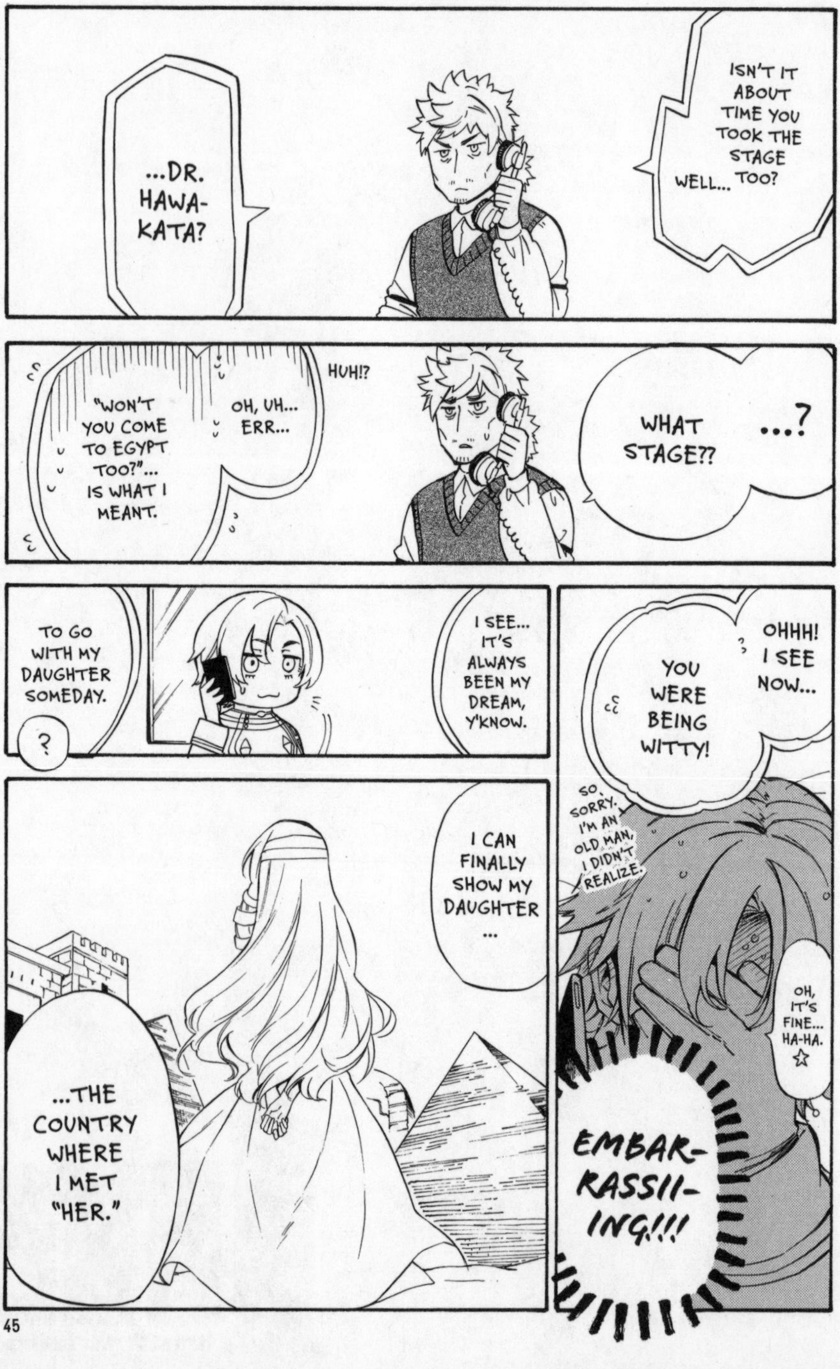
ISN'T IT ABOUT TIME YOU TOOK THE STAGE TOO?
WELL...
...DR. HAWAKATA?
...?
WHAT STAGE??
HUH!?
OH, UH... ERR...
"WON'T YOU COME TO EGYPT TOO?"... IS WHAT I MEANT.
OHHH! I SEE NOW...
YOU WERE BEING WITTY!
SO SORRY. I'M AN OLD MAN, I DIDN'T REALIZE.
OH, IT'S FINE... HA-HA. ☆
EMBARRASSIING!!!
I SEE... IT'S ALWAYS BEEN MY DREAM, Y'KNOW.
TO GO WITH MY DAUGHTER SOMEDAY.
?
I CAN FINALLY SHOW MY DAUGHTER...
...THE COUNTRY WHERE I MET "HER."

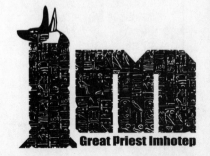
Great Priest Imhotep

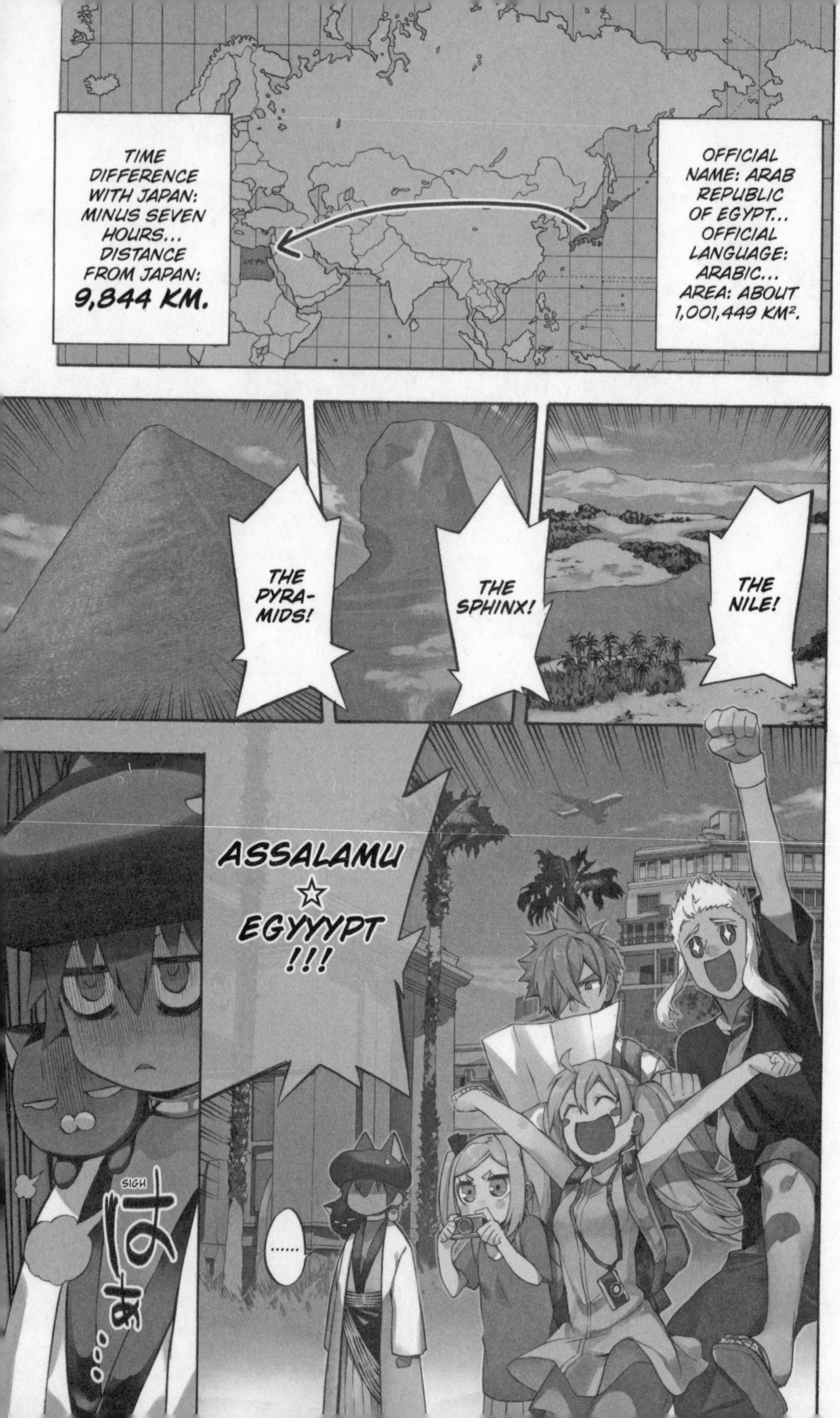

OFFICIAL NAME: ARAB REPUBLIC OF EGYPT... OFFICIAL LANGUAGE: ARABIC... AREA: ABOUT 1,001,449 KM².
TIME DIFFERENCE WITH JAPAN: MINUS SEVEN HOURS... DISTANCE FROM JAPAN: 9,844 KM.
THE NILE!
THE SPHINX!
THE PYRAMIDS!
ASSALAMU ☆ EGYYYPT!!!
......
SIGH
はぁ

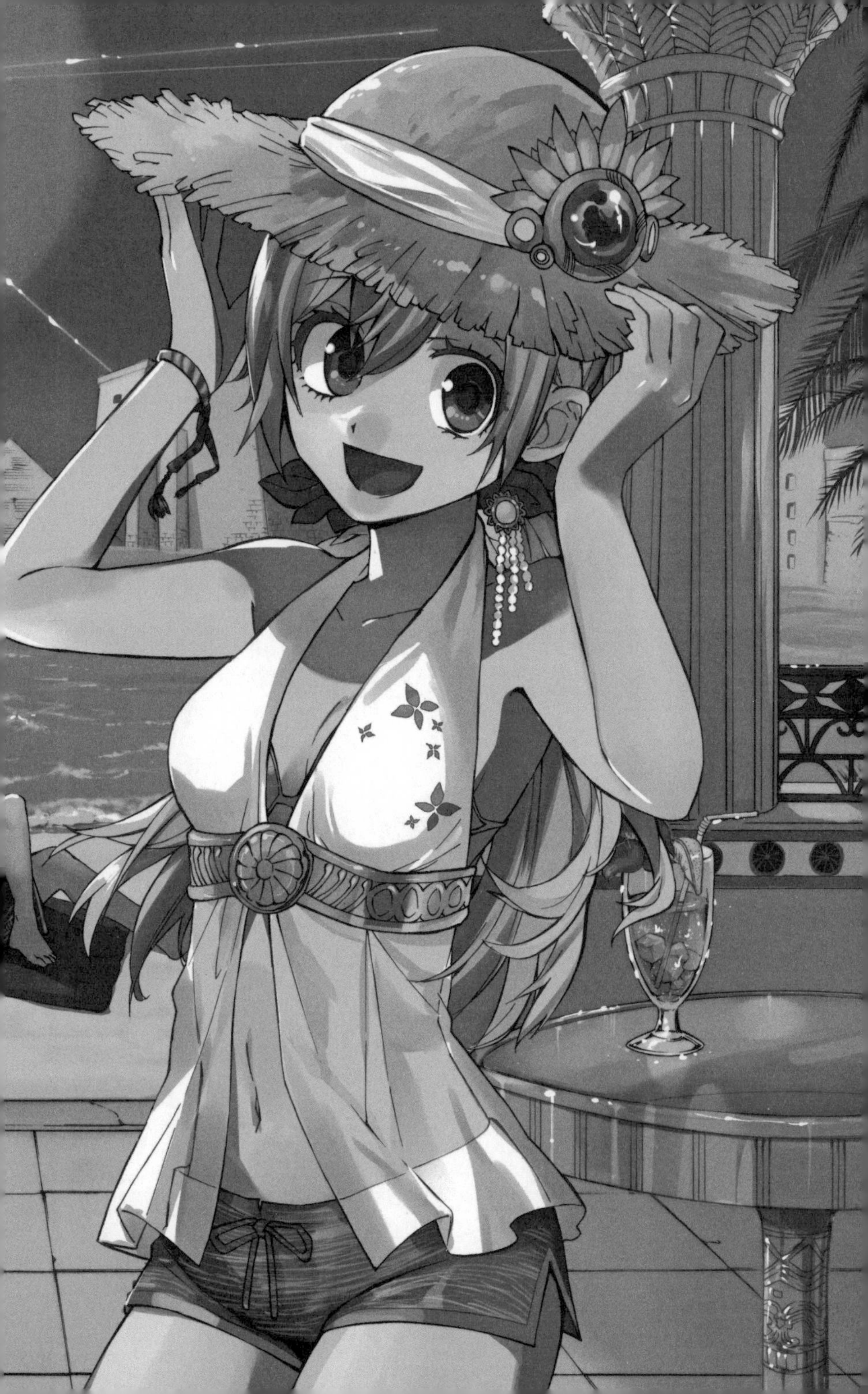

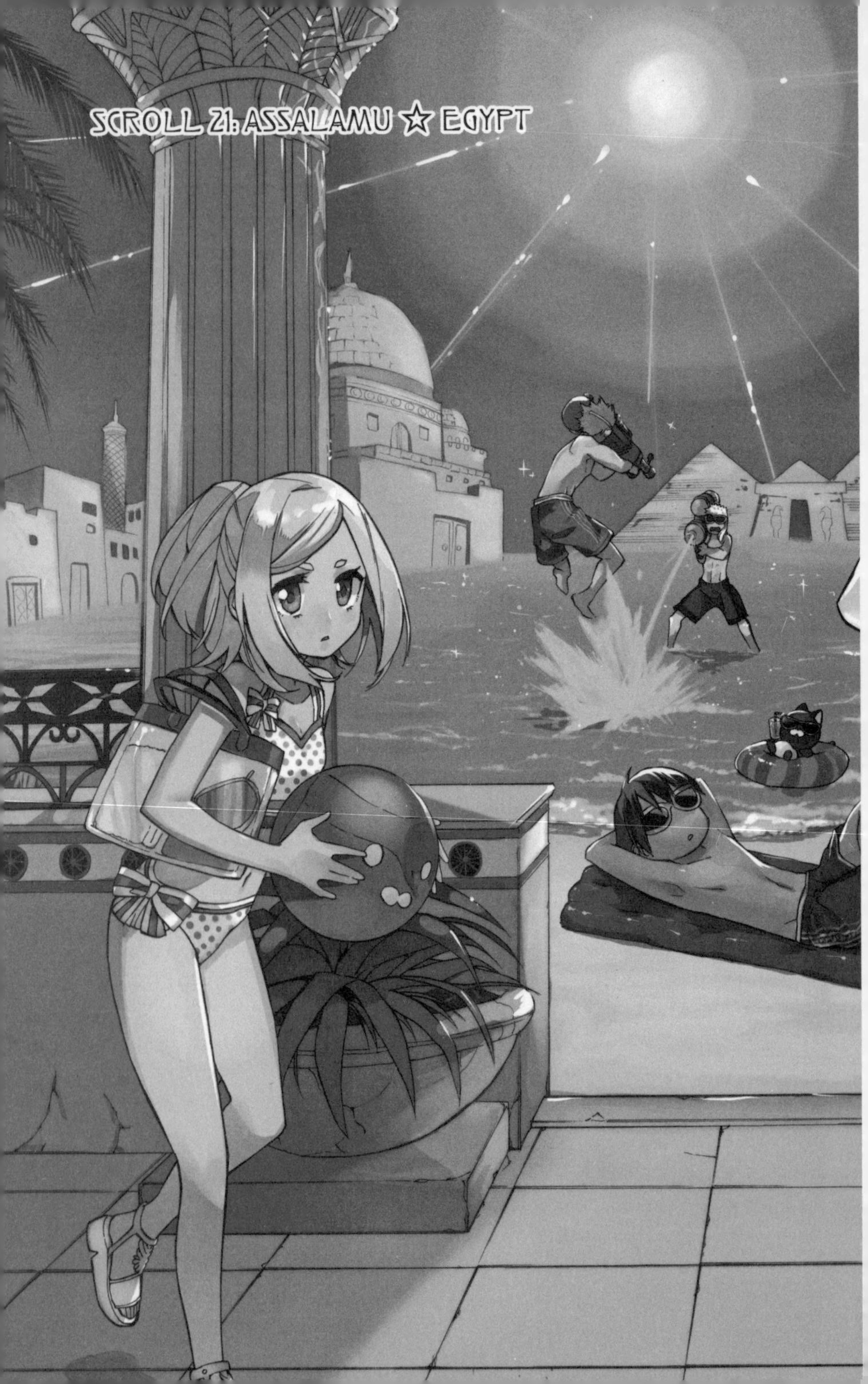
SCROLL 21: ASSALAMU ☆ EGYPT

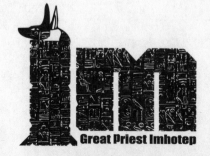
Great Priest Imhotep

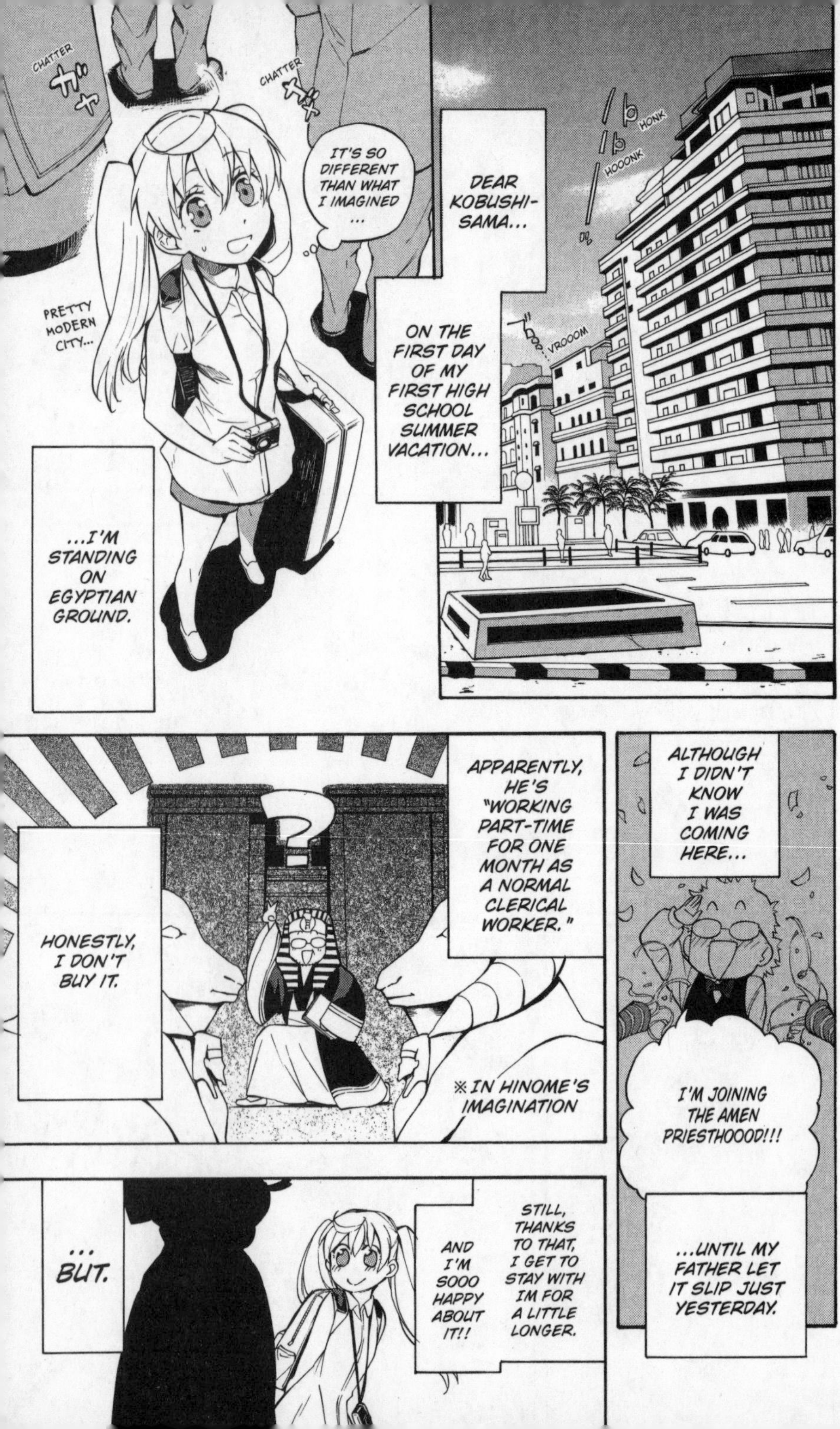
DEAR KOBUSHI-SAMA...
HONK
HOOONK
ON THE FIRST DAY OF MY FIRST HIGH SCHOOL SUMMER VACATION...
VROOOM
CHATTER
CHATTER
IT'S SO DIFFERENT THAN WHAT I IMAGINED ...
PRETTY MODERN CITY...
...I'M STANDING ON EGYPTIAN GROUND.
ALTHOUGH I DIDN'T KNOW I WAS COMING HERE...
I'M JOINING THE AMEN PRIESTHOOOD!!!
...UNTIL MY FATHER LET IT SLIP JUST YESTERDAY.
APPARENTLY, HE'S "WORKING PART-TIME FOR ONE MONTH AS A NORMAL CLERICAL WORKER."
HONESTLY, I DON'T BUY IT.
※IN HINOME'S IMAGINATION
STILL, THANKS TO THAT, I GET TO STAY WITH IM FOR A LITTLE LONGER.
AND I'M SOOO HAPPY ABOUT IT!!
... BUT.

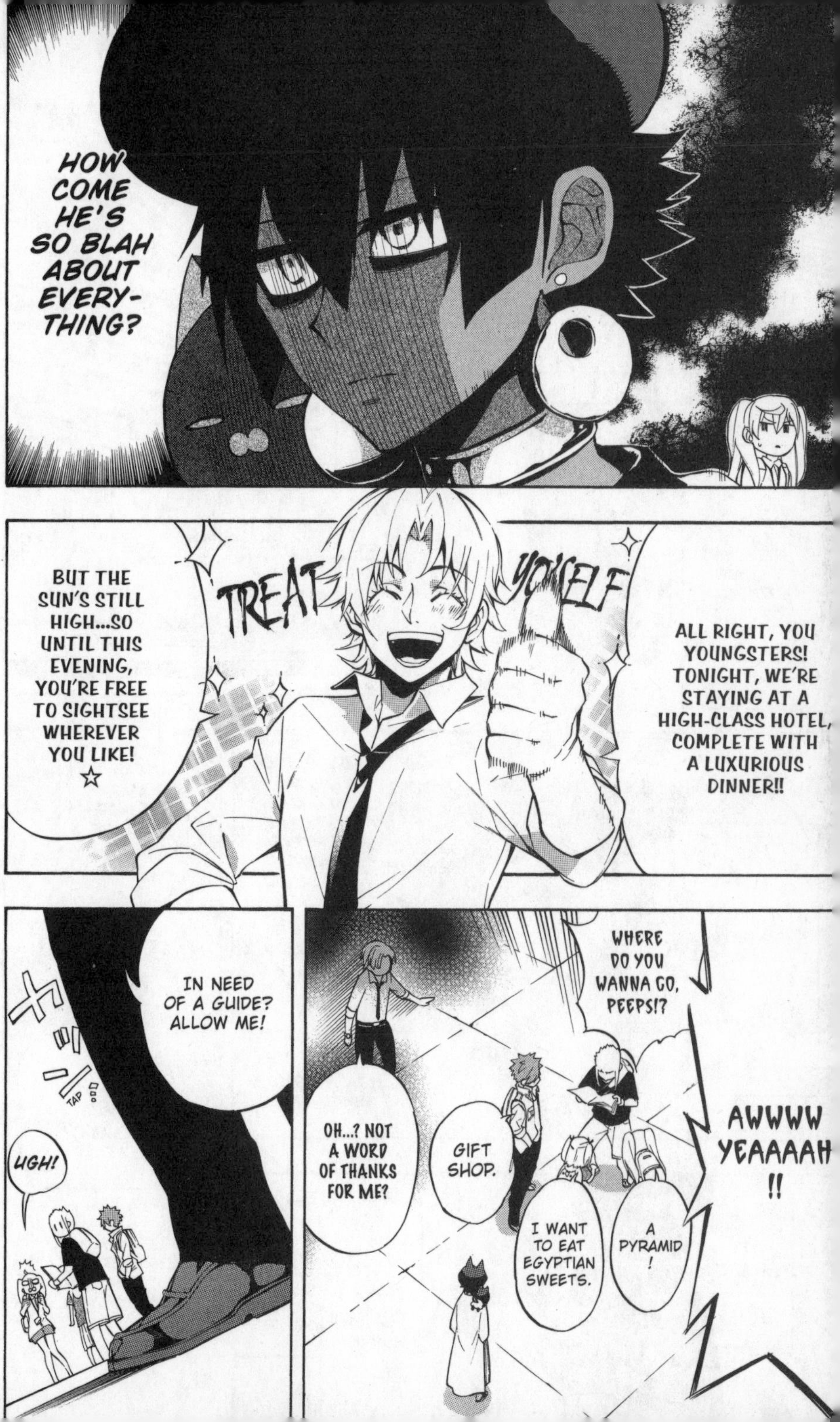
HOW COME HE'S SO BLAH ABOUT EVERY-THING?
ALL RIGHT, YOU YOUNGSTERS! TONIGHT, WE'RE STAYING AT A HIGH-CLASS HOTEL, COMPLETE WITH A LUXURIOUS DINNER!!
TREAT YOSELF
BUT THE SUN'S STILL HIGH...SO UNTIL THIS EVENING, YOU'RE FREE TO SIGHTSEE WHEREVER YOU LIKE! ☆
WHERE DO YOU WANNA GO, PEEPS!?
AWWWW YEAAAAH!!
A PYRAMID!
I WANT TO EAT EGYPTIAN SWEETS.
GIFT SHOP.
OH...? NOT A WORD OF THANKS FOR ME?
IN NEED OF A GUIDE? ALLOW ME!
TAP
UGH!

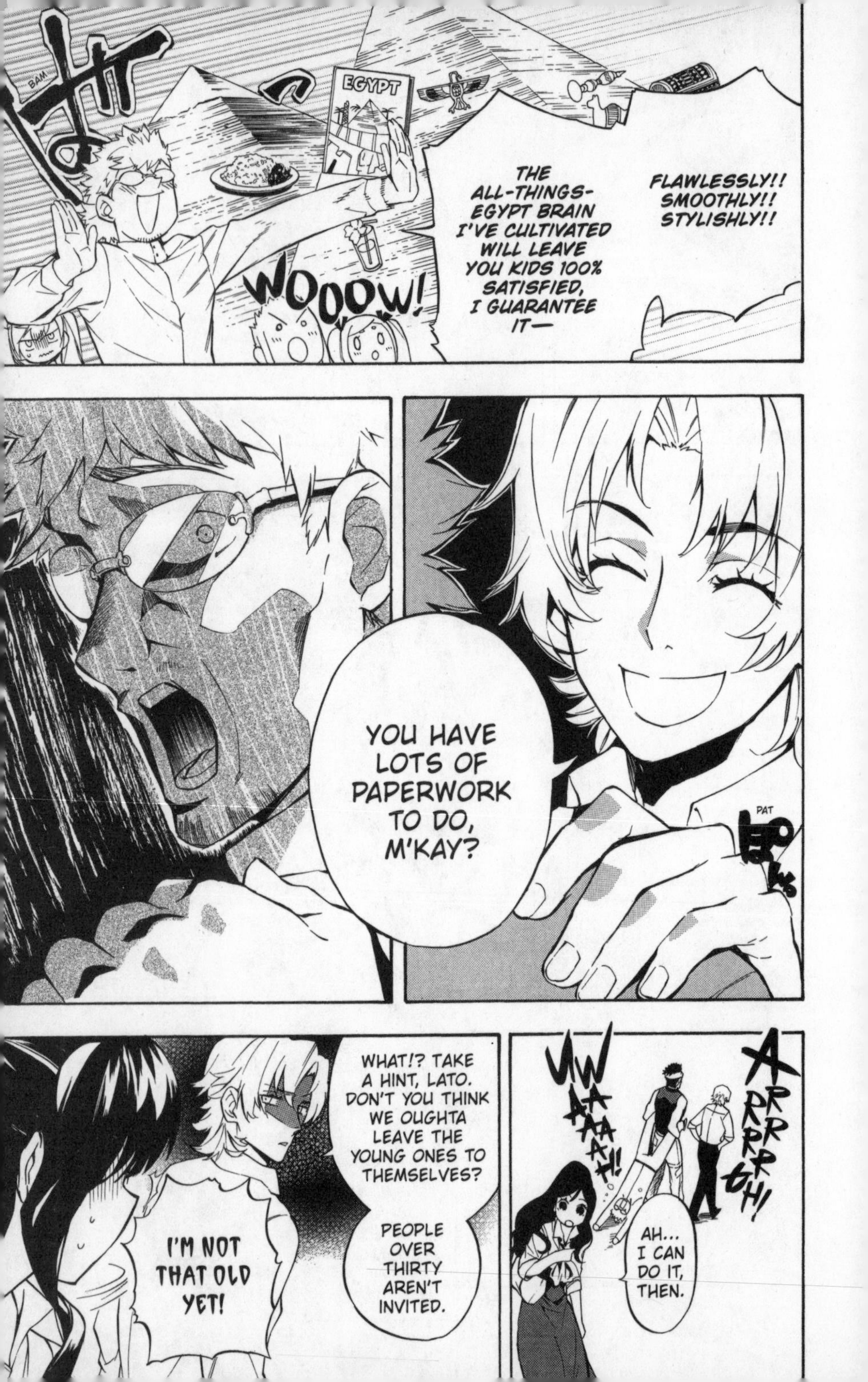
FLAWLESSLY!! SMOOTHLY!! STYLISHLY!!
THE ALL-THINGS-EGYPT BRAIN I'VE CULTIVATED WILL LEAVE YOU KIDS 100% SATISFIED, I GUARANTEE IT—
BAM
EGYPT
WOOOW!
YOU HAVE LOTS OF PAPERWORK TO DO, M'KAY?
PAT
ARRRRGH!
UWAAAAAH!
AH... I CAN DO IT, THEN.
WHAT!? TAKE A HINT, LATO. DON'T YOU THINK WE OUGHTA LEAVE THE YOUNG ONES TO THEMSELVES?
PEOPLE OVER THIRTY AREN'T INVITED.
I'M NOT THAT OLD YET!

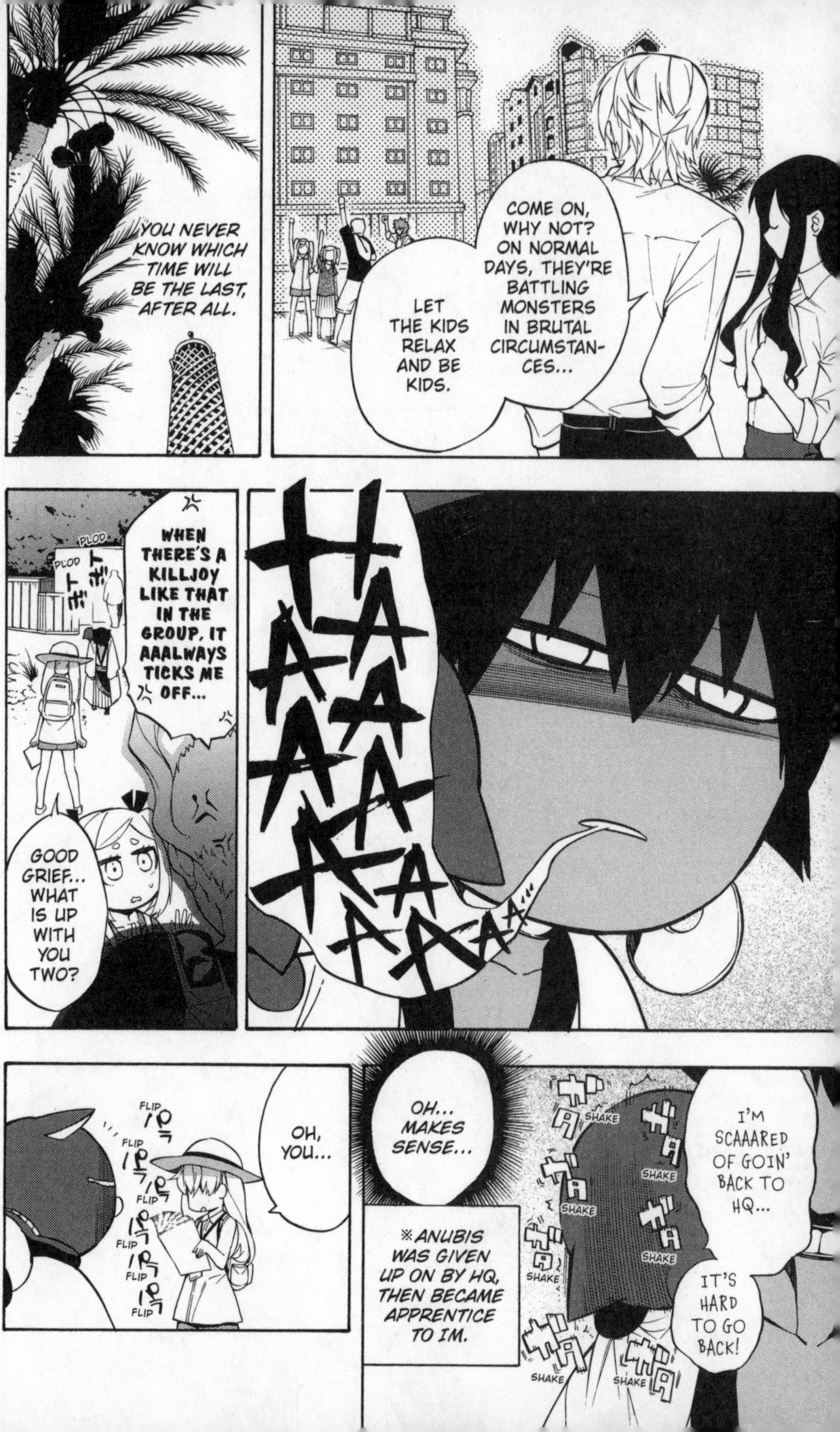
COME ON, WHY NOT? ON NORMAL DAYS, THEY'RE BATTLING MONSTERS IN BRUTAL CIRCUMSTAN-CES...
LET THE KIDS RELAX AND BE KIDS.
YOU NEVER KNOW WHICH TIME WILL BE THE LAST, AFTER ALL.
HAAAAAAAAAAAA
PLOD
PLOD
WHEN THERE'S A KILLJOY LIKE THAT IN THE GROUP, IT AAALWAYS TICKS ME OFF...
GOOD GRIEF... WHAT IS UP WITH YOU TWO?
SHAKE SHAKE SHAKE SHAKE SHAKE SHAKE SHAKE
I'M SCAAARED OF GOIN' BACK TO HQ...
IT'S HARD TO GO BACK!
OH... MAKES SENSE...
※ANUBIS WAS GIVEN UP ON BY HQ, THEN BECAME APPRENTICE TO IM.
OH, YOU...
FLIP FLIP FLIP FLIP FLIP FLIP

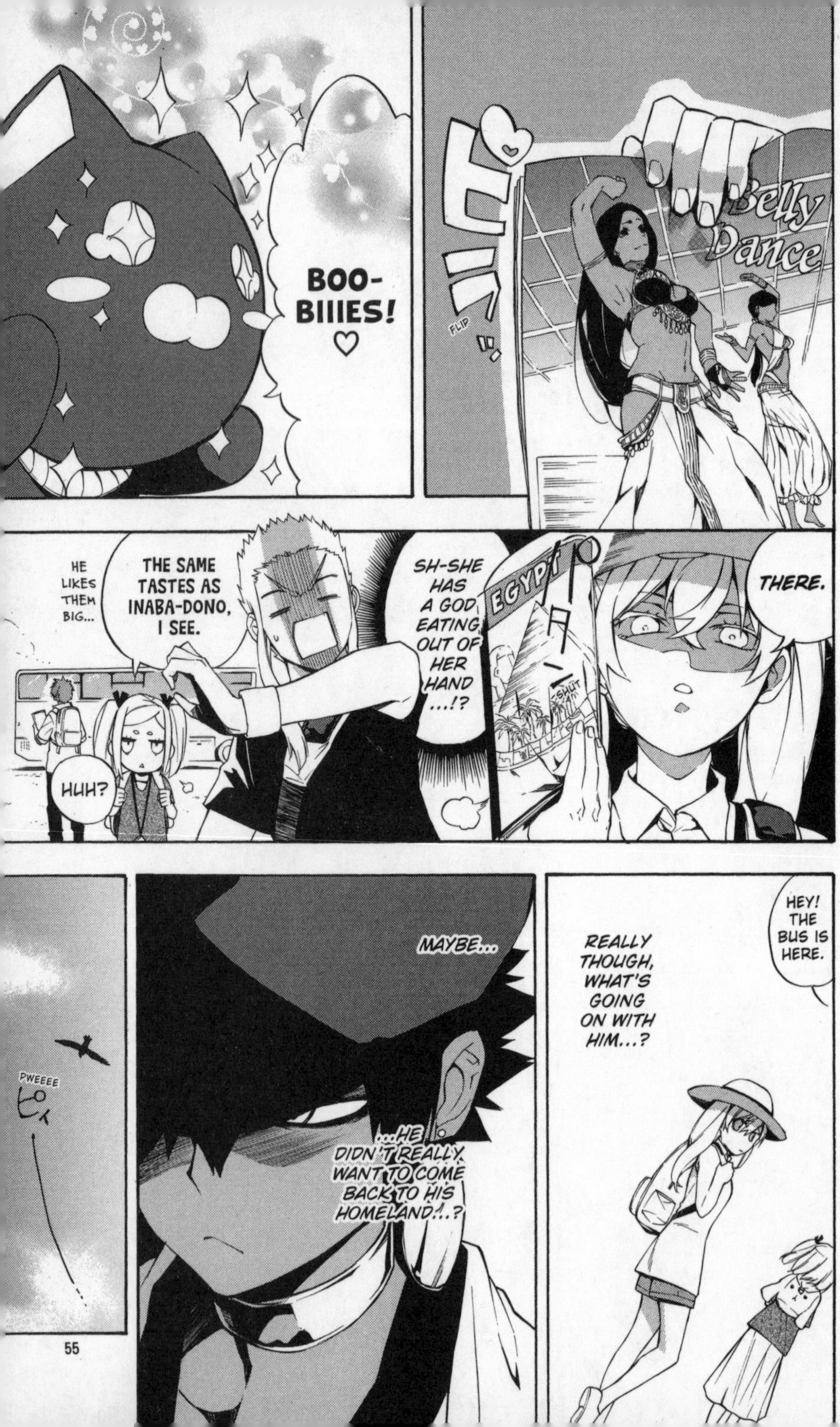

Belly Dance
FLIP
BOO-BIIIES! ♡
THERE.
EGYPT
SHUT
SH-SHE HAS A GOD EATING OUT OF HER HAND...!?
THE SAME TASTES AS INABA-DONO, I SEE.
HE LIKES THEM BIG...
HUH?
HEY! THE BUS IS HERE.
REALLY THOUGH, WHAT'S GOING ON WITH HIM...?
MAYBE...
...HE DIDN'T REALLY WANT TO COME BACK TO HIS HOMELAND...?
PWEEEE

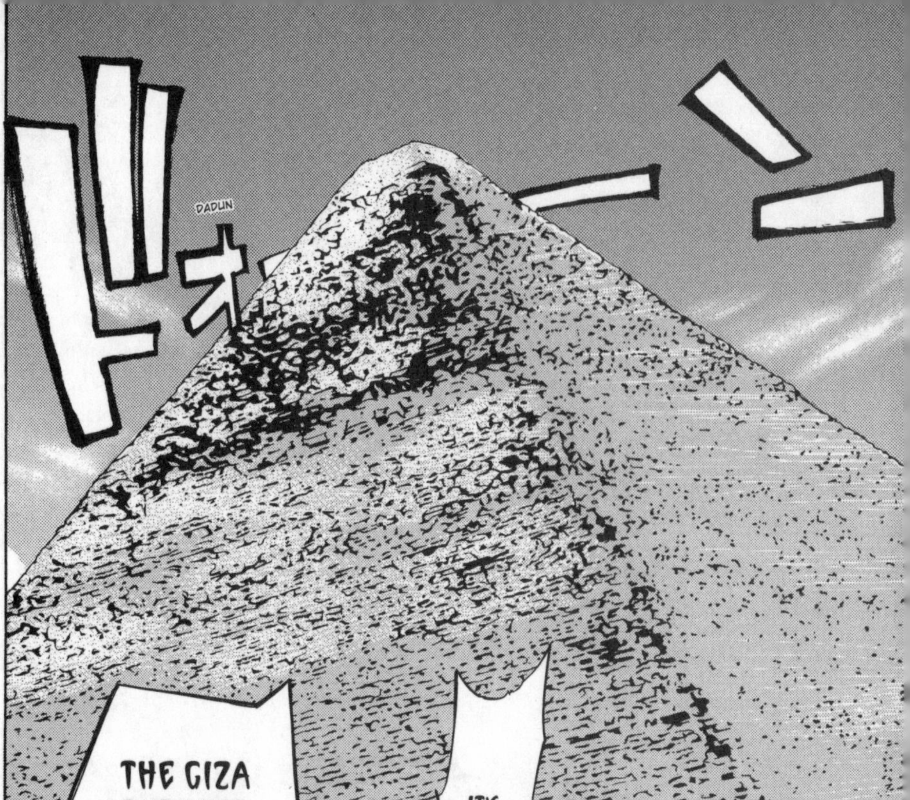
DADUN
IT'S HUUUGE !!
THE GIZA PYRAMID COMPLEX IS HUUUGE !!!
HERE.

※GIZA PYRAMID COMPLEX: INCLUDES THE GREAT PYRAMIDS OF THE PHARAOHS KHUFU, KHAFRE, AND MENKAURE.

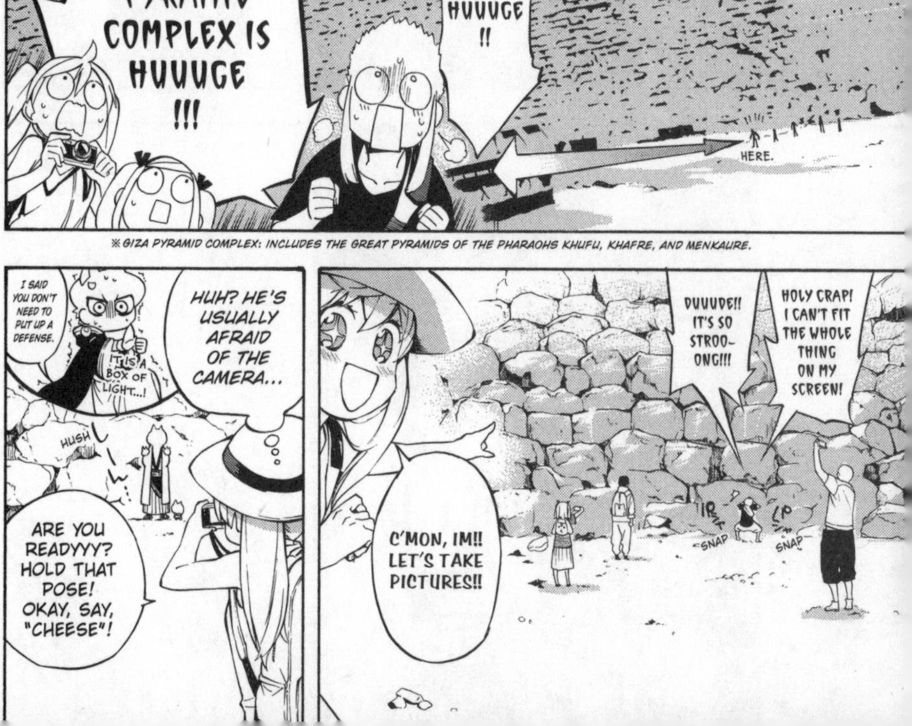
HOLY CRAP! I CAN'T FIT THE WHOLE THING ON MY SCREEN!
DUUUDE!! IT'S SO STROO-ONG!!!
SNAP
SNAP
C'MON, IM!! LET'S TAKE PICTURES!!
HUH? HE'S USUALLY AFRAID OF THE CAMERA...
I SAID YOU DON'T NEED TO PUT UP A DEFENSE.
IT IS A BOX OF LIGHT...!
HUSH
ARE YOU READYYY? HOLD THAT POSE! OKAY, SAY, "CHEESE"!

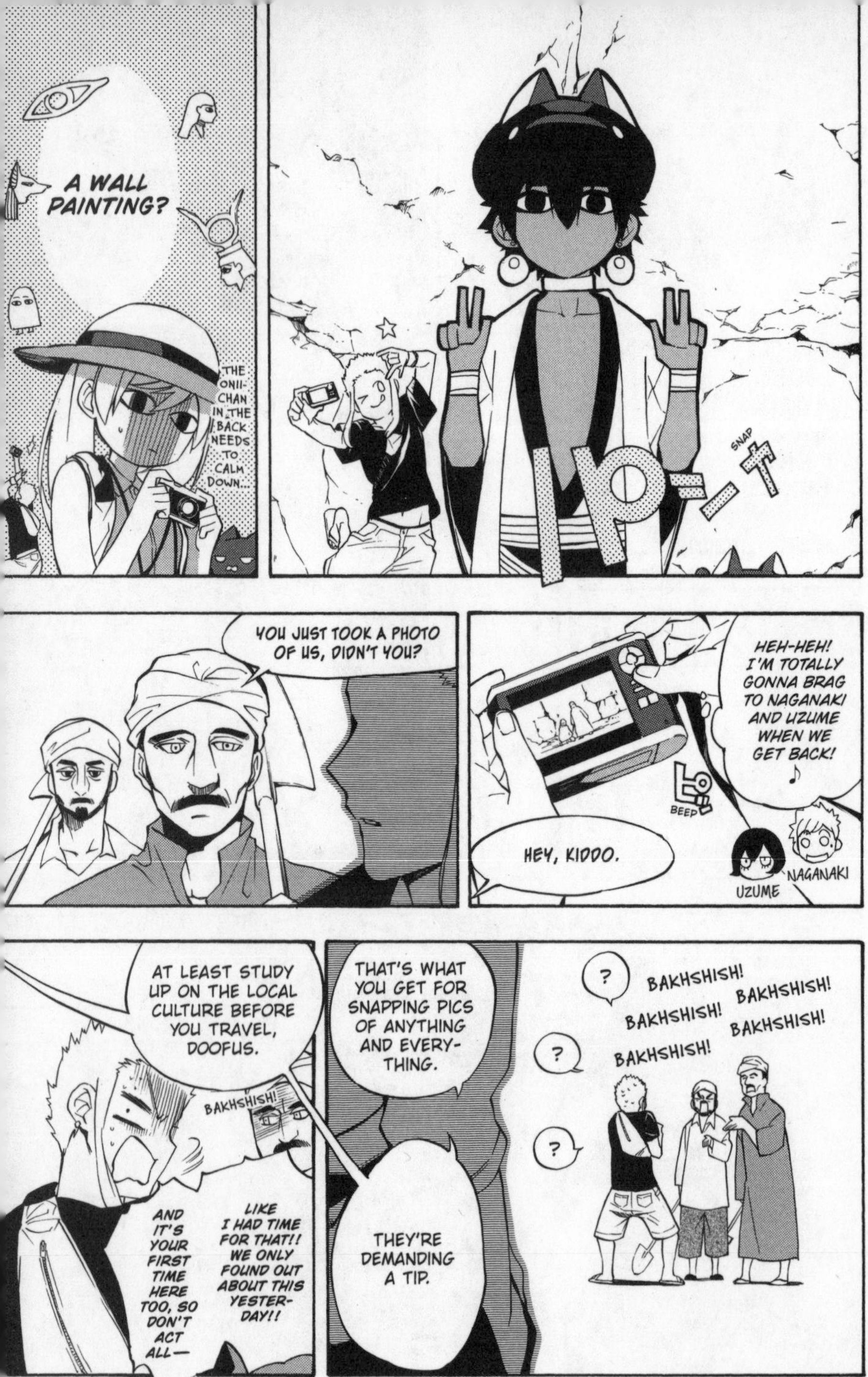
SNAP
A WALL PAINTING?
THE ONII-CHAN IN THE BACK NEEDS TO CALM DOWN...
HEH-HEH! I'M TOTALLY GONNA BRAG TO NAGANAKI AND UZUME WHEN WE GET BACK! ♪
BEEP
NAGANAKI
UZUME
HEY, KIDDO.
YOU JUST TOOK A PHOTO OF US, DIDN'T YOU?
?
?
?
BAKHSHISH!
BAKHSHISH!
BAKHSHISH!
BAKHSHISH!
BAKHSHISH!
THAT'S WHAT YOU GET FOR SNAPPING PICS OF ANYTHING AND EVERYTHING.
THEY'RE DEMANDING A TIP.
AT LEAST STUDY UP ON THE LOCAL CULTURE BEFORE YOU TRAVEL, DOOFUS.
BAKHSHISH!
LIKE I HAD TIME FOR THAT!! WE ONLY FOUND OUT ABOUT THIS YESTERDAY!!
AND IT'S YOUR FIRST TIME HERE TOO, SO DON'T ACT ALL—

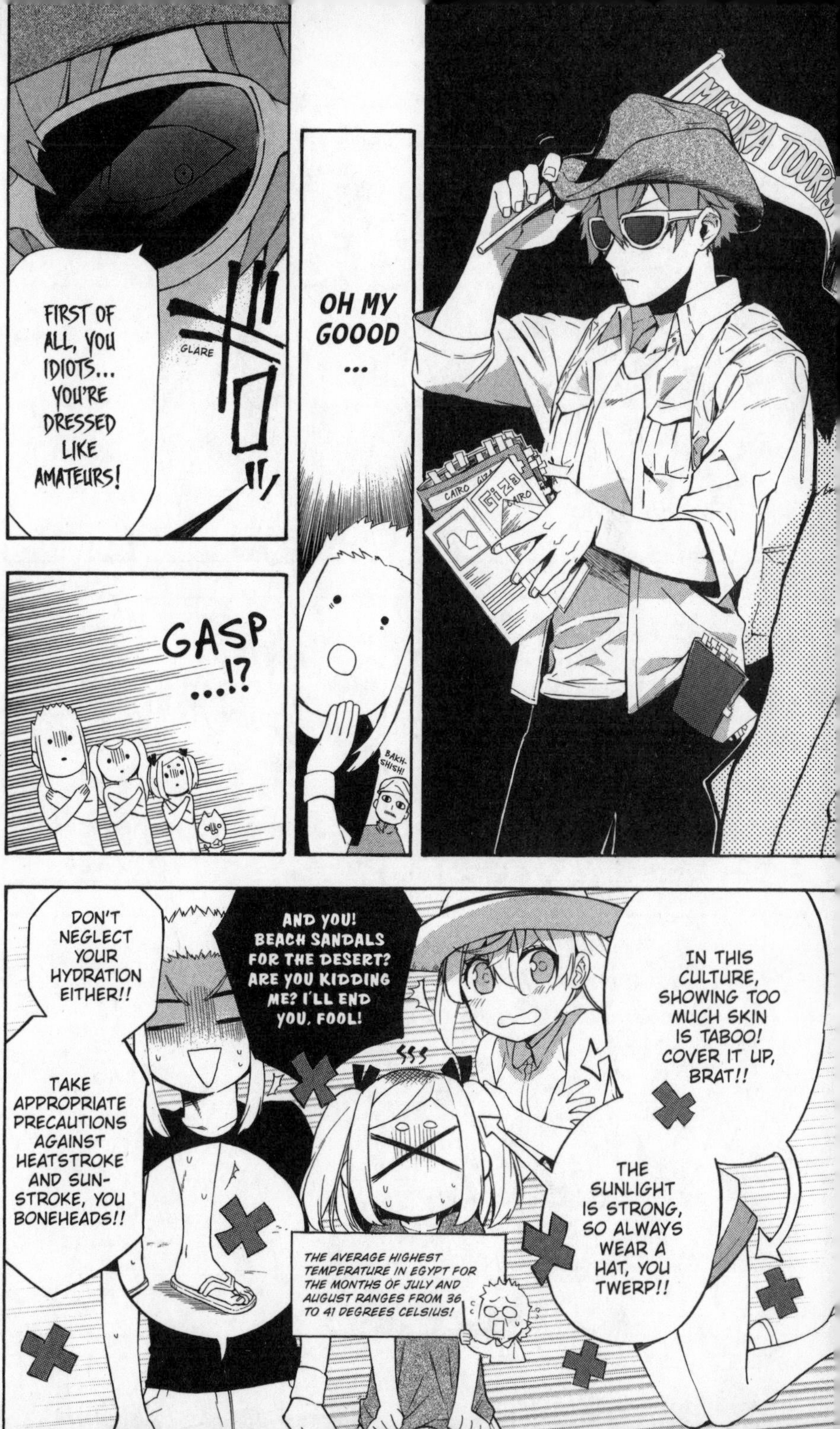
MICORA TOUR
CAIRO
GIZA
GIZA
CAIRO
OH MY GOOOD ...
BAKH-SHISH!
FIRST OF ALL, YOU IDIOTS... YOU'RE DRESSED LIKE AMATEURS!
GLARE
GASP ...!?
IN THIS CULTURE, SHOWING TOO MUCH SKIN IS TABOO! COVER IT UP, BRAT!!
AND YOU! BEACH SANDALS FOR THE DESERT? ARE YOU KIDDING ME? I'LL END YOU, FOOL!
DON'T NEGLECT YOUR HYDRATION EITHER!!
THE SUNLIGHT IS STRONG, SO ALWAYS WEAR A HAT, YOU TWERP!!
TAKE APPROPRIATE PRECAUTIONS AGAINST HEATSTROKE AND SUN-STROKE, YOU BONEHEADS!!
THE AVERAGE HIGHEST TEMPERATURE IN EGYPT FOR THE MONTHS OF JULY AND AUGUST RANGES FROM 36 TO 41 DEGREES CELSIUS!

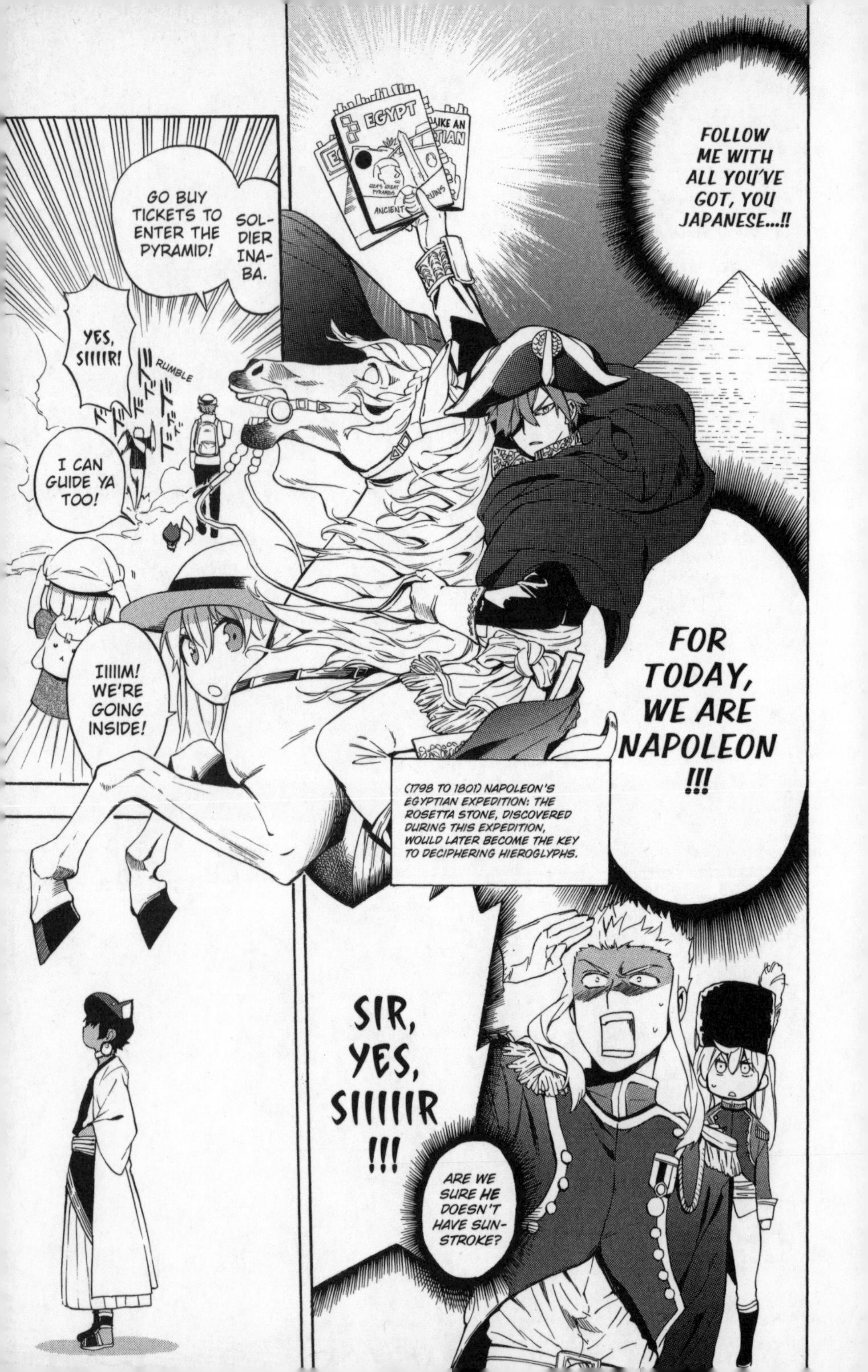
EGYPT
FOLLOW ME WITH ALL YOU'VE GOT, YOU JAPANESE...!!
FOR TODAY, WE ARE NAPOLEON!!!
(1798 TO 1801) NAPOLEON'S EGYPTIAN EXPEDITION: THE ROSETTA STONE, DISCOVERED DURING THIS EXPEDITION, WOULD LATER BECOME THE KEY TO DECIPHERING HIEROGLYPHS.
GO BUY TICKETS TO ENTER THE PYRAMID!
SOLDIER INABA.
YES, SIIIIR!
RUMBLE
I CAN GUIDE YA TOO!
IIIIIM! WE'RE GOING INSIDE!
SIR, YES, SIIIIIR!!!
ARE WE SURE HE DOESN'T HAVE SUNSTROKE?

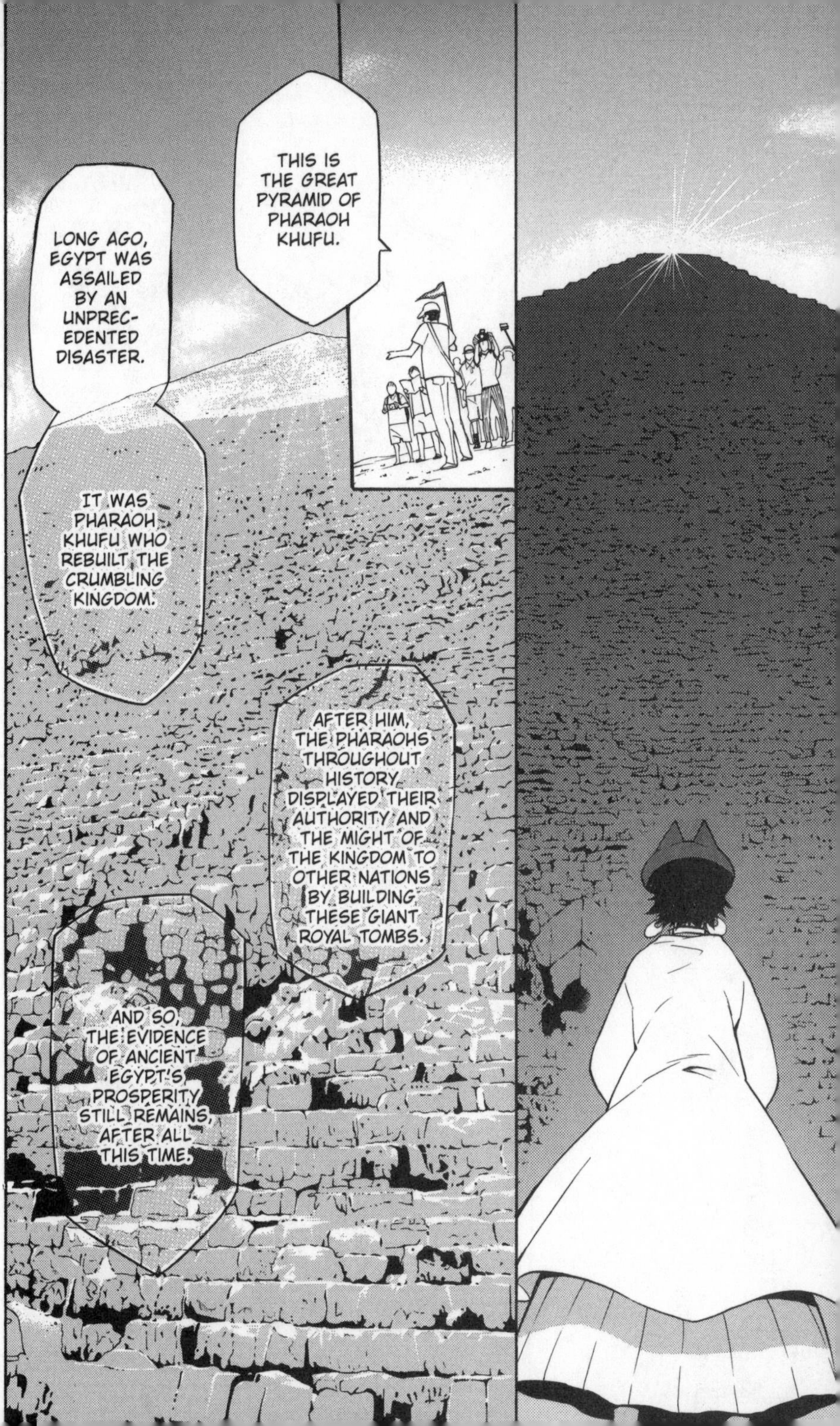
THIS IS THE GREAT PYRAMID OF PHARAOH KHUFU.
LONG AGO, EGYPT WAS ASSAILED BY AN UNPREC-EDENTED DISASTER.
IT WAS PHARAOH KHUFU WHO REBUILT THE CRUMBLING KINGDOM.
AFTER HIM, THE PHARAOHS THROUGHOUT HISTORY DISPLAYED THEIR AUTHORITY AND THE MIGHT OF THE KINGDOM TO OTHER NATIONS BY BUILDING THESE GIANT ROYAL TOMBS.
AND SO, THE EVIDENCE OF ANCIENT EGYPT'S PROSPERITY STILL REMAINS, AFTER ALL THIS TIME.

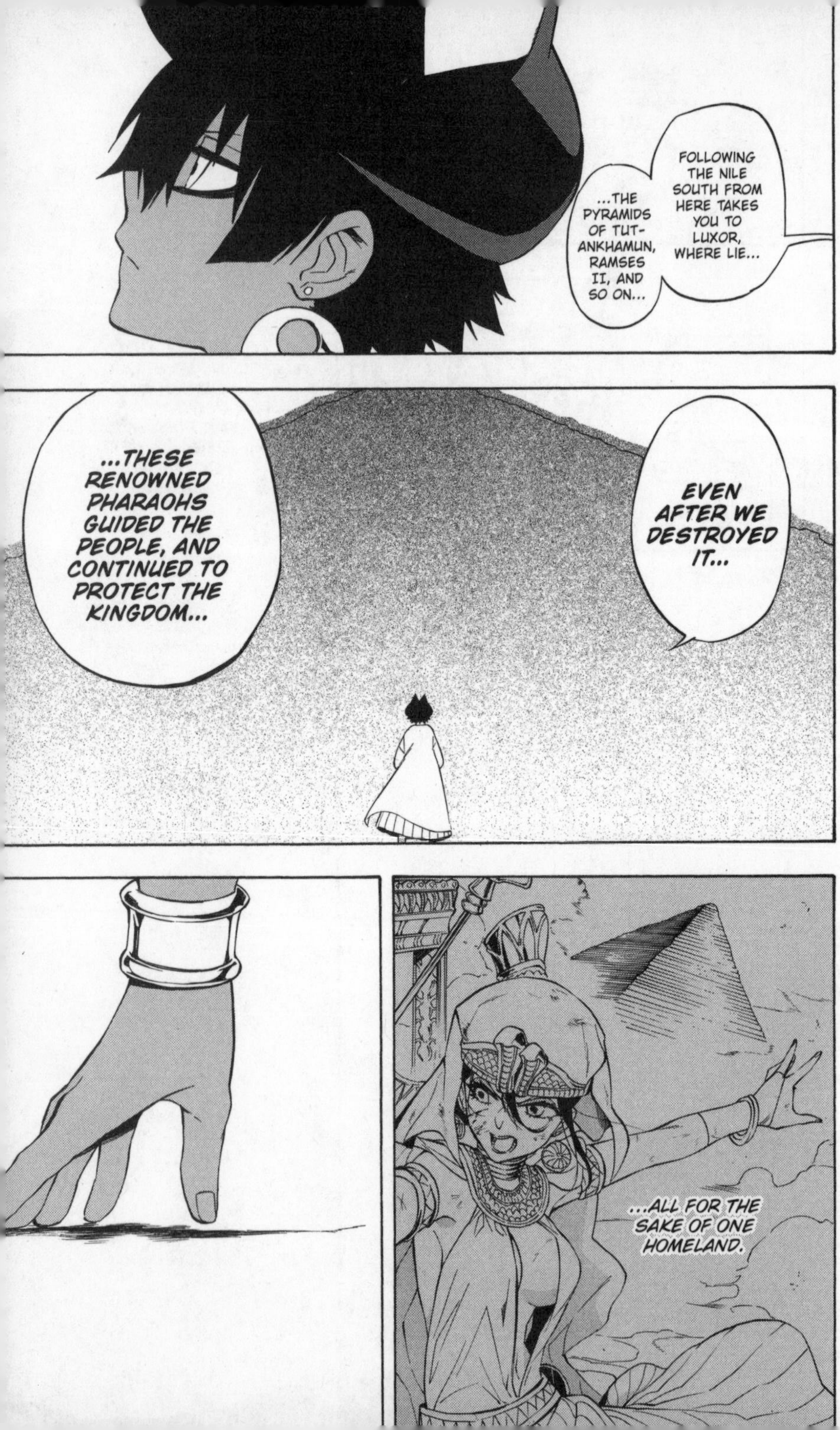
FOLLOWING THE NILE SOUTH FROM HERE TAKES YOU TO LUXOR, WHERE LIE...
...THE PYRAMIDS OF TUT-ANKHAMUN, RAMSES II, AND SO ON...
EVEN AFTER WE DESTROYED IT...
...THESE RENOWNED PHARAOHS GUIDED THE PEOPLE, AND CONTINUED TO PROTECT THE KINGDOM...
...ALL FOR THE SAKE OF ONE HOMELAND.

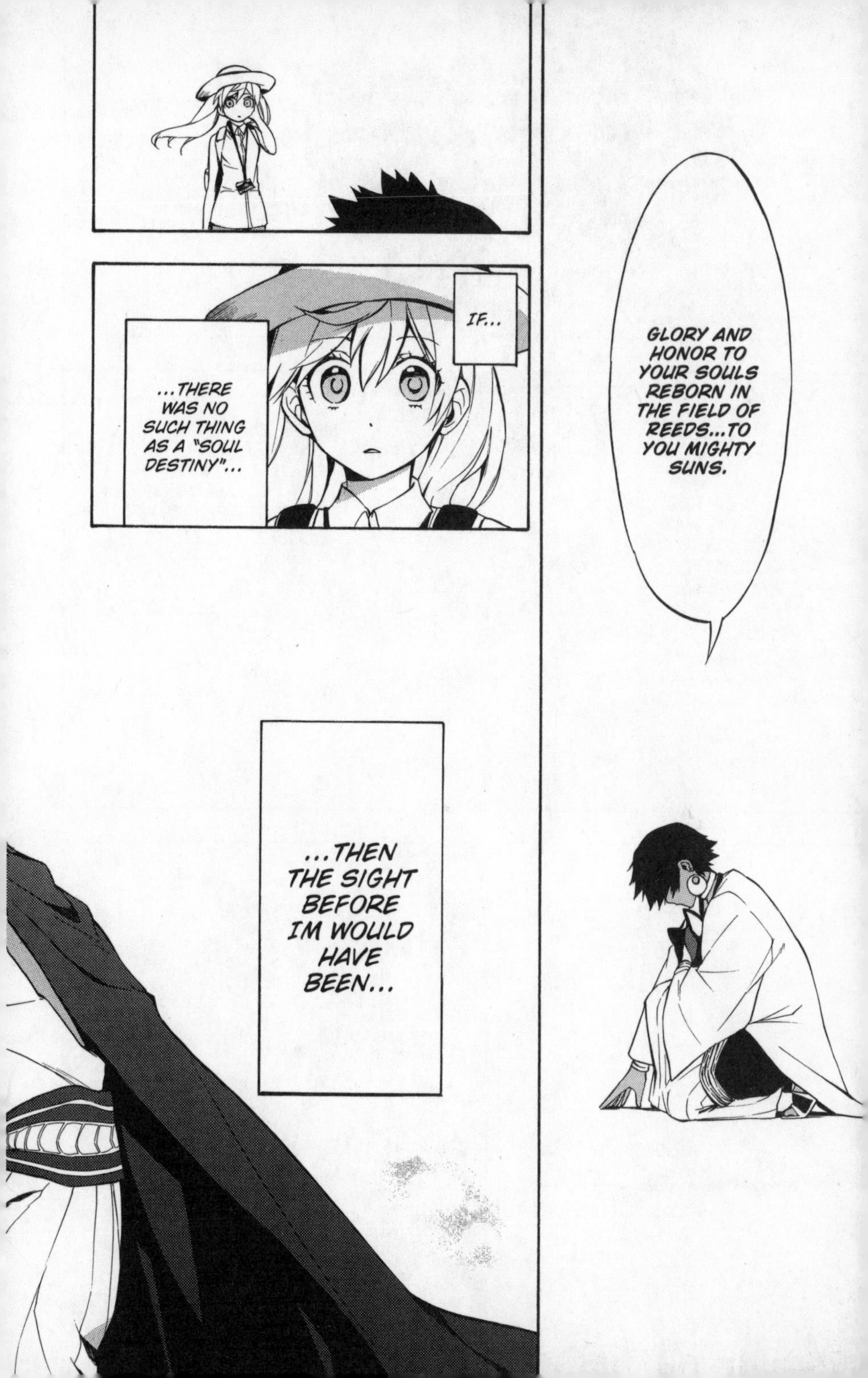
GLORY AND HONOR TO YOUR SOULS REBORN IN THE FIELD OF REEDS...TO YOU MIGHTY SUNS.
IF...
...THERE WAS NO SUCH THING AS A "SOUL DESTINY"...
...THEN THE SIGHT BEFORE IM WOULD HAVE BEEN...

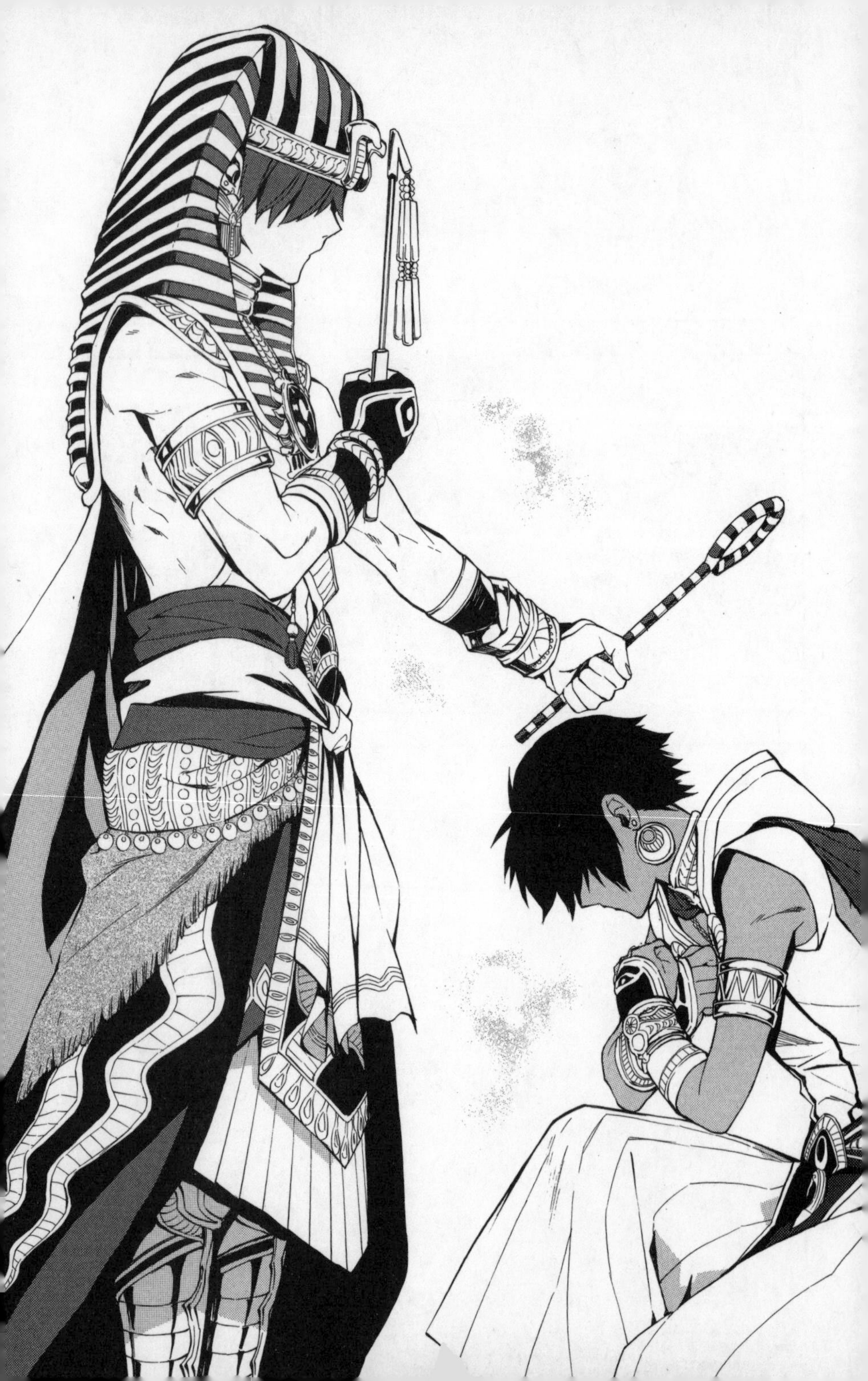

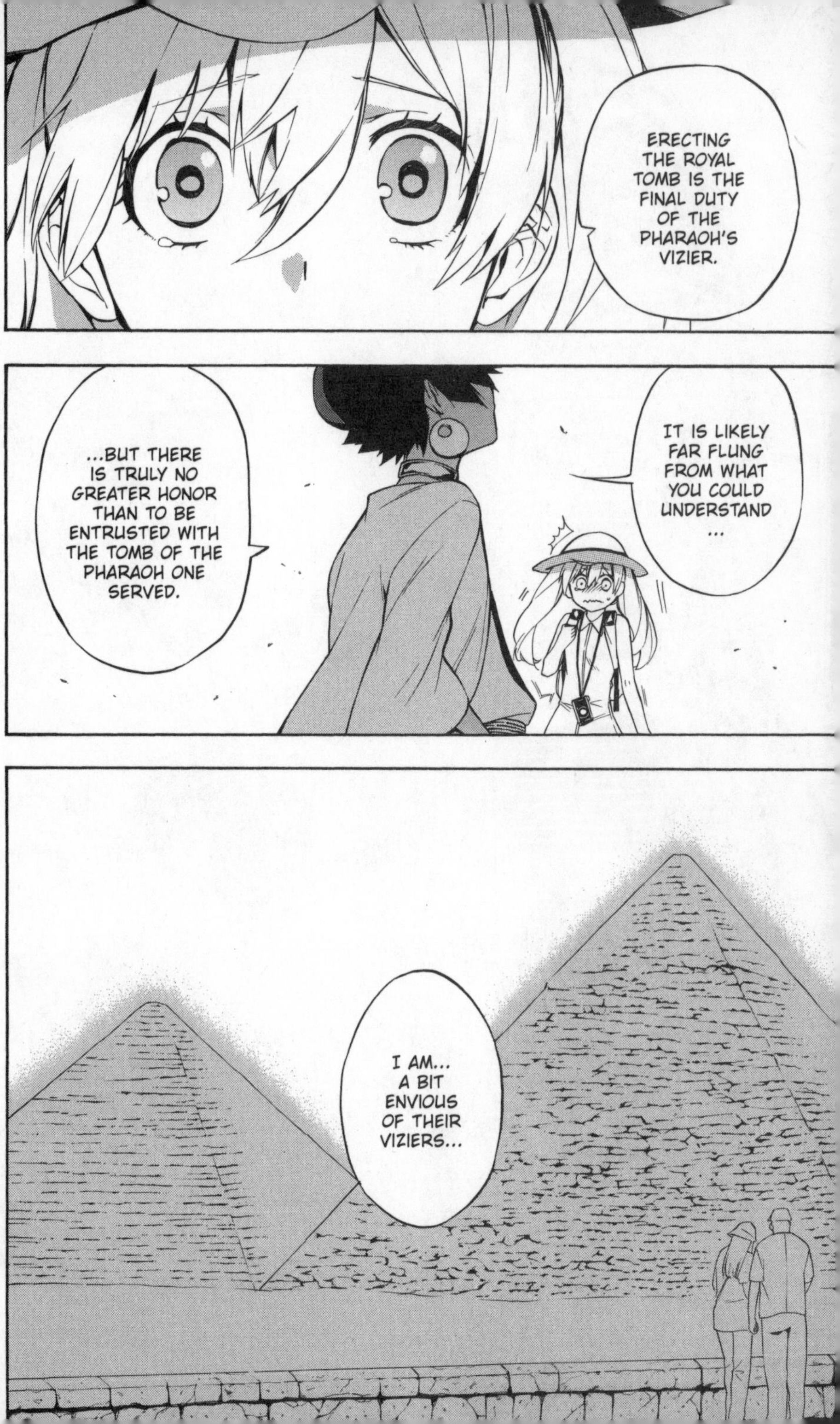
ERECTING THE ROYAL TOMB IS THE FINAL DUTY OF THE PHARAOH'S VIZIER.
IT IS LIKELY FAR FLUNG FROM WHAT YOU COULD UNDERSTAND ...
...BUT THERE IS TRULY NO GREATER HONOR THAN TO BE ENTRUSTED WITH THE TOMB OF THE PHARAOH ONE SERVED.
I AM... A BIT ENVIOUS OF THEIR VIZIERS...

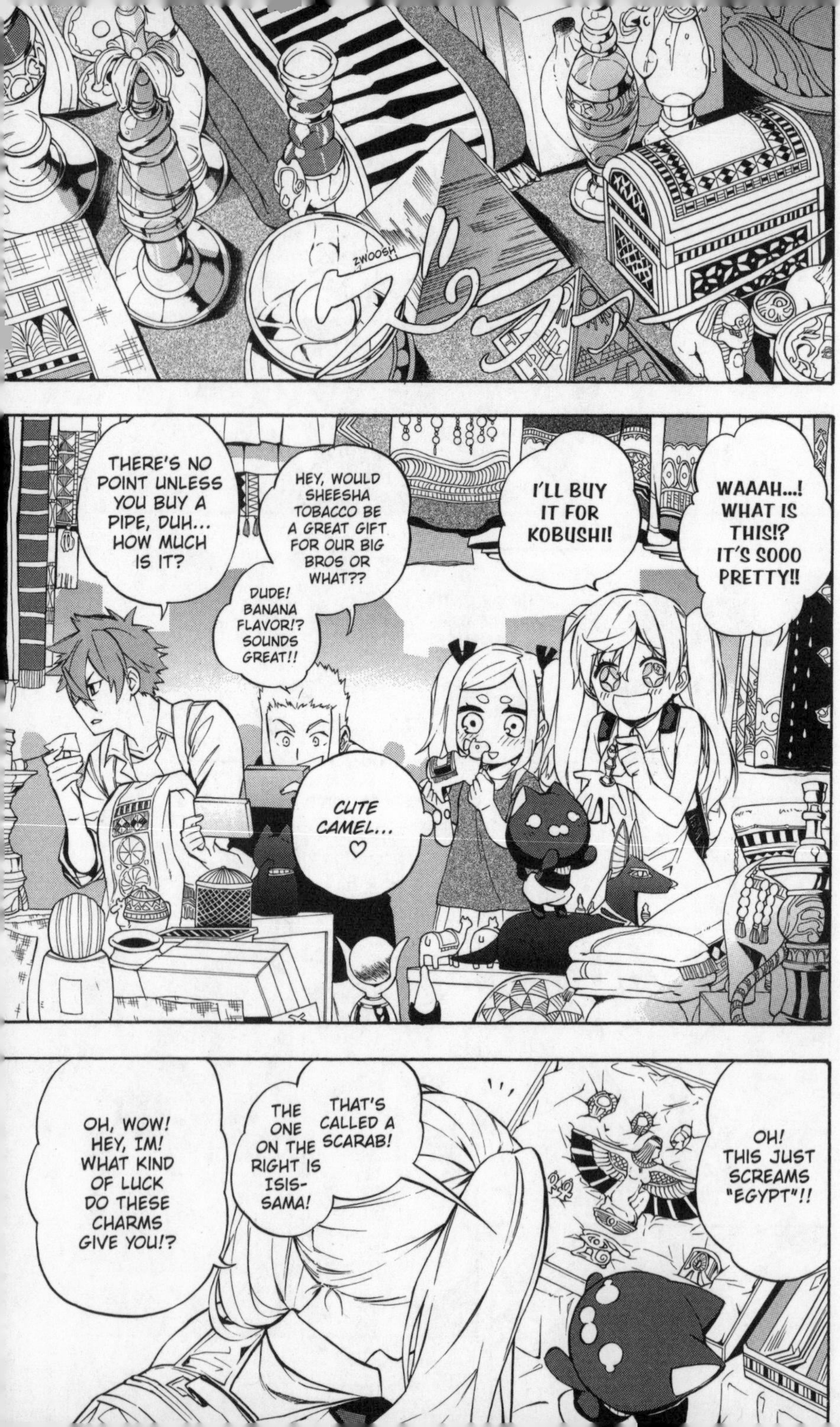
ZWOOSH
WAAAH...! WHAT IS THIS!? IT'S SOOO PRETTY!!
I'LL BUY IT FOR KOBUSHI!
CUTE CAMEL... ♡
HEY, WOULD SHEESHA TOBACCO BE A GREAT GIFT FOR OUR BIG BROS OR WHAT??
DUDE! BANANA FLAVOR!? SOUNDS GREAT!!
THERE'S NO POINT UNLESS YOU BUY A PIPE, DUH... HOW MUCH IS IT?
OH! THIS JUST SCREAMS "EGYPT"!!
THAT'S CALLED A SCARAB!
THE ONE ON THE RIGHT IS ISIS-SAMA!
OH, WOW! HEY, IM! WHAT KIND OF LUCK DO THESE CHARMS GIVE YOU!?

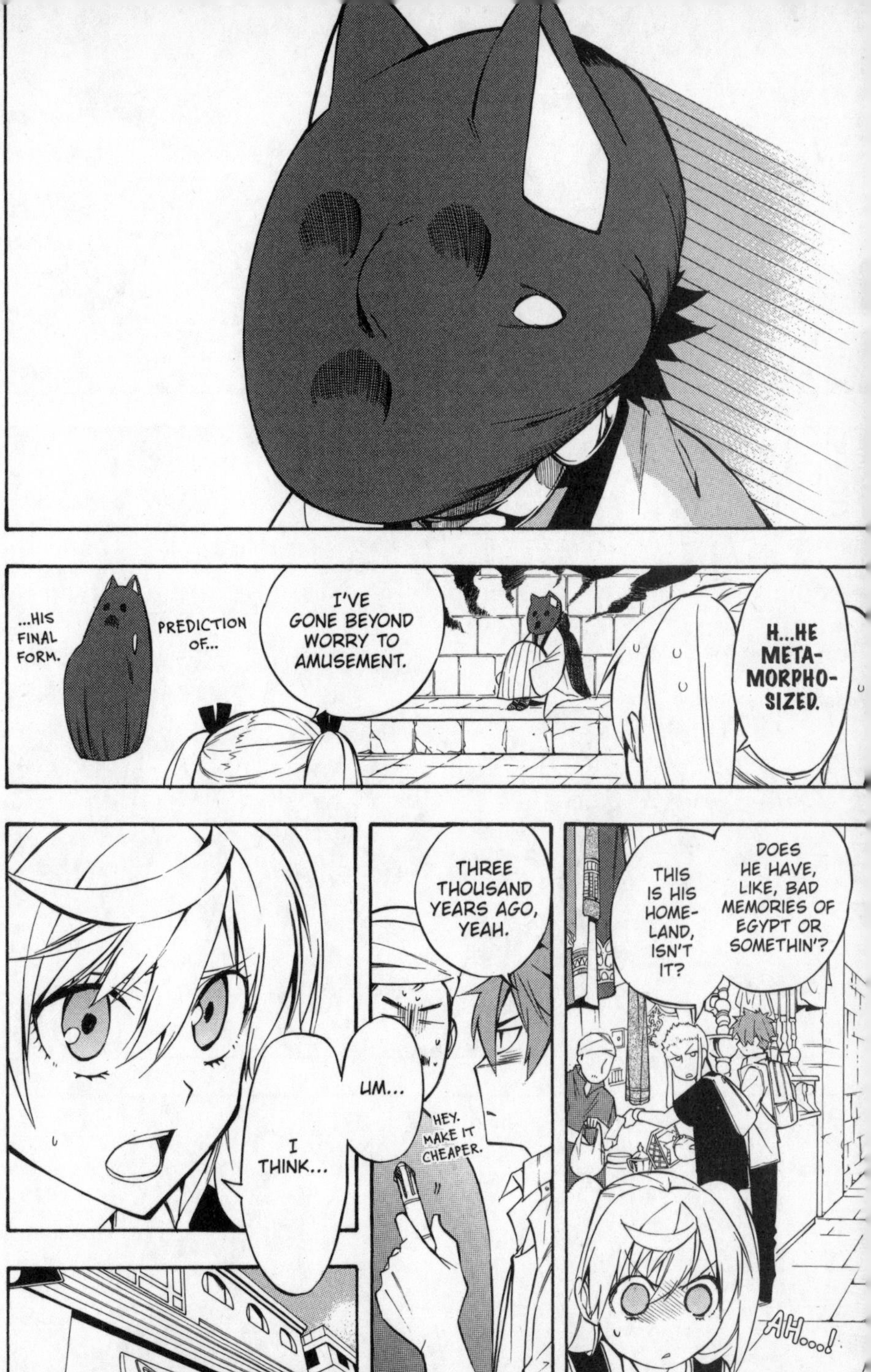
H...HE METAMORPHOSIZED.
I'VE GONE BEYOND WORRY TO AMUSEMENT.
PREDICTION OF...
...HIS FINAL FORM.
DOES HE HAVE, LIKE, BAD MEMORIES OF EGYPT OR SOMETHIN'?
THIS IS HIS HOMELAND, ISN'T IT?
AH...!
THREE THOUSAND YEARS AGO, YEAH.
HEY. MAKE IT CHEAPER.
UM...
I THINK...

SPECIAL MOVE: BALLPOINT PEN PRICE KNOCKDOWN. AT ONE TIME, JAPANESE-MADE BALLPOINT PENS WERE POPULAR IN EGYPT, AND THERE ARE CASES OF PEOPLE SUCCESSFULLY BARTERING FOR GOODS WITH THEM.

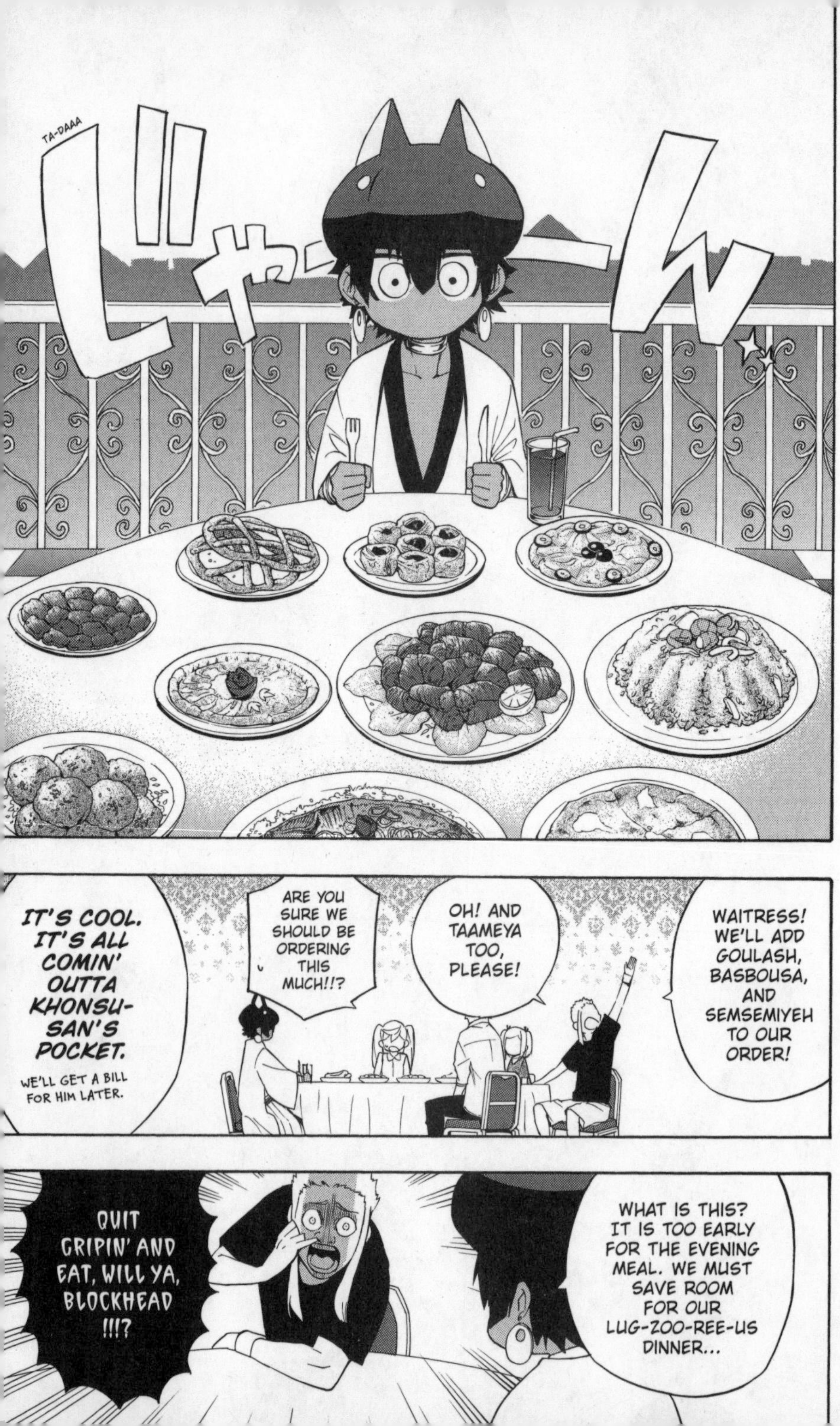
じゃーん
TA-DAAA
WAITRESS! WE'LL ADD GOULASH, BASBOUSA, AND SEMSEMIYEH TO OUR ORDER!
OH! AND TAAMEYA TOO, PLEASE!
ARE YOU SURE WE SHOULD BE ORDERING THIS MUCH!!?
IT'S COOL. IT'S ALL COMIN' OUTTA KHONSU-SAN'S POCKET.
WE'LL GET A BILL FOR HIM LATER.
WHAT IS THIS? IT IS TOO EARLY FOR THE EVENING MEAL. WE MUST SAVE ROOM FOR OUR LUG-ZOO-REE-US DINNER...
QUIT GRIPIN' AND EAT, WILL YA, BLOCKHEAD !!!?

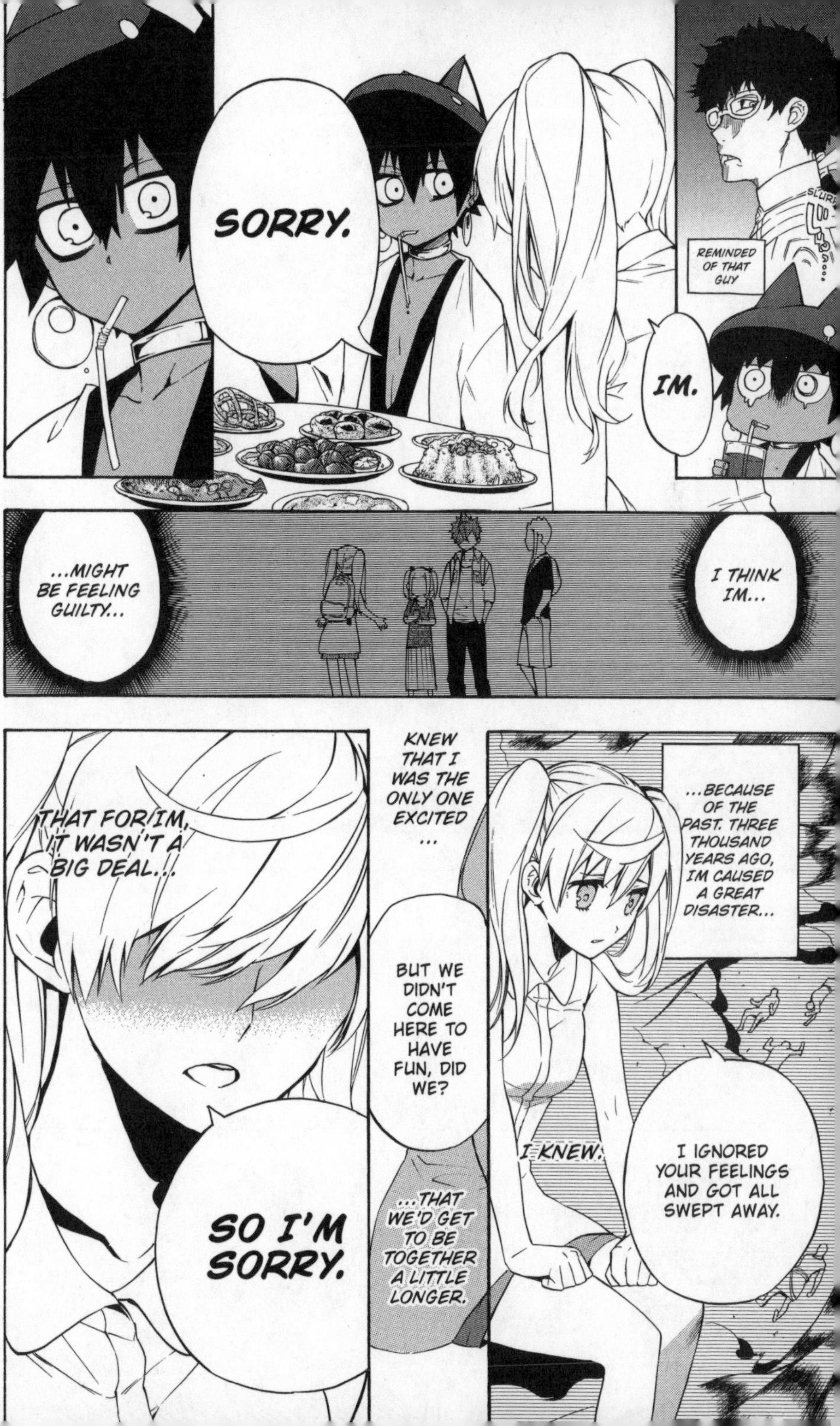
REMINDED OF THAT GUY
SLURP
IM.
SORRY.
I THINK IM...
...MIGHT BE FEELING GUILTY...
...BECAUSE OF THE PAST. THREE THOUSAND YEARS AGO, IM CAUSED A GREAT DISASTER...
I IGNORED YOUR FEELINGS AND GOT ALL SWEPT AWAY.
I KNEW.
...THAT WE'D GET TO BE TOGETHER A LITTLE LONGER.
KNEW THAT I WAS THE ONLY ONE EXCITED ...
BUT WE DIDN'T COME HERE TO HAVE FUN, DID WE?
THAT FOR IM, IT WASN'T A BIG DEAL...
SO I'M SORRY.

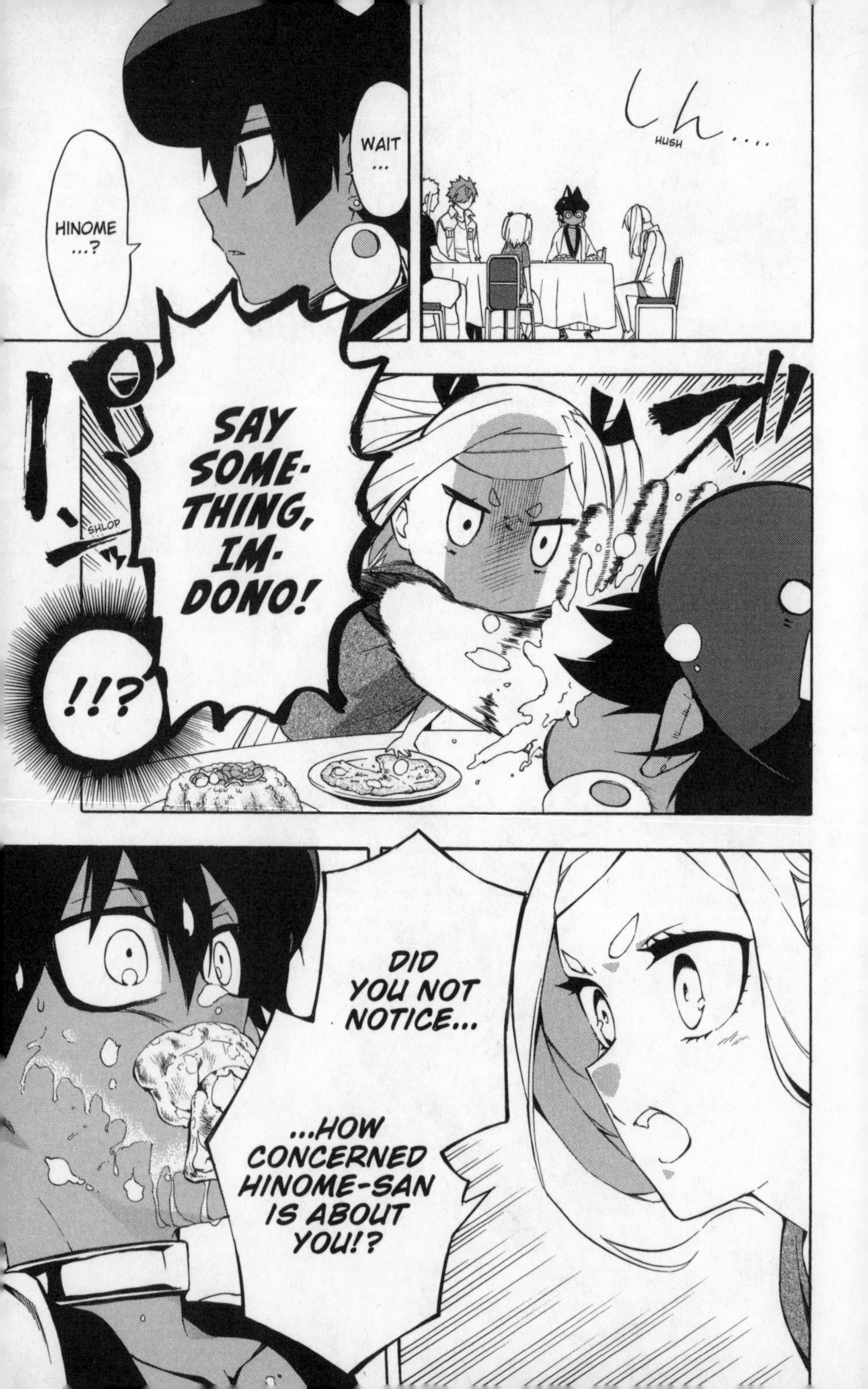

しん....
HUSH
WAIT ...
HINOME ...?
SAY SOME-THING, IM-DONO!
SHLOP
!!?
DID YOU NOT NOTICE...
...HOW CONCERNED HINOME-SAN IS ABOUT YOU!?

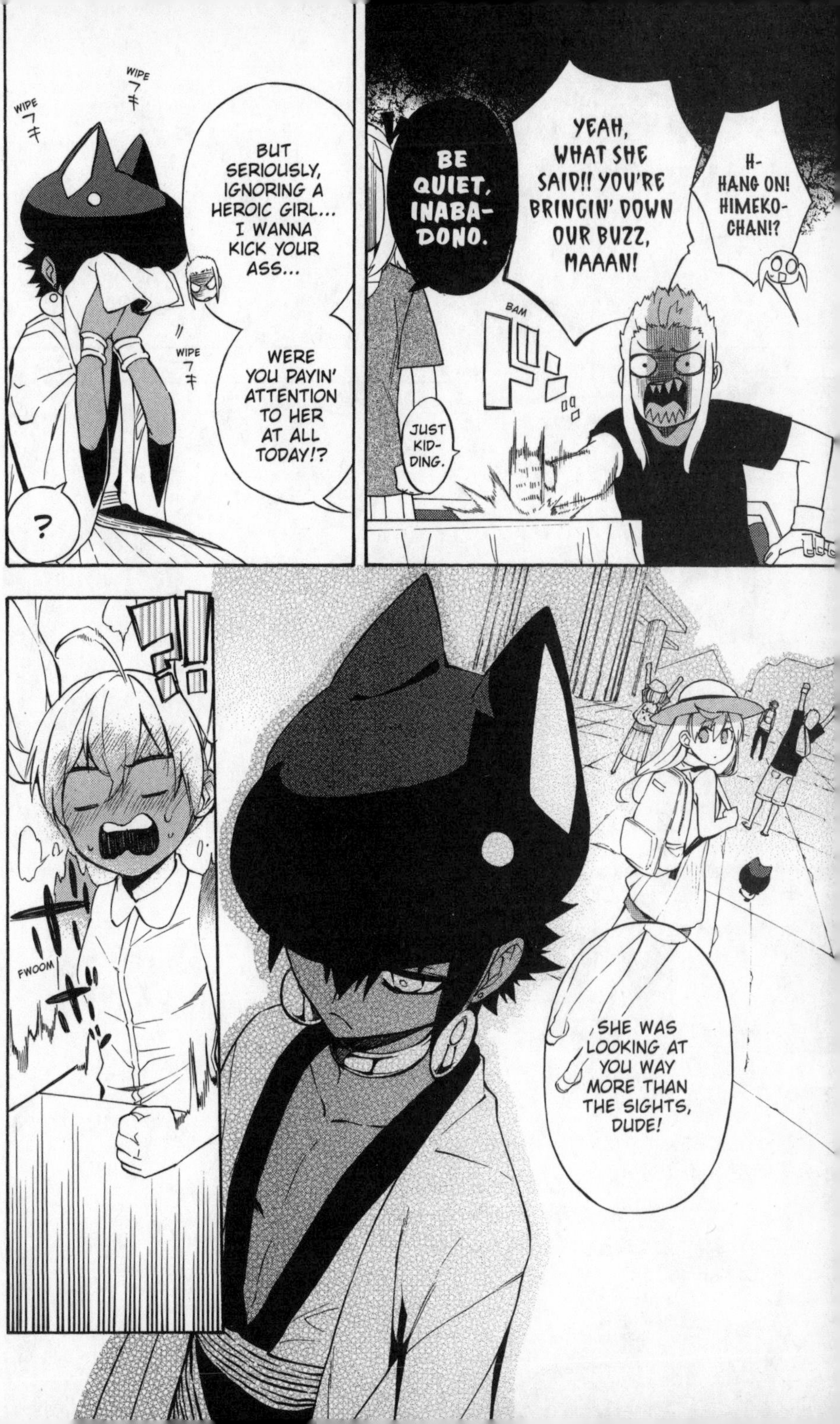
H-HANG ON! HIMEKO-CHAN!?
YEAH, WHAT SHE SAID!! YOU'RE BRINGIN' DOWN OUR BUZZ, MAAAN!
BE QUIET, INABA-DONO.
BAM
JUST KID-DING.
WIPE
WIPE
BUT SERIOUSLY, IGNORING A HEROIC GIRL... I WANNA KICK YOUR ASS...
WIPE
WERE YOU PAYIN' ATTENTION TO HER AT ALL TODAY!?
?
SHE WAS LOOKING AT YOU WAY MORE THAN THE SIGHTS, DUDE!
FWOOM

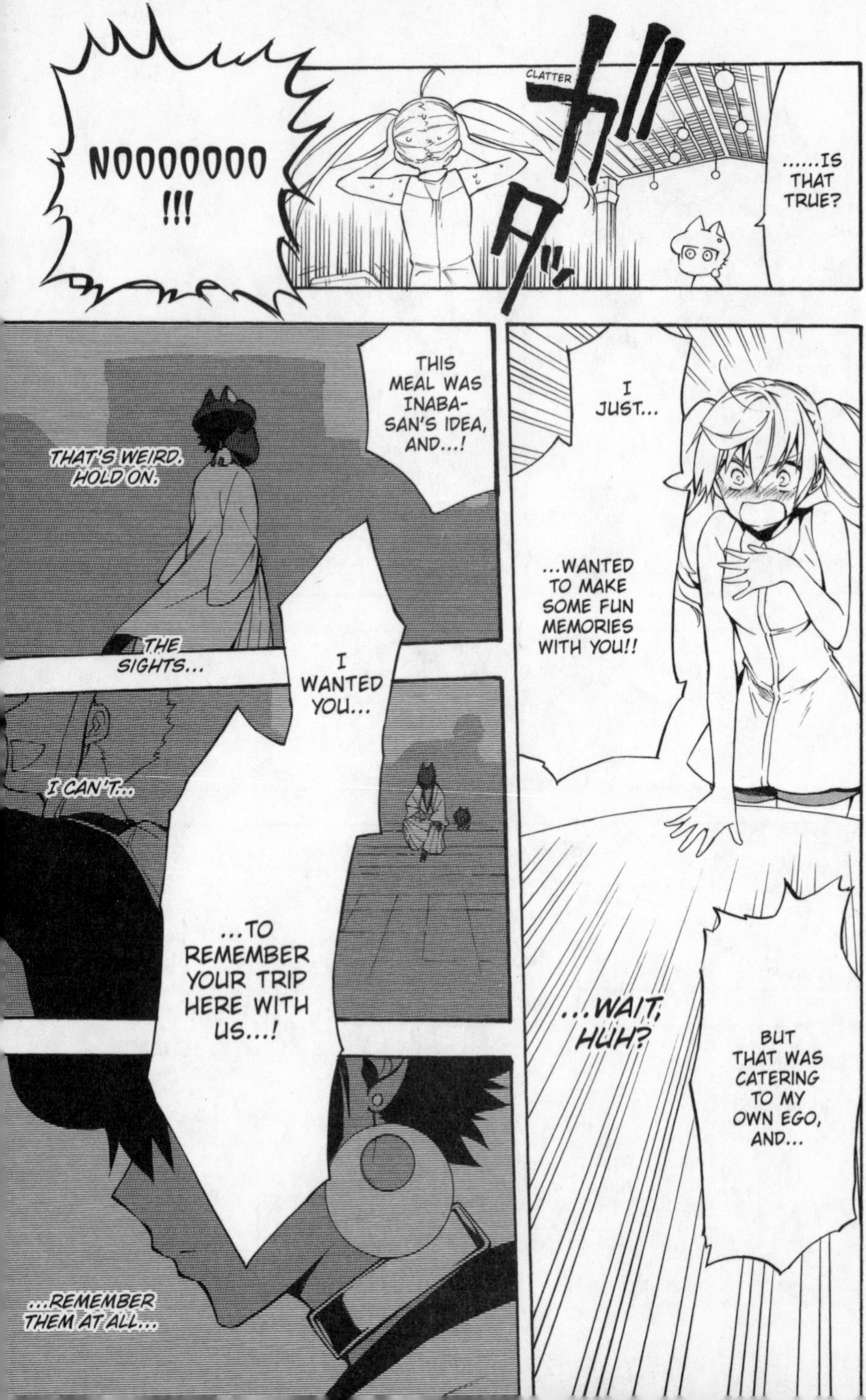
......IS THAT TRUE?
CLATTER
NOOOOOOO!!!
I JUST...
...WANTED TO MAKE SOME FUN MEMORIES WITH YOU!!
BUT THAT WAS CATERING TO MY OWN EGO, AND...
...WAIT, HUH?
THIS MEAL WAS INABA-SAN'S IDEA, AND...!
THAT'S WEIRD. HOLD ON.
THE SIGHTS...
I WANTED YOU...
I CAN'T...
...TO REMEMBER YOUR TRIP HERE WITH US...!
...REMEMBER THEM AT ALL...

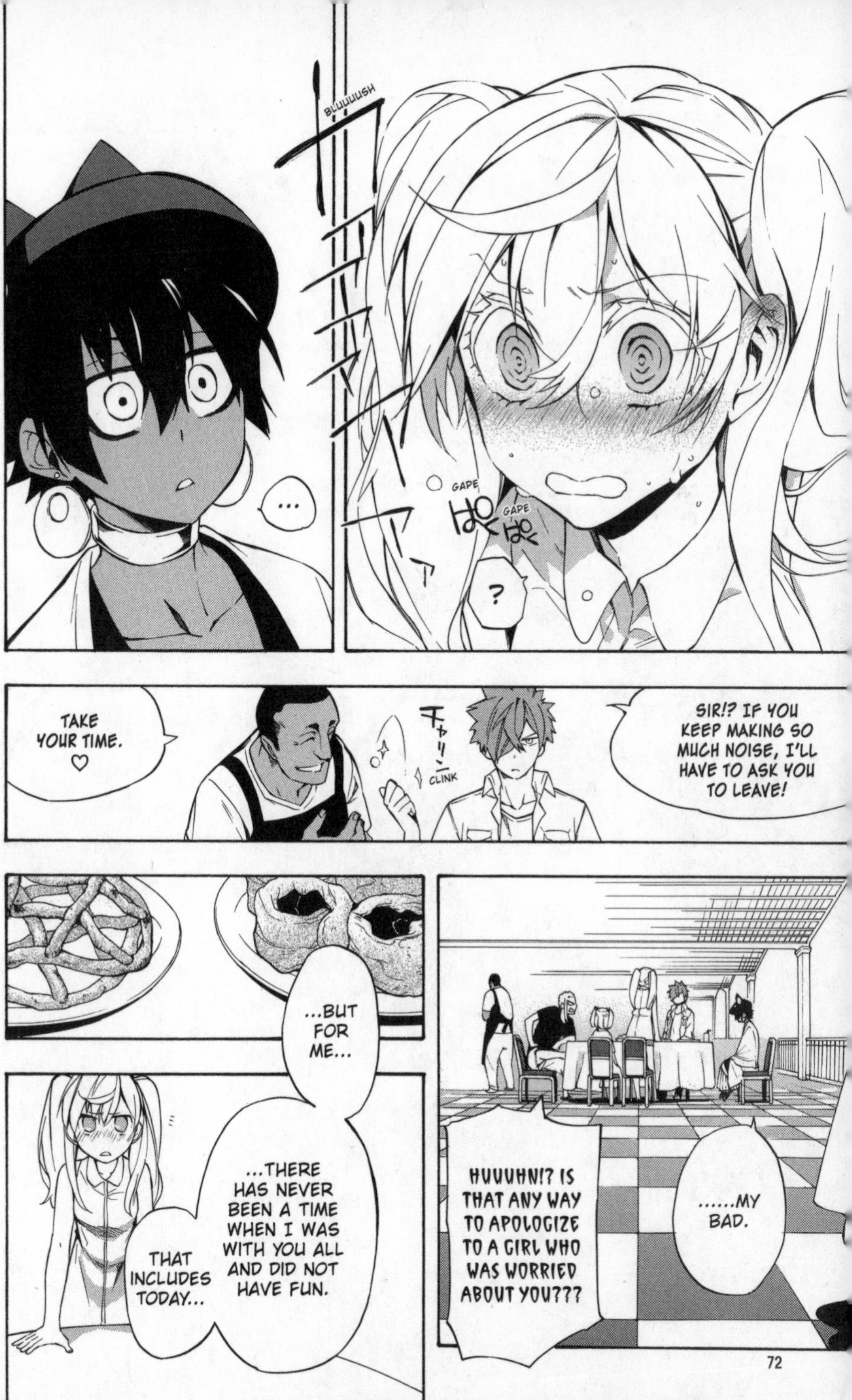
BLUUUUSH
GAPE
GAPE
?
...
SIR!? IF YOU KEEP MAKING SO MUCH NOISE, I'LL HAVE TO ASK YOU TO LEAVE!
CLINK
TAKE YOUR TIME. ♡
......MY BAD.
HUUUHN!? IS THAT ANY WAY TO APOLOGIZE TO A GIRL WHO WAS WORRIED ABOUT YOU???
...BUT FOR ME...
...THERE HAS NEVER BEEN A TIME WHEN I WAS WITH YOU ALL AND DID NOT HAVE FUN.
THAT INCLUDES TODAY...

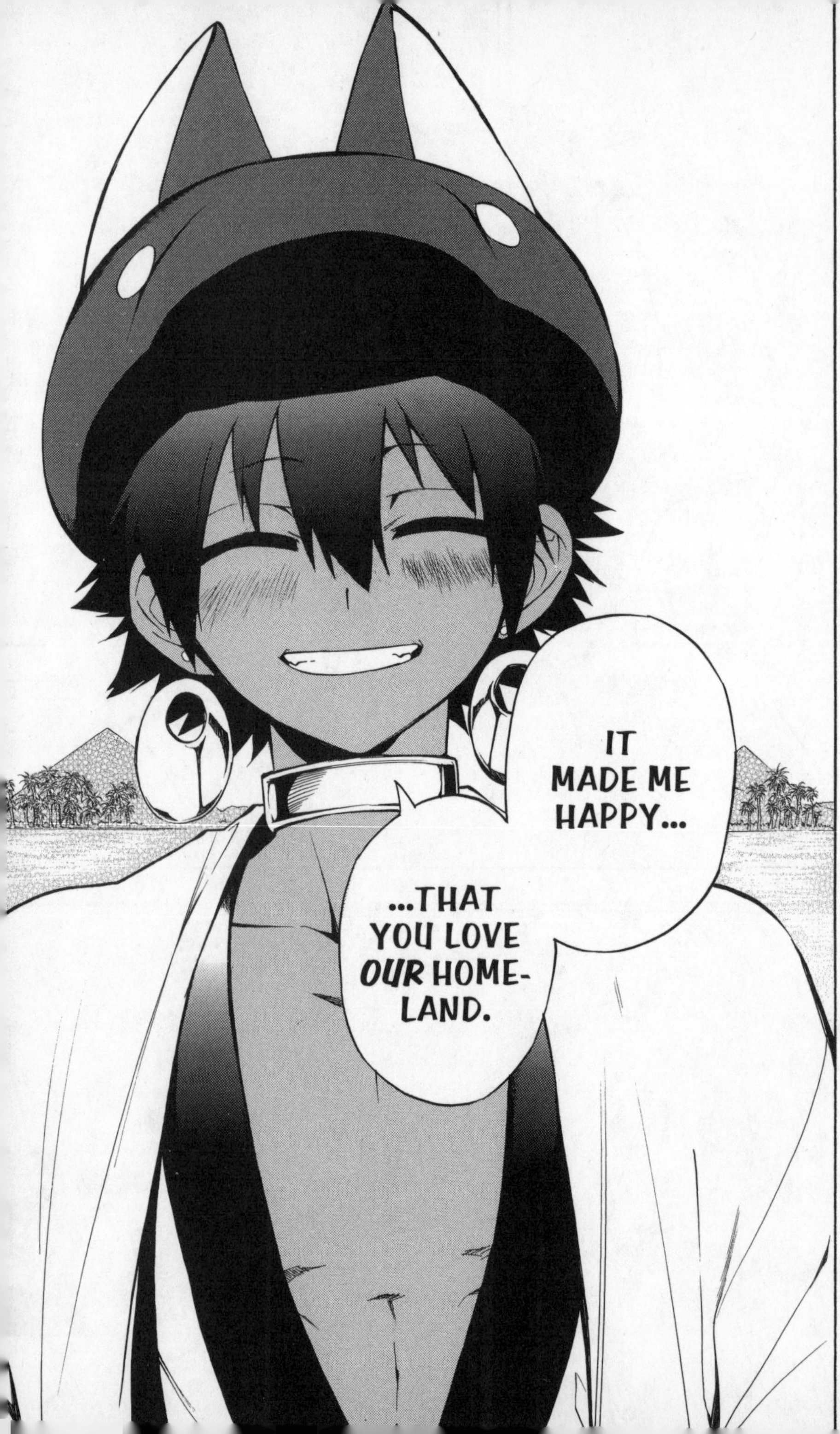
IT MADE ME HAPPY...
...THAT YOU LOVE *OUR* HOME-LAND.

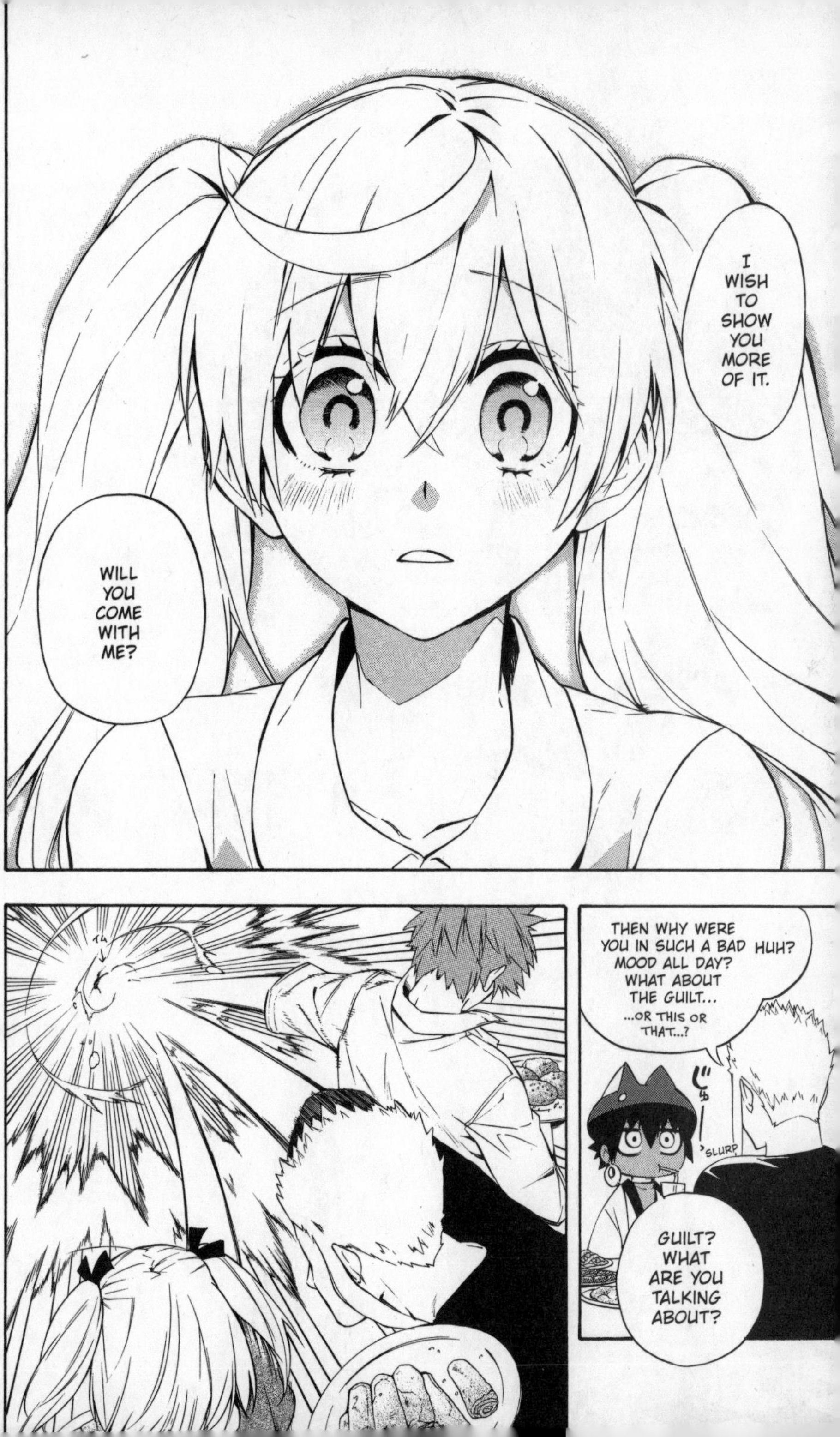
I WISH TO SHOW YOU MORE OF IT.
WILL YOU COME WITH ME?
HUH?
THEN WHY WERE YOU IN SUCH A BAD MOOD ALL DAY? WHAT ABOUT THE GUILT...
...OR THIS OR THAT...?
SLURP
GUILT? WHAT ARE YOU TALKING ABOUT?

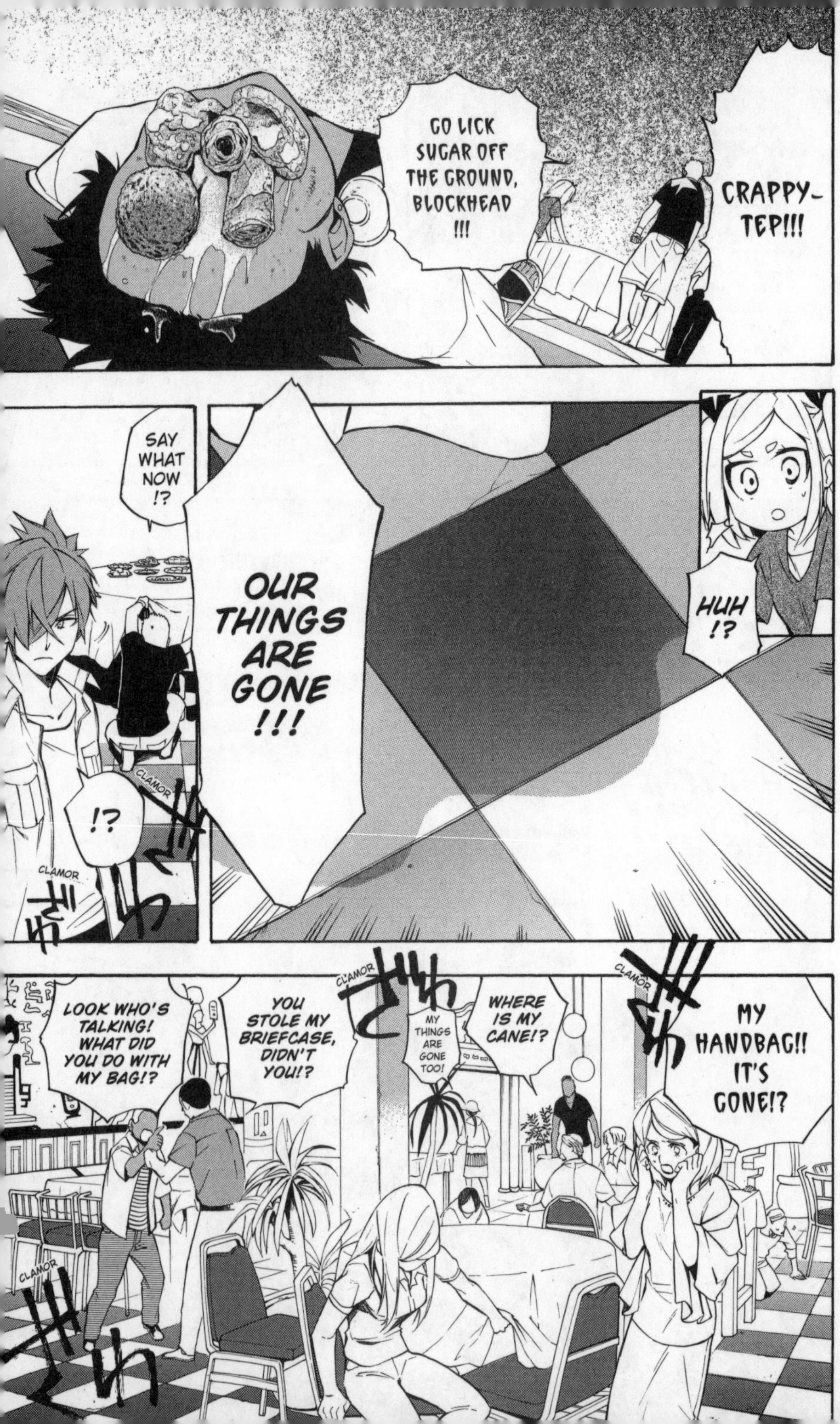
CRAPPY-TEP!!!
GO LICK SUGAR OFF THE GROUND, BLOCKHEAD!!!
HUH!?
OUR THINGS ARE GONE!!!
SAY WHAT NOW!?
CLAMOR
!?
CLAMOR
MY HANDBAG!! IT'S GONE!?
CLAMOR
WHERE IS MY CANE!?
MY THINGS ARE GONE TOO!
CLAMOR
YOU STOLE MY BRIEFCASE, DIDN'T YOU!?
LOOK WHO'S TALKING! WHAT DID YOU DO WITH MY BAG!?
CLAMOR

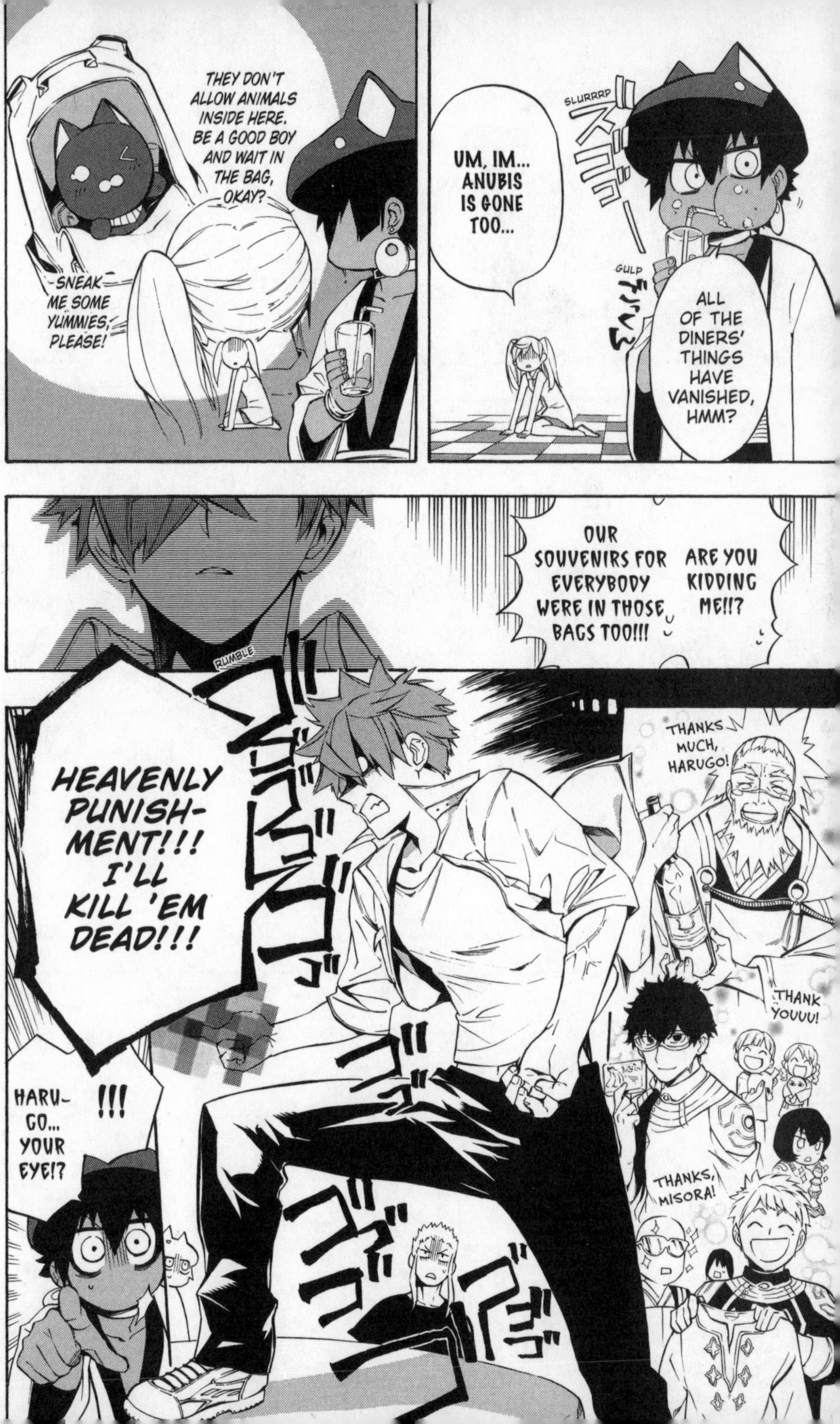
SLURRRP
UM, IM... ANUBIS IS GONE TOO...
GULP
ALL OF THE DINERS' THINGS HAVE VANISHED, HMM?
THEY DON'T ALLOW ANIMALS INSIDE HERE. BE A GOOD BOY AND WAIT IN THE BAG, OKAY?
SNEAK ME SOME YUMMIES, PLEASE!
ARE YOU KIDDING ME!!?
OUR SOUVENIRS FOR EVERYBODY WERE IN THOSE BAGS TOO!!!
RUMBLE
THANKS MUCH, HARUGO!
HEAVENLY PUNISHMENT!!! I'LL KILL 'EM DEAD!!!
THANK YOUUU!
THANKS, MISORA!
!!!
HARU-GO... YOUR EYE!?

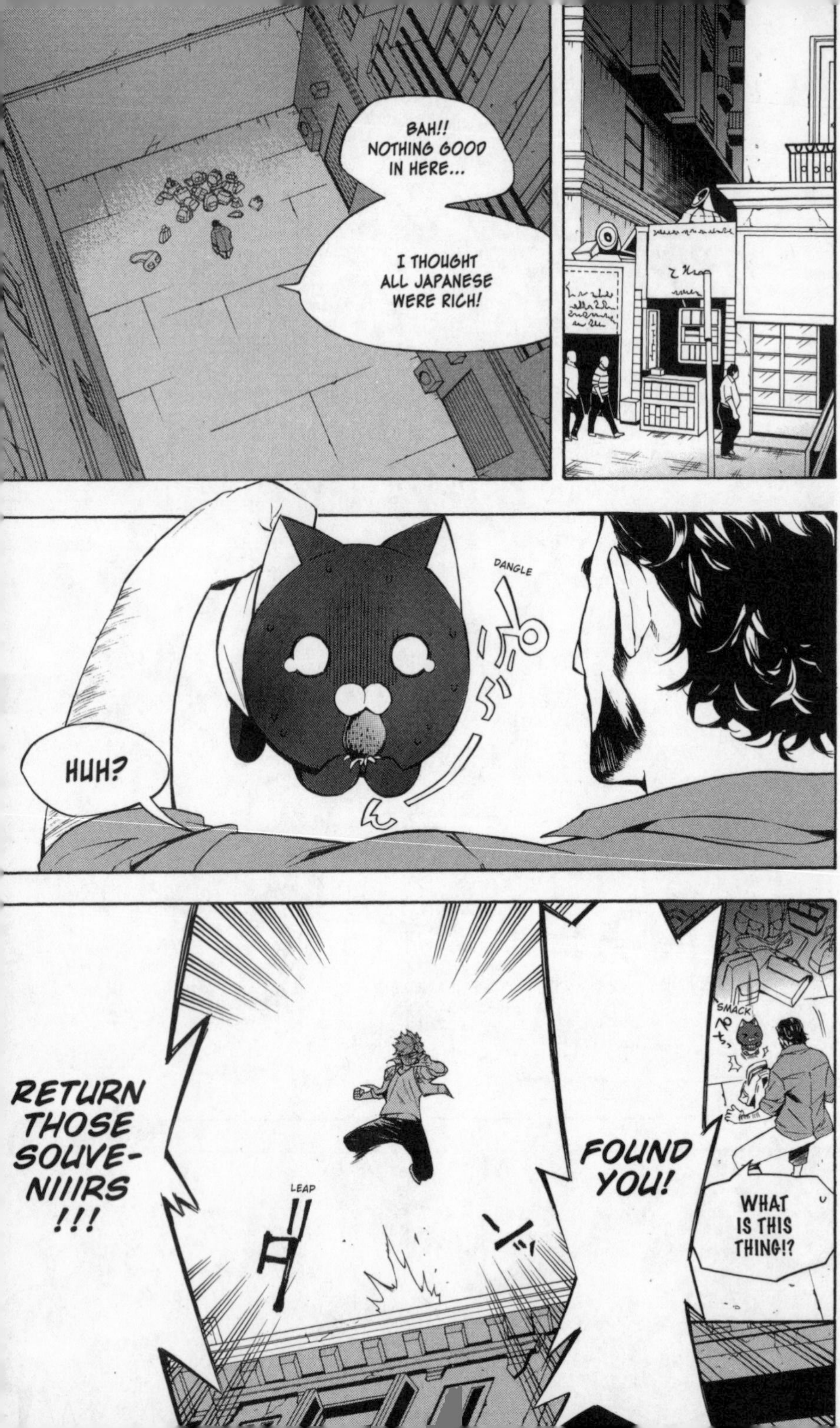
BAH!! NOTHING GOOD IN HERE...
I THOUGHT ALL JAPANESE WERE RICH!
DANGLE
HUH?
SMACK
WHAT IS THIS THING!?
FOUND YOU!
LEAP
RETURN THOSE SOUVE-NIIIRS!!!

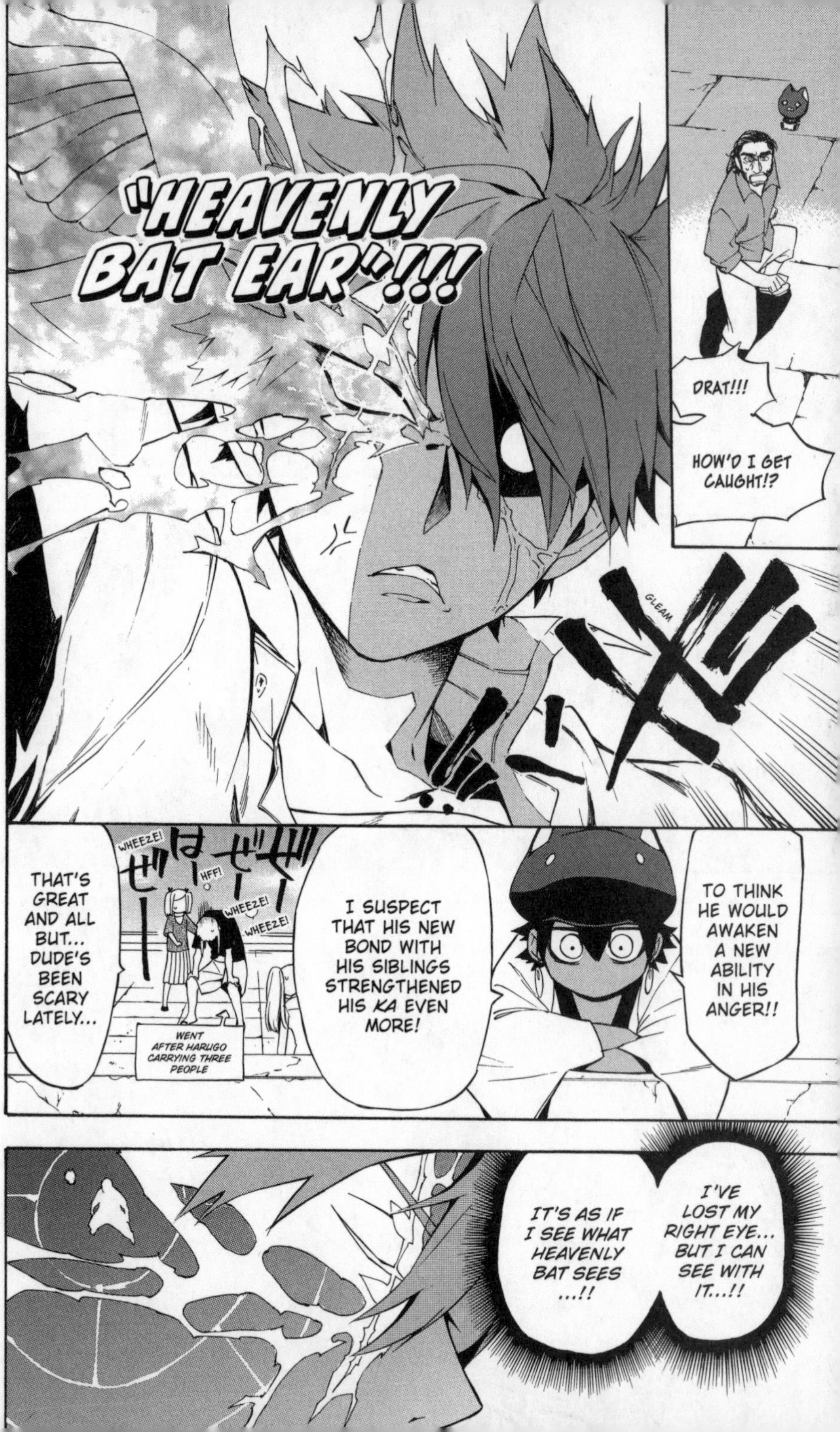
DRAT!!!
HOW'D I GET CAUGHT!?
"HEAVENLY BAT EAR"!!!
GLEAM
TO THINK HE WOULD AWAKEN A NEW ABILITY IN HIS ANGER!!
I SUSPECT THAT HIS NEW BOND WITH HIS SIBLINGS STRENGTHENED HIS *KA* EVEN MORE!
WHEEZE!
HFF!
WHEEZE!
WHEEZE!
WENT AFTER HARUGO CARRYING THREE PEOPLE
THAT'S GREAT AND ALL BUT... DUDE'S BEEN SCARY LATELY...
I'VE LOST MY RIGHT EYE... BUT I CAN SEE WITH IT...!!
IT'S AS IF I SEE WHAT HEAVENLY BAT SEES ...!!

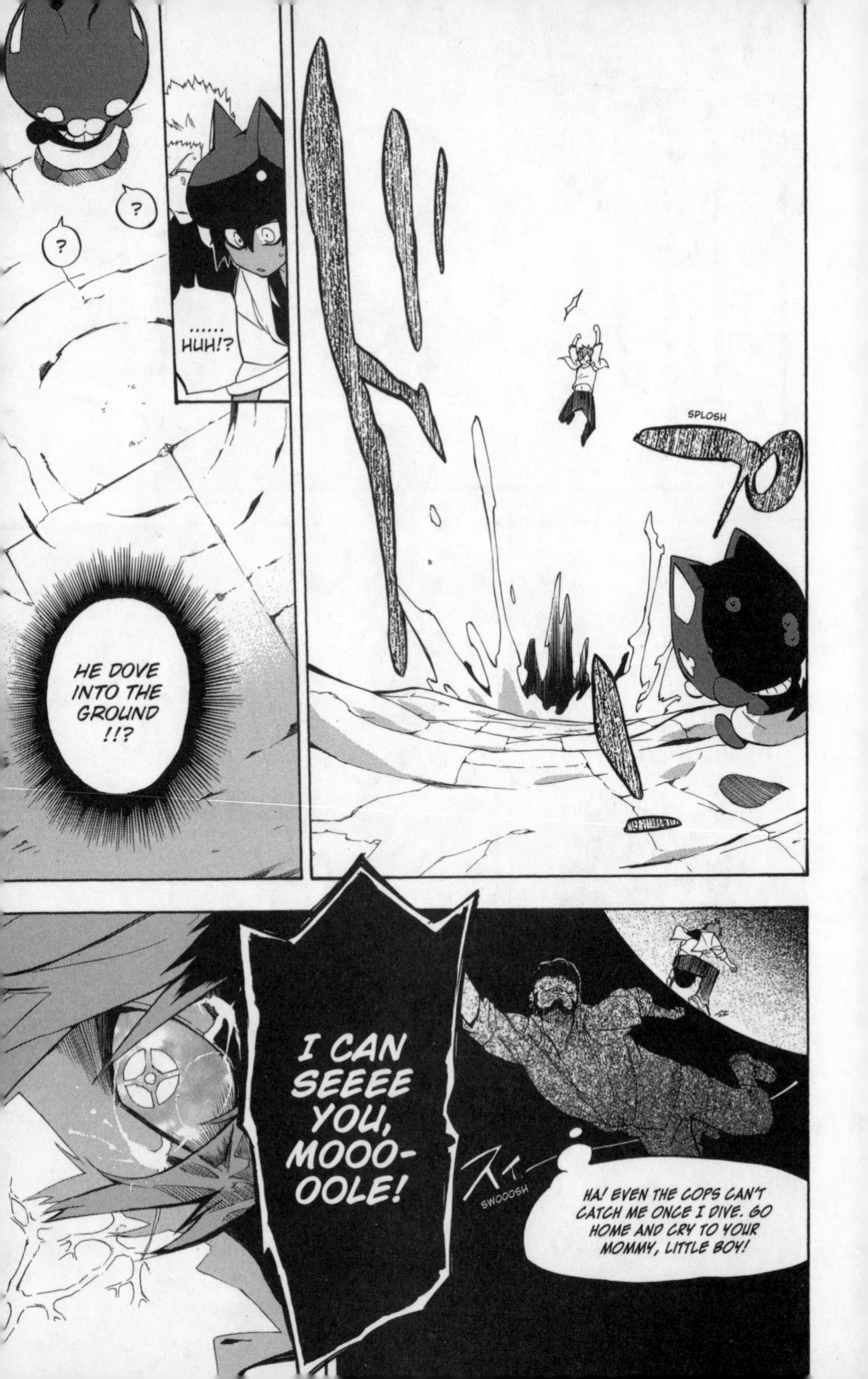
SPLOSH
......
HUH!?
?
?
HE DOVE INTO THE GROUND !!?
HA! EVEN THE COPS CAN'T CATCH ME ONCE I DIVE. GO HOME AND CRY TO YOUR MOMMY, LITTLE BOY!
スィー
SWOOOSH
I CAN SEEEE YOU, MOOO-OOLE!

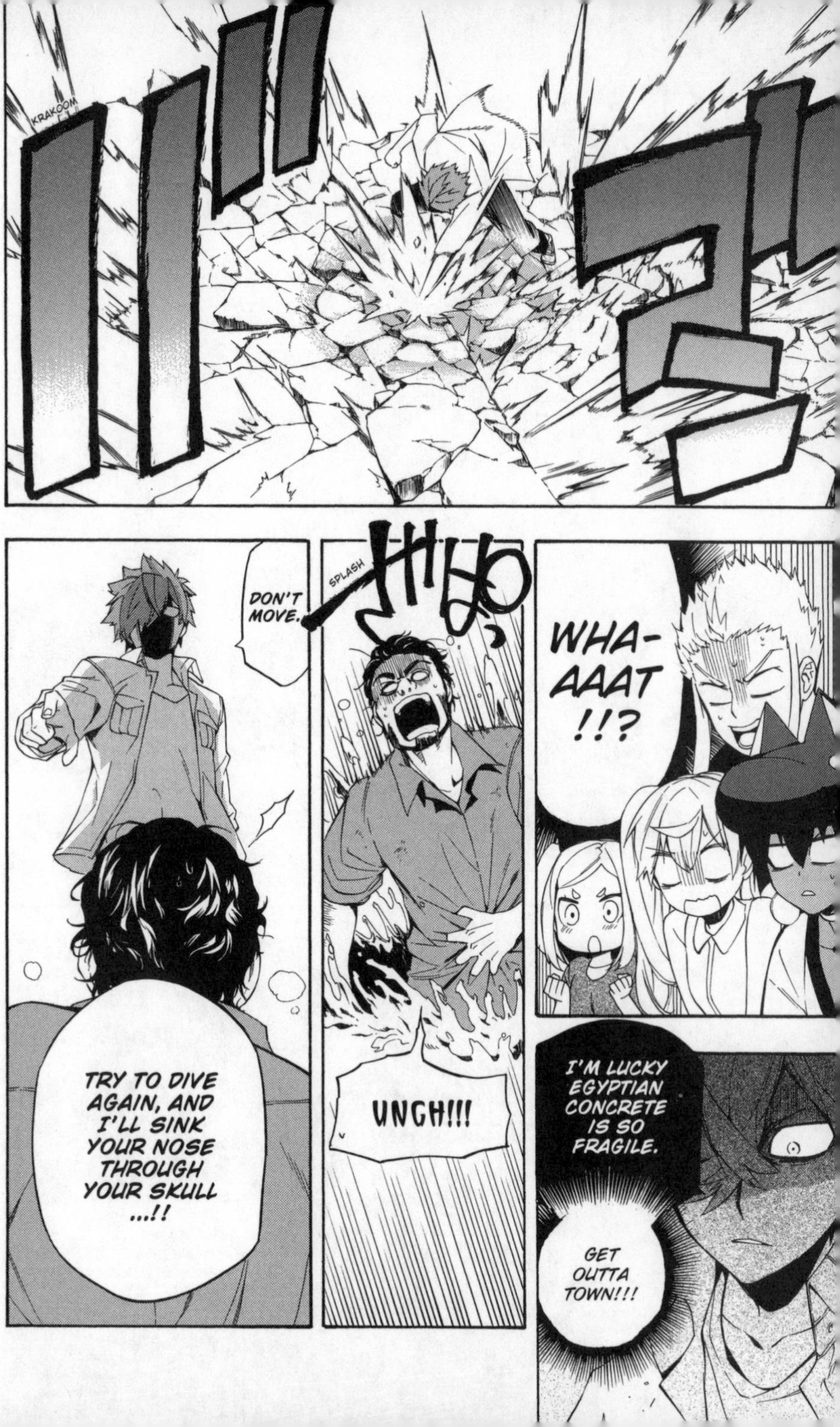
KRAKOOM
WHA-AAAT!!?
I'M LUCKY EGYPTIAN CONCRETE IS SO FRAGILE.
GET OUTTA TOWN!!!
SPLASH
UNGH!!!
DON'T MOVE...
TRY TO DIVE AGAIN, AND I'LL SINK YOUR NOSE THROUGH YOUR SKULL ...!!

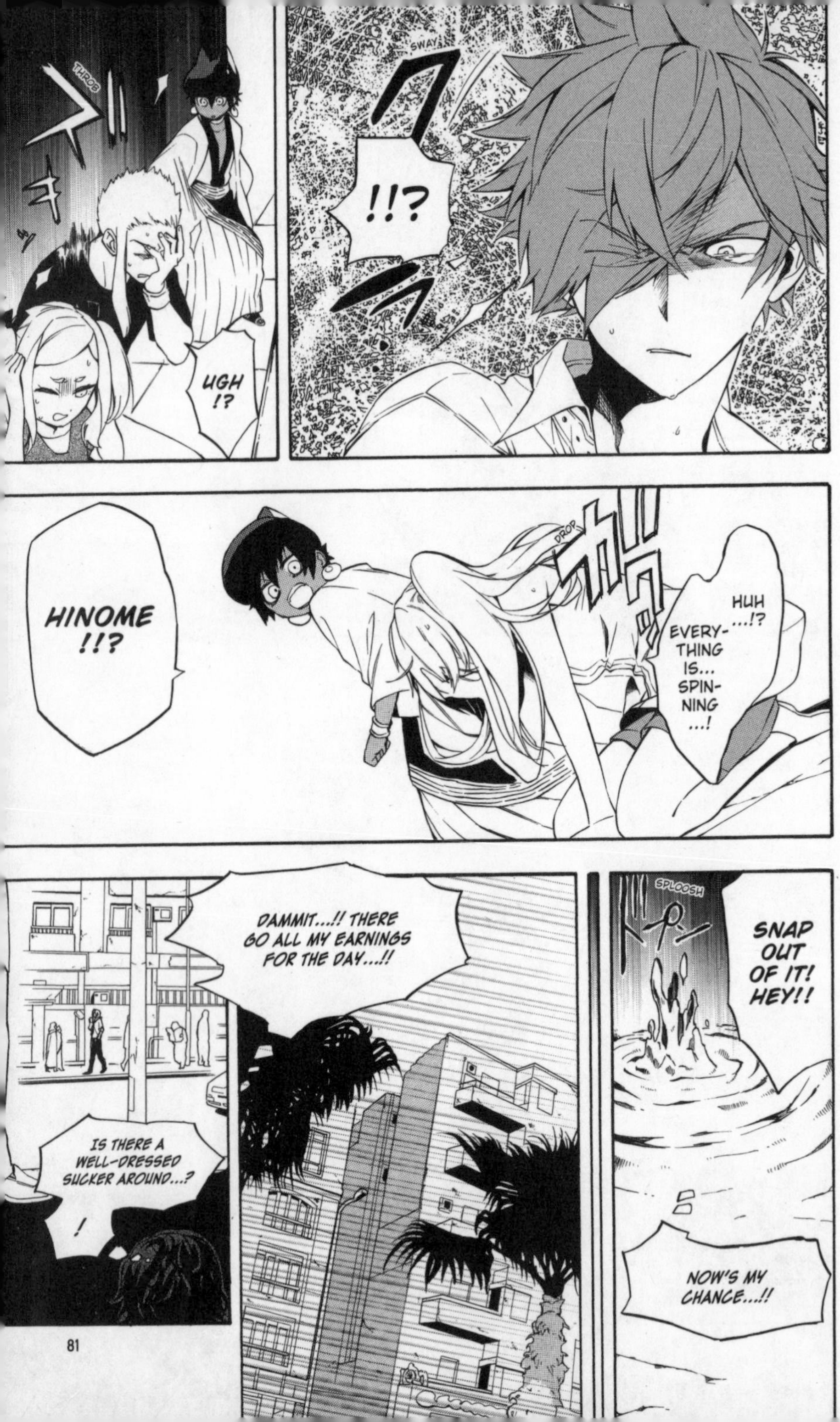
SWAY
!!?
THROB
UGH!?
HUH...!? EVERYTHING IS... SPINNING...!
DROP
HINOME!!?
SPLOOSH
SNAP OUT OF IT! HEY!!
NOW'S MY CHANCE...!!
DAMMIT...!! THERE GO ALL MY EARNINGS FOR THE DAY...!!
IS THERE A WELL-DRESSED SUCKER AROUND...?
!

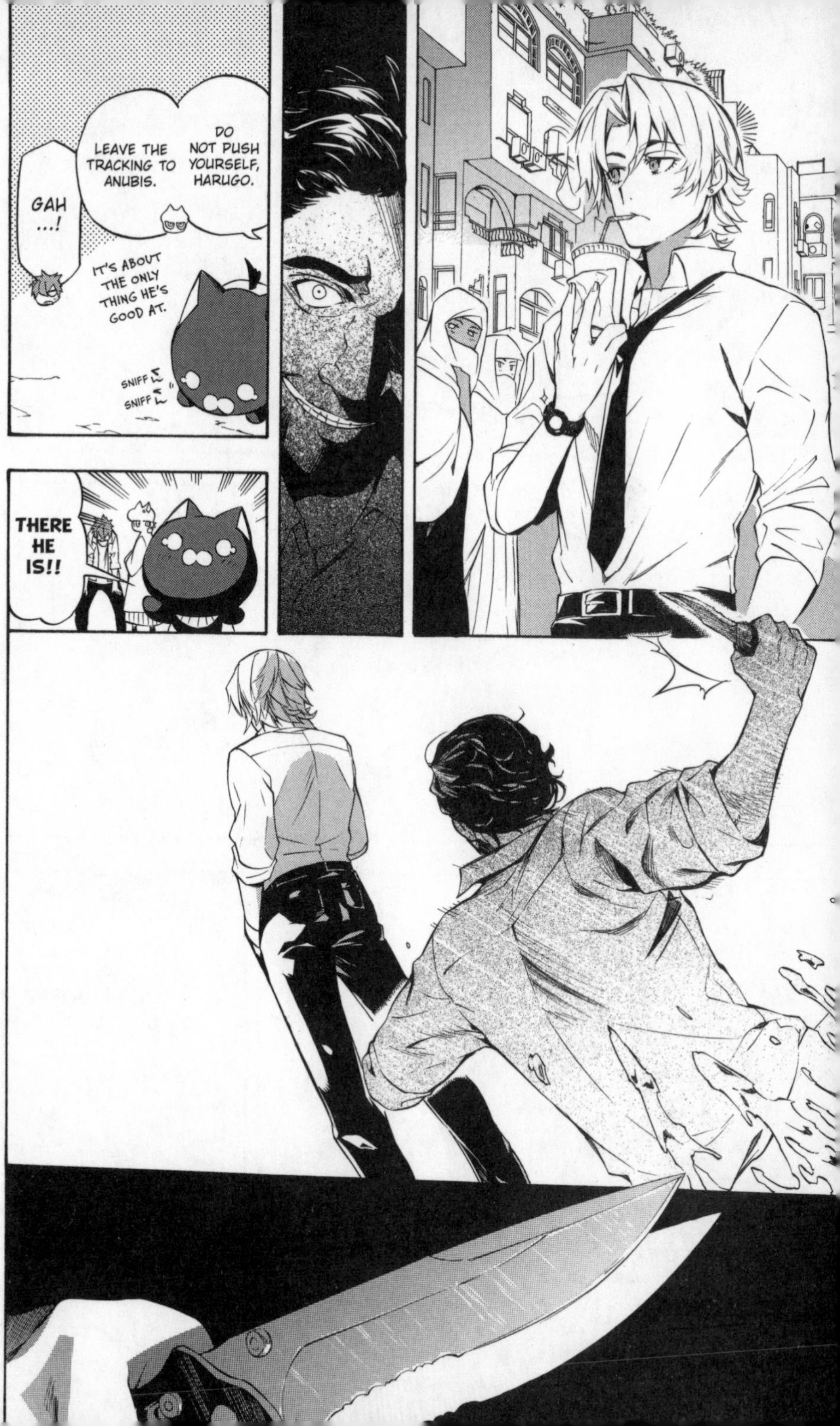
DO NOT PUSH YOURSELF, HARUGO.
LEAVE THE TRACKING TO ANUBIS.
GAH ...!
IT'S ABOUT THE ONLY THING HE'S GOOD AT.
SNIFF
SNIFF
THERE HE IS!!

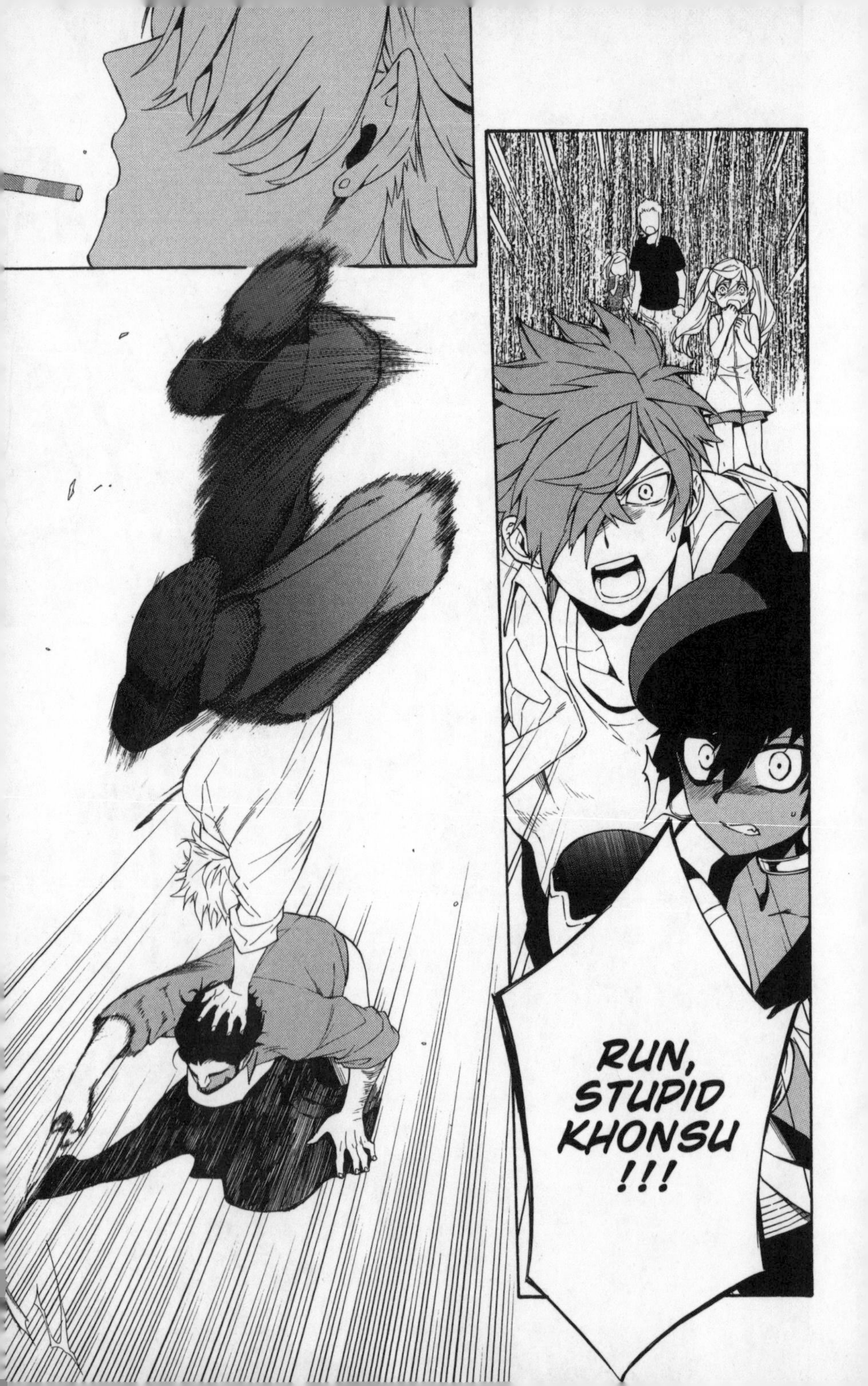
RUN, STUPID KHONSU !!!

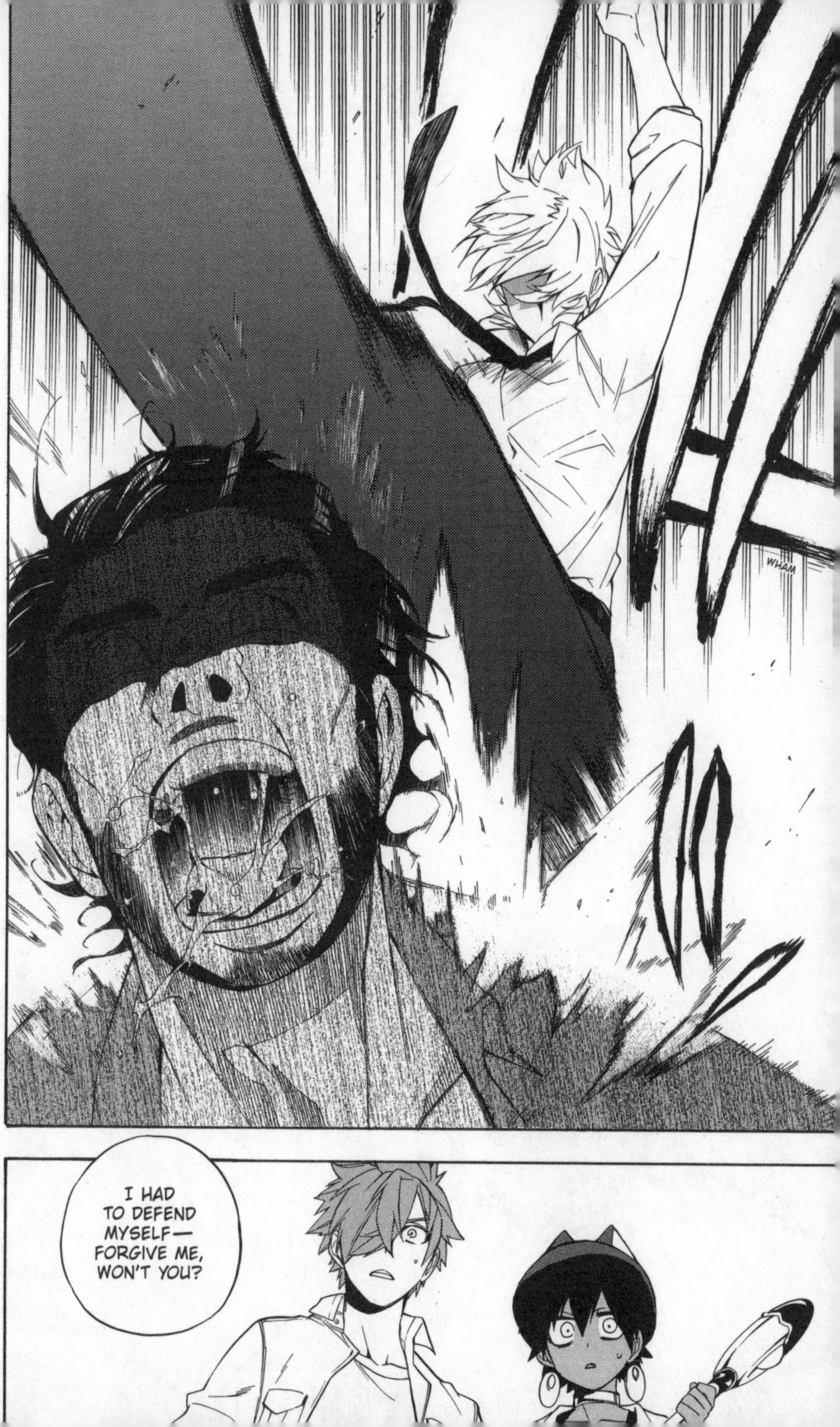
WHAM
I HAD TO DEFEND MYSELF— FORGIVE ME, WON'T YOU?

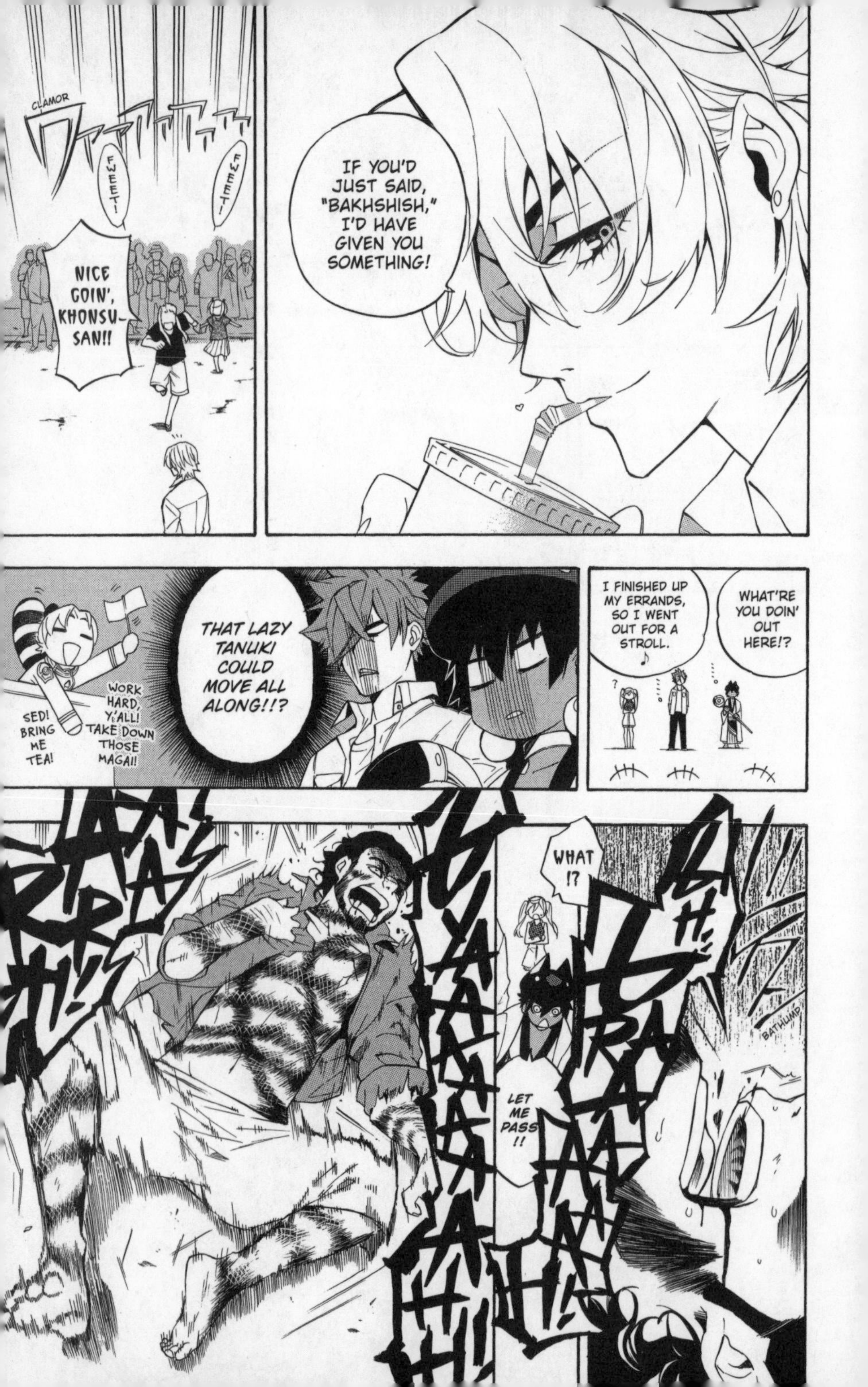
IF YOU'D JUST SAID, "BAKHSHISH," I'D HAVE GIVEN YOU SOMETHING!
CLAMOR
FWEET!
FWEET!
NICE GOIN', KHONSU-SAN!!
WHAT'RE YOU DOIN' OUT HERE!?
I FINISHED UP MY ERRANDS, SO I WENT OUT FOR A STROLL. ♪
THAT LAZY TANUKI COULD MOVE ALL ALONG!!?
WORK HARD, Y'ALL! TAKE DOWN THOSE MAGA!!
SED! BRING ME TEA!
WHAT!?
BATHUMP
LET ME PASS!!

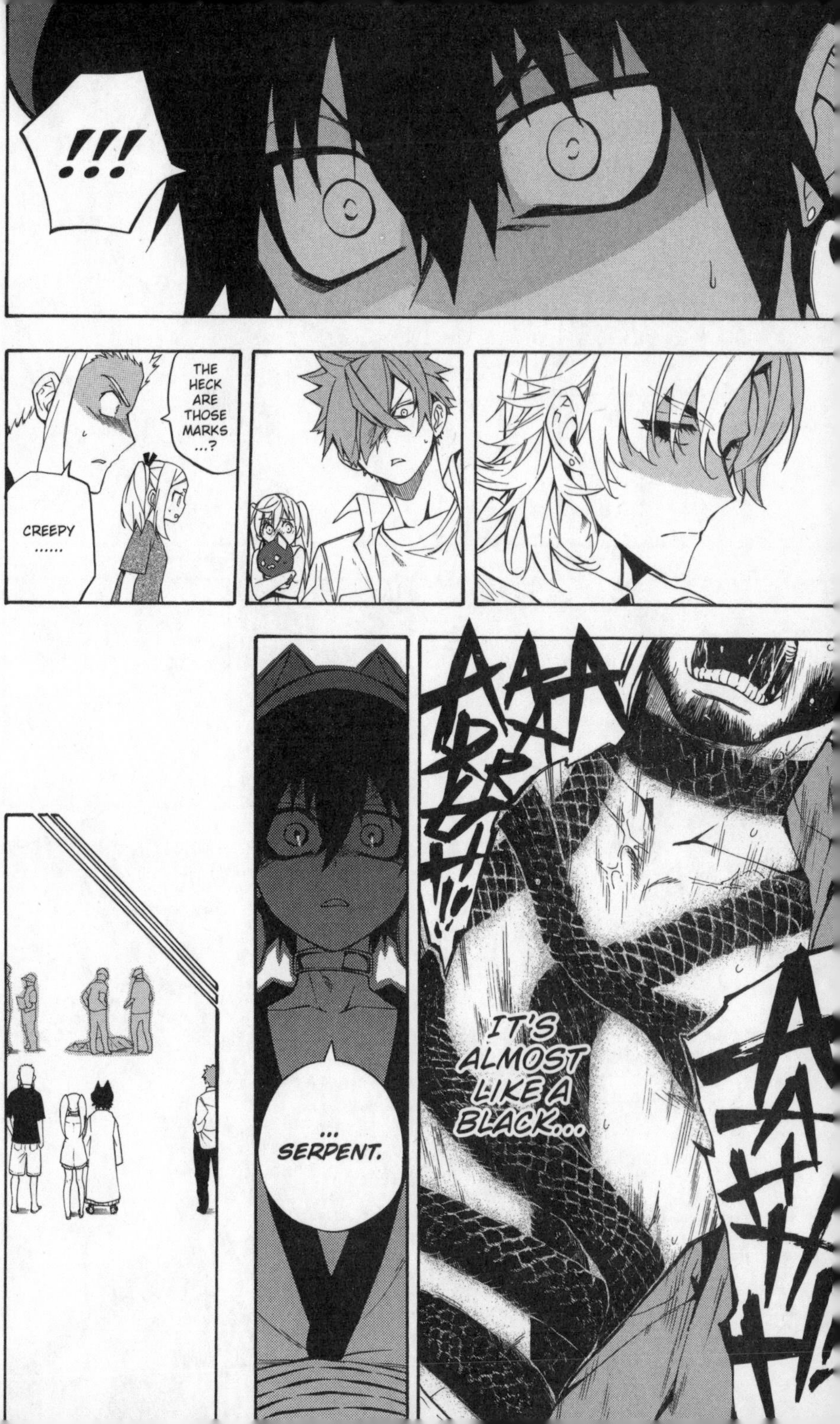
!!!
THE HECK ARE THOSE MARKS ...?
CREEPY ......
IT'S ALMOST LIKE A BLACK...
... SERPENT.

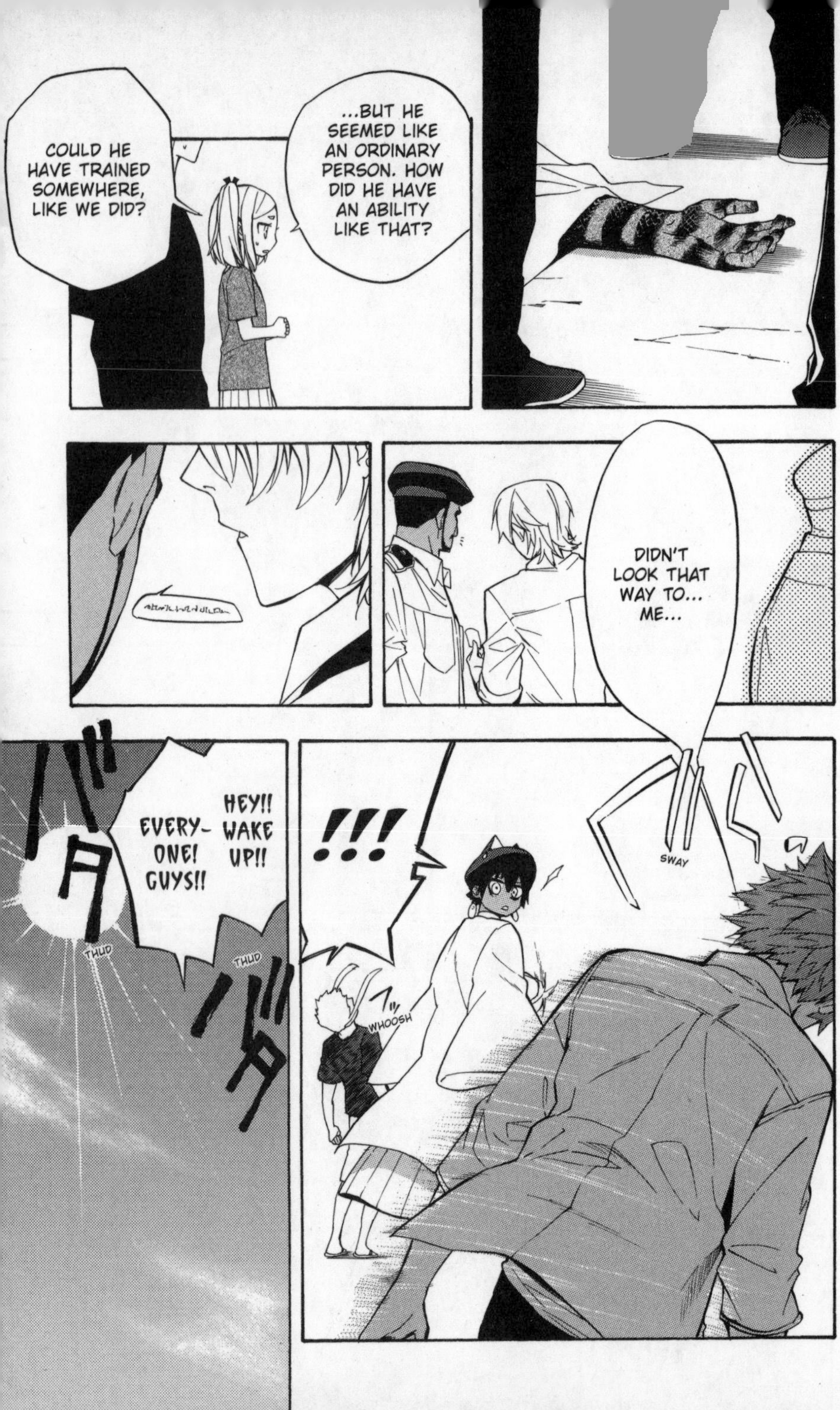
...BUT HE SEEMED LIKE AN ORDINARY PERSON. HOW DID HE HAVE AN ABILITY LIKE THAT?
COULD HE HAVE TRAINED SOMEWHERE, LIKE WE DID?
DIDN'T LOOK THAT WAY TO... ME...
SWAY
!!!
WHOOSH
HEY!! WAKE UP!!
EVERY-ONE! GUYS!!
THUD
THUD

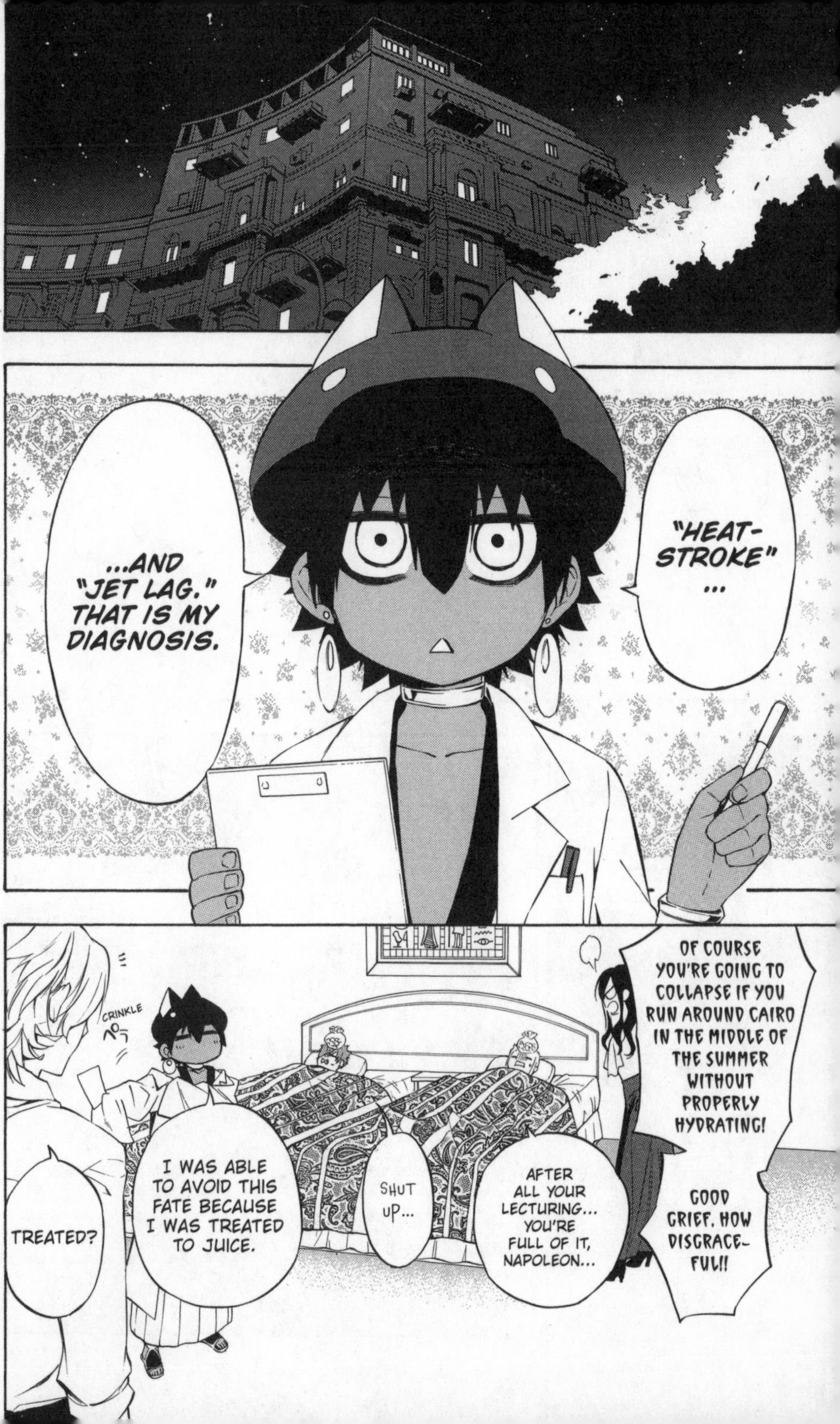
"HEAT-STROKE"...
...AND "JET LAG." THAT IS MY DIAGNOSIS.
OF COURSE YOU'RE GOING TO COLLAPSE IF YOU RUN AROUND CAIRO IN THE MIDDLE OF THE SUMMER WITHOUT PROPERLY HYDRATING!
GOOD GRIEF. HOW DISGRACE-FUL!!
AFTER ALL YOUR LECTURING... YOU'RE FULL OF IT, NAPOLEON...
SHUT UP...
I WAS ABLE TO AVOID THIS FATE BECAUSE I WAS TREATED TO JUICE.
CRINKLE
TREATED?

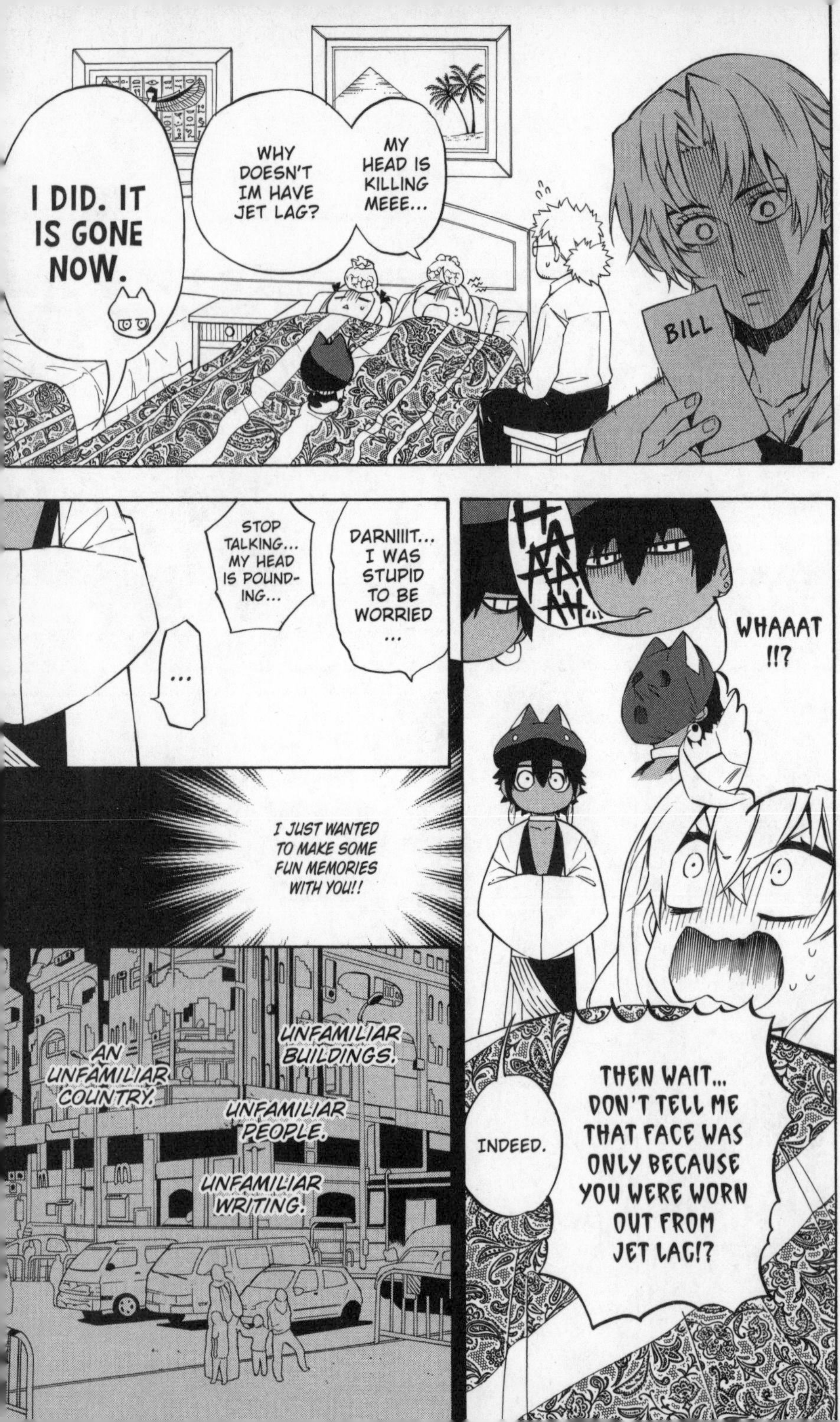
MY HEAD IS KILLING MEEE...
WHY DOESN'T IM HAVE JET LAG?
I DID. IT IS GONE NOW.
BILL
HAHAAH
WHAAAT !!?
THEN WAIT... DON'T TELL ME THAT FACE WAS ONLY BECAUSE YOU WERE WORN OUT FROM JET LAG!?
INDEED.
DARNIIIT... I WAS STUPID TO BE WORRIED...
STOP TALKING... MY HEAD IS POUNDING...
...
I JUST WANTED TO MAKE SOME FUN MEMORIES WITH YOU!!
AN UNFAMILIAR COUNTRY.
UNFAMILIAR BUILDINGS.
UNFAMILIAR PEOPLE.
UNFAMILIAR WRITING.

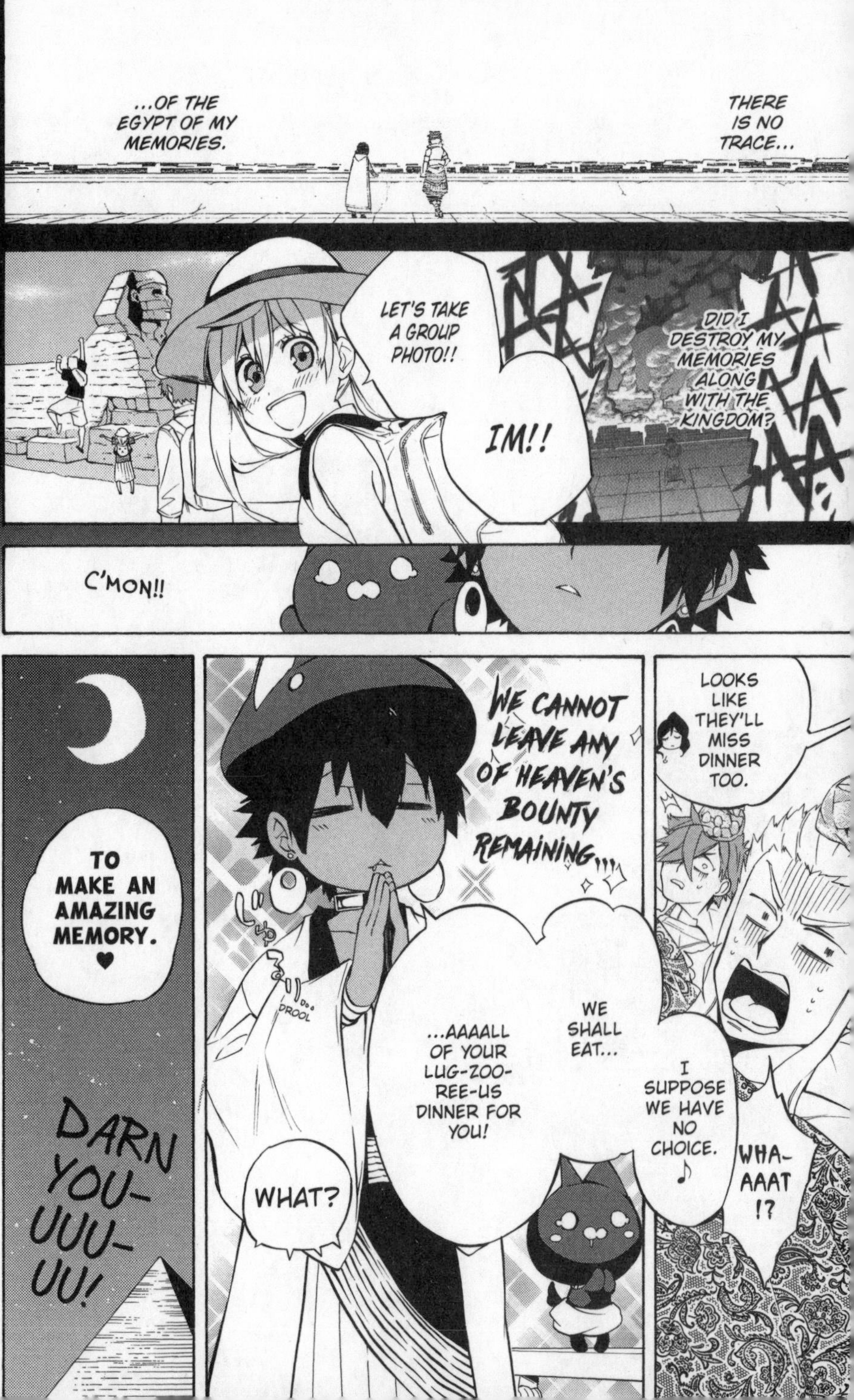
THERE IS NO TRACE...
...OF THE EGYPT OF MY MEMORIES.
DID I DESTROY MY MEMORIES ALONG WITH THE KINGDOM?
LET'S TAKE A GROUP PHOTO!!
IM!!
C'MON!!
LOOKS LIKE THEY'LL MISS DINNER TOO.
WHA-AAAT!?
I SUPPOSE WE HAVE NO CHOICE. ♪
WE CANNOT LEAVE ANY OF HEAVEN'S BOUNTY REMAINING...!!!
WE SHALL EAT...
...AAAALL OF YOUR LUG-ZOO-REE-US DINNER FOR YOU!
DROOL
WHAT?
TO MAKE AN AMAZING MEMORY. ♥
DARN YOU-UUU-UU!

FOOD REPORT!! EGYPTIAN FOOD NEXT DOOR

REPORTER: IMHOTEP

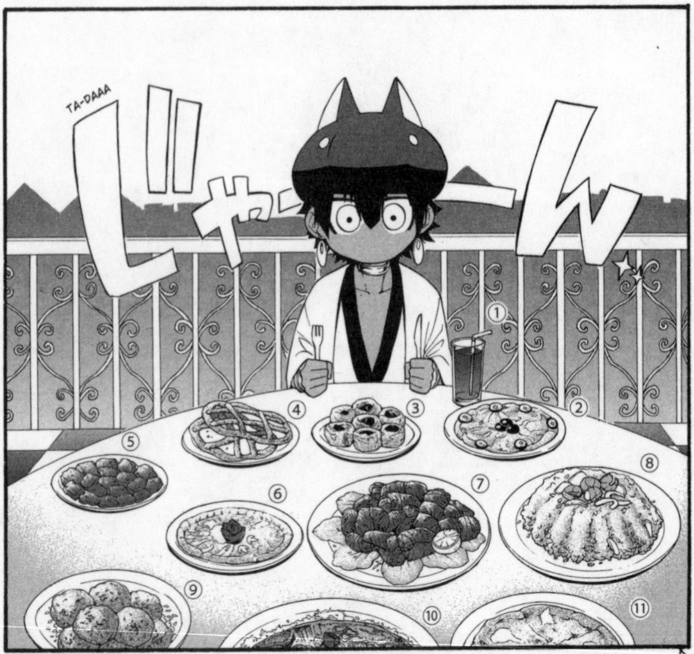
TA-DAAA
じゃーん

① POMEGRANATE JUICE
A MAJOR FRUIT IN EGYPT SINCE ANCIENT TIMES, THEY'RE VERY ATTACHED TO IT. IT'S SWEET AND SOUR.

② TAHINA
A COMMON DISH IN EGYPT, BREAD WITH A SESAME PASTE SPREAD.

③ BAKLAVA
THIS IS A PASTRY MADE OF LAYERS OF THIN PIE DOUGH, FILLED WITH NUTS AND COVERED IN SYRUP.

④ SIMIT
A TYPE OF EGYPTIAN BREAD. IN A NUTSHELL, IT'S A RING OF BREAD TOPPED WITH SESAME SEEDS.

⑤ KOFTA GAMBARI
MINCED SHRIMP FORMED INTO NUGGETS AND FRIED. GAMBARI MEANS "SHRIMP."

⑥ LABNEH
GOES WITH BREAD, A CREAM CHEESE PASTE.

⑦ MOMBAR
INTESTINES STUFFED WITH BLOOD-FLAVORED RICE.

⑧ ROS BI GAMBARI
FRIED RICE PACKED WITH SAVORY SHRIMP FLAVOR.

⑨ TAAMEYA (#1 RECOM-MENDATION)
CROQUETTES MADE WITH BROAD BEANS AND VEGGIES. THEIR CRUNCHY TEXTURE IS ADDICTING INDEED.

⑩ UKARU MA'LI
FRIED SEA BASS. ITS NAME SOUNDS LIKE IT COULD GIVE GOOD LUCK TO STUDENTS STUDYING FOR ENTRANCE EXAMS.

⑪ FETEER
EGYPT-STYLE PANCAKES. I LIKE MINE TOPPED WITH LOTS OF HONEY, CREAM, AND POWDERED SUGAR.

HARUGO LURCHED AWAY WHEN HE SAW THEM.

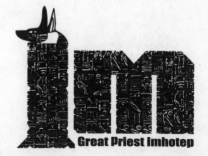
Great Priest Imhotep

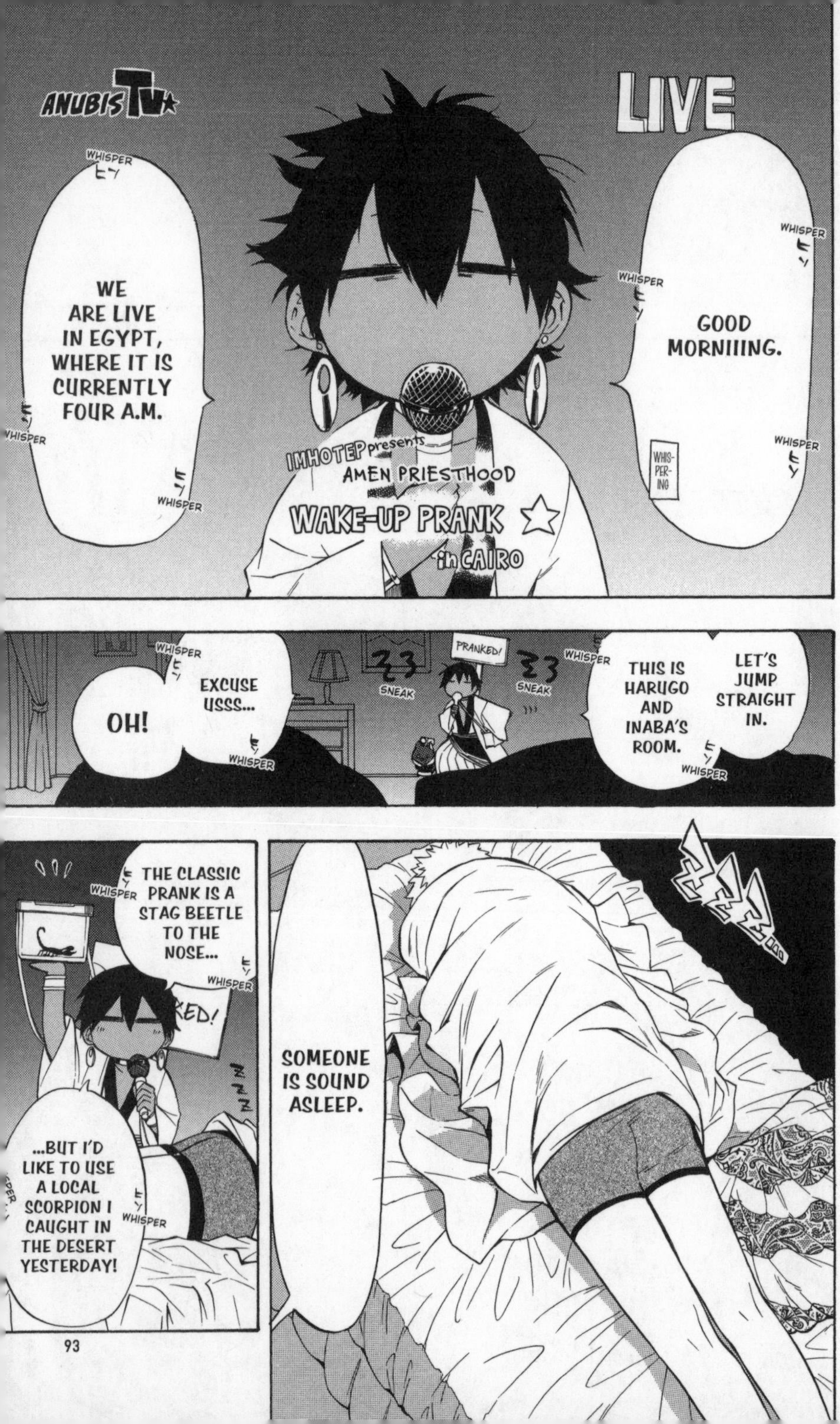
ANUBIS TV★
LIVE
WHISPER
GOOD MORNIIIING.
WHISPER
WE ARE LIVE IN EGYPT, WHERE IT IS CURRENTLY FOUR A.M.
WHISPER
WHISPERING
IMHOTEP presents AMEN PRIESTHOOD WAKE-UP PRANK ☆ in CAIRO
WHISPER
LET'S JUMP STRAIGHT IN.
THIS IS HARUGO AND INABA'S ROOM.
PRANKED!
SNEAK
SNEAK
WHISPER
EXCUSE USSS...
OH!
SOMEONE IS SOUND ASLEEP.
WHISPER
THE CLASSIC PRANK IS A STAG BEETLE TO THE NOSE...
WHISPER
...BUT I'D LIKE TO USE A LOCAL SCORPION I CAUGHT IN THE DESERT YESTERDAY!

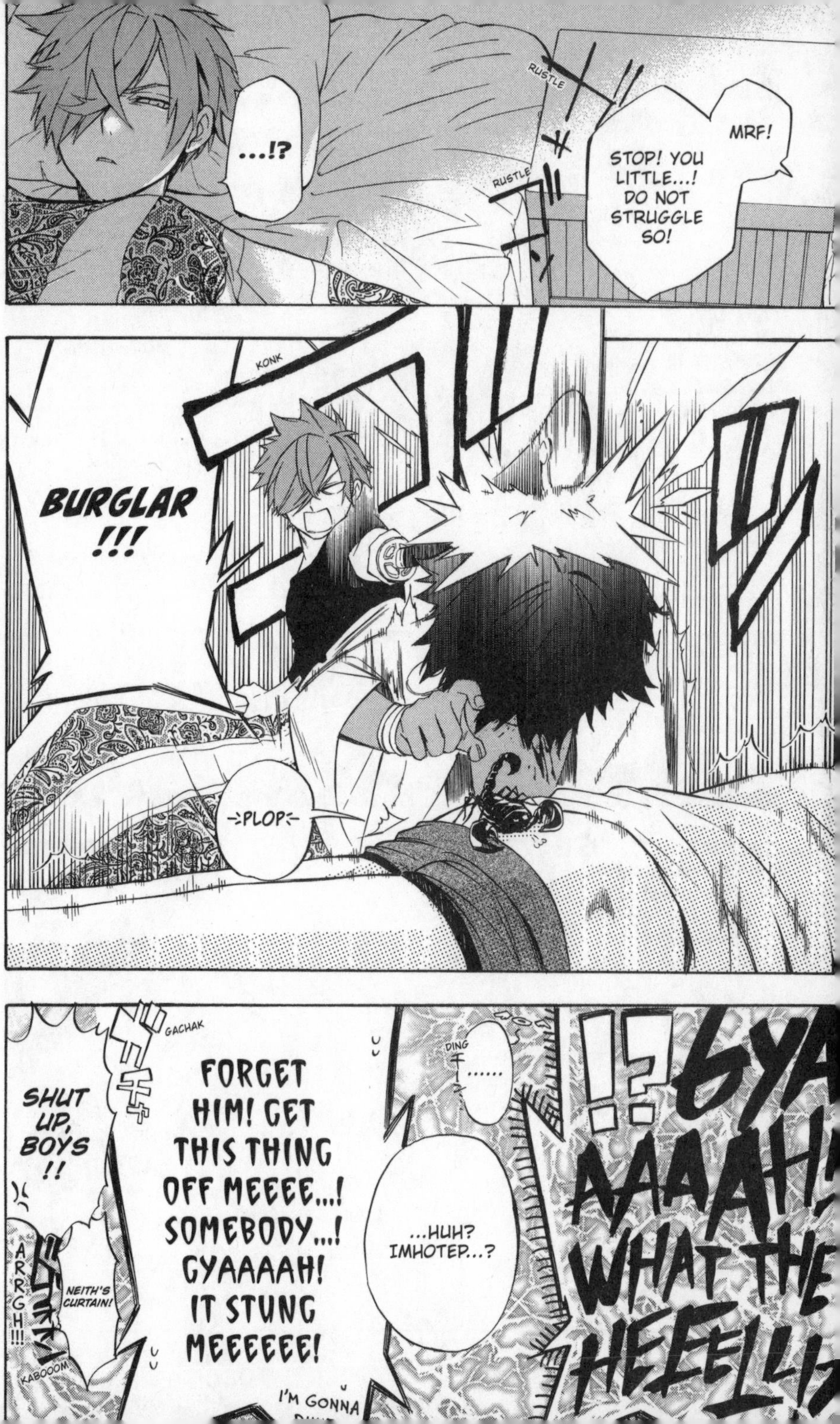
MRF!
STOP! YOU LITTLE...! DO NOT STRUGGLE SO!
RUSTLE
RUSTLE
...!?
KONK
BURGLAR!!!
PLOP
!? GYA AAAAH! WHAT THE HEEELL!
DING
......
...HUH? IMHOTEP...?
FORGET HIM! GET THIS THING OFF MEEEE...! SOMEBODY...! GYAAAAH! IT STUNG MEEEEEEE!
I'M GONNA
GACHAK
SHUT UP, BOYS!!
ARRGH!!!
NEITH'S CURTAIN!
KABOOOM

SCROLL 22: THE SEED THAT HAS YET TO SPROUT

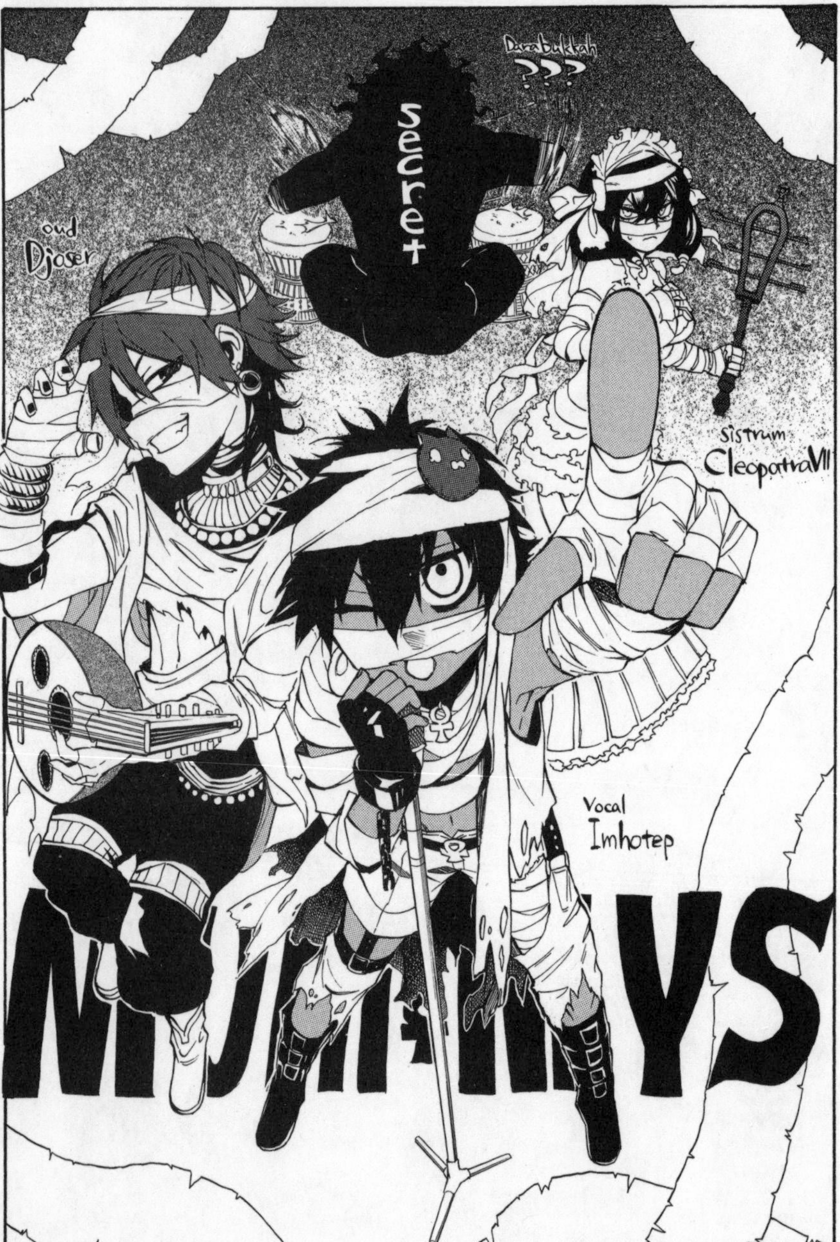
Darabukkah
???
secret
oud
Djoser
sistrum
CleopatraVII
Vocal
Imhotep

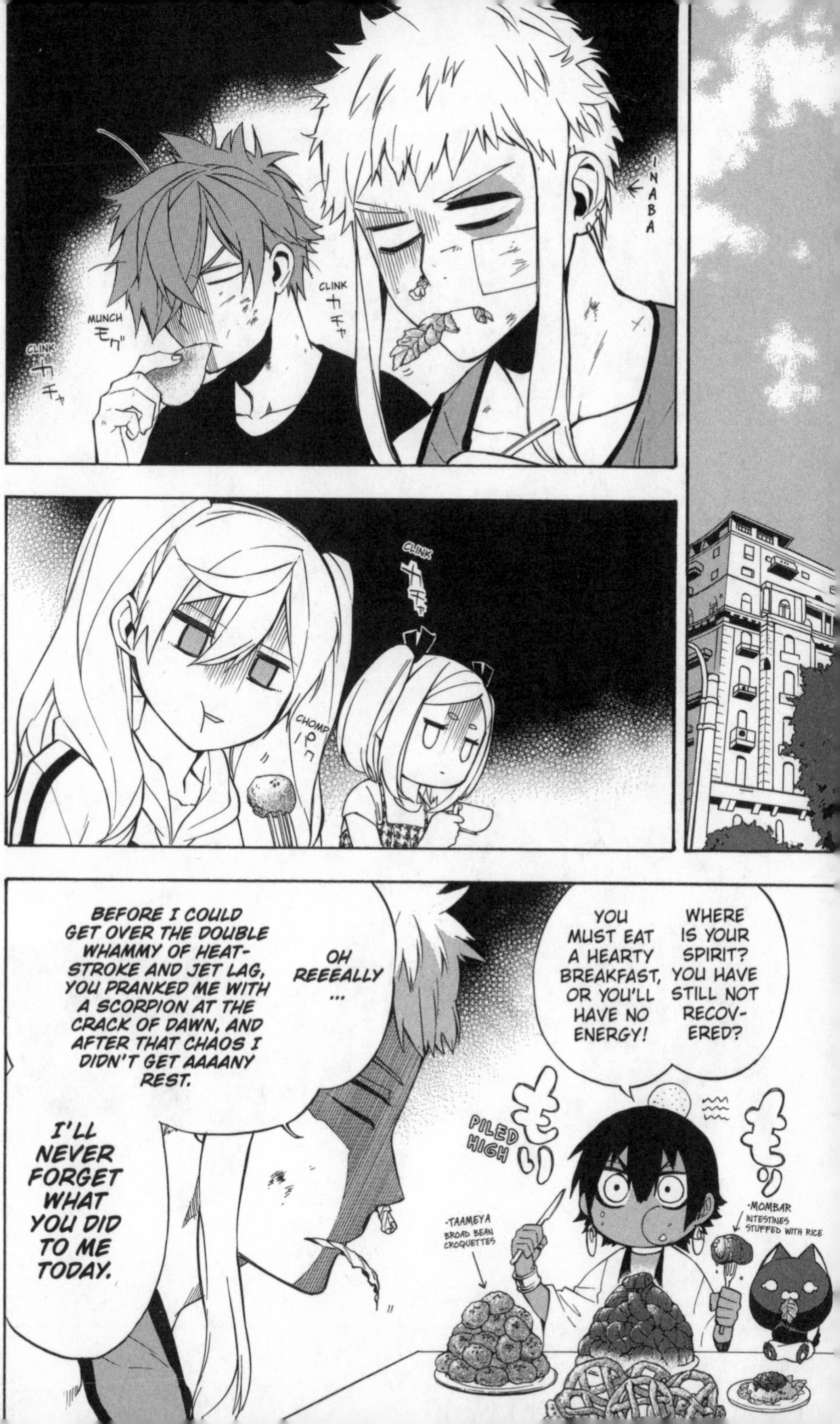
INABA
CLINK
カチャ
MUNCH
モグ
CLINK
カチャ
CLINK
カチャ
CHOMP
パク
WHERE IS YOUR SPIRIT? YOU HAVE STILL NOT RECOV-ERED?
YOU MUST EAT A HEARTY BREAKFAST, OR YOU'LL HAVE NO ENERGY!
OH REEEALLY ...
BEFORE I COULD GET OVER THE DOUBLE WHAMMY OF HEAT-STROKE AND JET LAG, YOU PRANKED ME WITH A SCORPION AT THE CRACK OF DAWN, AND AFTER THAT CHAOS I DIDN'T GET AAAANY REST.
I'LL NEVER FORGET WHAT YOU DID TO ME TODAY.
もり
PILED HIGH
·MOMBAR
INTESTINES STUFFED WITH RICE
·TAAMEYA
BROAD BEAN CROQUETTES

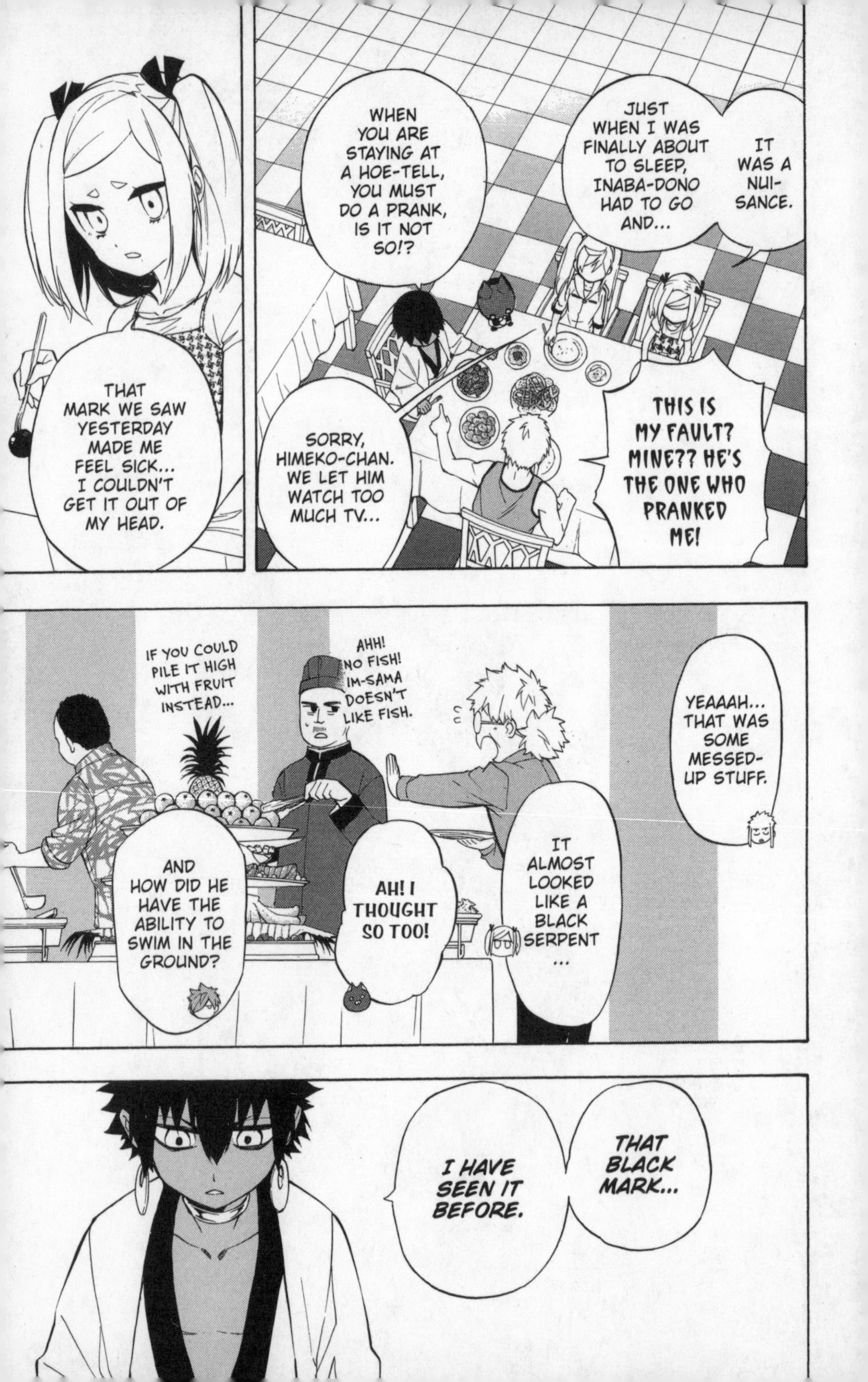
IT WAS A NUISANCE.
JUST WHEN I WAS FINALLY ABOUT TO SLEEP, INABA-DONO HAD TO GO AND...
WHEN YOU ARE STAYING AT A HOE-TELL, YOU MUST DO A PRANK, IS IT NOT SO!?
THIS IS MY FAULT? MINE?? HE'S THE ONE WHO PRANKED ME!
SORRY, HIMEKO-CHAN. WE LET HIM WATCH TOO MUCH TV...
THAT MARK WE SAW YESTERDAY MADE ME FEEL SICK... I COULDN'T GET IT OUT OF MY HEAD.
YEAAAH... THAT WAS SOME MESSED-UP STUFF.
IT ALMOST LOOKED LIKE A BLACK SERPENT...
AHH! NO FISH! IM-SAMA DOESN'T LIKE FISH.
AH! I THOUGHT SO TOO!
IF YOU COULD PILE IT HIGH WITH FRUIT INSTEAD...
AND HOW DID HE HAVE THE ABILITY TO SWIM IN THE GROUND?
THAT BLACK MARK...
I HAVE SEEN IT BEFORE.

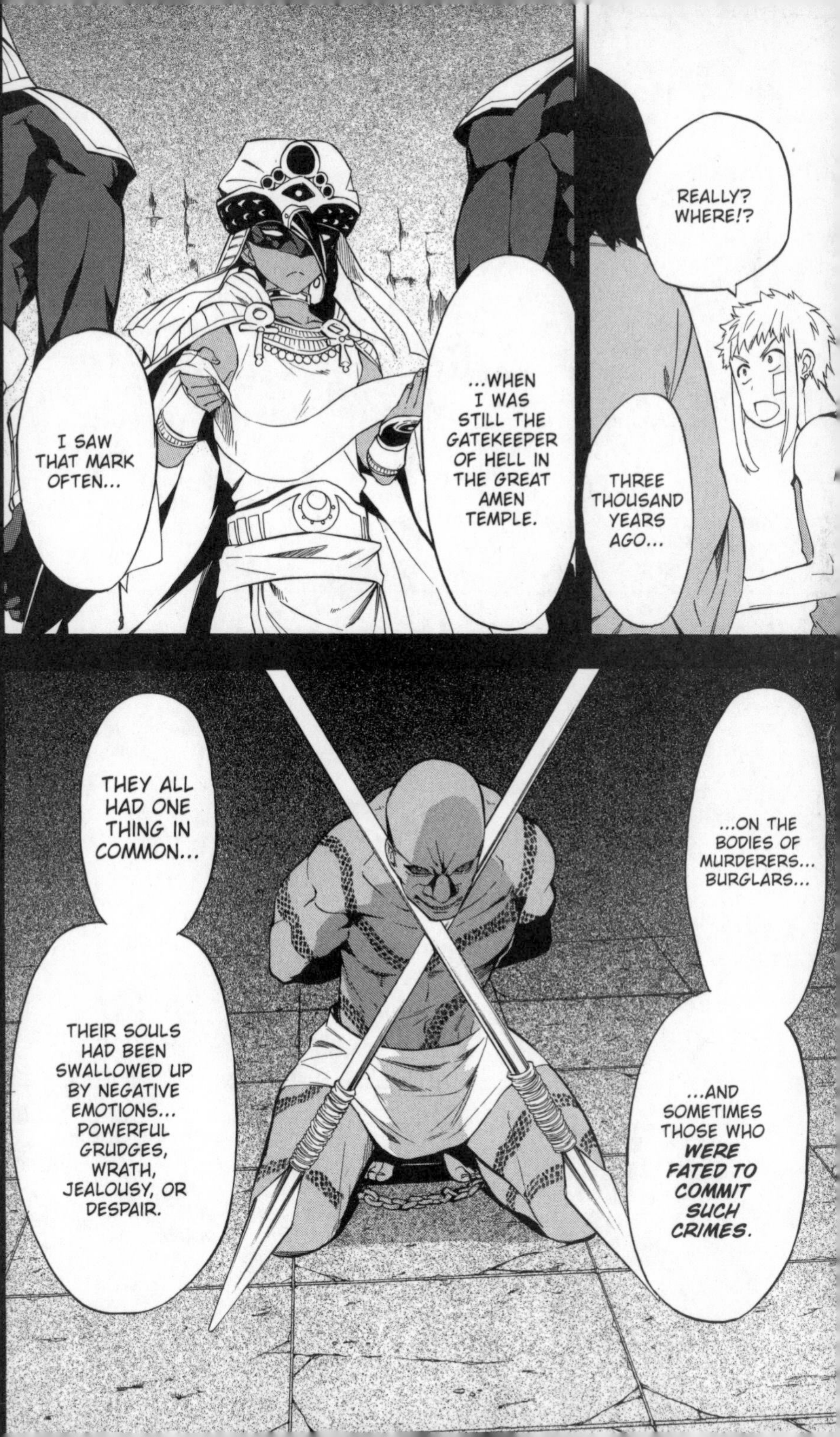
REALLY? WHERE!?
THREE THOUSAND YEARS AGO...
...WHEN I WAS STILL THE GATEKEEPER OF HELL IN THE GREAT AMEN TEMPLE.
I SAW THAT MARK OFTEN...
...ON THE BODIES OF MURDERERS... BURGLARS...
...AND SOMETIMES THOSE WHO *WERE FATED TO COMMIT SUCH CRIMES.*
THEY ALL HAD ONE THING IN COMMON...
THEIR SOULS HAD BEEN SWALLOWED UP BY NEGATIVE EMOTIONS... POWERFUL GRUDGES, WRATH, JEALOUSY, OR DESPAIR.

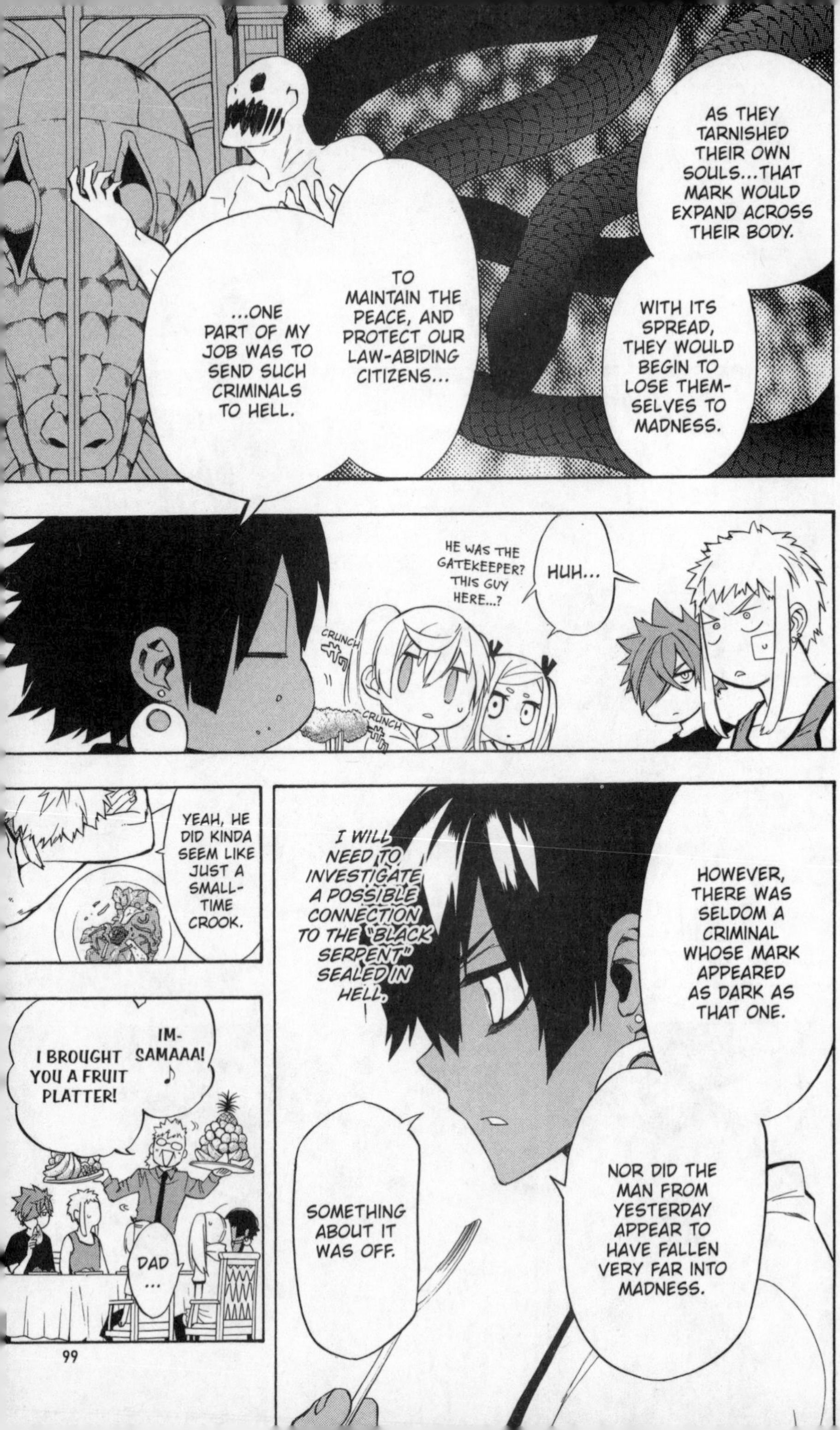
AS THEY TARNISHED THEIR OWN SOULS...THAT MARK WOULD EXPAND ACROSS THEIR BODY.
WITH ITS SPREAD, THEY WOULD BEGIN TO LOSE THEMSELVES TO MADNESS.
TO MAINTAIN THE PEACE, AND PROTECT OUR LAW-ABIDING CITIZENS...
...ONE PART OF MY JOB WAS TO SEND SUCH CRIMINALS TO HELL.
HUH...
HE WAS THE GATEKEEPER? THIS GUY HERE...?
CRUNCH
CRUNCH
HOWEVER, THERE WAS SELDOM A CRIMINAL WHOSE MARK APPEARED AS DARK AS THAT ONE.
I WILL NEED TO INVESTIGATE A POSSIBLE CONNECTION TO THE "BLACK SERPENT" SEALED IN HELL.
NOR DID THE MAN FROM YESTERDAY APPEAR TO HAVE FALLEN VERY FAR INTO MADNESS.
SOMETHING ABOUT IT WAS OFF.
YEAH, HE DID KINDA SEEM LIKE JUST A SMALL-TIME CROOK.
IM-SAMAAA! ♪
I BROUGHT YOU A FRUIT PLATTER!
DAD ...

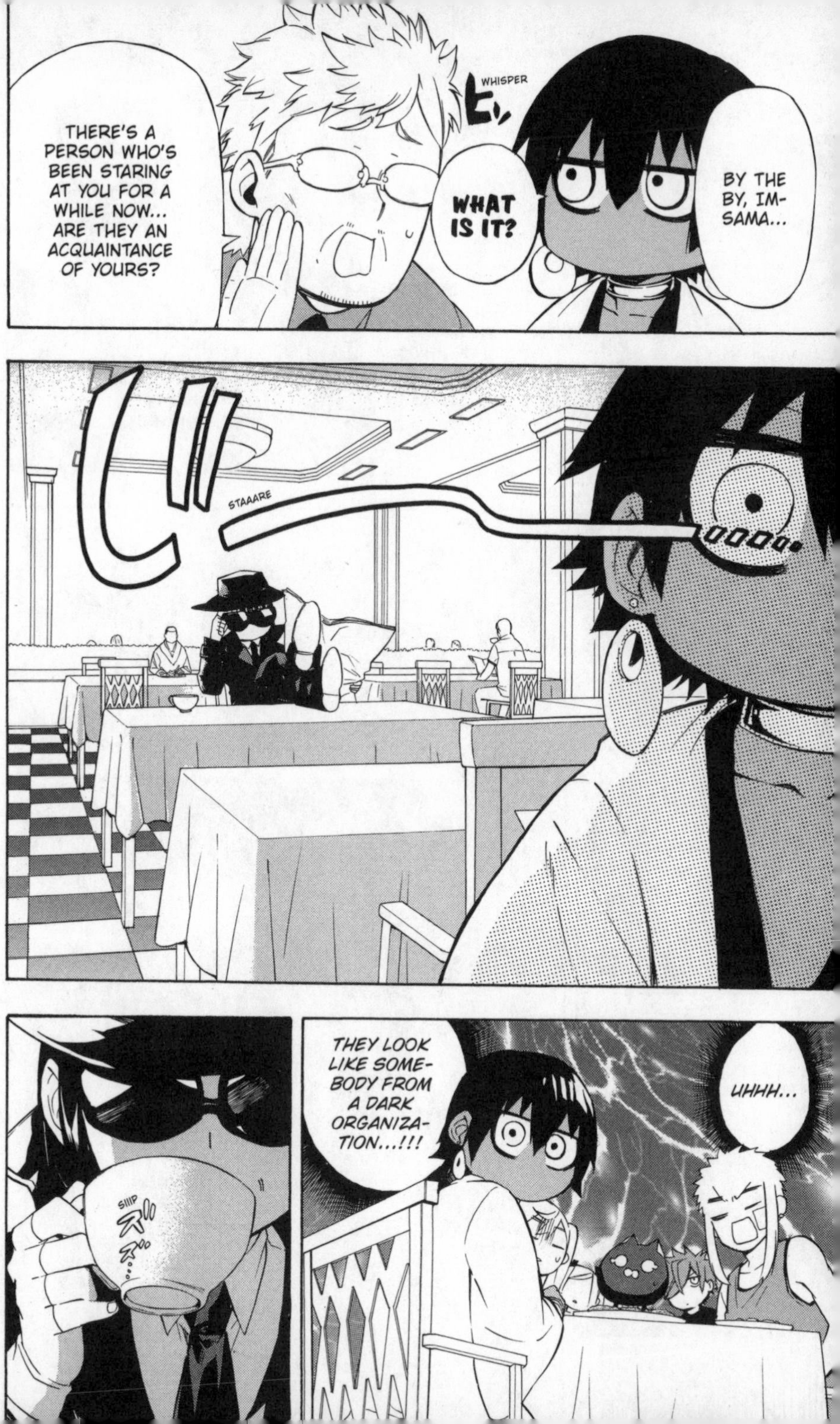
BY THE BY, IM-SAMA...
WHISPER
WHAT IS IT?
THERE'S A PERSON WHO'S BEEN STARING AT YOU FOR A WHILE NOW... ARE THEY AN ACQUAINTANCE OF YOURS?
STAAARE
UHHH...
THEY LOOK LIKE SOME-BODY FROM A DARK ORGANIZA-TION...!!!
SIIIP

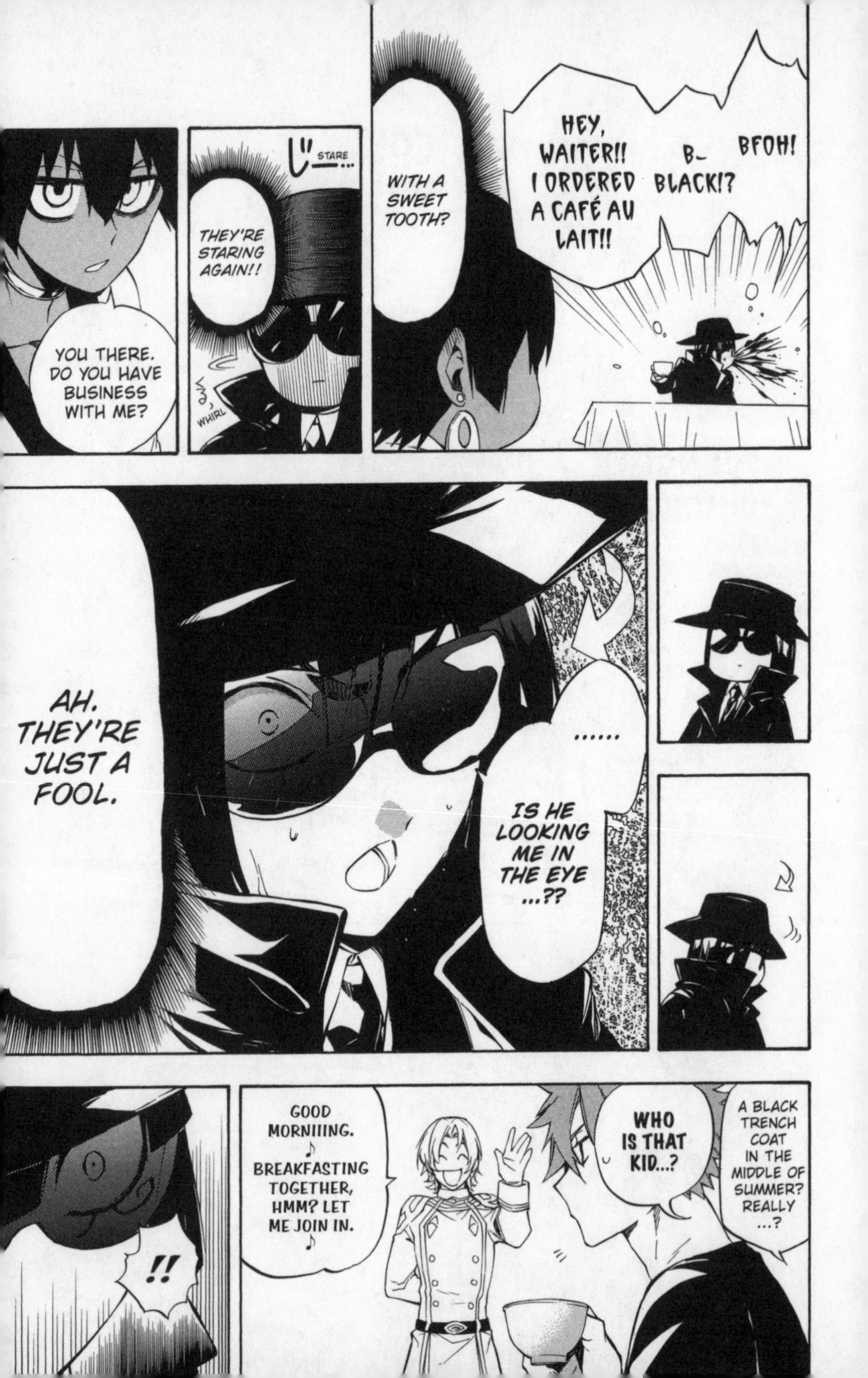
BFOH!
B- BLACK!?
HEY, WAITER!! I ORDERED A CAFÉ AU LAIT!!
WITH A SWEET TOOTH?
じー STARE...
THEY'RE STARING AGAIN!!
WHIRL
YOU THERE. DO YOU HAVE BUSINESS WITH ME?
......
IS HE LOOKING ME IN THE EYE ...??
AH. THEY'RE JUST A FOOL.
A BLACK TRENCH COAT IN THE MIDDLE OF SUMMER? REALLY ...?
WHO IS THAT KID...?
GOOD MORNIIING. ♪ BREAKFASTING TOGETHER, HMM? LET ME JOIN IN. ♪
!!

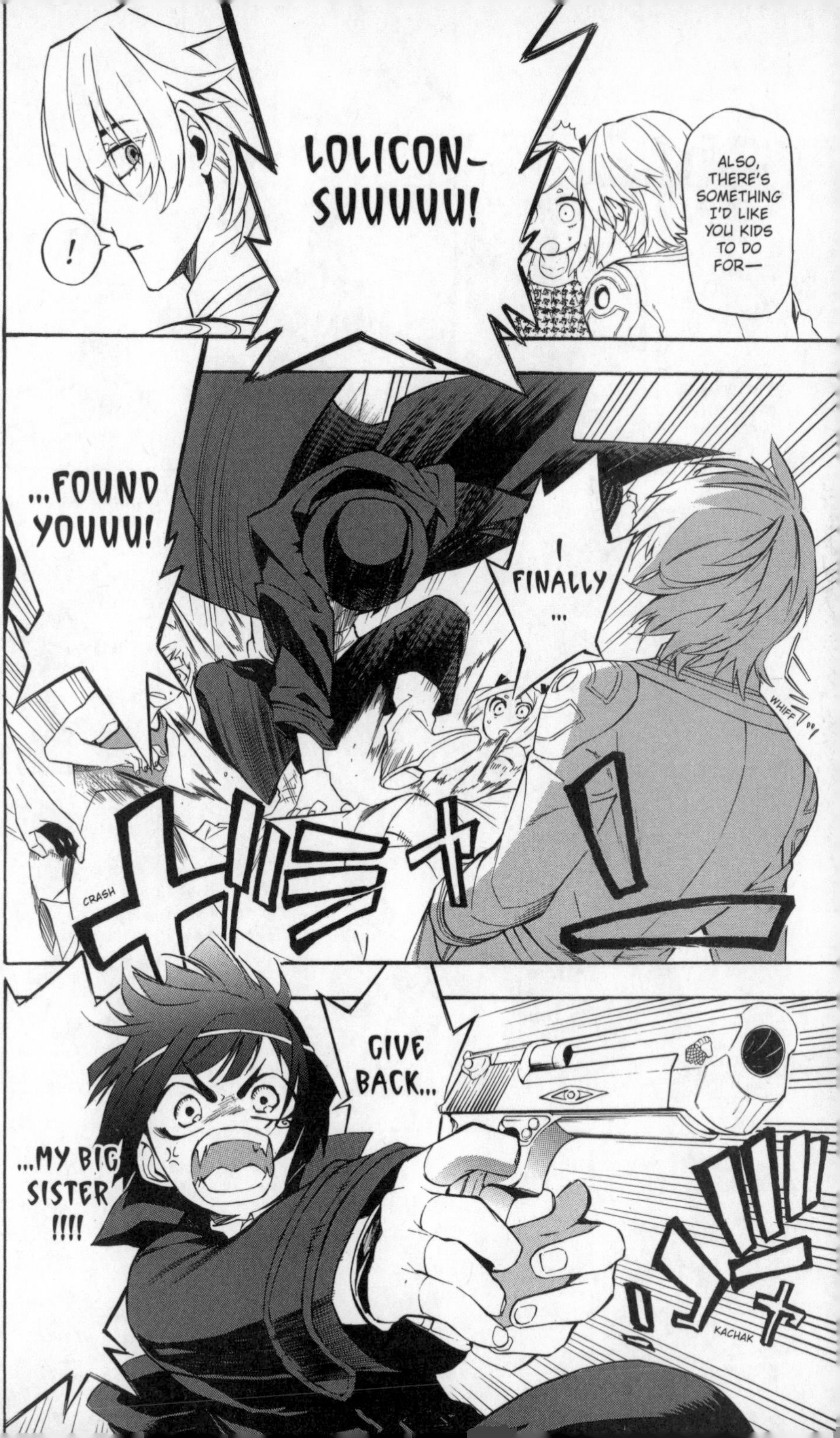
ALSO, THERE'S SOMETHING I'D LIKE YOU KIDS TO DO FOR—
LOLICON-SUUUUUU!
!
I FINALLY...
...FOUND YOUUU!
WHIFF
CRASH
GIVE BACK...
...MY BIG SISTER!!!!
KACHAK

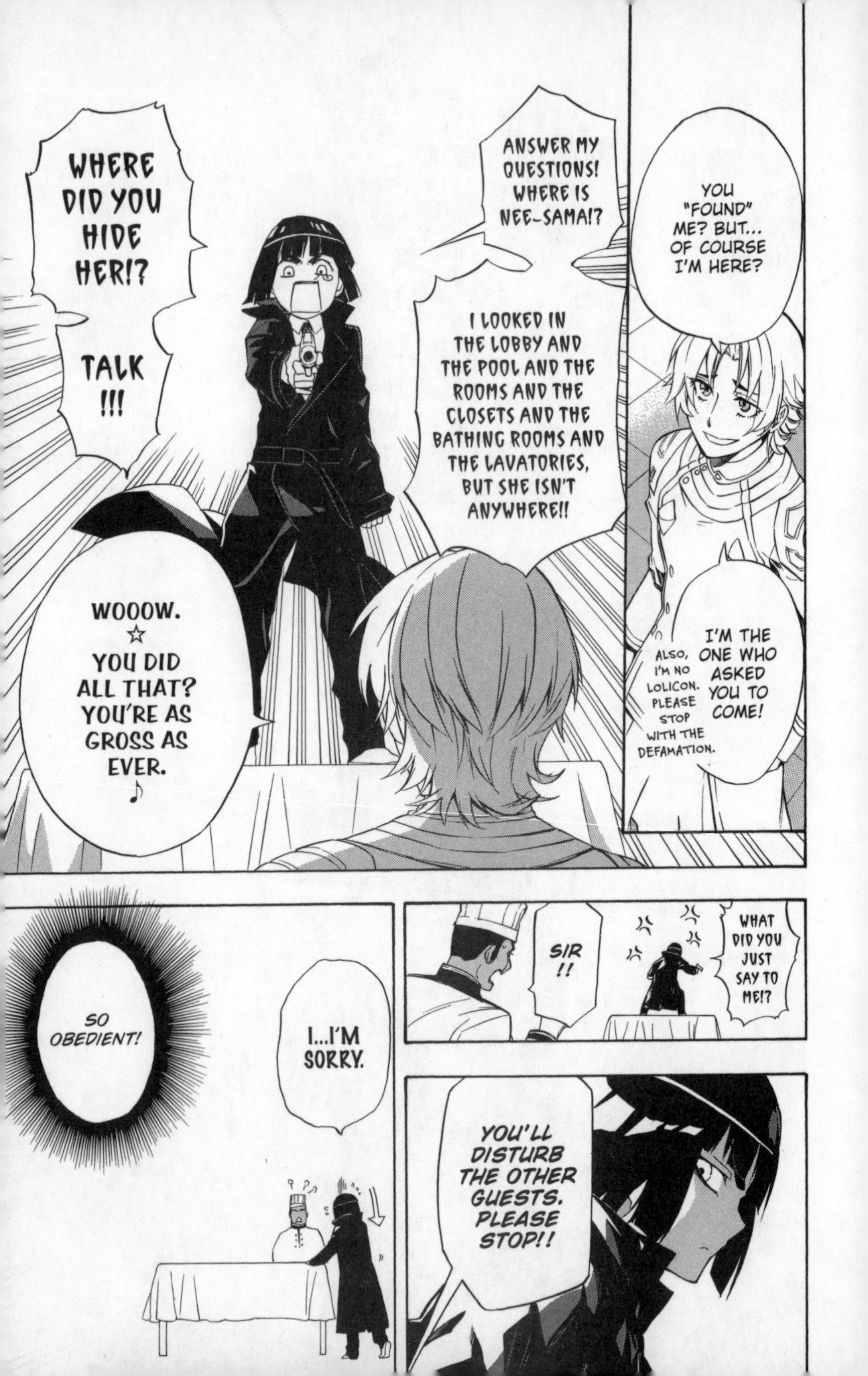
YOU "FOUND" ME? BUT... OF COURSE I'M HERE?
I'M THE ONE WHO ASKED YOU TO COME!
ALSO, I'M NO LOLICON. PLEASE STOP WITH THE DEFAMATION.
ANSWER MY QUESTIONS! WHERE IS NEE-SAMA!?
WHERE DID YOU HIDE HER!?
TALK!!!
I LOOKED IN THE LOBBY AND THE POOL AND THE ROOMS AND THE CLOSETS AND THE BATHING ROOMS AND THE LAVATORIES, BUT SHE ISN'T ANYWHERE!!
WOOOW. ☆ YOU DID ALL THAT? YOU'RE AS GROSS AS EVER. ♪
WHAT DID YOU JUST SAY TO ME!?
SIR!!
YOU'LL DISTURB THE OTHER GUESTS. PLEASE STOP!!
I...I'M SORRY.
SO OBEDIENT!

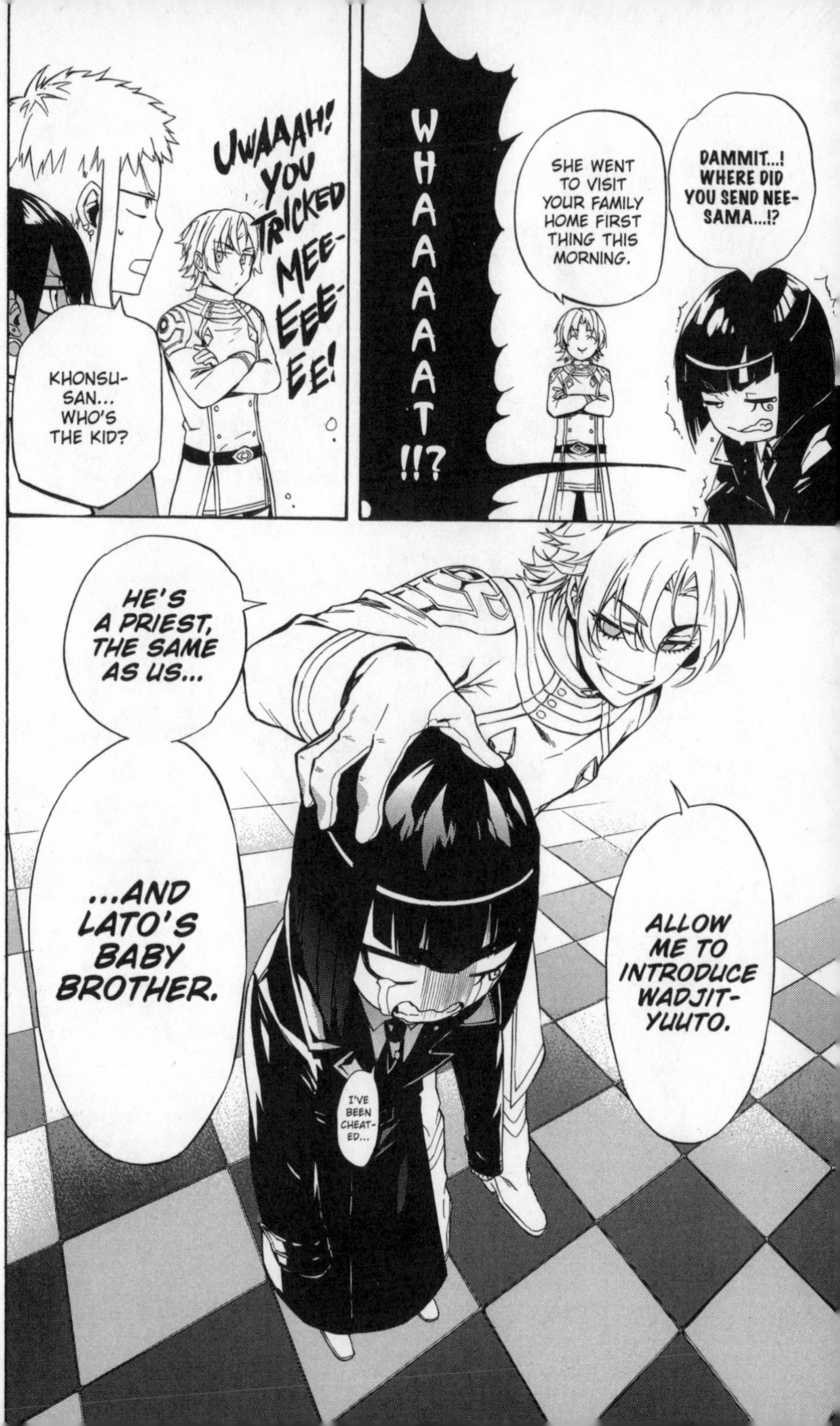
DAMMIT...! WHERE DID YOU SEND NEE-SAMA...!?
SHE WENT TO VISIT YOUR FAMILY HOME FIRST THING THIS MORNING.
WHAAAAAAT!!?
UWAAAH! YOU TRICKED MEE-EEE-EE!
KHONSU-SAN... WHO'S THE KID?
HE'S A PRIEST, THE SAME AS US...
...AND LATO'S BABY BROTHER.
ALLOW ME TO INTRODUCE WADJIT-YUUTO.
I'VE BEEN CHEATED...

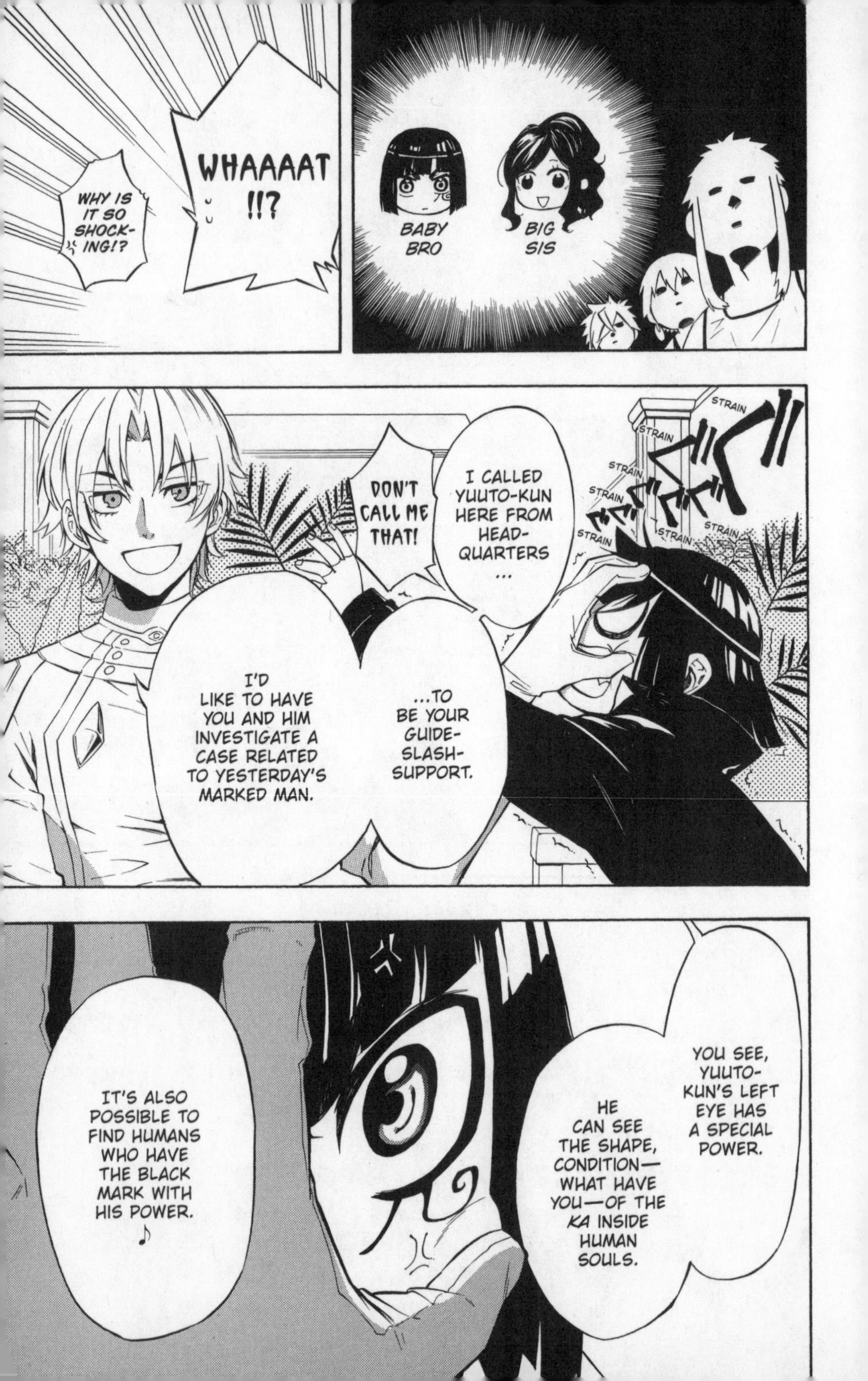
BABY BRO
BIG SIS
WHAAAAT!!?
WHY IS IT SO SHOCKING!?
STRAIN STRAIN STRAIN STRAIN STRAIN STRAIN STRAIN
I CALLED YUUTO-KUN HERE FROM HEADQUARTERS...
DON'T CALL ME THAT!
...TO BE YOUR GUIDE-SLASH-SUPPORT.
I'D LIKE TO HAVE YOU AND HIM INVESTIGATE A CASE RELATED TO YESTERDAY'S MARKED MAN.
YOU SEE, YUUTO-KUN'S LEFT EYE HAS A SPECIAL POWER.
HE CAN SEE THE SHAPE, CONDITION—WHAT HAVE YOU—OF THE *KA* INSIDE HUMAN SOULS.
IT'S ALSO POSSIBLE TO FIND HUMANS WHO HAVE THE BLACK MARK WITH HIS POWER. ♪

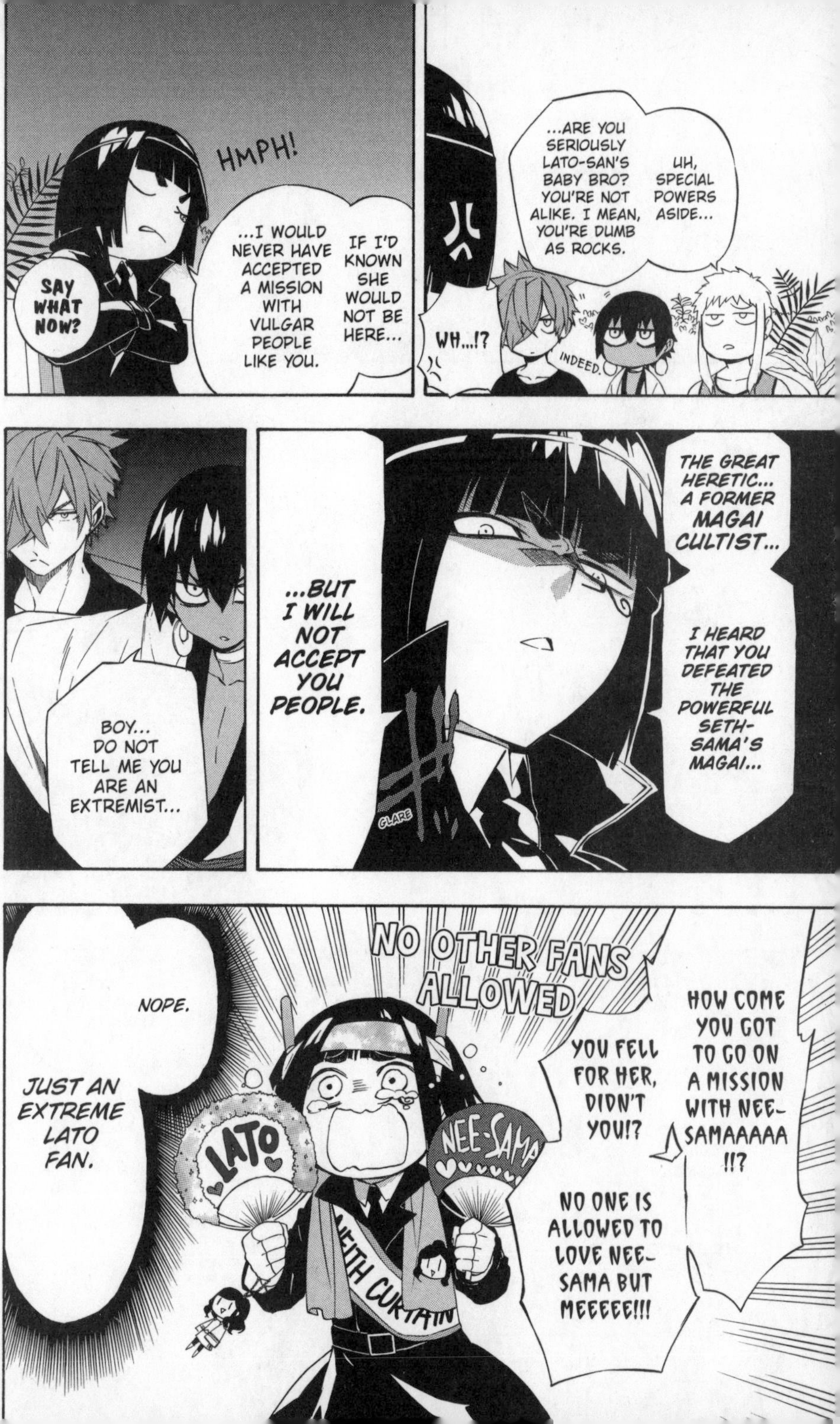
...ARE YOU SERIOUSLY LATO-SAN'S BABY BRO? YOU'RE NOT ALIKE. I MEAN, YOU'RE DUMB AS ROCKS.
UH, SPECIAL POWERS ASIDE...
INDEED.
WH...!?
HMPH!
IF I'D KNOWN SHE WOULD NOT BE HERE...
...I WOULD NEVER HAVE ACCEPTED A MISSION WITH VULGAR PEOPLE LIKE YOU.
SAY WHAT NOW?
THE GREAT HERETIC... A FORMER MAGAI CULTIST...
I HEARD THAT YOU DEFEATED THE POWERFUL SETH-SAMA'S MAGAI...
...BUT I WILL NOT ACCEPT YOU PEOPLE.
GLARE
BOY... DO NOT TELL ME YOU ARE AN EXTREMIST...
HOW COME YOU GOT TO GO ON A MISSION WITH NEE-SAMAAAAA!!?
YOU FELL FOR HER, DIDN'T YOU!?
NO OTHER FANS ALLOWED
NO ONE IS ALLOWED TO LOVE NEE-SAMA BUT MEEEEE!!!
NEE-SAMA
LATO
NEITH CURTAIN
NOPE.
JUST AN EXTREME LATO FAN.

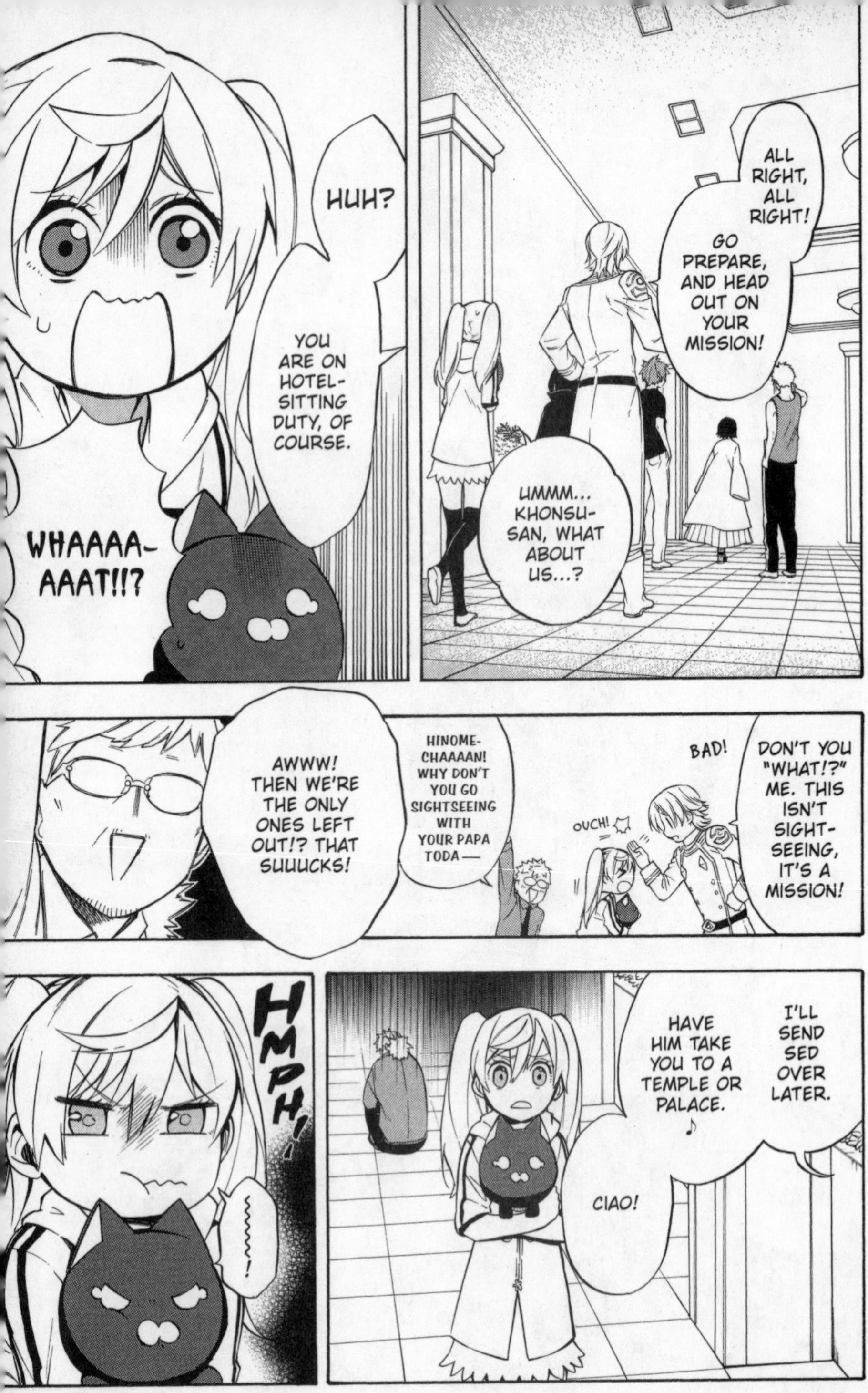
ALL RIGHT, ALL RIGHT!
GO PREPARE, AND HEAD OUT ON YOUR MISSION!
UMMM... KHONSU-SAN, WHAT ABOUT US...?
HUH?
YOU ARE ON HOTEL-SITTING DUTY, OF COURSE.
WHAAAA-AAAT!!?
DON'T YOU "WHAT!?" ME. THIS ISN'T SIGHT-SEEING, IT'S A MISSION!
BAD!
OUCH!
HINOME-CHAAAAN! WHY DON'T YOU GO SIGHTSEEING WITH YOUR PAPA TODA—
AWWW! THEN WE'RE THE ONLY ONES LEFT OUT!? THAT SUUUCKS!
I'LL SEND SED OVER LATER.
HAVE HIM TAKE YOU TO A TEMPLE OR PALACE. ♪
CIAO!
HMPH!
......!

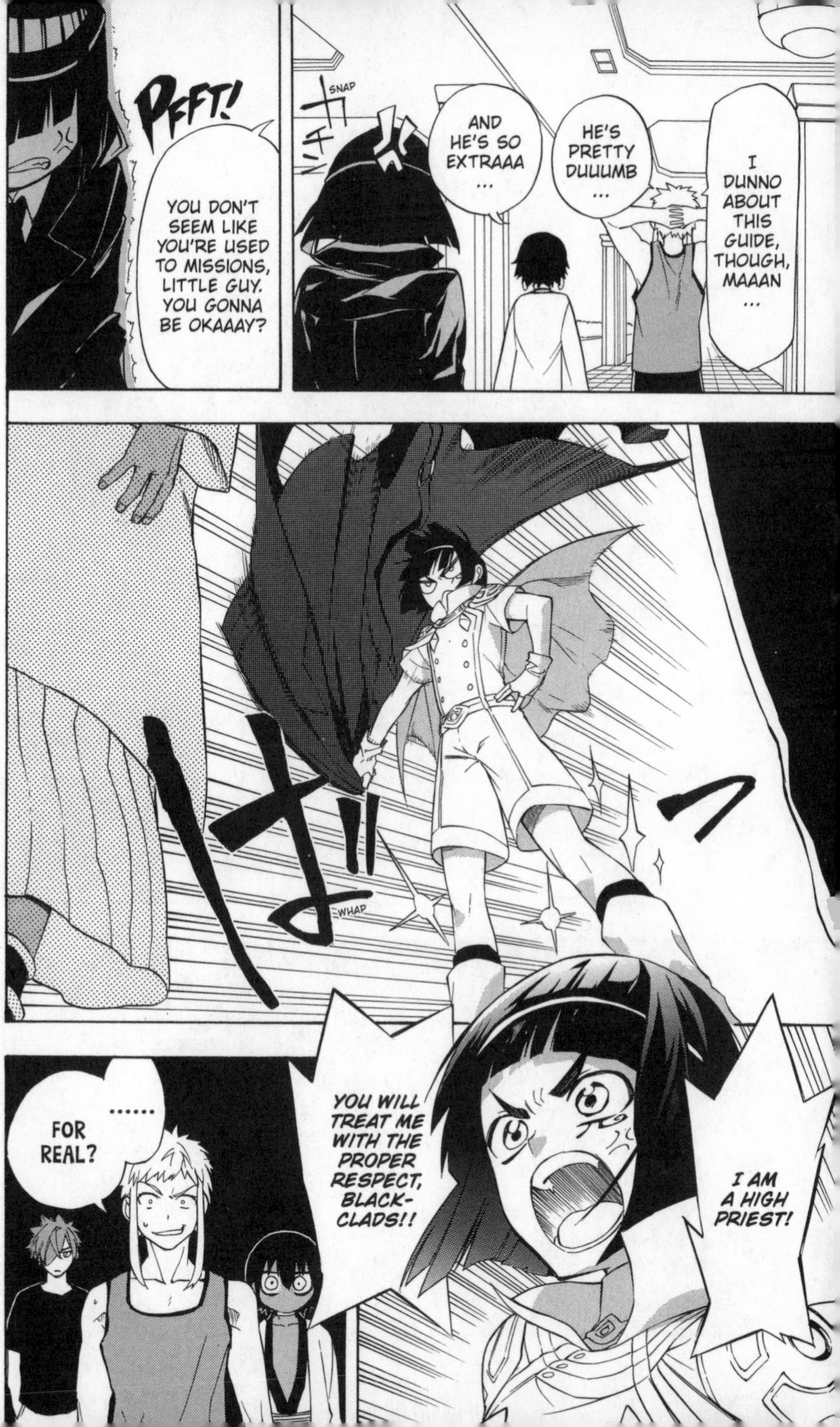
I DUNNO ABOUT THIS GUIDE, THOUGH, MAAAN...
HE'S PRETTY DUUUMB...
AND HE'S SO EXTRAAA...
SNAP
PFFT!
YOU DON'T SEEM LIKE YOU'RE USED TO MISSIONS, LITTLE GUY. YOU GONNA BE OKAAAY?
WHAP
I AM A HIGH PRIEST!
YOU WILL TREAT ME WITH THE PROPER RESPECT, BLACK-CLADS!!
......
FOR REAL?

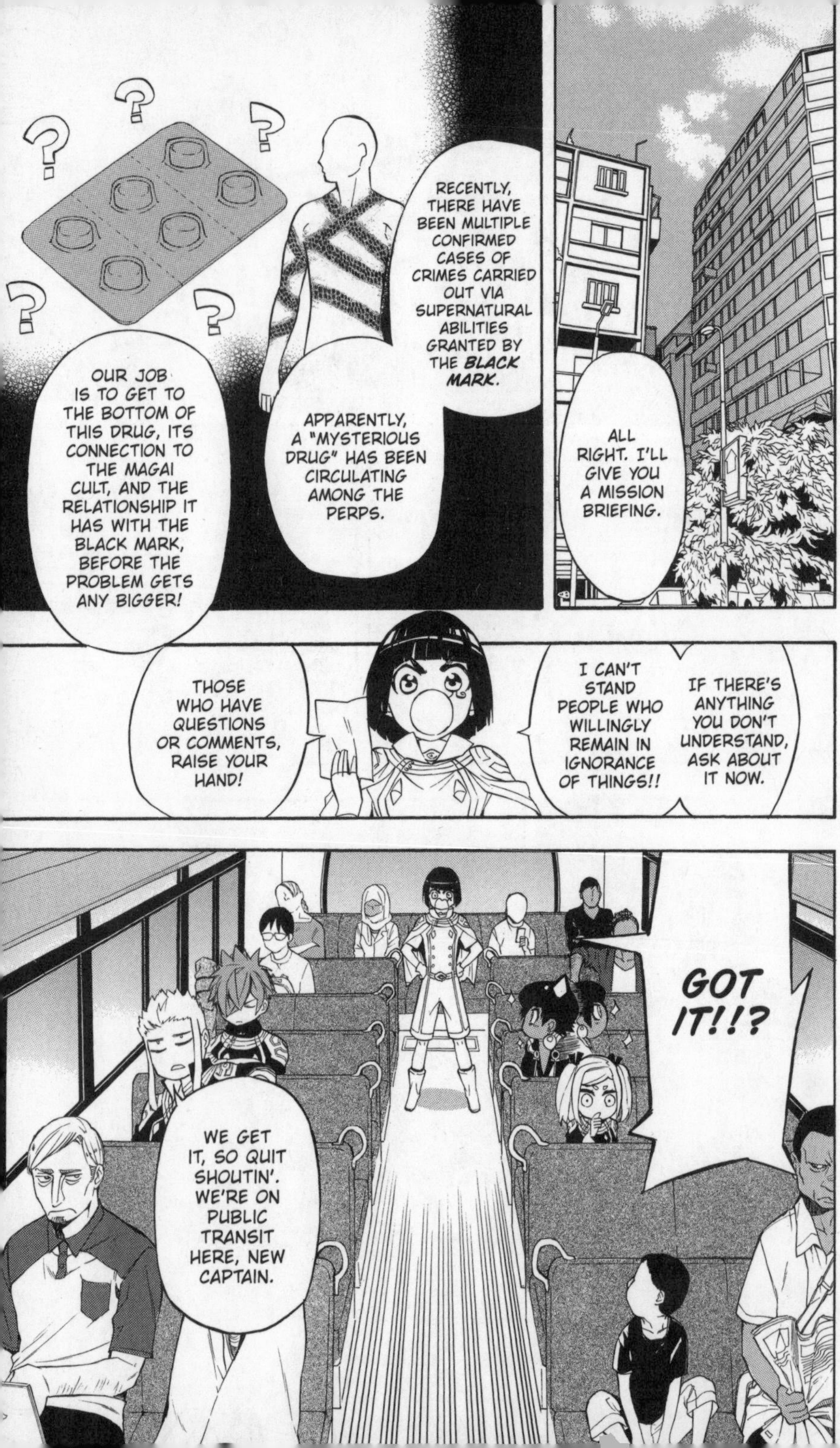
ALL RIGHT. I'LL GIVE YOU A MISSION BRIEFING.
RECENTLY, THERE HAVE BEEN MULTIPLE CONFIRMED CASES OF CRIMES CARRIED OUT VIA SUPERNATURAL ABILITIES GRANTED BY THE *BLACK MARK*.
APPARENTLY, A "MYSTERIOUS DRUG" HAS BEEN CIRCULATING AMONG THE PERPS.
OUR JOB IS TO GET TO THE BOTTOM OF THIS DRUG, ITS CONNECTION TO THE MAGAI CULT, AND THE RELATIONSHIP IT HAS WITH THE BLACK MARK, BEFORE THE PROBLEM GETS ANY BIGGER!
IF THERE'S ANYTHING YOU DON'T UNDERSTAND, ASK ABOUT IT NOW.
I CAN'T STAND PEOPLE WHO WILLINGLY REMAIN IN IGNORANCE OF THINGS!!
THOSE WHO HAVE QUESTIONS OR COMMENTS, RAISE YOUR HAND!
GOT IT!!?
WE GET IT, SO QUIT SHOUTIN'. WE'RE ON PUBLIC TRANSIT HERE, NEW CAPTAIN.

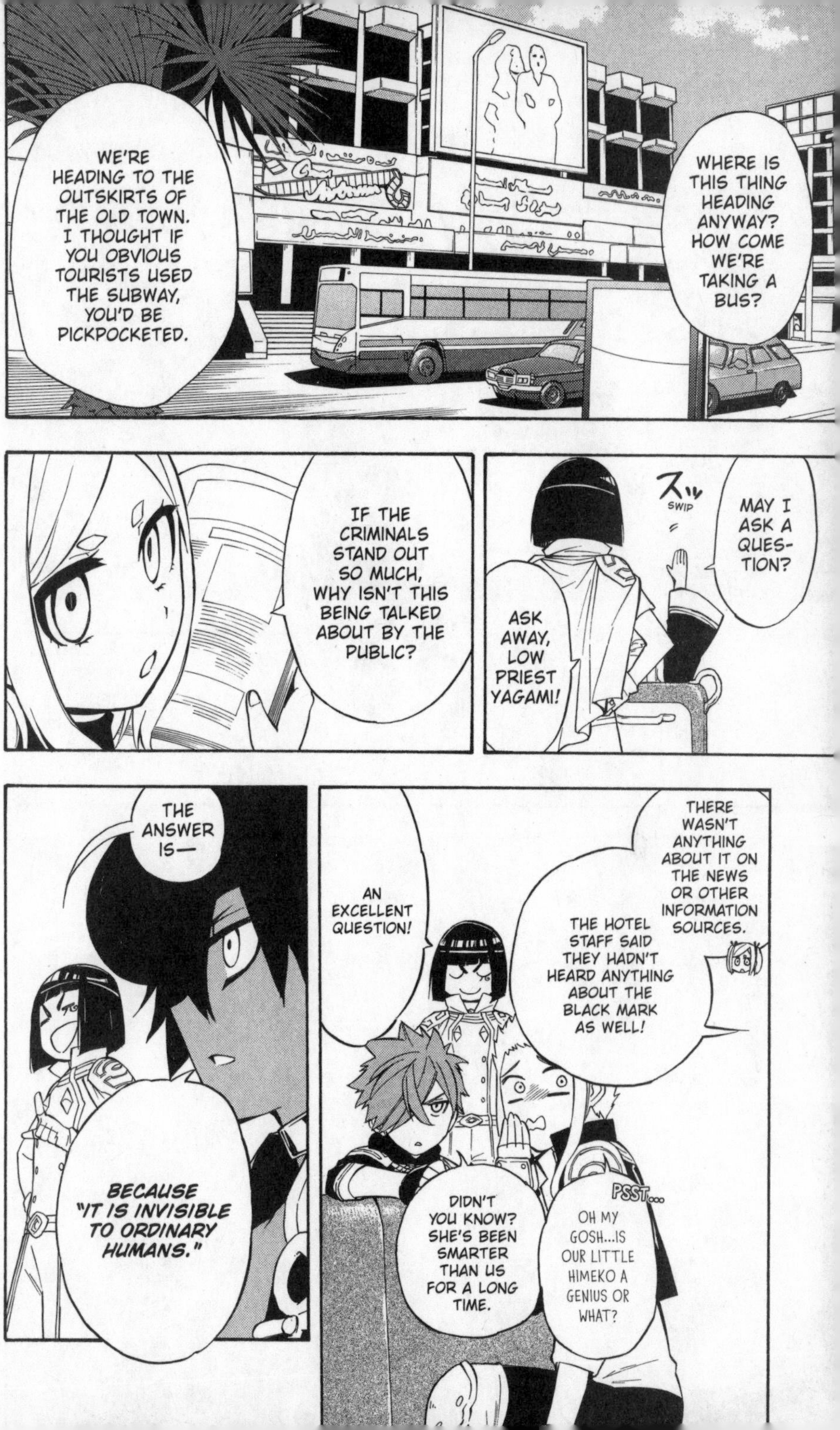
WHERE IS THIS THING HEADING ANYWAY? HOW COME WE'RE TAKING A BUS?
WE'RE HEADING TO THE OUTSKIRTS OF THE OLD TOWN. I THOUGHT IF YOU OBVIOUS TOURISTS USED THE SUBWAY, YOU'D BE PICKPOCKETED.
スッ SWIP
MAY I ASK A QUES-TION?
ASK AWAY, LOW PRIEST YAGAMI!
IF THE CRIMINALS STAND OUT SO MUCH, WHY ISN'T THIS BEING TALKED ABOUT BY THE PUBLIC?
THERE WASN'T ANYTHING ABOUT IT ON THE NEWS OR OTHER INFORMATION SOURCES.
THE HOTEL STAFF SAID THEY HADN'T HEARD ANYTHING ABOUT THE BLACK MARK AS WELL!
AN EXCELLENT QUESTION!
PSST...
OH MY GOSH...IS OUR LITTLE HIMEKO A GENIUS OR WHAT?
DIDN'T YOU KNOW? SHE'S BEEN SMARTER THAN US FOR A LONG TIME.
THE ANSWER IS—
BECAUSE "IT IS INVISIBLE TO ORDINARY HUMANS."

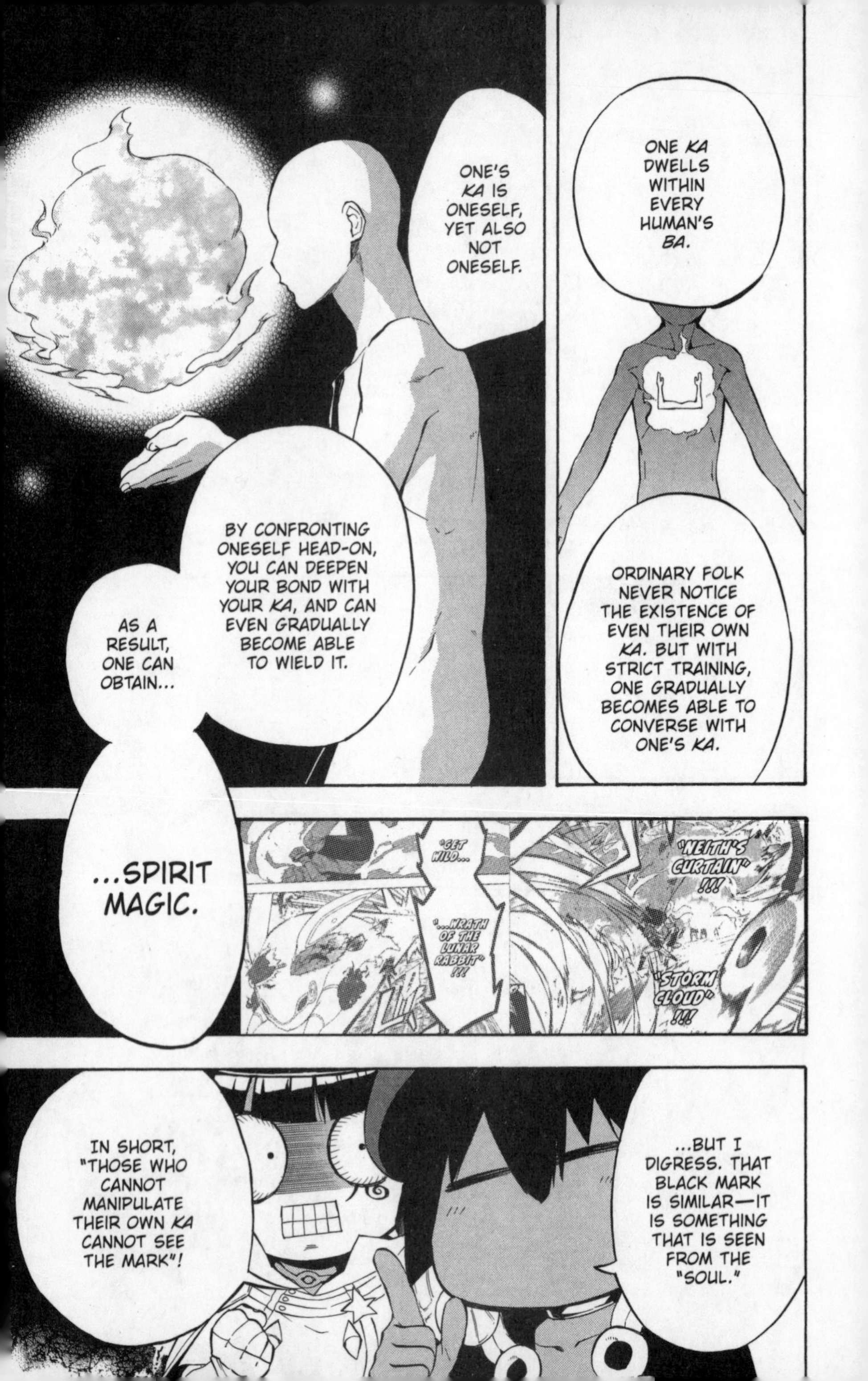
ONE KA DWELLS WITHIN EVERY HUMAN'S BA.
ORDINARY FOLK NEVER NOTICE THE EXISTENCE OF EVEN THEIR OWN KA. BUT WITH STRICT TRAINING, ONE GRADUALLY BECOMES ABLE TO CONVERSE WITH ONE'S KA.
ONE'S KA IS ONESELF, YET ALSO NOT ONESELF.
BY CONFRONTING ONESELF HEAD-ON, YOU CAN DEEPEN YOUR BOND WITH YOUR KA, AND CAN EVEN GRADUALLY BECOME ABLE TO WIELD IT.
AS A RESULT, ONE CAN OBTAIN...
...SPIRIT MAGIC.
"NEITH'S CURTAIN"!!!
"STORM CLOUD"!!!
"GET WILD...
"...WRATH OF THE LUNAR RABBIT"!!!
...BUT I DIGRESS. THAT BLACK MARK IS SIMILAR—IT IS SOMETHING THAT IS SEEN FROM THE "SOUL."
IN SHORT, "THOSE WHO CANNOT MANIPULATE THEIR OWN KA CANNOT SEE THE MARK"!

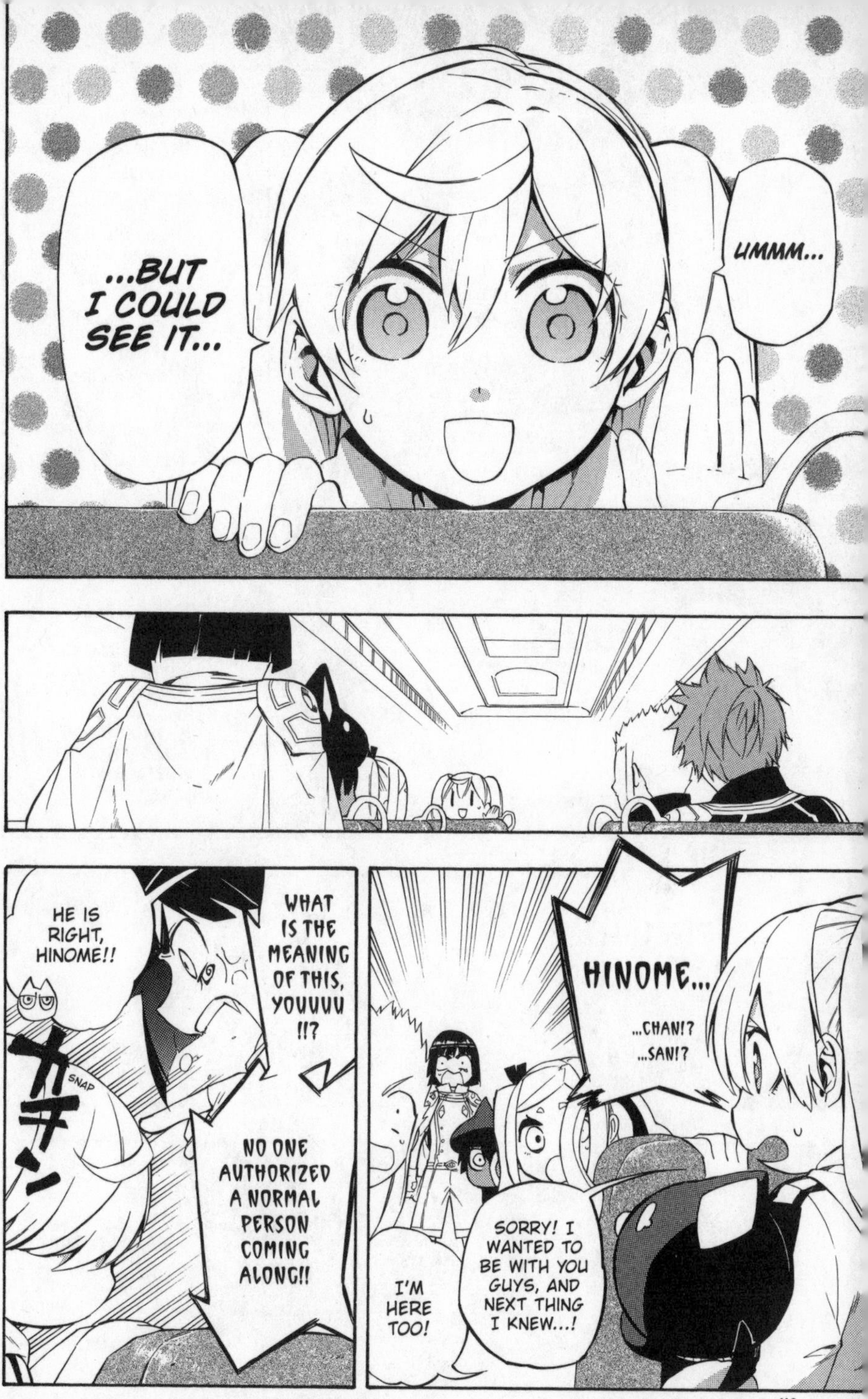
UMMM...
...BUT I COULD SEE IT...
HINOME...
...CHAN!? ...SAN!?
SORRY! I WANTED TO BE WITH YOU GUYS, AND NEXT THING I KNEW...!
I'M HERE TOO!
WHAT IS THE MEANING OF THIS, YOUUUU!!?
NO ONE AUTHORIZED A NORMAL PERSON COMING ALONG!!
HE IS RIGHT, HINOME!!
SNAP

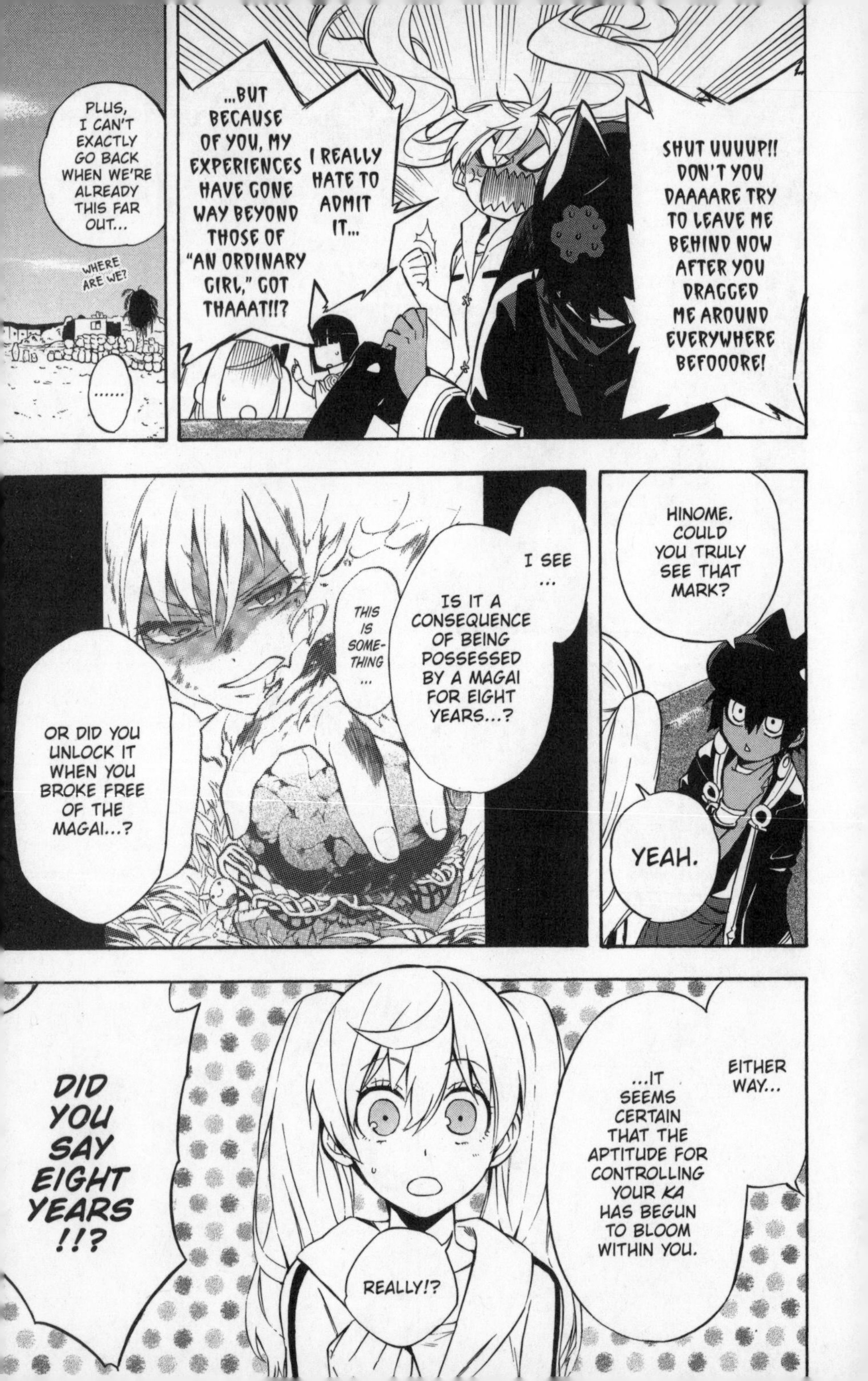
SHUT UUUUP!! DON'T YOU DAAAARE TRY TO LEAVE ME BEHIND NOW AFTER YOU DRAGGED ME AROUND EVERYWHERE BEFOOORE!
I REALLY HATE TO ADMIT IT...
...BUT BECAUSE OF YOU, MY EXPERIENCES HAVE GONE WAY BEYOND THOSE OF "AN ORDINARY GIRL," GOT THAAAT!!?
PLUS, I CAN'T EXACTLY GO BACK WHEN WE'RE ALREADY THIS FAR OUT...
WHERE ARE WE?
......
HINOME. COULD YOU TRULY SEE THAT MARK?
YEAH.
I SEE...
IS IT A CONSEQUENCE OF BEING POSSESSED BY A MAGAI FOR EIGHT YEARS...?
THIS IS SOMETHING...
OR DID YOU UNLOCK IT WHEN YOU BROKE FREE OF THE MAGAI...?
EITHER WAY...
...IT SEEMS CERTAIN THAT THE APTITUDE FOR CONTROLLING YOUR *KA* HAS BEGUN TO BLOOM WITHIN YOU.
REALLY!?
DID YOU SAY EIGHT YEARS!!?

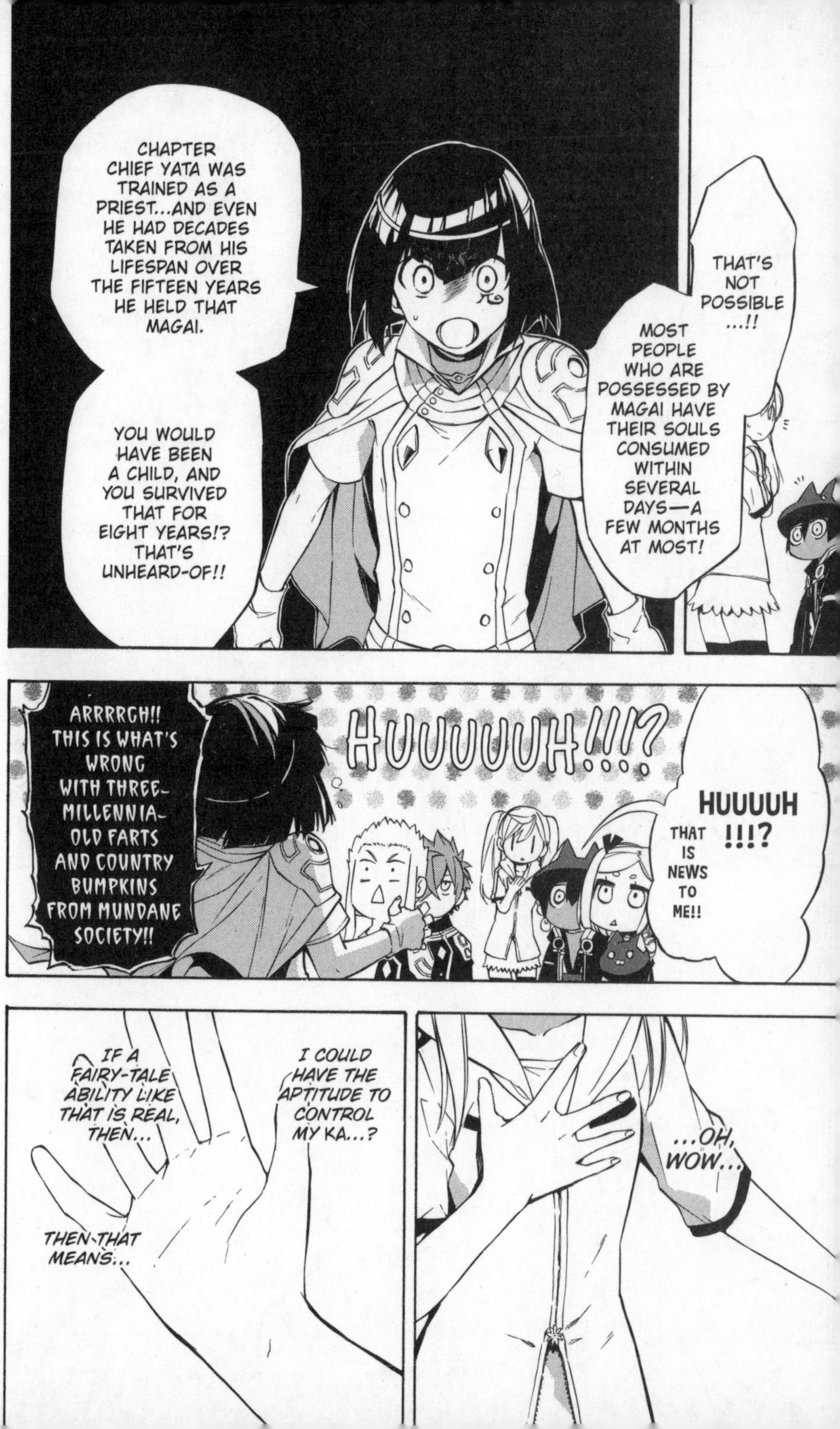
THAT'S NOT POSSIBLE...!!
MOST PEOPLE WHO ARE POSSESSED BY MAGAI HAVE THEIR SOULS CONSUMED WITHIN SEVERAL DAYS—A FEW MONTHS AT MOST!
CHAPTER CHIEF YATA WAS TRAINED AS A PRIEST...AND EVEN HE HAD DECADES TAKEN FROM HIS LIFESPAN OVER THE FIFTEEN YEARS HE HELD THAT MAGAI.
YOU WOULD HAVE BEEN A CHILD, AND YOU SURVIVED THAT FOR EIGHT YEARS!? THAT'S UNHEARD-OF!!
HUUUUH!!!? THAT IS NEWS TO ME!!
HUUUUUH!!!?
ARRRRGH!! THIS IS WHAT'S WRONG WITH THREE-MILLENNIA-OLD FARTS AND COUNTRY BUMPKINS FROM MUNDANE SOCIETY!!
...OH, WOW...
I COULD HAVE THE APTITUDE TO CONTROL MY KA...?
IF A FAIRY-TALE ABILITY LIKE THAT IS REAL, THEN...
THEN THAT MEANS...

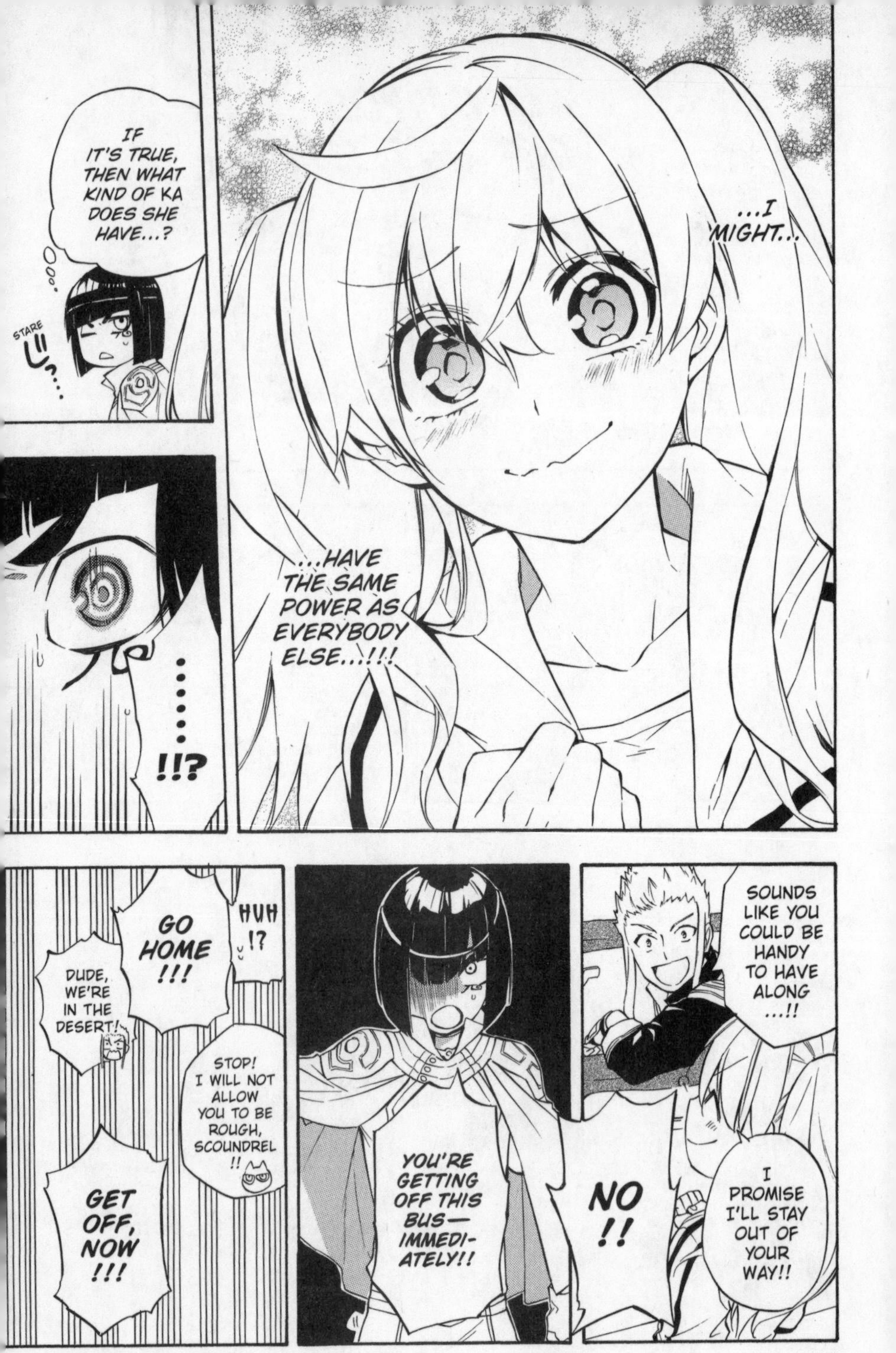
...I MIGHT...
...HAVE THE SAME POWER AS EVERYBODY ELSE...!!!
IF IT'S TRUE, THEN WHAT KIND OF KA DOES SHE HAVE...?
STARE
......
!!?
SOUNDS LIKE YOU COULD BE HANDY TO HAVE ALONG ...!!
I PROMISE I'LL STAY OUT OF YOUR WAY!!
NO !!
YOU'RE GETTING OFF THIS BUS—IMMEDI-ATELY!!
HUH !?
GO HOME !!!
DUDE, WE'RE IN THE DESERT!
STOP! I WILL NOT ALLOW YOU TO BE ROUGH, SCOUNDREL !!
GET OFF, NOW !!!

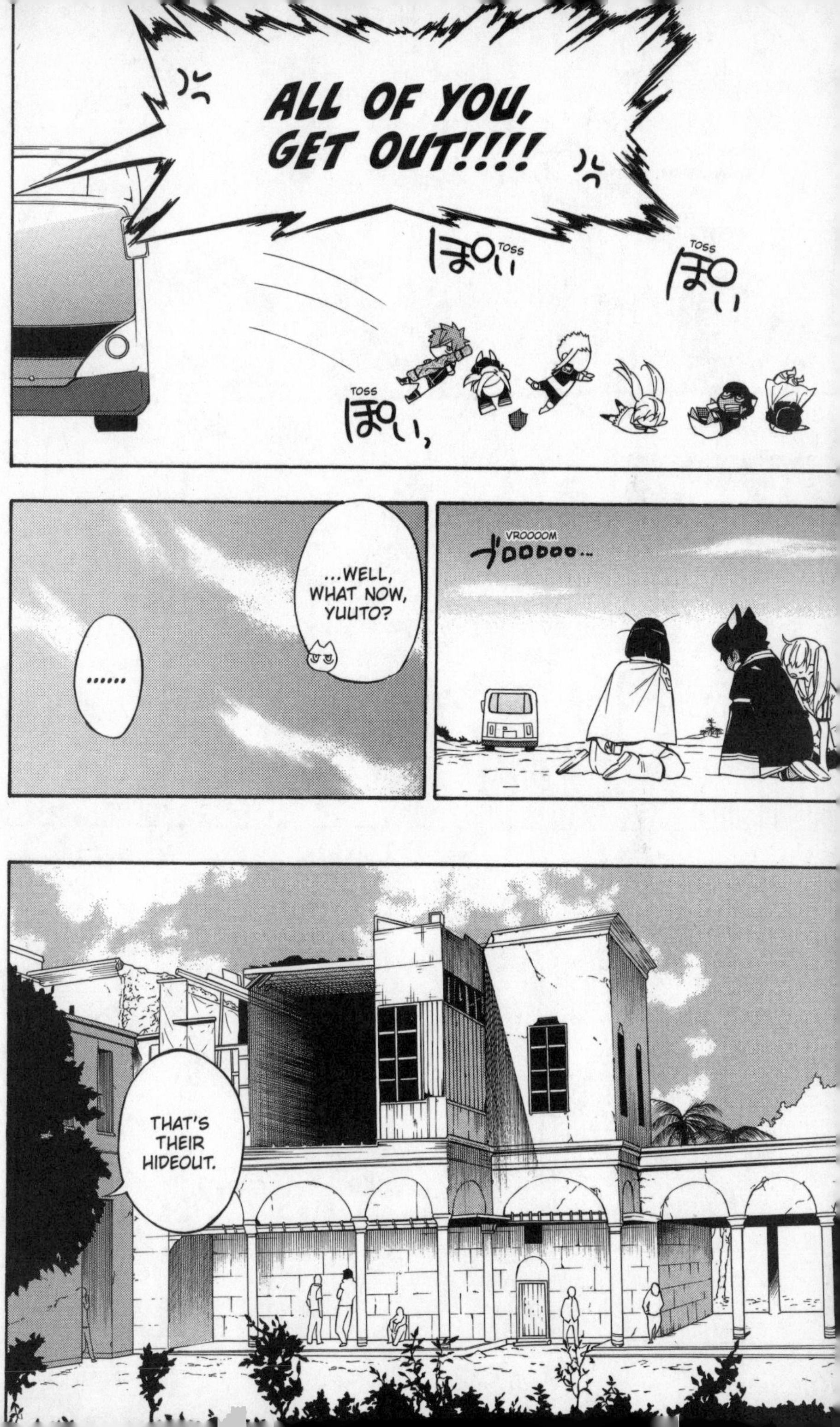
ALL OF YOU, GET OUT!!!!
ぽい
TOSS
ぽい
TOSS
ぽい,
TOSS
VROOOOM
...WELL, WHAT NOW, YUUTO?
....
THAT'S THEIR HIDEOUT.

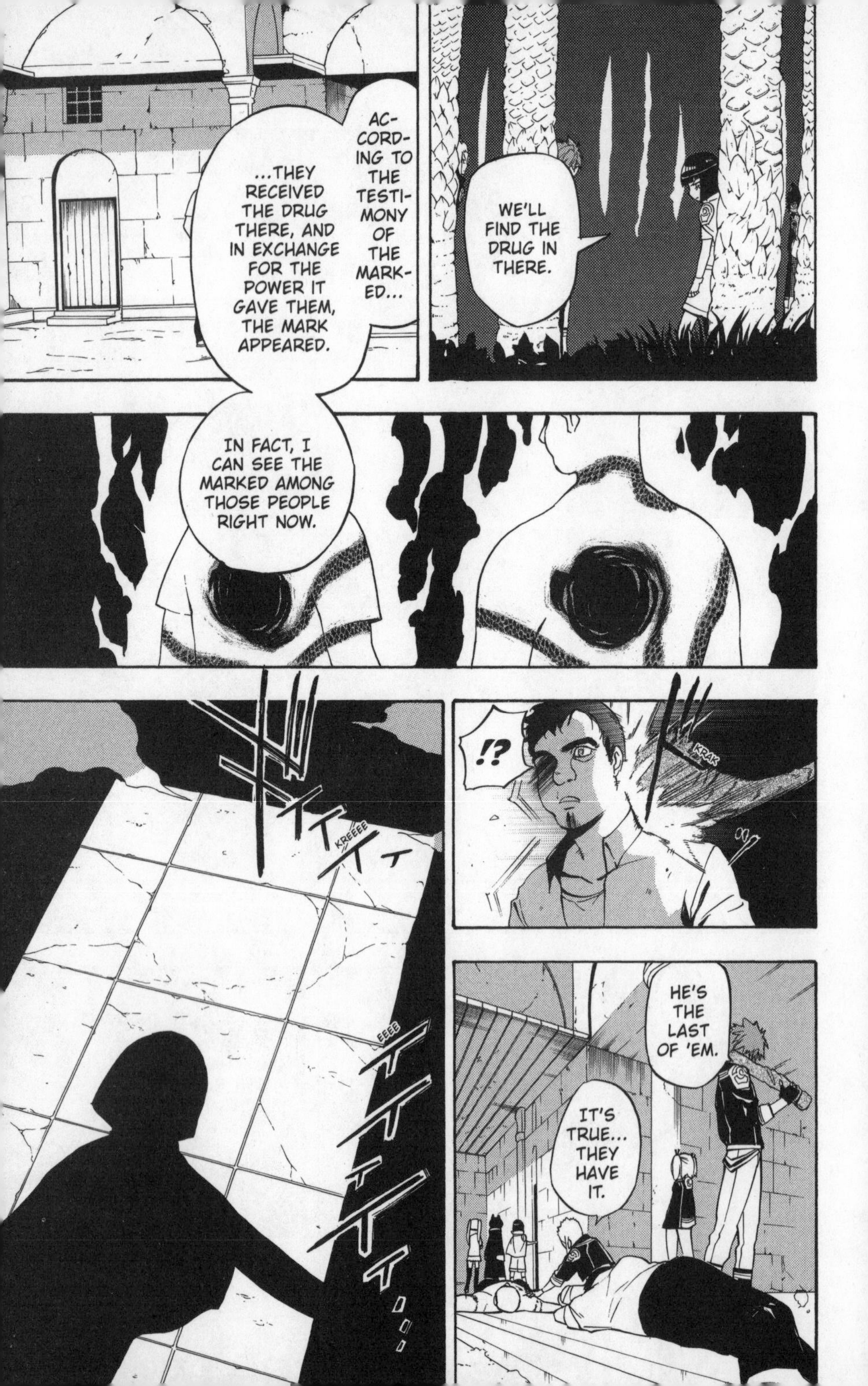
WE'LL FIND THE DRUG IN THERE.
AC-CORD-ING TO THE TESTI-MONY OF THE MARK-ED...
...THEY RECEIVED THE DRUG THERE, AND IN EXCHANGE FOR THE POWER IT GAVE THEM, THE MARK APPEARED.
IN FACT, I CAN SEE THE MARKED AMONG THOSE PEOPLE RIGHT NOW.
!?
KRAK
HE'S THE LAST OF 'EM.
IT'S TRUE... THEY HAVE IT.
KREEEE
EEEE

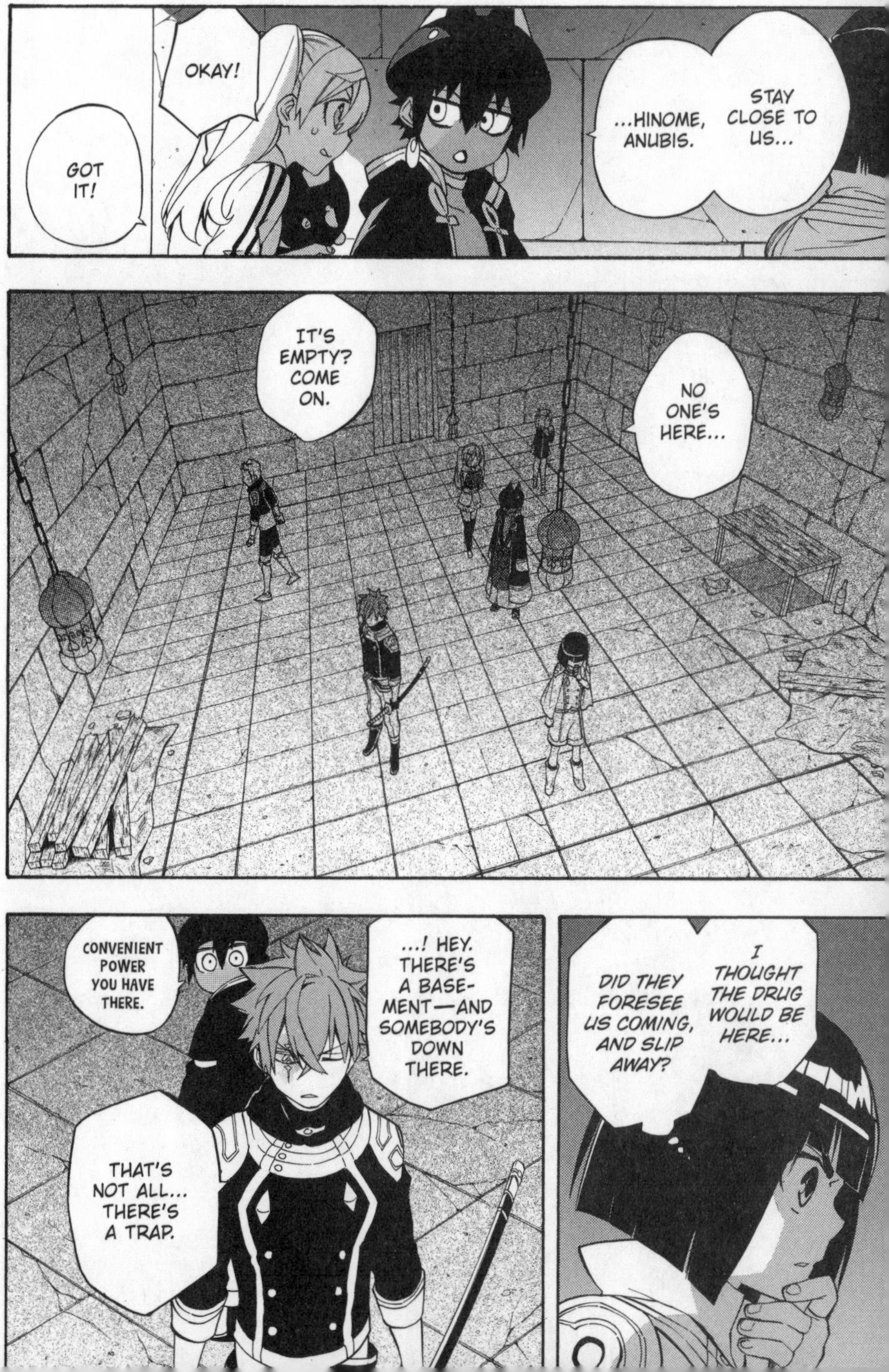
STAY CLOSE TO US...
...HINOME, ANUBIS.
OKAY!
GOT IT!
NO ONE'S HERE...
IT'S EMPTY? COME ON.
I THOUGHT THE DRUG WOULD BE HERE...
DID THEY FORESEE US COMING, AND SLIP AWAY?
...! HEY. THERE'S A BASE-MENT—AND SOMEBODY'S DOWN THERE.
CONVENIENT POWER YOU HAVE THERE.
THAT'S NOT ALL... THERE'S A TRAP.

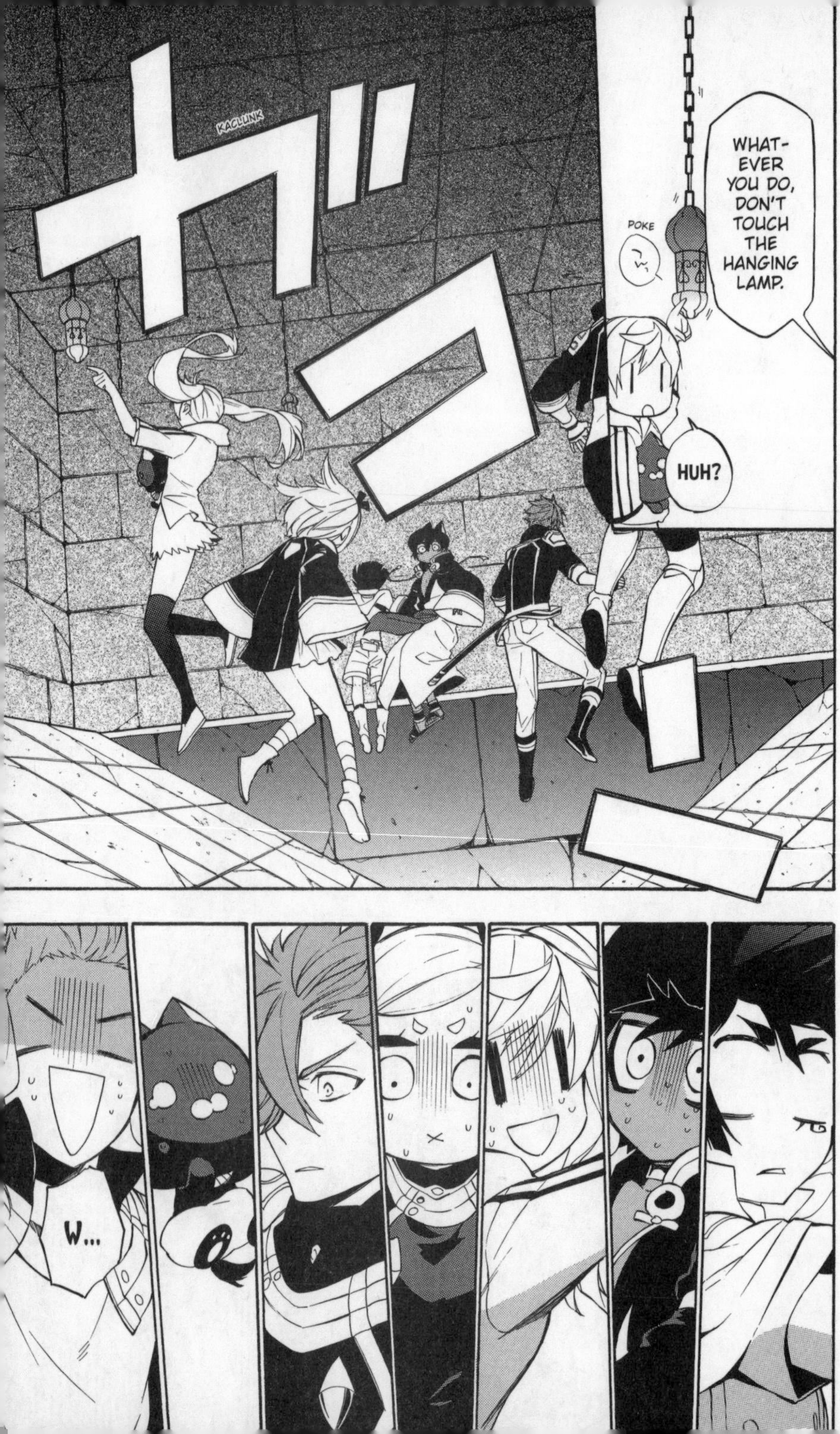
WHAT-EVER YOU DO, DON'T TOUCH THE HANGING LAMP.
POKE
HUH?
KACLUNK
W...

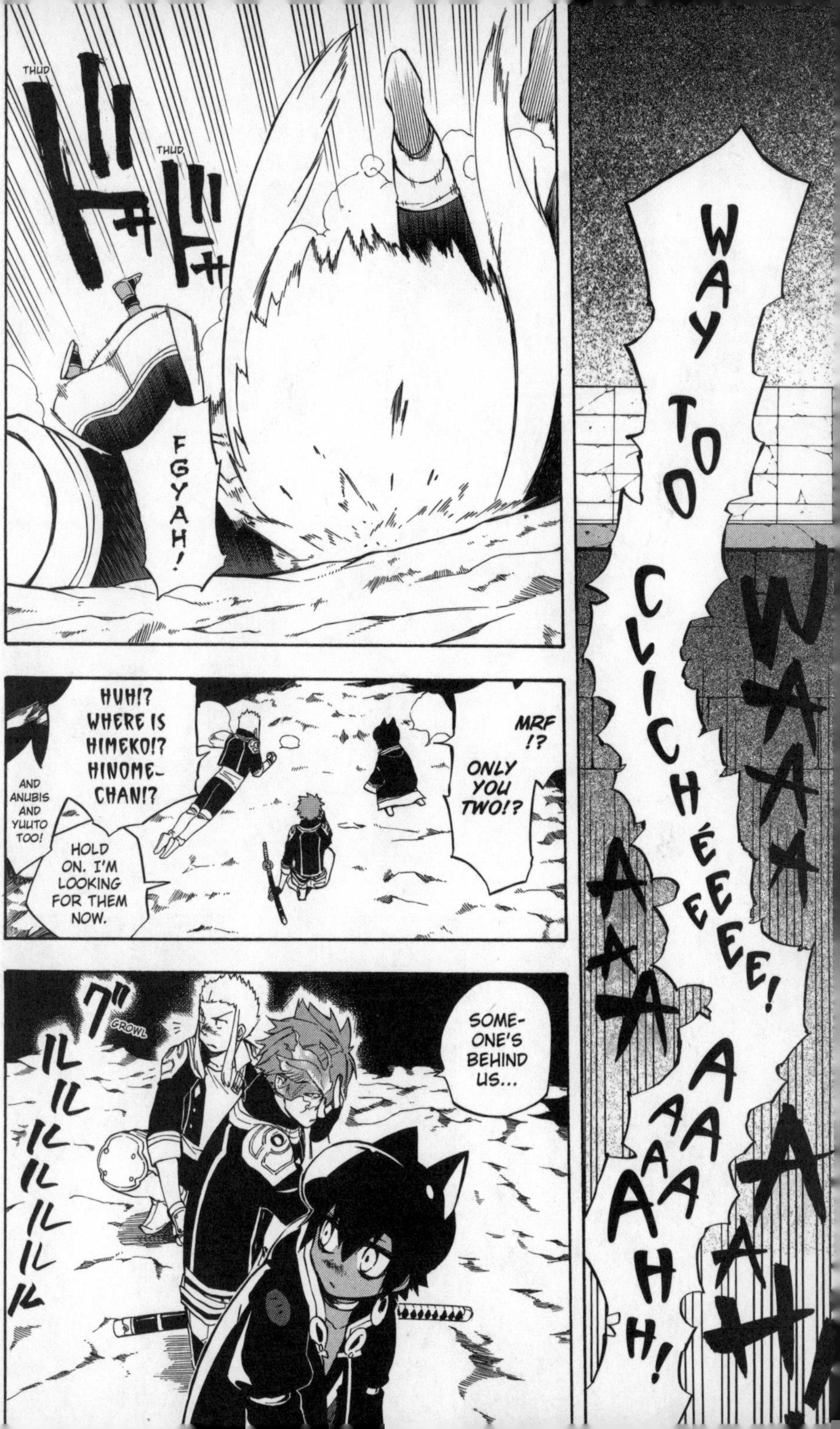
WAY TOO CLICHÉEEEEE!
WAAAAAAAH!
AAAAAAAHH!
THUD
THUD
FGYAH!
MRF!?
ONLY YOU TWO!?
HUH!? WHERE IS HIMEKO!? HINOME-CHAN!?
AND ANUBIS AND YUUTO TOO!
HOLD ON. I'M LOOKING FOR THEM NOW.
SOME-ONE'S BEHIND US...
GROWL

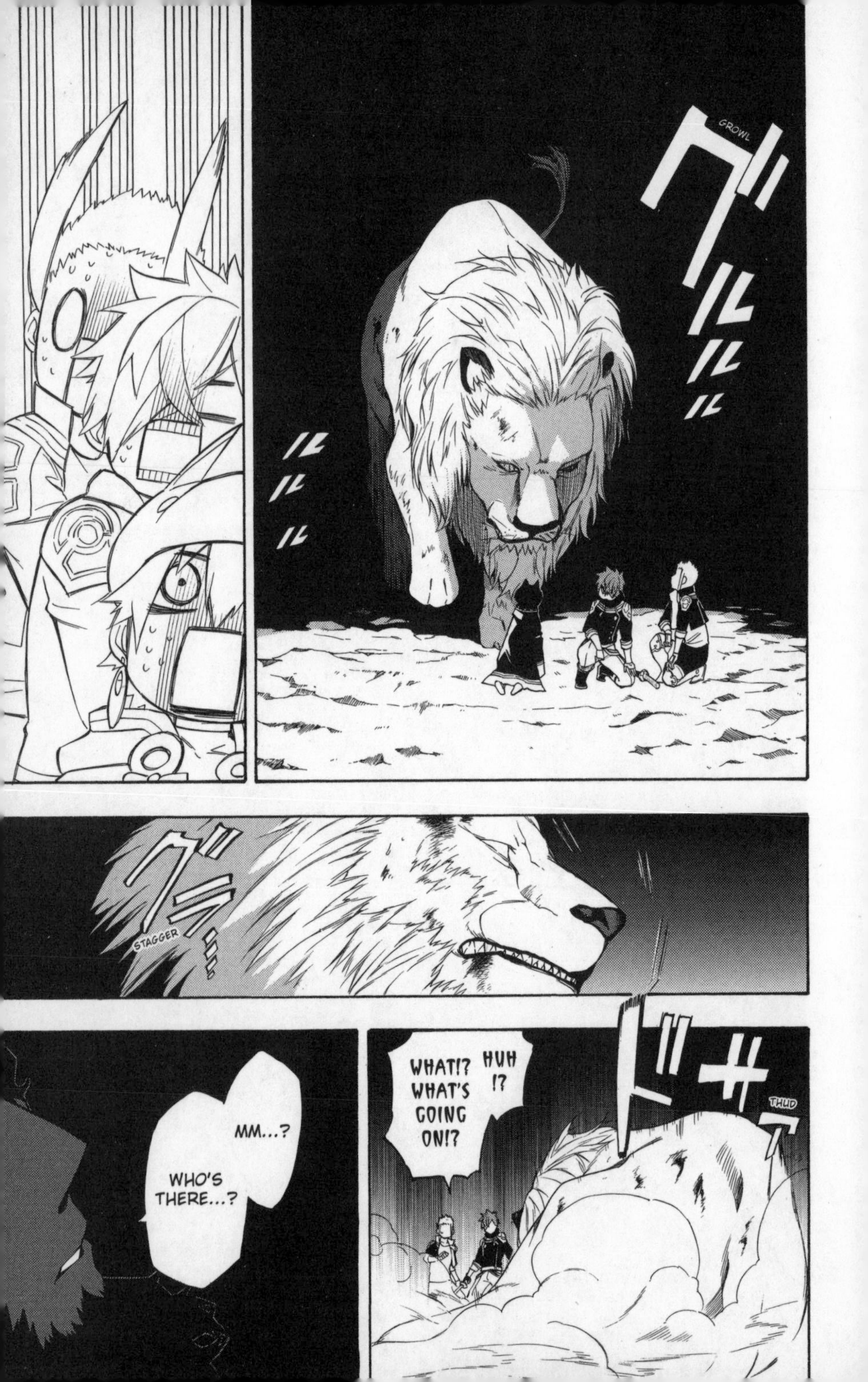
グルルル
GROWL
ルルル
グラ…
STAGGER
ドサッ
THUD
HUH !?
WHAT!? WHAT'S GOING ON!?
MM...?
WHO'S THERE...?

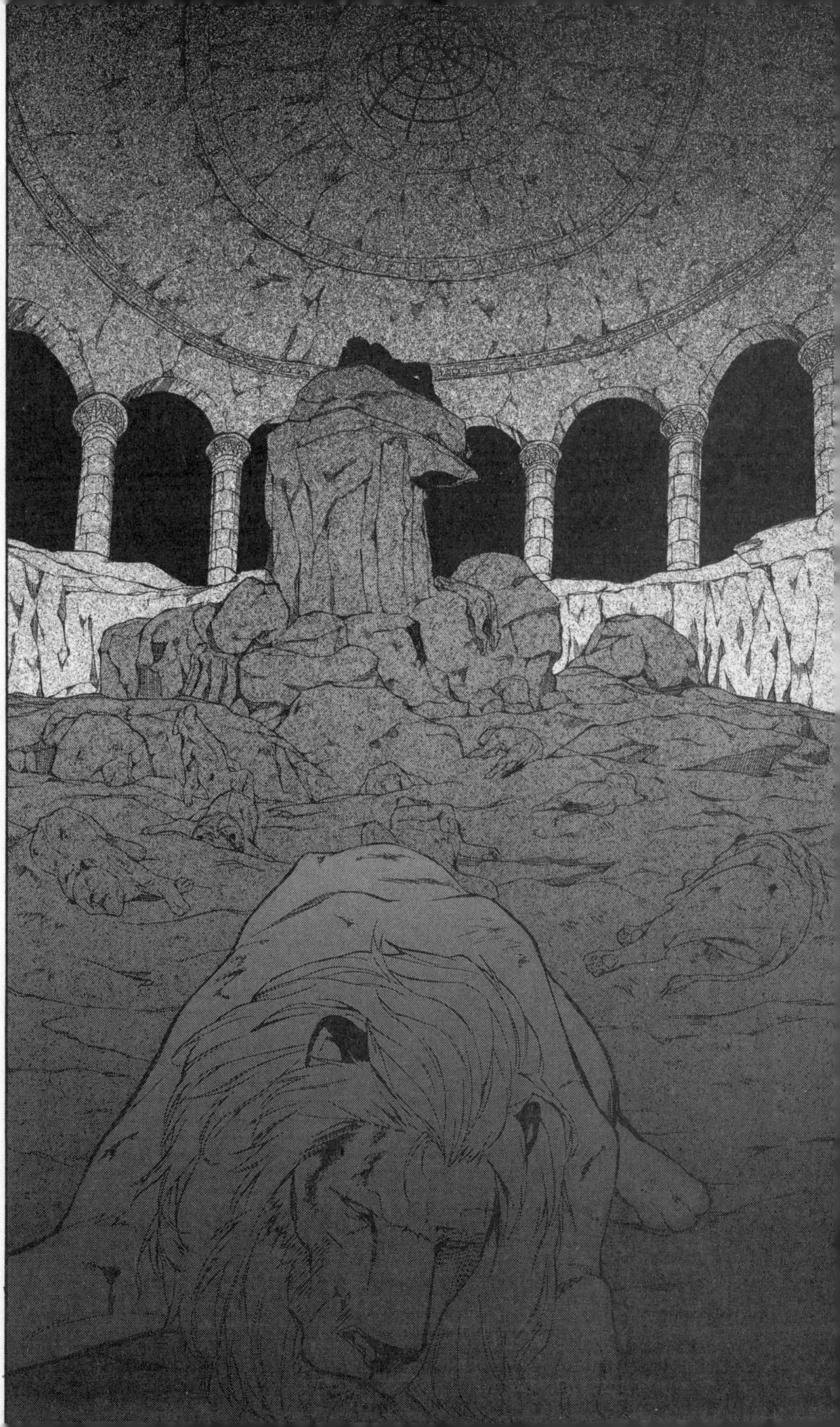

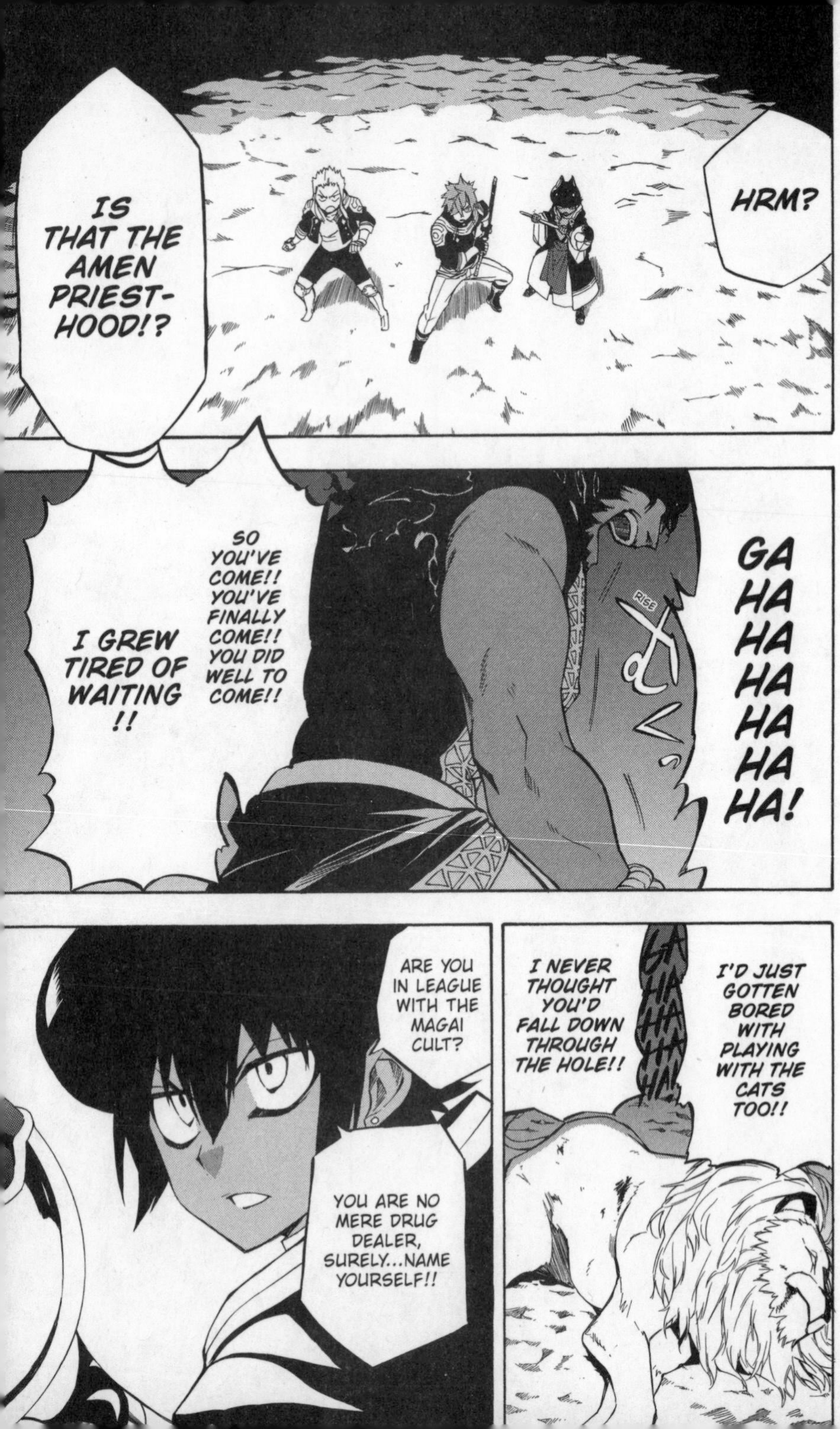
HRM?
IS THAT THE AMEN PRIEST-HOOD!?
GA HA HA HA HA HA HA!
SO YOU'VE COME!! YOU'VE FINALLY COME!! YOU DID WELL TO COME!!
I GREW TIRED OF WAITING!!
I'D JUST GOTTEN BORED WITH PLAYING WITH THE CATS TOO!!
I NEVER THOUGHT YOU'D FALL DOWN THROUGH THE HOLE!!
ARE YOU IN LEAGUE WITH THE MAGAI CULT?
YOU ARE NO MERE DRUG DEALER, SURELY...NAME YOURSELF!!

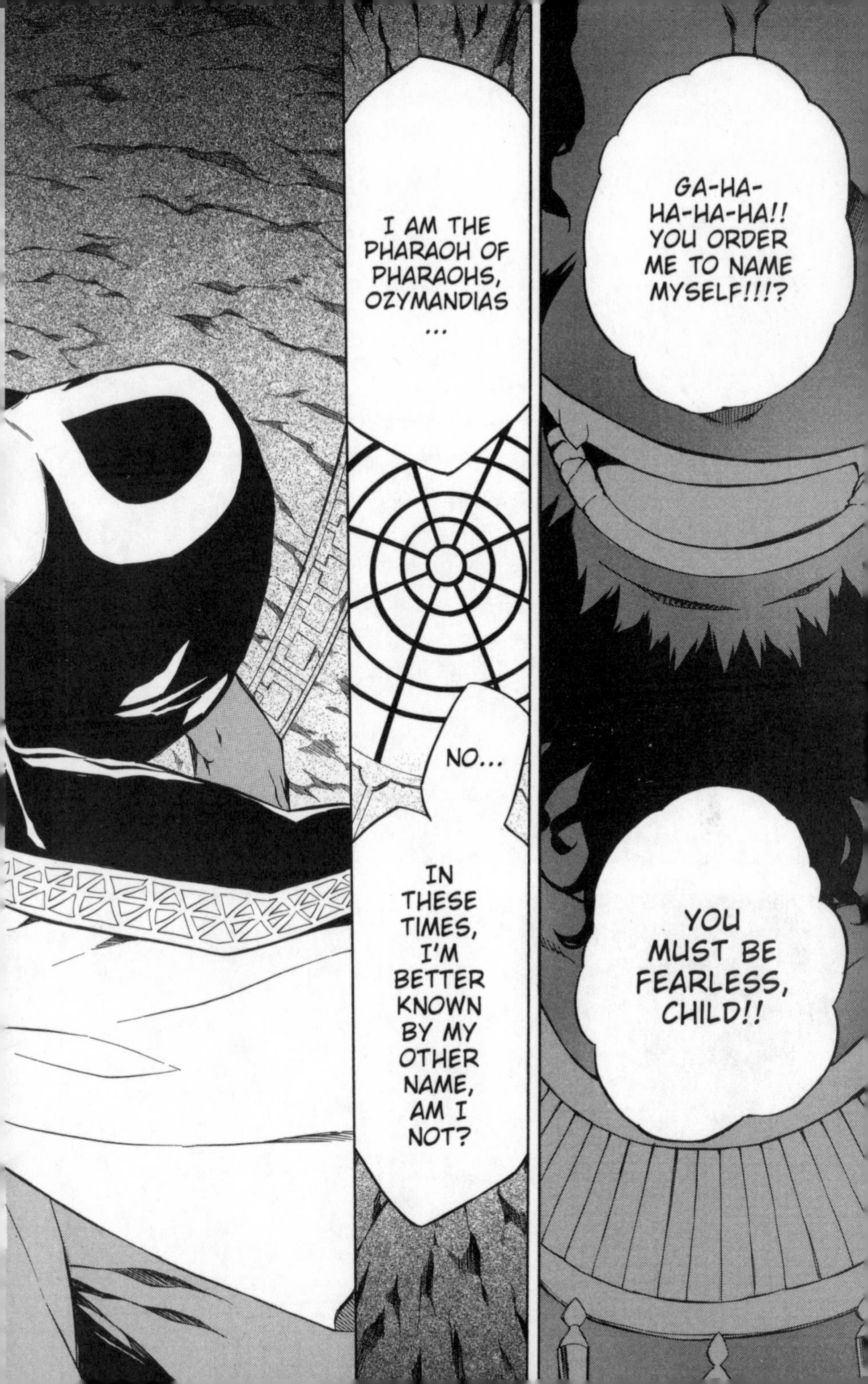
GA-HA-HA-HA-HA!! YOU ORDER ME TO NAME MYSELF!!!?
YOU MUST BE FEARLESS, CHILD!!
I AM THE PHARAOH OF PHARAOHS, OZYMANDIAS...
NO...
IN THESE TIMES, I'M BETTER KNOWN BY MY OTHER NAME, AM I NOT?

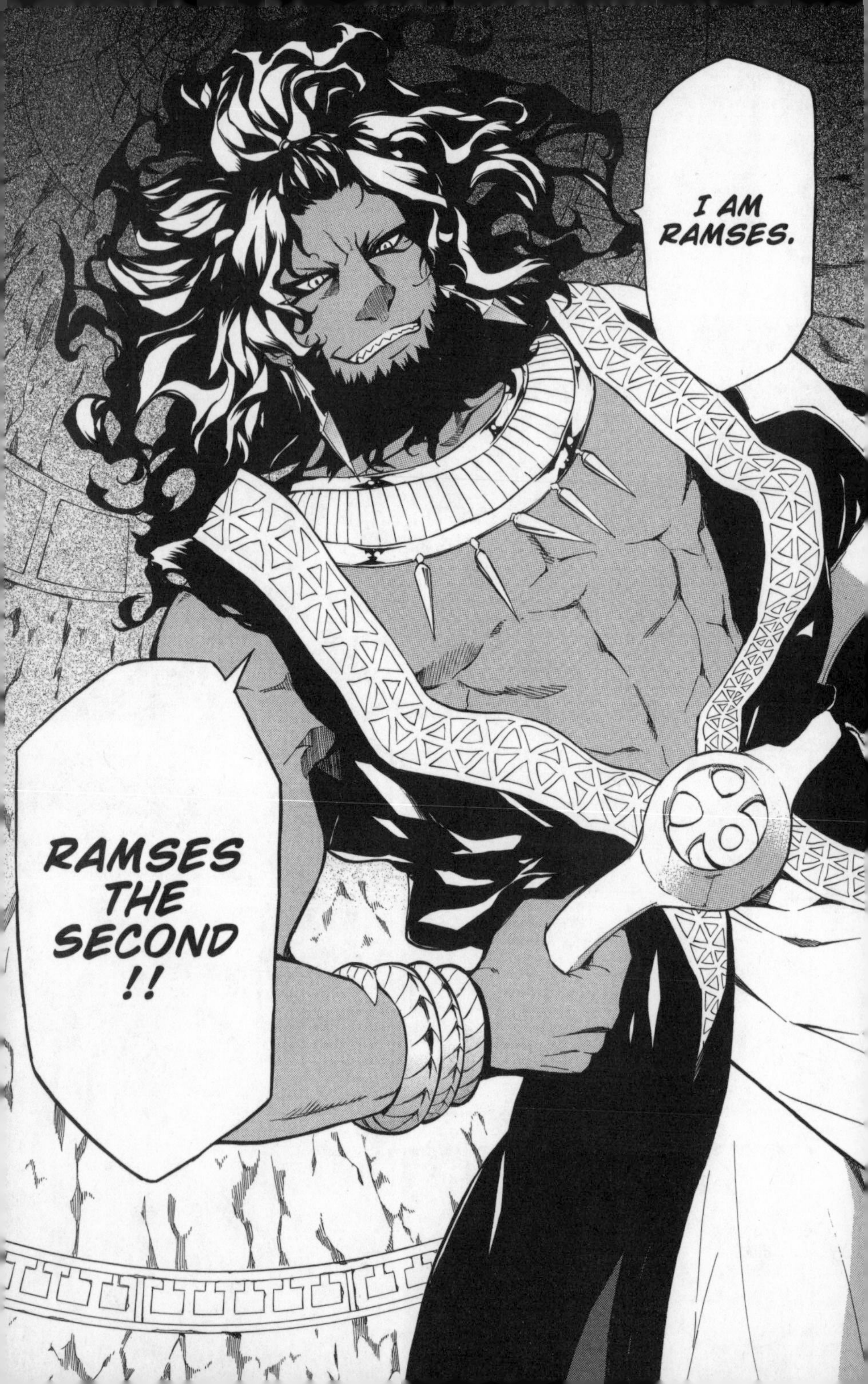
I AM RAMSES.
RAMSES THE SECOND !!

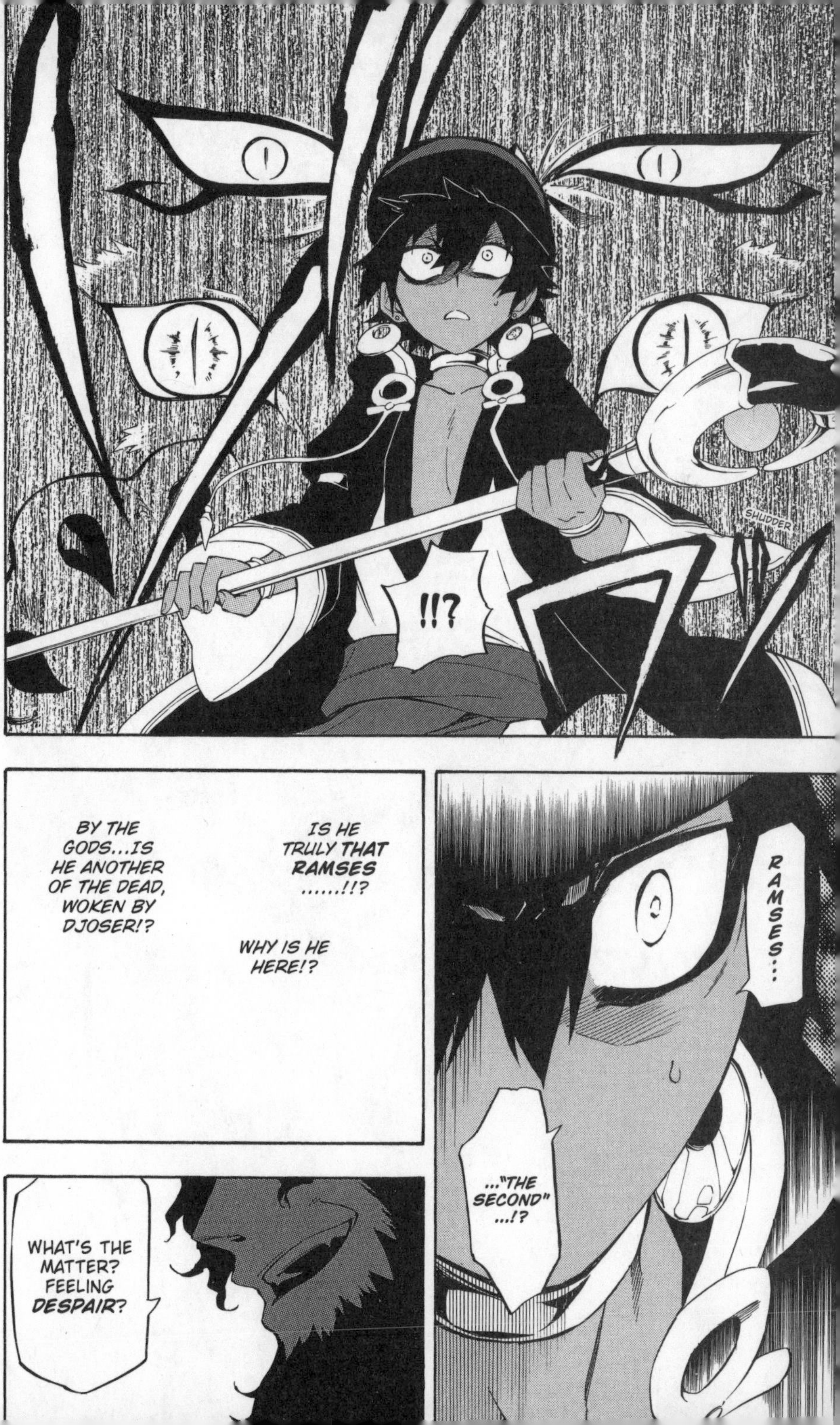
SHUDDER
!!?
RAMSES...
..."THE SECOND" ...!?
IS HE TRULY THAT RAMSES ......!!?
BY THE GODS...IS HE ANOTHER OF THE DEAD, WOKEN BY DJOSER!?
WHY IS HE HERE!?
WHAT'S THE MATTER? FEELING DESPAIR?

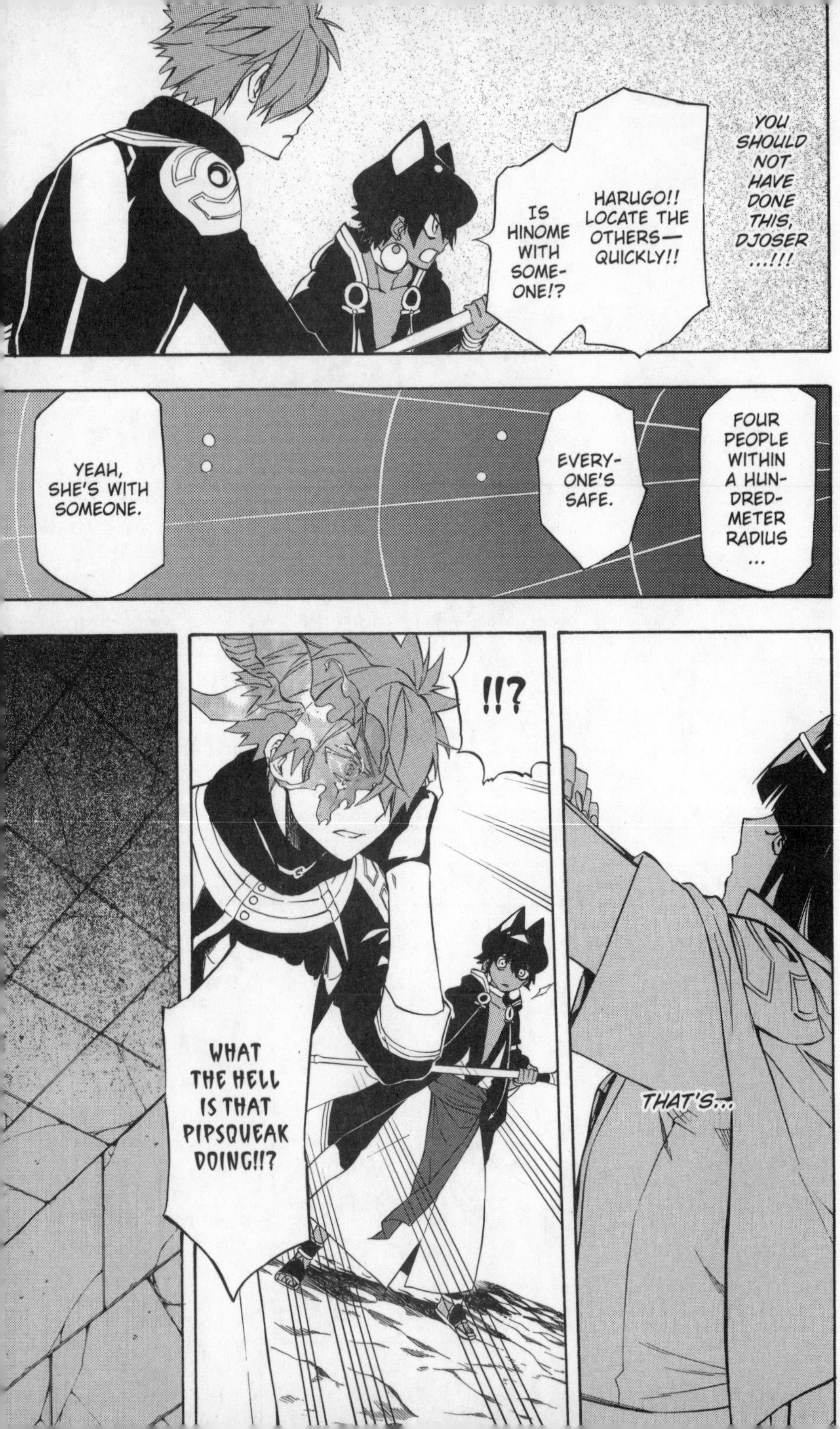
YOU SHOULD NOT HAVE DONE THIS, DJOSER ...!!!
HARUGO!! LOCATE THE OTHERS—QUICKLY!!
IS HINOME WITH SOME-ONE!?
FOUR PEOPLE WITHIN A HUN-DRED-METER RADIUS ...
EVERY-ONE'S SAFE.
YEAH, SHE'S WITH SOMEONE.
THAT'S...
!!?
WHAT THE HELL IS THAT PIPSQUEAK DOING!!?

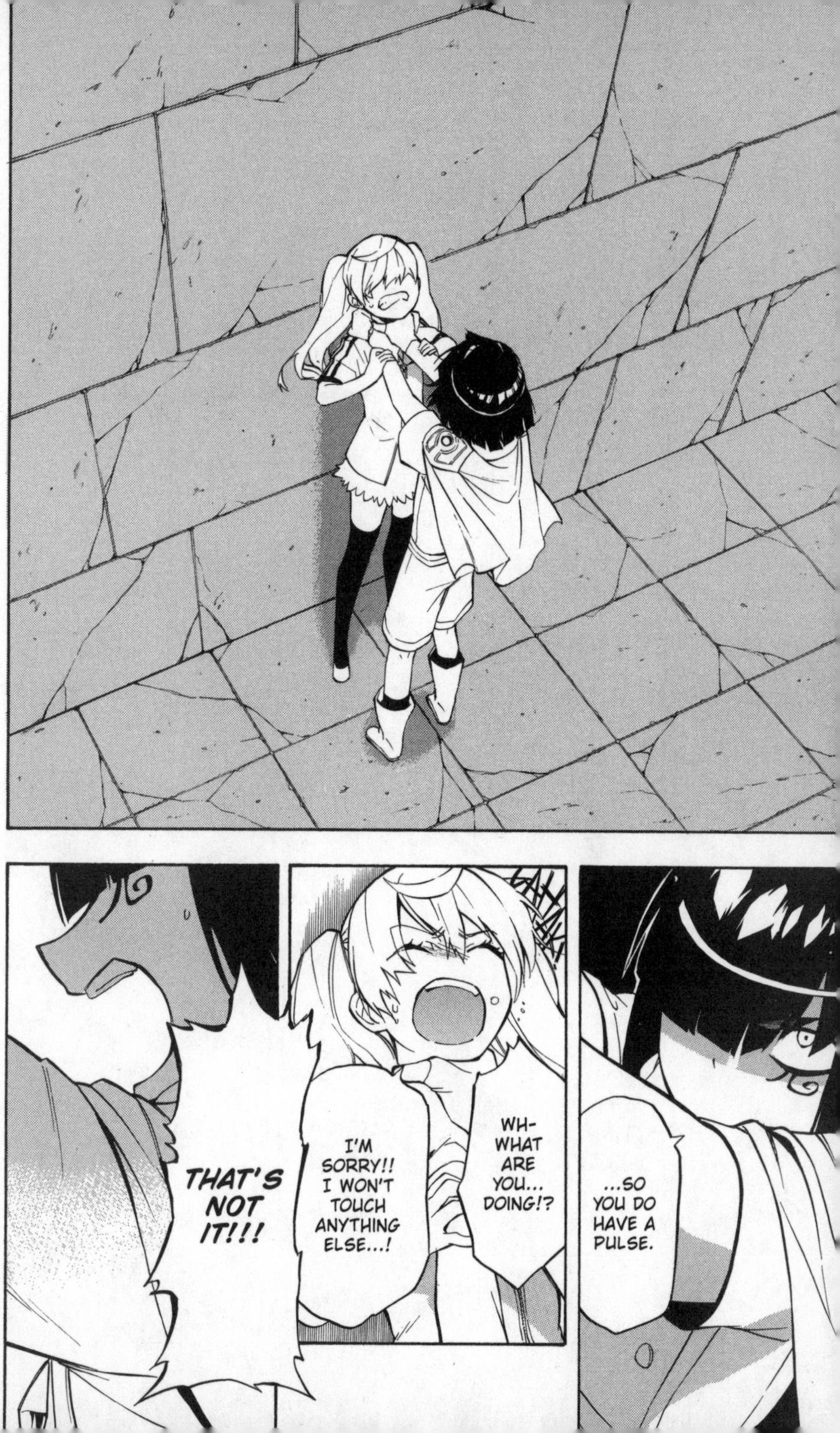
...SO YOU DO HAVE A PULSE.
WH- WHAT ARE YOU... DOING!?
I'M SORRY!! I WON'T TOUCH ANYTHING ELSE...!
THAT'S NOT IT!!!

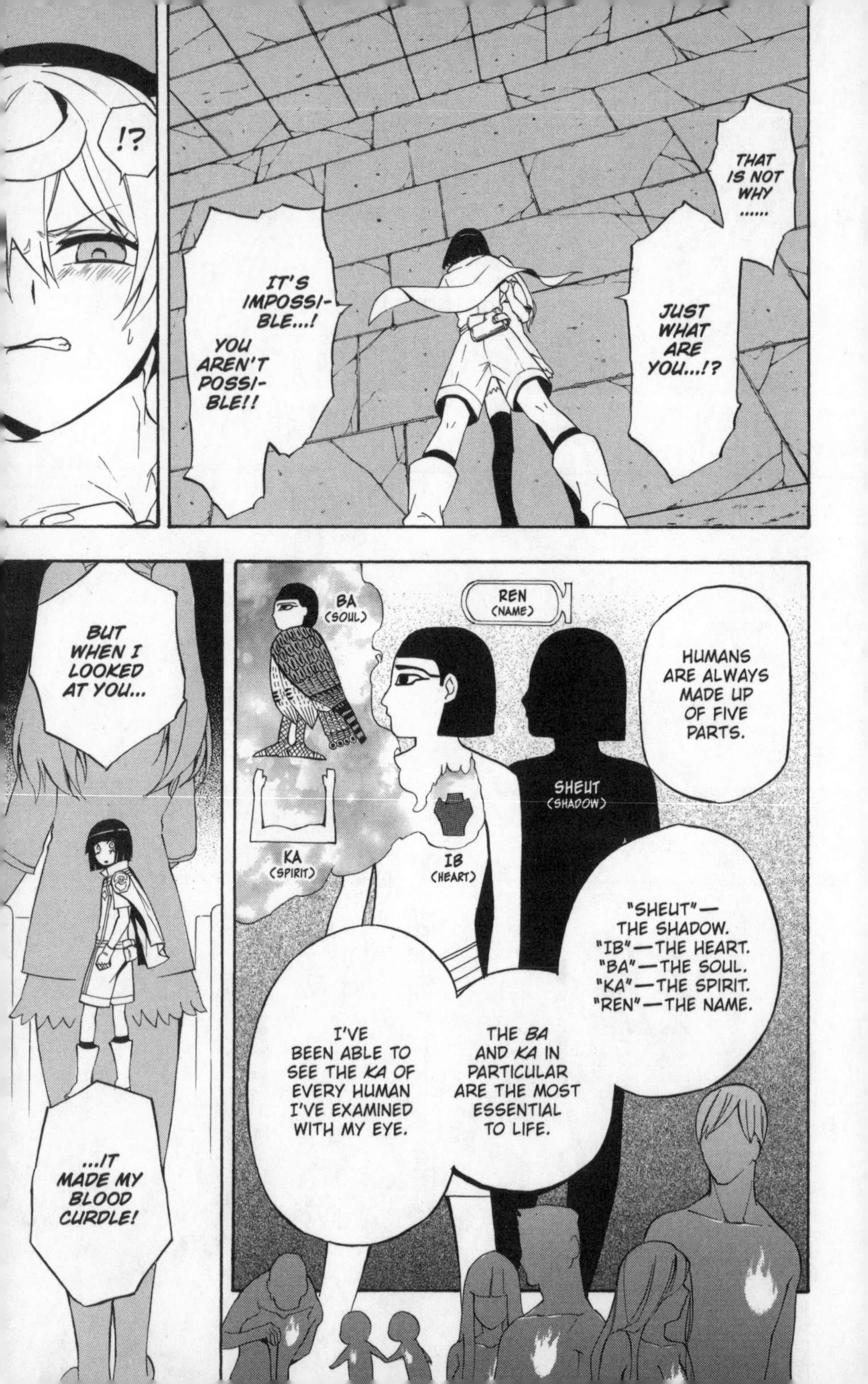
THAT IS NOT WHY ......
JUST WHAT ARE YOU...!?
IT'S IMPOSSI-BLE...!
YOU AREN'T POSSI-BLE!!
!?
HUMANS ARE ALWAYS MADE UP OF FIVE PARTS.
REN (NAME)
BA (SOUL)
SHEUT (SHADOW)
IB (HEART)
KA (SPIRIT)
"SHEUT"—THE SHADOW. "IB"—THE HEART. "BA"—THE SOUL. "KA"—THE SPIRIT. "REN"—THE NAME.
THE BA AND KA IN PARTICULAR ARE THE MOST ESSENTIAL TO LIFE.
I'VE BEEN ABLE TO SEE THE KA OF EVERY HUMAN I'VE EXAMINED WITH MY EYE.
BUT WHEN I LOOKED AT YOU...
...IT MADE MY BLOOD CURDLE!

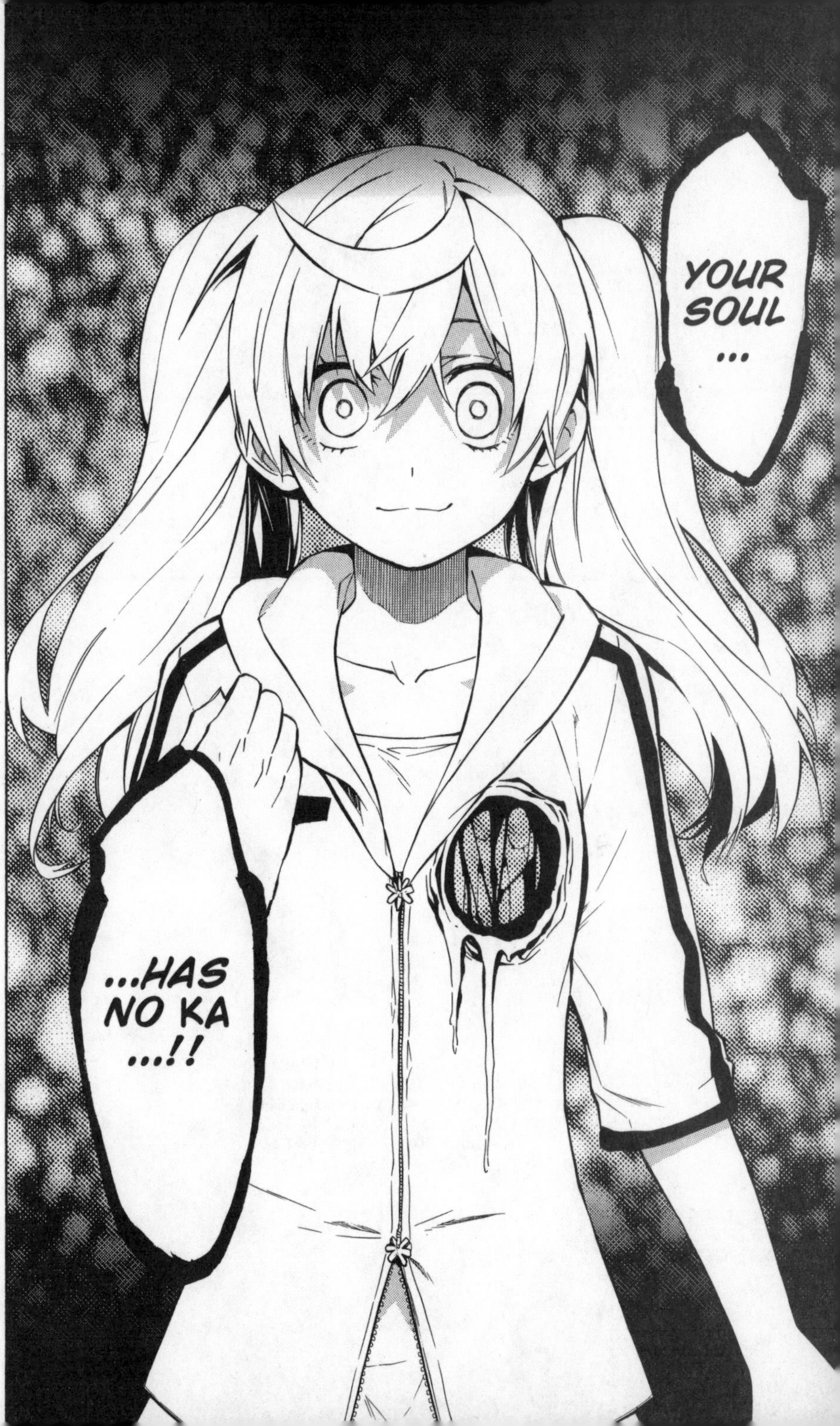
YOUR SOUL ...
...HAS NO KA ...!!

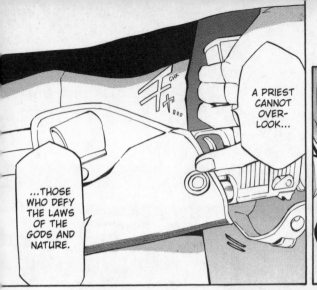

A PRIEST CANNOT OVERLOOK...

...THOSE WHO DEFY THE LAWS OF THE GODS AND NATURE.

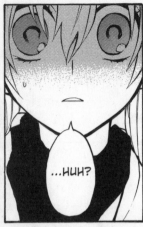

...HUH?

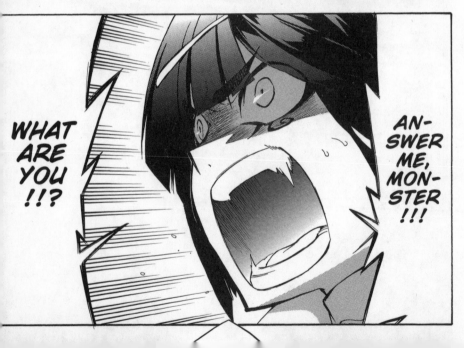

WHAT ARE YOU!!?

ANSWER ME, MONSTER!!!

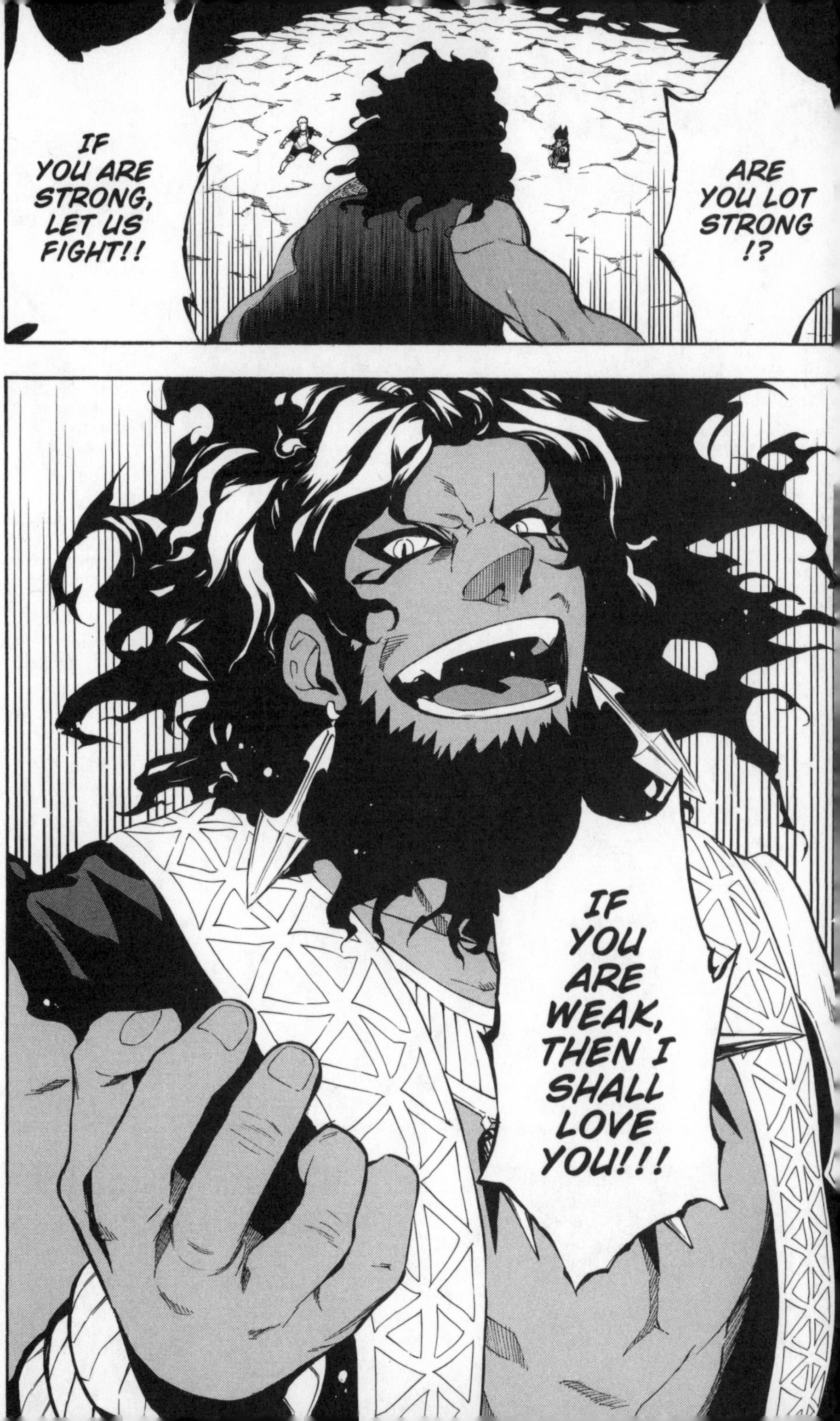
ARE YOU LOT STRONG !?
IF YOU ARE STRONG, LET US FIGHT!!
IF YOU ARE WEAK, THEN I SHALL LOVE YOU!!!

MEANWHILE, HIMEKO & ANUBIS

WAAAAH!
どてち────ん
KERSPLAT
OH NO...! WE'VE BEEN SEPARATED FROM THE OTHERS.
BOO-HOOOO... I'M SCARED... IT'S DAAARK...
AH!
AH!
SO SMALL...
HE...
...NEEDS MY PROTECTION ...!!!
SHE...

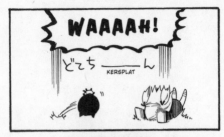

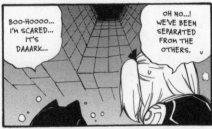

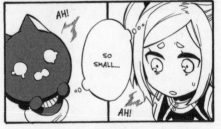

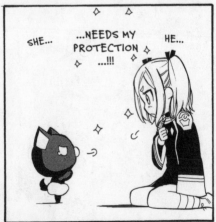

THEIR HEARTS HAD BECOME ONE.

A SLIGHTLY EARLY

Special Thanks!

- Arisa Yukimiya
- Ui Kizuki
- Mai Kurozuki

SPECIAL HELP FROM:

- You Omura-sensei (Thank you so much for offering your photos from a trip to Egypt!!)
- Shinome-san
- Makoto Kisaragi-san

My editor, Yuuichi Shimomura-sama

森下真
Morishita Makoto

⇦ KEEP READING FOR MORE OF THE MAIN STORY!!!

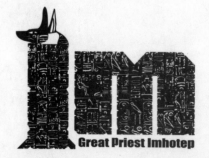
Great Priest Imhotep

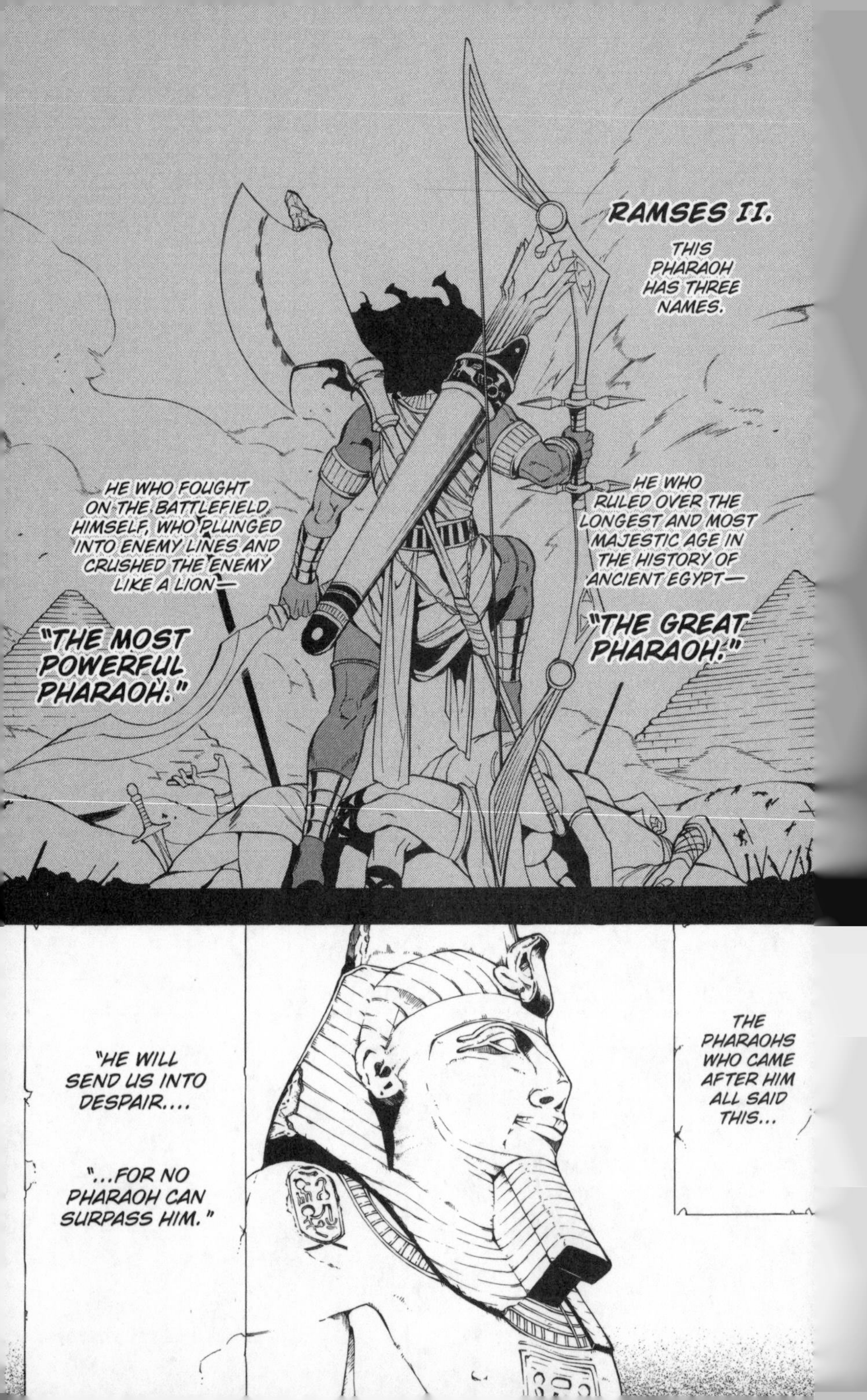
RAMSES II.
THIS PHARAOH HAS THREE NAMES.
HE WHO RULED OVER THE LONGEST AND MOST MAJESTIC AGE IN THE HISTORY OF ANCIENT EGYPT—
"THE GREAT PHARAOH."
HE WHO FOUGHT ON THE BATTLEFIELD HIMSELF, WHO PLUNGED INTO ENEMY LINES AND CRUSHED THE ENEMY LIKE A LION—
"THE MOST POWERFUL PHARAOH."
THE PHARAOHS WHO CAME AFTER HIM ALL SAID THIS...
"HE WILL SEND US INTO DESPAIR....
"...FOR NO PHARAOH CAN SURPASS HIM."

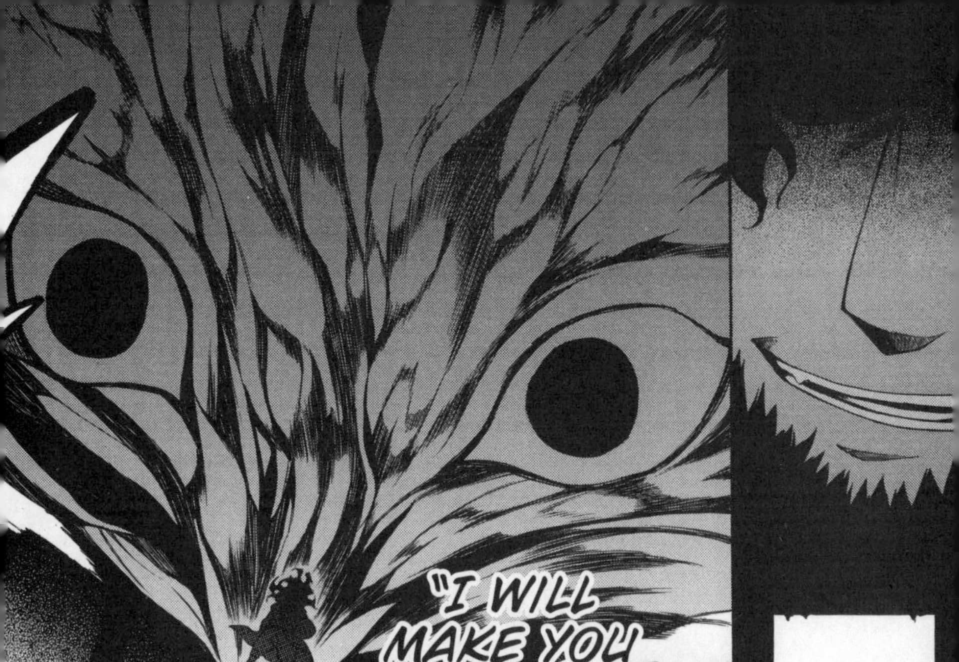
THE KING HIMSELF HAD LEFT THIS MESSAGE IN HISTORY—
"I WILL MAKE YOU DESPAIR."

SCROLL 23: SUN'S BUD, HINOME

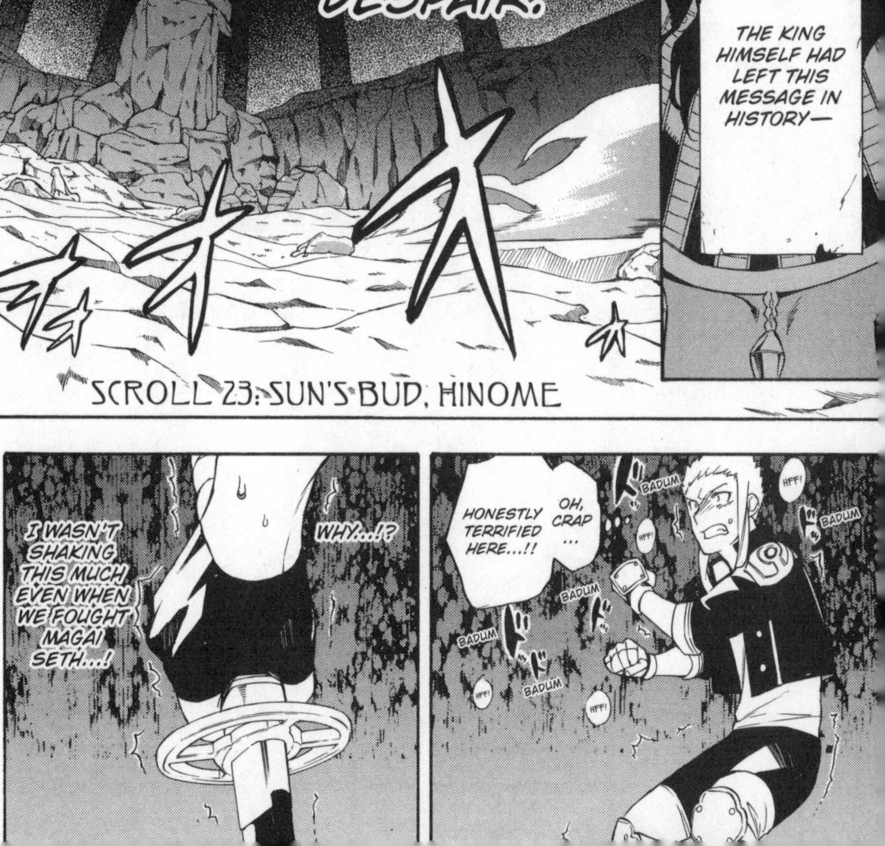
HFF!
BADUM
BADUM
HFF!
OH, CRAP...
HONESTLY TERRIFIED HERE...!!
BADUM
BADUM
BADUM
HFF!
HFF!
WHY...!?
I WASN'T SHAKING THIS MUCH EVEN WHEN WE FOUGHT MAGAI SETH...!

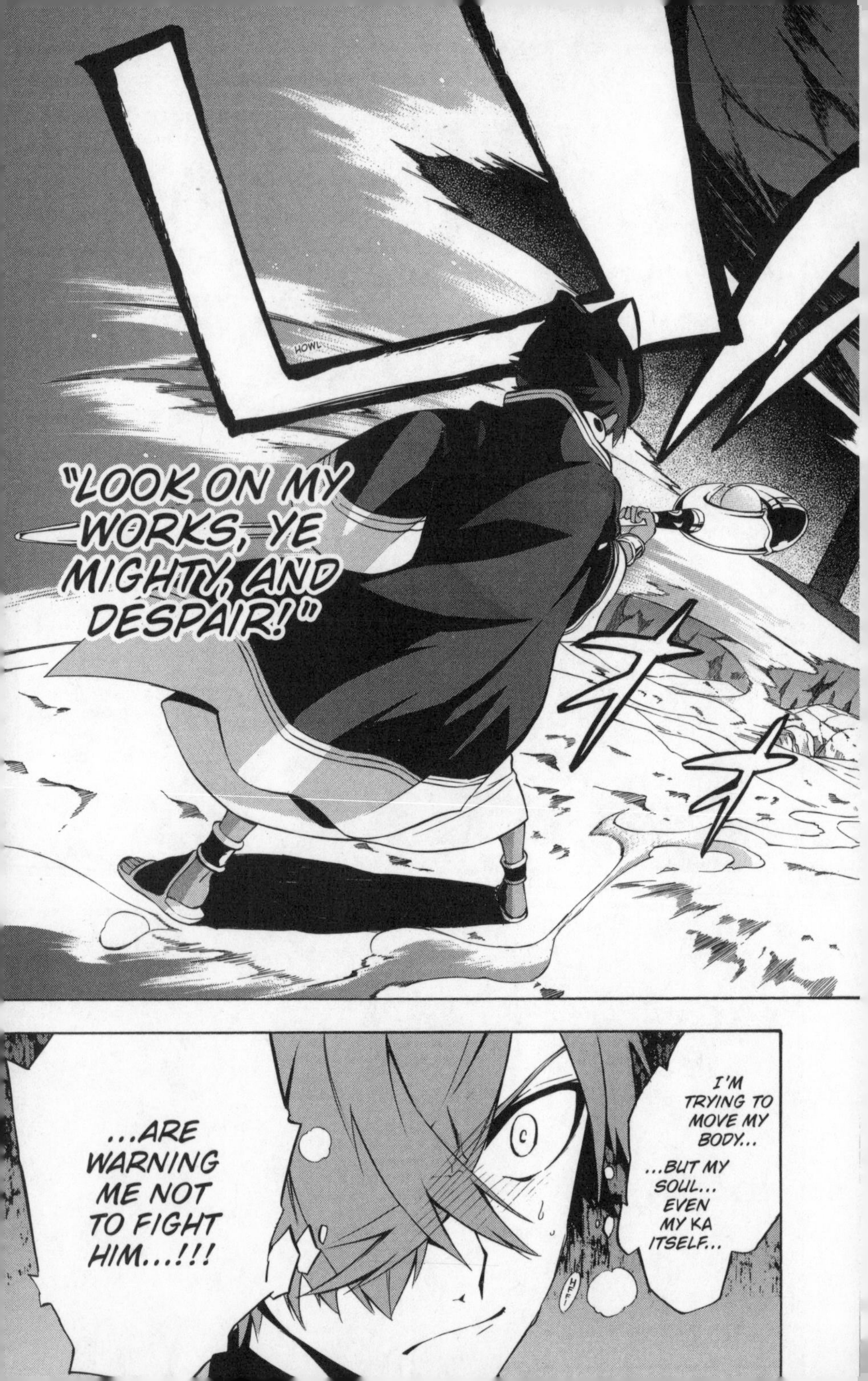
HOWL
"LOOK ON MY WORKS, YE MIGHTY, AND DESPAIR!"
I'M TRYING TO MOVE MY BODY...
...BUT MY SOUL... EVEN MY KA ITSELF...
...ARE WARNING ME NOT TO FIGHT HIM...!!!

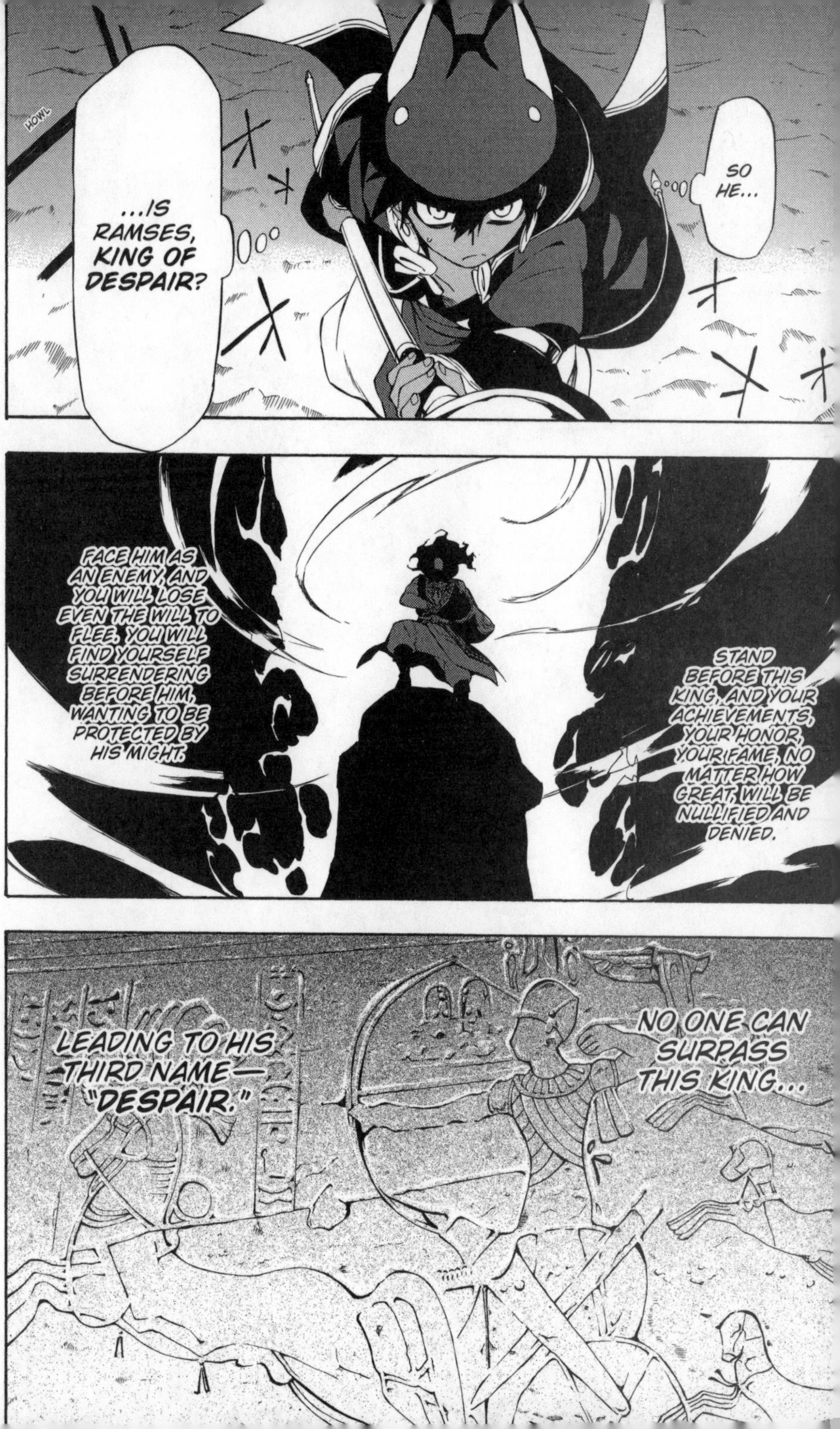
SO HE...
...IS RAMSES, KING OF DESPAIR?
HOWL
STAND BEFORE THIS KING, AND YOUR ACHIEVEMENTS, YOUR HONOR, YOUR FAME, NO MATTER HOW GREAT, WILL BE NULLIFIED AND DENIED.
FACE HIM AS AN ENEMY, AND YOU WILL LOSE EVEN THE WILL TO FLEE. YOU WILL FIND YOURSELF SURRENDERING BEFORE HIM, WANTING TO BE PROTECTED BY HIS MIGHT.
NO ONE CAN SURPASS THIS KING...
LEADING TO HIS THIRD NAME—"DESPAIR."

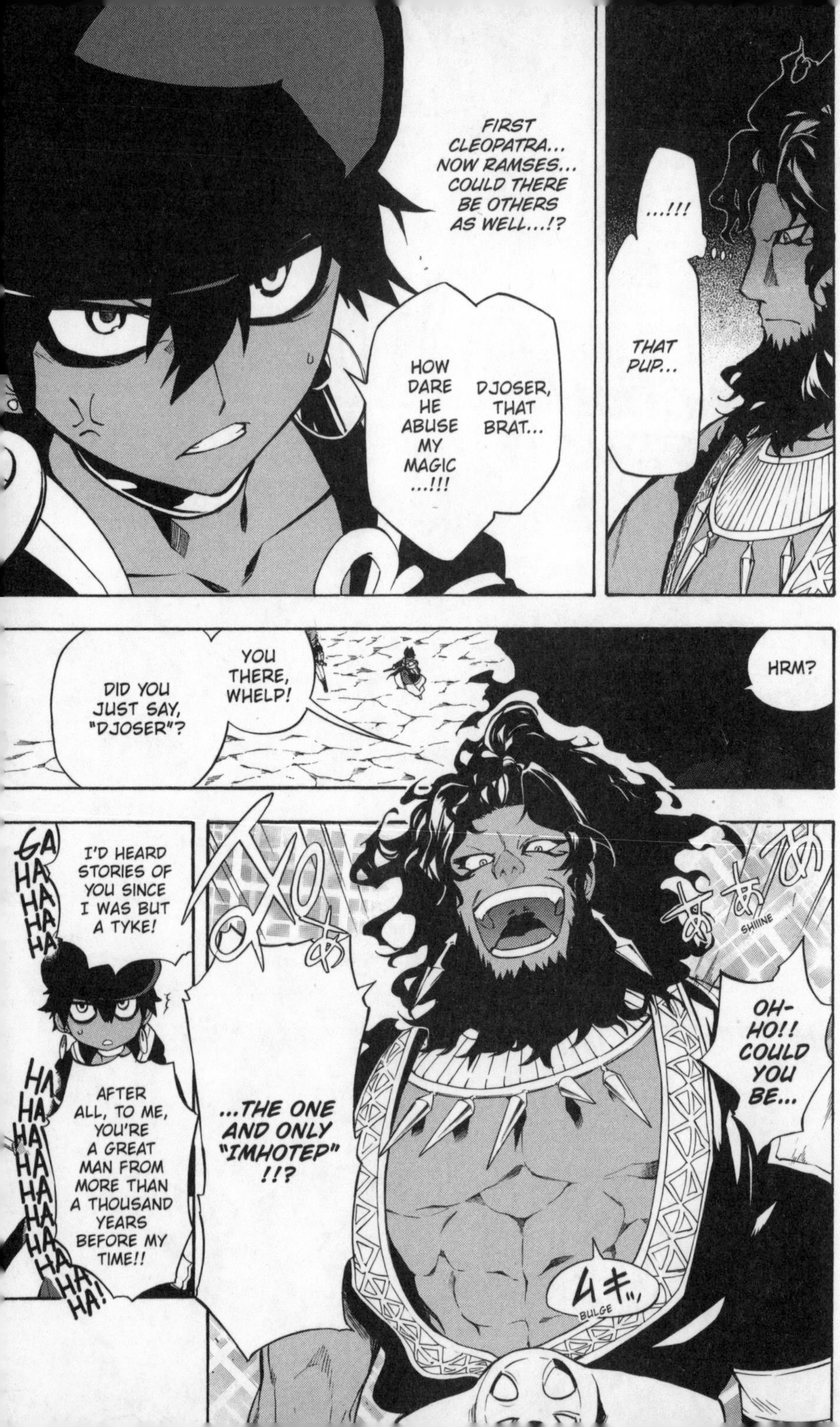
...!!!
THAT PUP...
FIRST CLEOPATRA... NOW RAMSES... COULD THERE BE OTHERS AS WELL...!?
DJOSER, THAT BRAT...
HOW DARE HE ABUSE MY MAGIC ...!!!
HRM?
YOU THERE, WHELP!
DID YOU JUST SAY, "DJOSER"?
SHIIINE
OH-HO!! COULD YOU BE...
...THE ONE AND ONLY "IMHOTEP" !!?
ムキッ
BULGE
GAHAHAHAHA
I'D HEARD STORIES OF YOU SINCE I WAS BUT A TYKE!
AFTER ALL, TO ME, YOU'RE A GREAT MAN FROM MORE THAN A THOUSAND YEARS BEFORE MY TIME!!
HAHAHAHAHAHAHAHAHA!

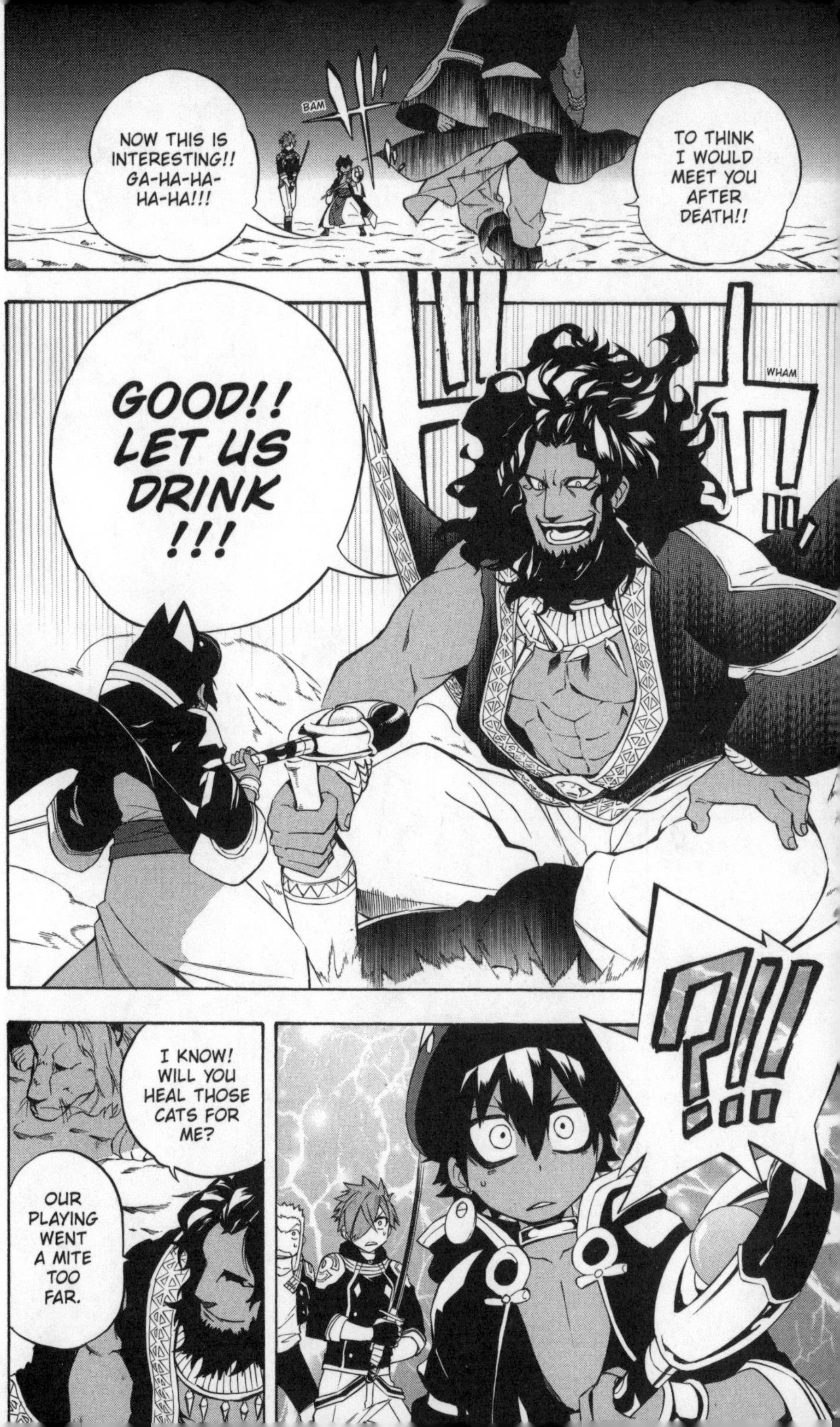
TO THINK I WOULD MEET YOU AFTER DEATH!!
BAM
NOW THIS IS INTERESTING!! GA-HA-HA-HA-HA!!!
WHAM
GOOD!! LET US DRINK!!!
?!!
I KNOW! WILL YOU HEAL THOSE CATS FOR ME?
OUR PLAYING WENT A MITE TOO FAR.

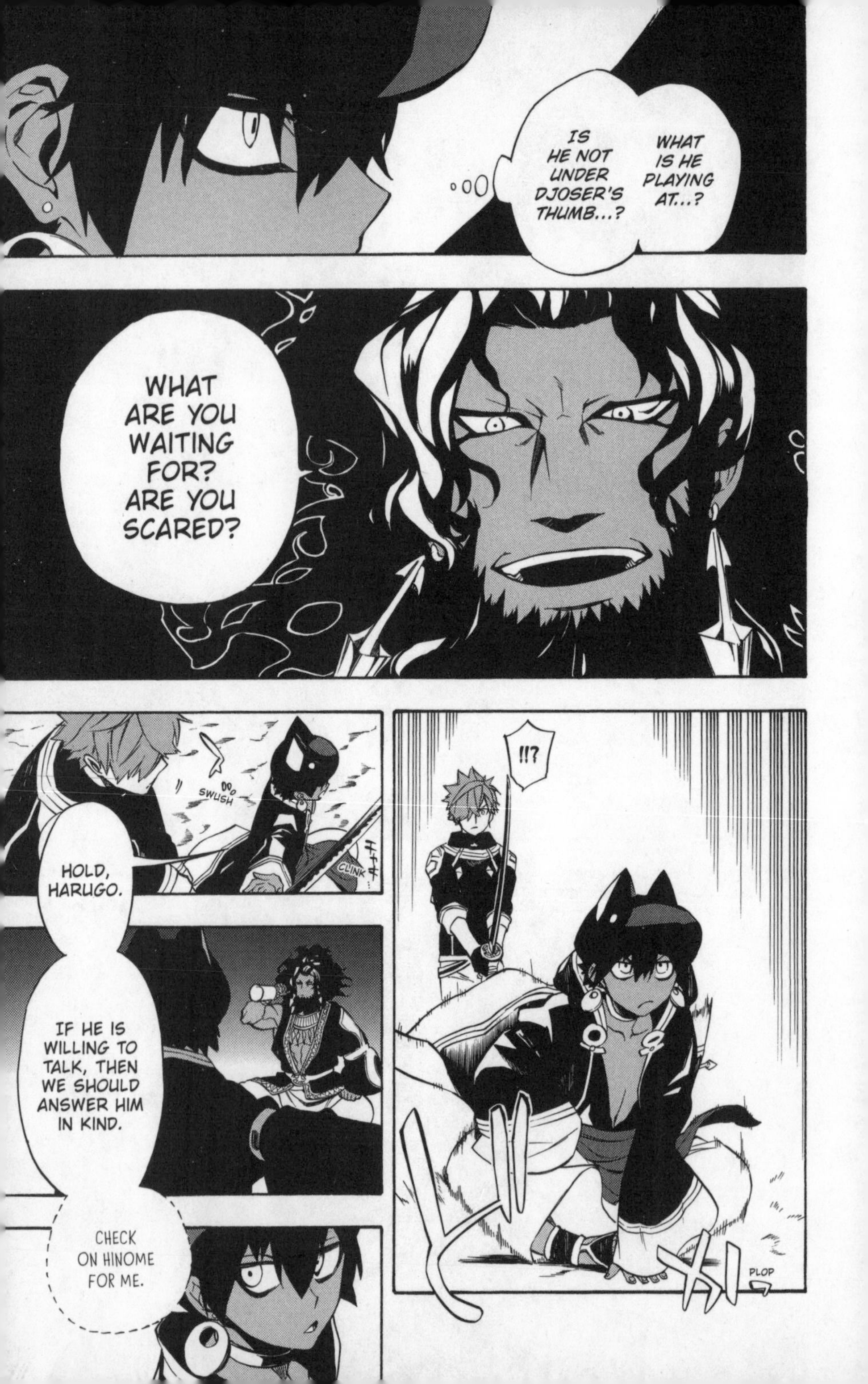
WHAT IS HE PLAYING AT...?
IS HE NOT UNDER DJOSER'S THUMB...?
WHAT ARE YOU WAITING FOR? ARE YOU SCARED?
!!?
PLOP
SWUSH
CLINK
HOLD, HARUGO.
IF HE IS WILLING TO TALK, THEN WE SHOULD ANSWER HIM IN KIND.
CHECK ON HINOME FOR ME.

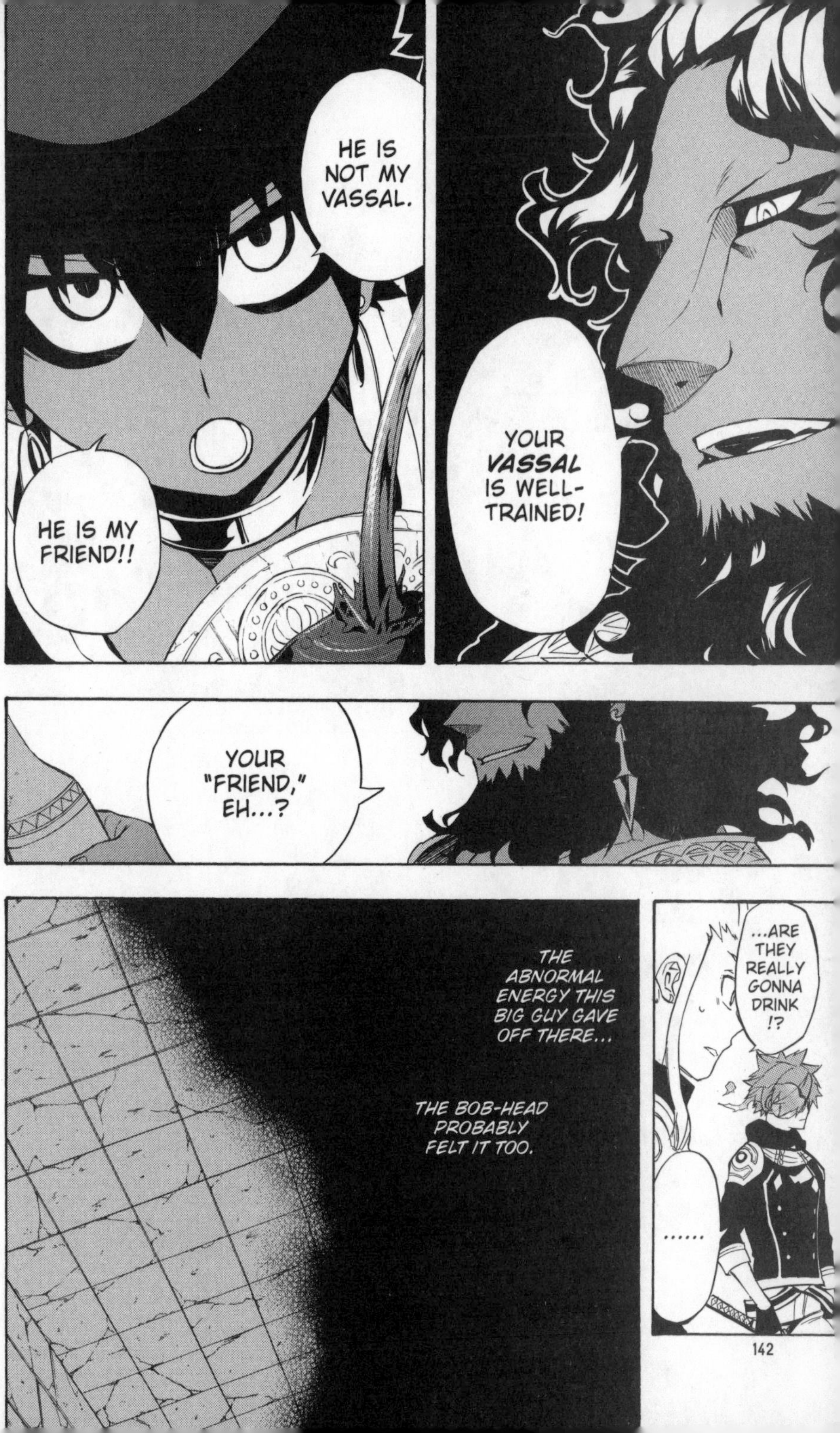
YOUR *VASSAL* IS WELL-TRAINED!
HE IS NOT MY VASSAL.
HE IS MY FRIEND!!
YOUR "FRIEND," EH...?
...ARE THEY REALLY GONNA DRINK !?
......
THE ABNORMAL ENERGY THIS BIG GUY GAVE OFF THERE...
THE BOB-HEAD PROBABLY FELT IT TOO.

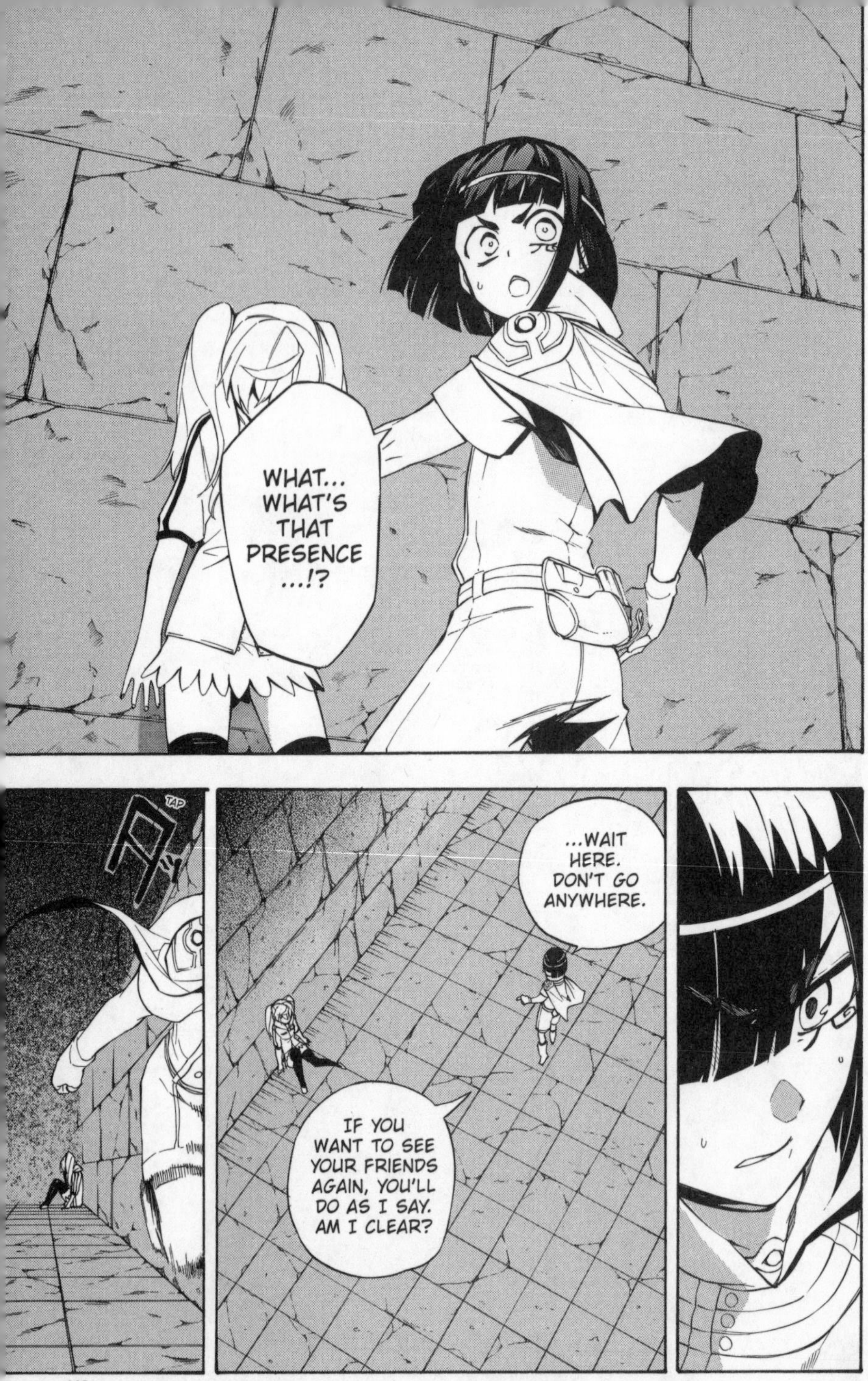
WHAT... WHAT'S THAT PRESENCE ...!?
...WAIT HERE. DON'T GO ANYWHERE.
IF YOU WANT TO SEE YOUR FRIENDS AGAIN, YOU'LL DO AS I SAY. AM I CLEAR?
TAP

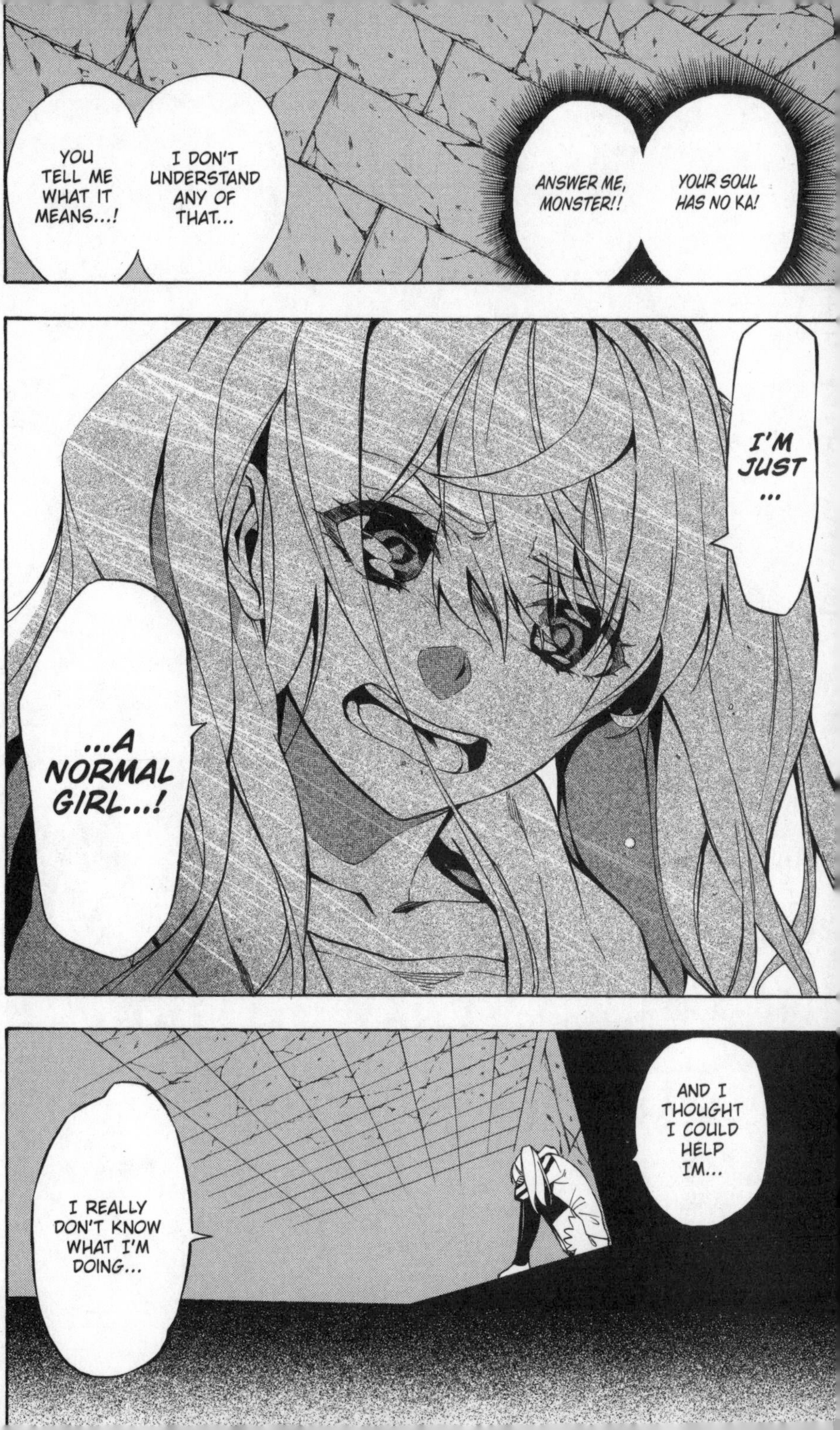
YOUR SOUL HAS NO KA!
ANSWER ME, MONSTER!!
I DON'T UNDERSTAND ANY OF THAT...
YOU TELL ME WHAT IT MEANS...!
I'M JUST ...
...A NORMAL GIRL...!
AND I THOUGHT I COULD HELP IM...
I REALLY DON'T KNOW WHAT I'M DOING...

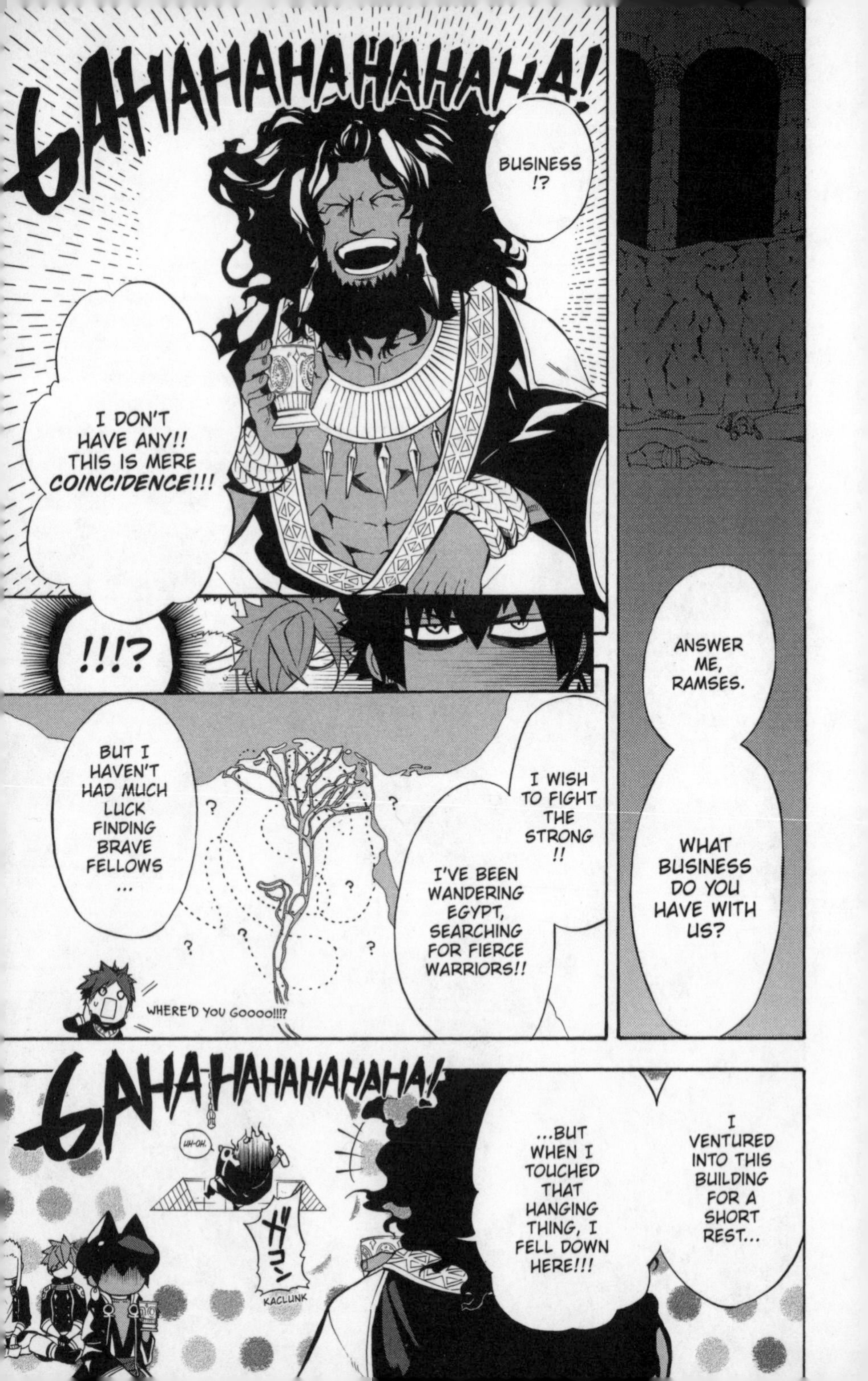
ANSWER ME, RAMSES.
WHAT BUSINESS DO YOU HAVE WITH US?
GAHAHAHAHAHAHAHA!
BUSINESS !?
I DON'T HAVE ANY!! THIS IS MERE COINCIDENCE!!!
!!!?
I WISH TO FIGHT THE STRONG !!
I'VE BEEN WANDERING EGYPT, SEARCHING FOR FIERCE WARRIORS!!
BUT I HAVEN'T HAD MUCH LUCK FINDING BRAVE FELLOWS ...
WHERE'D YOU GOOOO!!!?
I VENTURED INTO THIS BUILDING FOR A SHORT REST...
...BUT WHEN I TOUCHED THAT HANGING THING, I FELL DOWN HERE!!!
GAHAHAHAHAHAHA!
UH-OH.
ガコン
KACLUNK

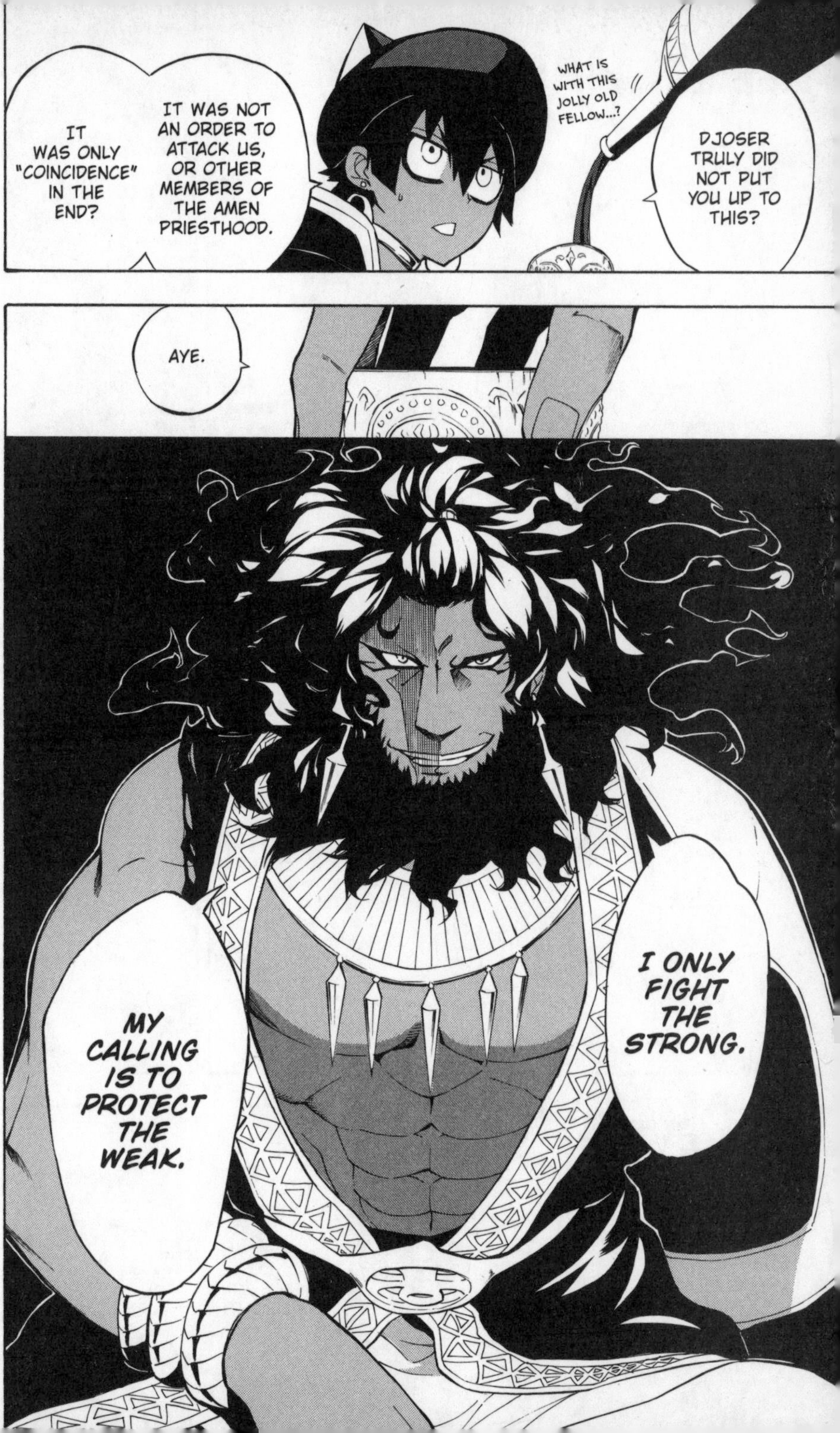
DJOSER TRULY DID NOT PUT YOU UP TO THIS?
WHAT IS WITH THIS JOLLY OLD FELLOW...?
IT WAS NOT AN ORDER TO ATTACK US, OR OTHER MEMBERS OF THE AMEN PRIESTHOOD.
IT WAS ONLY "COINCIDENCE" IN THE END?
AYE.
I ONLY FIGHT THE STRONG.
MY CALLING IS TO PROTECT THE WEAK.

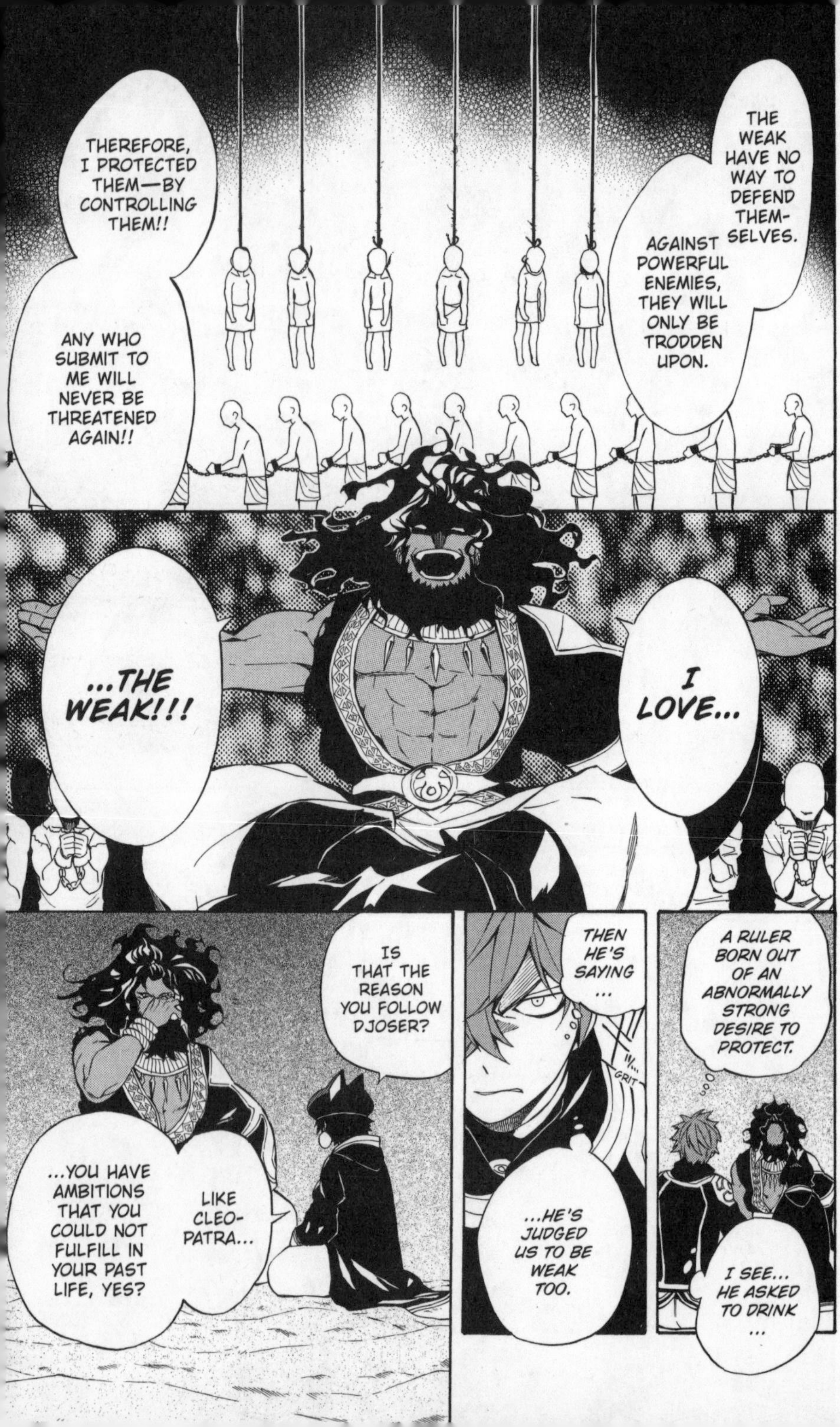
THE WEAK HAVE NO WAY TO DEFEND THEM-SELVES.
AGAINST POWERFUL ENEMIES, THEY WILL ONLY BE TRODDEN UPON.
THEREFORE, I PROTECTED THEM—BY CONTROLLING THEM!!
ANY WHO SUBMIT TO ME WILL NEVER BE THREATENED AGAIN!!
I LOVE...
...THE WEAK!!!
A RULER BORN OUT OF AN ABNORMALLY STRONG DESIRE TO PROTECT.
I SEE... HE ASKED TO DRINK ...
THEN HE'S SAYING ...
GRIT
...HE'S JUDGED US TO BE WEAK TOO.
IS THAT THE REASON YOU FOLLOW DJOSER?
LIKE CLEO-PATRA...
...YOU HAVE AMBITIONS THAT YOU COULD NOT FULFILL IN YOUR PAST LIFE, YES?

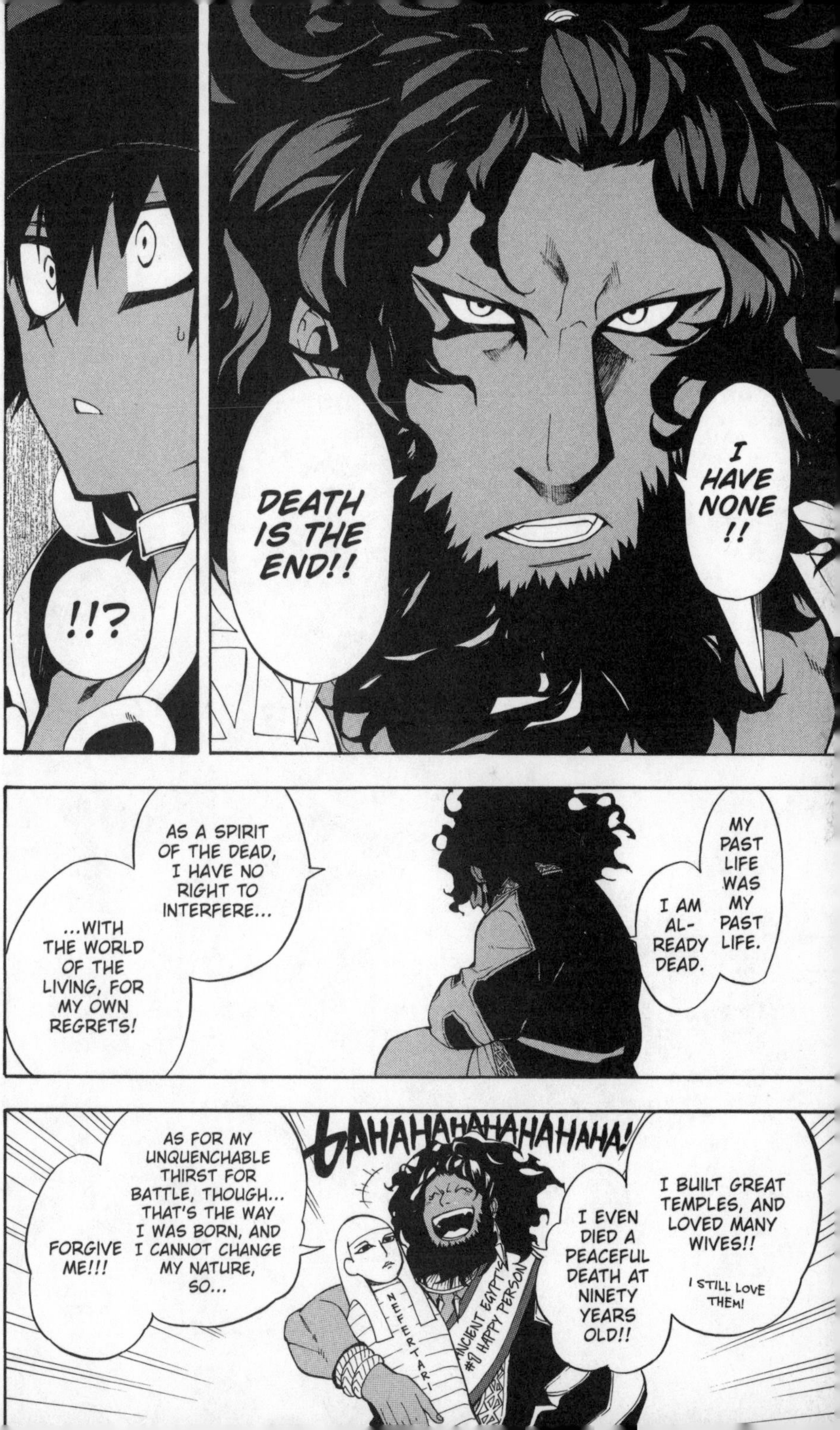
I HAVE NONE!!
DEATH IS THE END!!
!!?
MY PAST LIFE WAS MY PAST LIFE.
I AM AL-READY DEAD.
AS A SPIRIT OF THE DEAD, I HAVE NO RIGHT TO INTERFERE...
...WITH THE WORLD OF THE LIVING, FOR MY OWN REGRETS!
GAHAHAHAHAHAHAHAHA!
I BUILT GREAT TEMPLES, AND LOVED MANY WIVES!!
I STILL LOVE THEM!
I EVEN DIED A PEACEFUL DEATH AT NINETY YEARS OLD!!
ANCIENT EGYPT'S #1 HAPPY PERSON
NEFERTARI
AS FOR MY UNQUENCHABLE THIRST FOR BATTLE, THOUGH... THAT'S THE WAY I WAS BORN, AND I CANNOT CHANGE MY NATURE, SO...
FORGIVE ME!!!

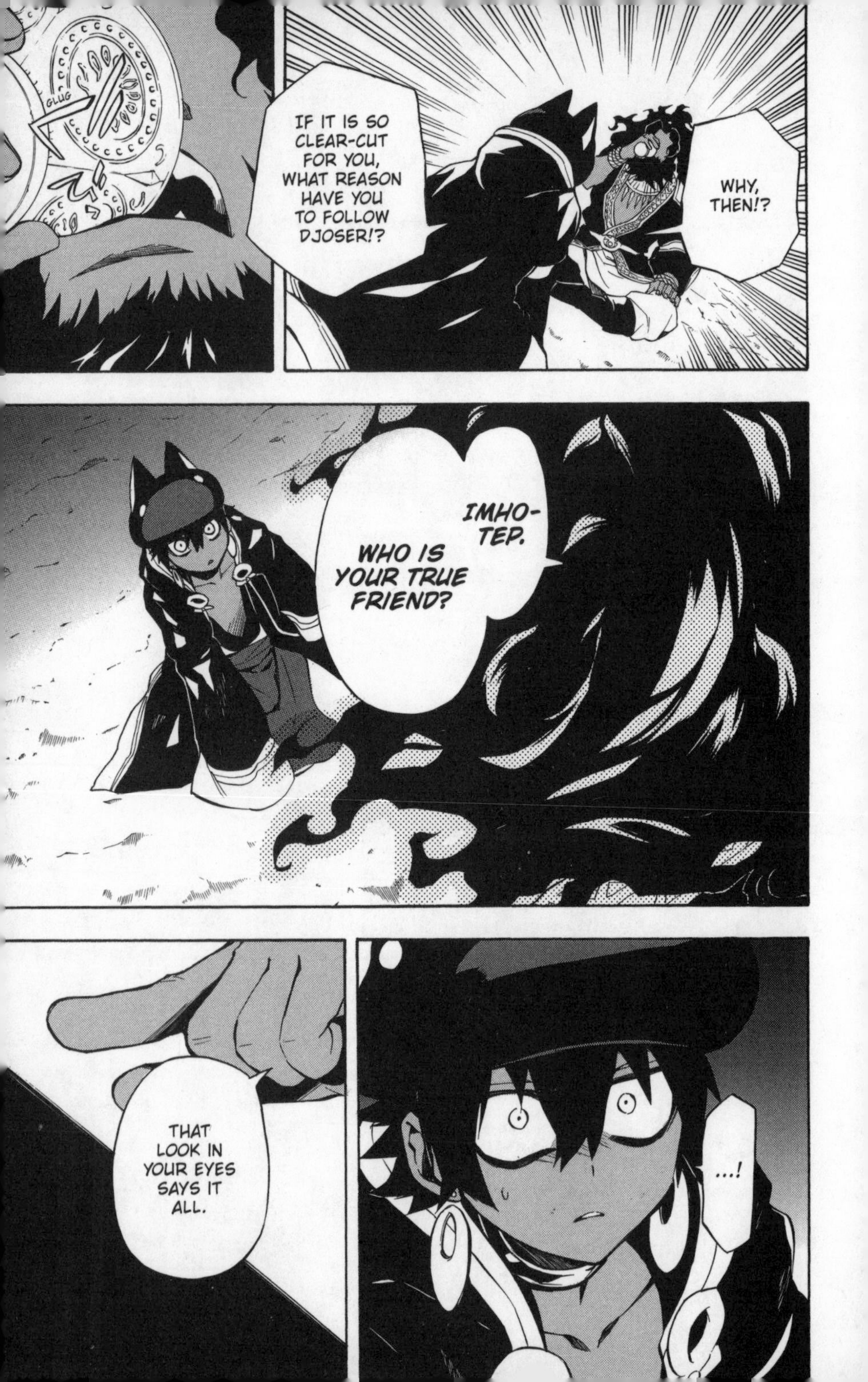
WHY, THEN!?
IF IT IS SO CLEAR-CUT FOR YOU, WHAT REASON HAVE YOU TO FOLLOW DJOSER!?
GLUG
IMHO-TEP.
WHO IS YOUR TRUE FRIEND?
...!
THAT LOOK IN YOUR EYES SAYS IT ALL.

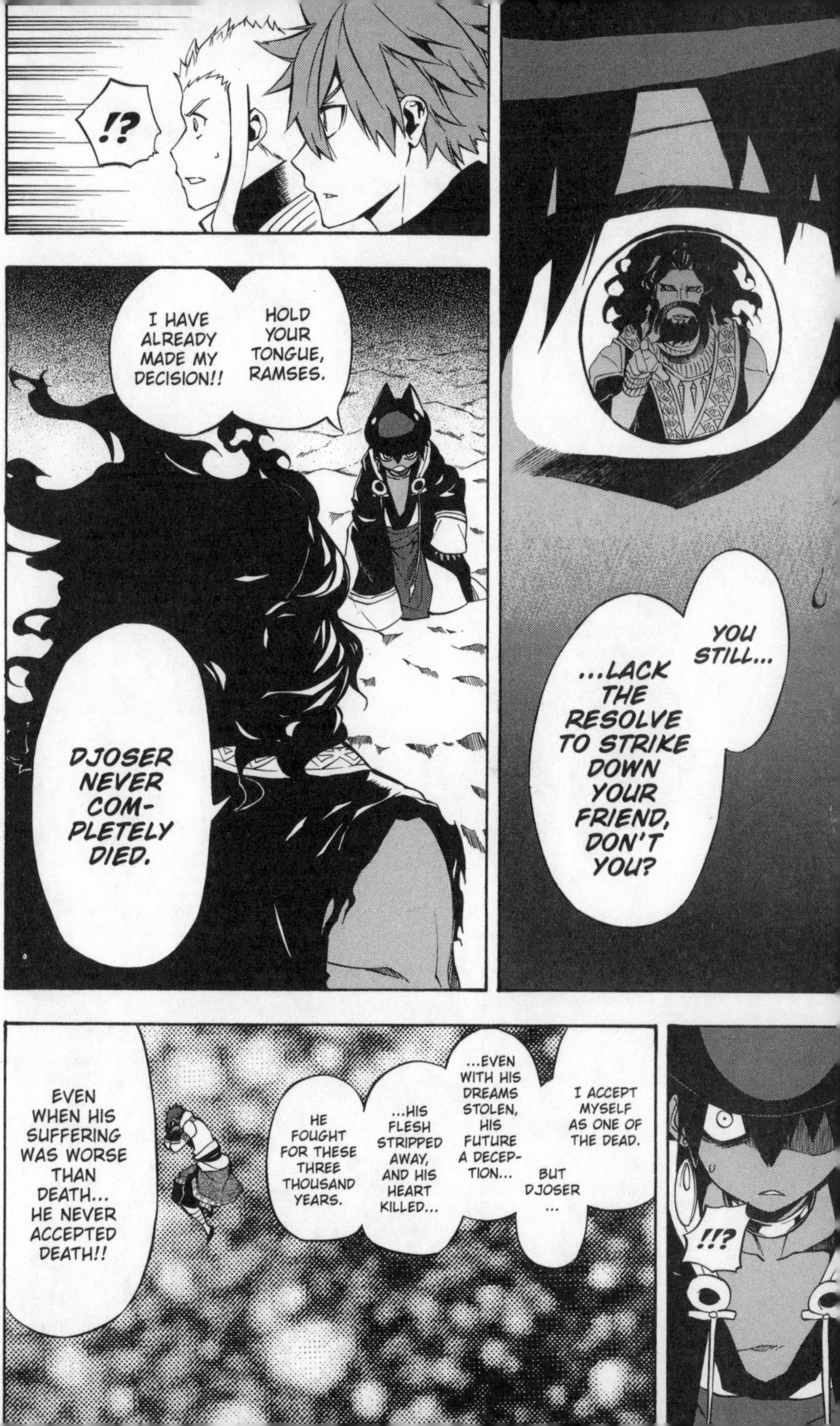
YOU STILL...
...LACK THE RESOLVE TO STRIKE DOWN YOUR FRIEND, DON'T YOU?
!?
HOLD YOUR TONGUE, RAMSES.
I HAVE ALREADY MADE MY DECISION!!
DJOSER NEVER COM-PLETELY DIED.
!!?
I ACCEPT MYSELF AS ONE OF THE DEAD.
BUT DJOSER...
...EVEN WITH HIS DREAMS STOLEN, HIS FUTURE A DECEP-TION...
...HIS FLESH STRIPPED AWAY, AND HIS HEART KILLED...
HE FOUGHT FOR THESE THREE THOUSAND YEARS.
EVEN WHEN HIS SUFFERING WAS WORSE THAN DEATH... HE NEVER ACCEPTED DEATH!!

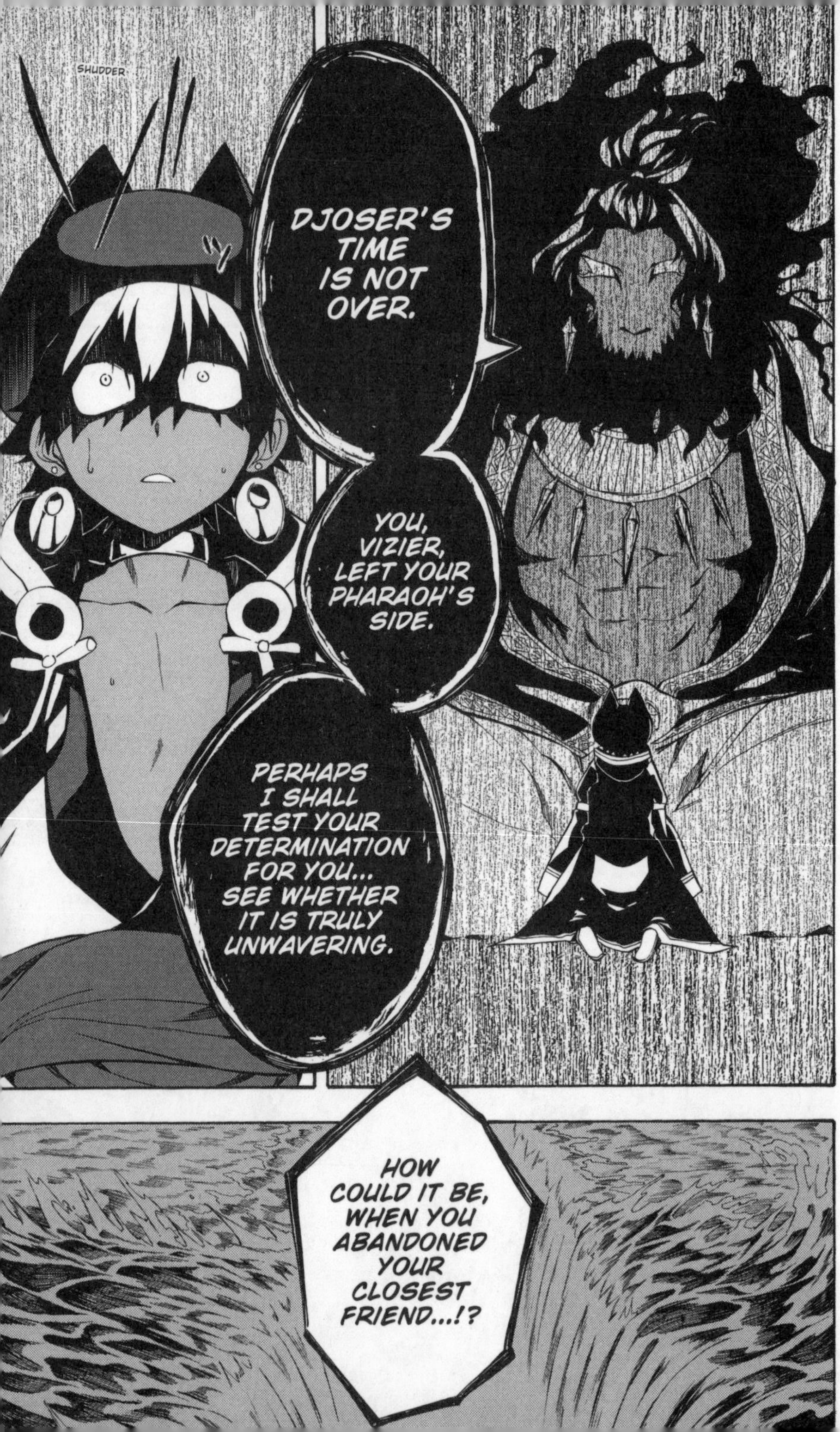
DJOSER'S TIME IS NOT OVER.
YOU, VIZIER, LEFT YOUR PHARAOH'S SIDE.
PERHAPS I SHALL TEST YOUR DETERMINATION FOR YOU... SEE WHETHER IT IS TRULY UNWAVERING.
SHUDDER
HOW COULD IT BE, WHEN YOU ABANDONED YOUR CLOSEST FRIEND...!?

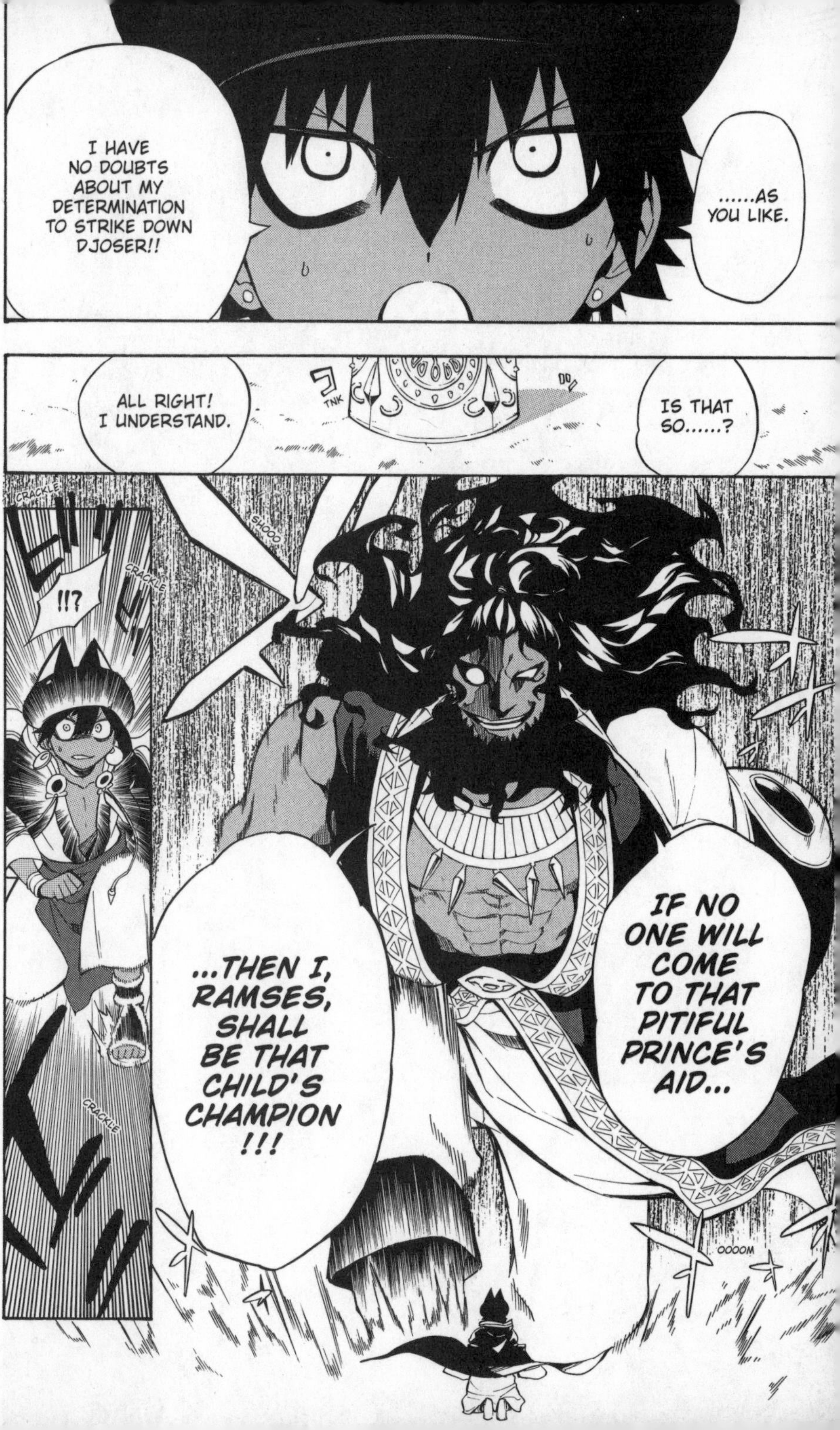
......AS YOU LIKE.
I HAVE NO DOUBTS ABOUT MY DETERMINATION TO STRIKE DOWN DJOSER!!
IS THAT SO......?
TNK
ALL RIGHT! I UNDERSTAND.
IF NO ONE WILL COME TO THAT PITIFUL PRINCE'S AID...
...THEN I, RAMSES, SHALL BE THAT CHILD'S CHAMPION!!!
SHOOO
OOOOM
CRACKLE
!!?
CRACKLE
CRACKLE

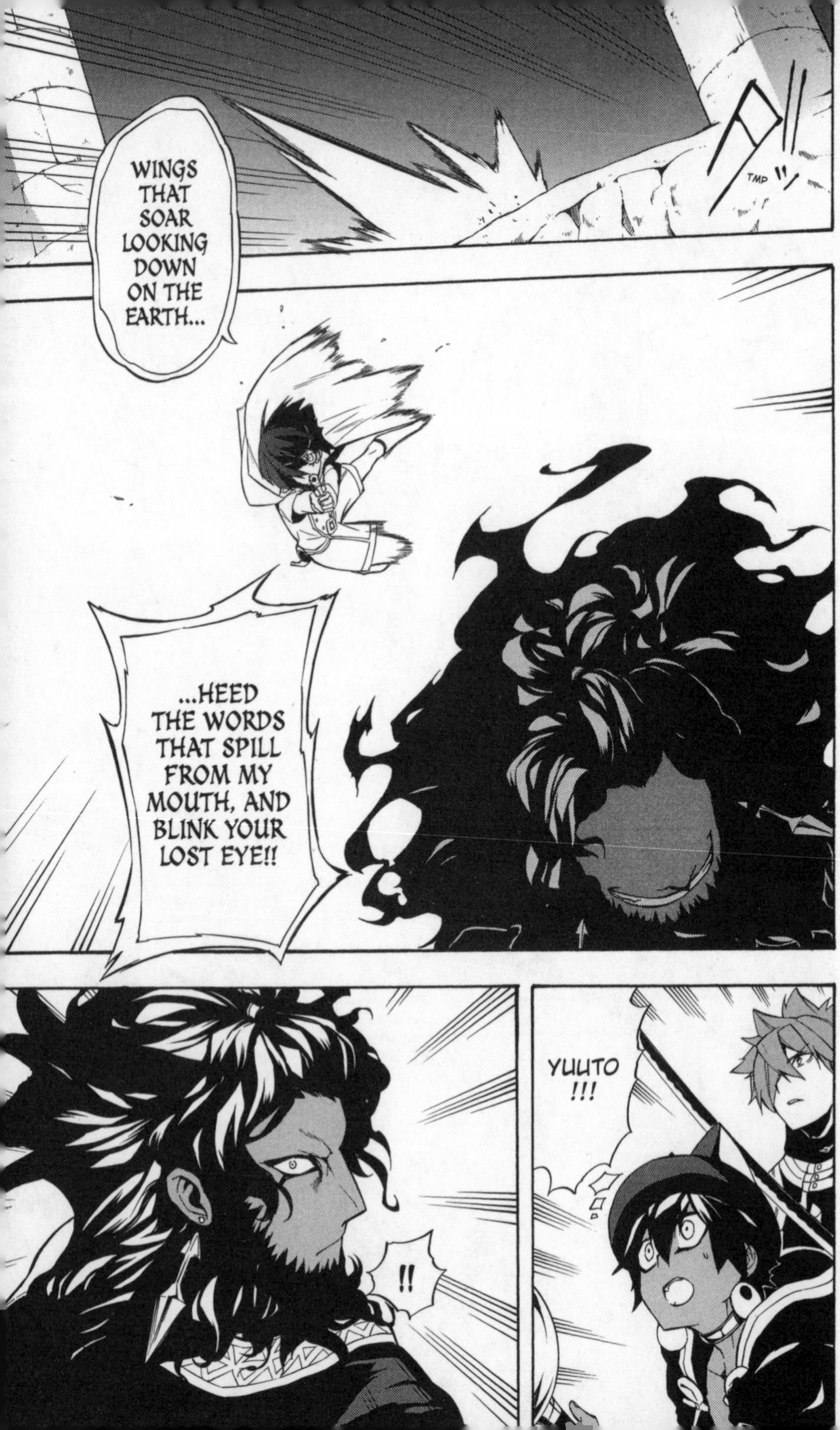
TMP
WINGS THAT SOAR LOOKING DOWN ON THE EARTH...
...HEED THE WORDS THAT SPILL FROM MY MOUTH, AND BLINK YOUR LOST EYE!!
YUUTO !!!
!!

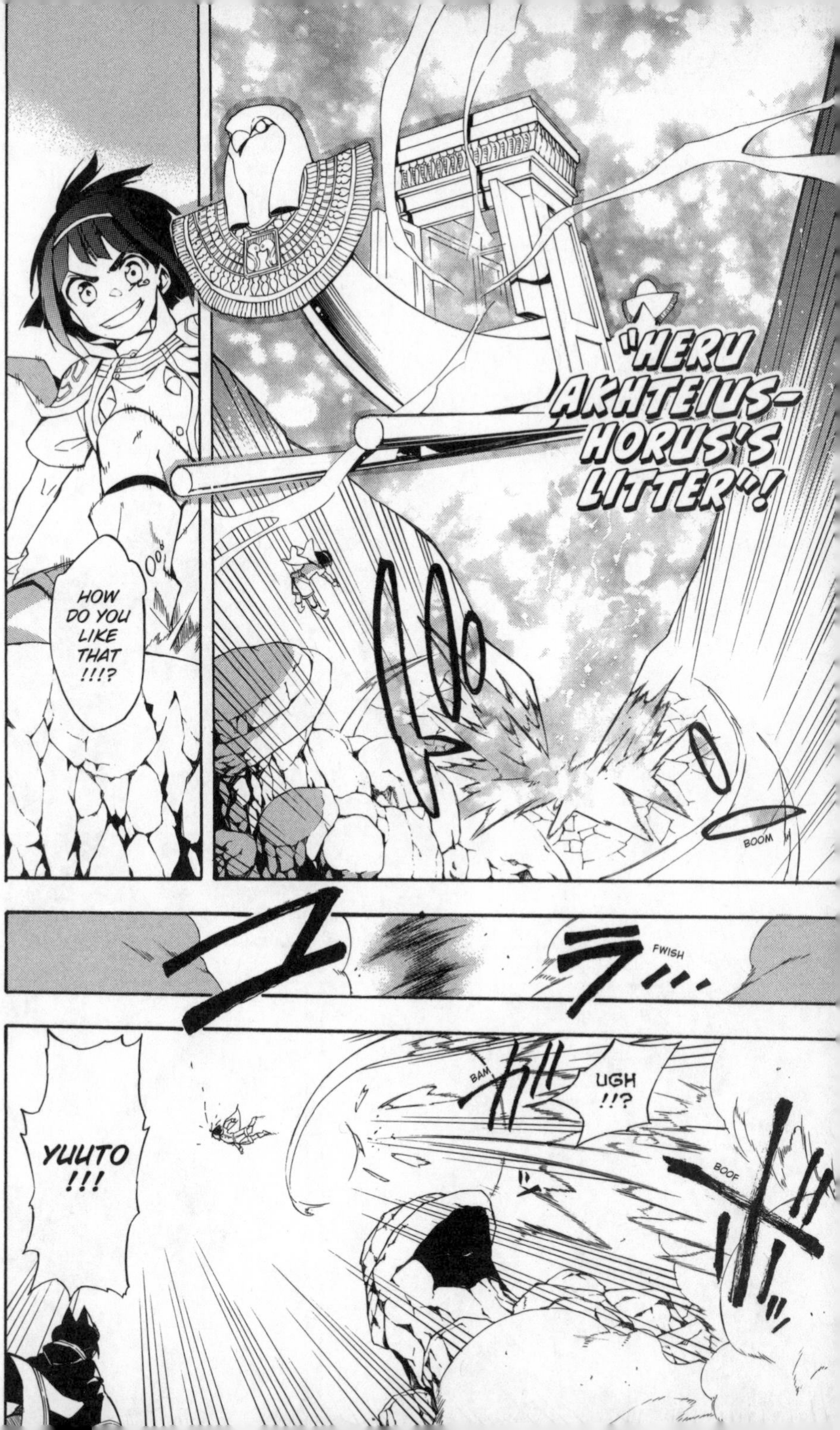
"HERU AKHTEIUS-HORUS'S LITTER"!
BOOM
HOW DO YOU LIKE THAT!!!?
FWISH
BAM
UGH!!?
BOOF
YUUTO!!!

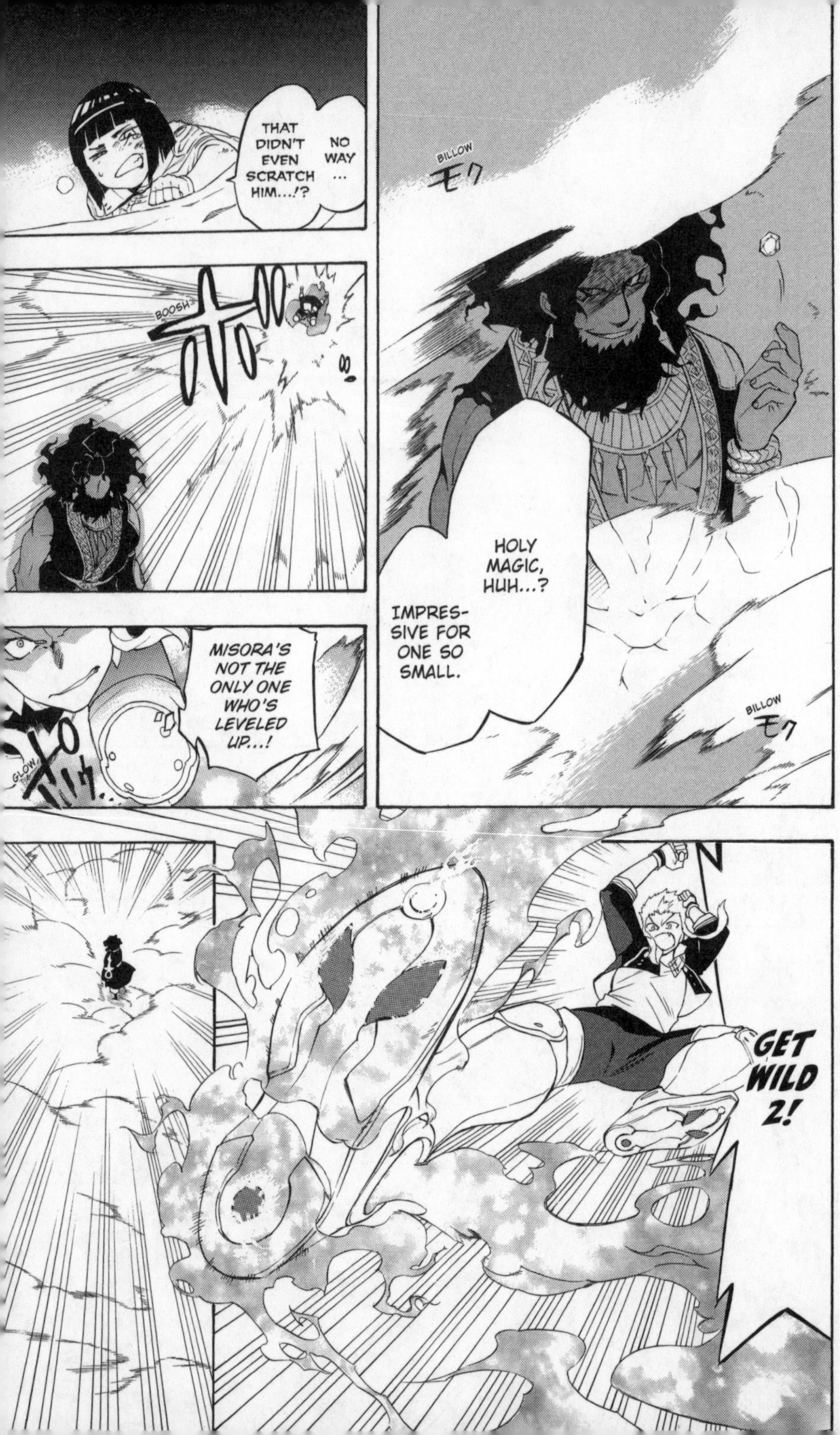
BILLOW
モク
HOLY MAGIC, HUH...?
IMPRESSIVE FOR ONE SO SMALL.
BILLOW
モク
NO WAY...
THAT DIDN'T EVEN SCRATCH HIM...!?
BOOSH
MISORA'S NOT THE ONLY ONE WHO'S LEVELED UP...!
GLOW
GET WILD 2!

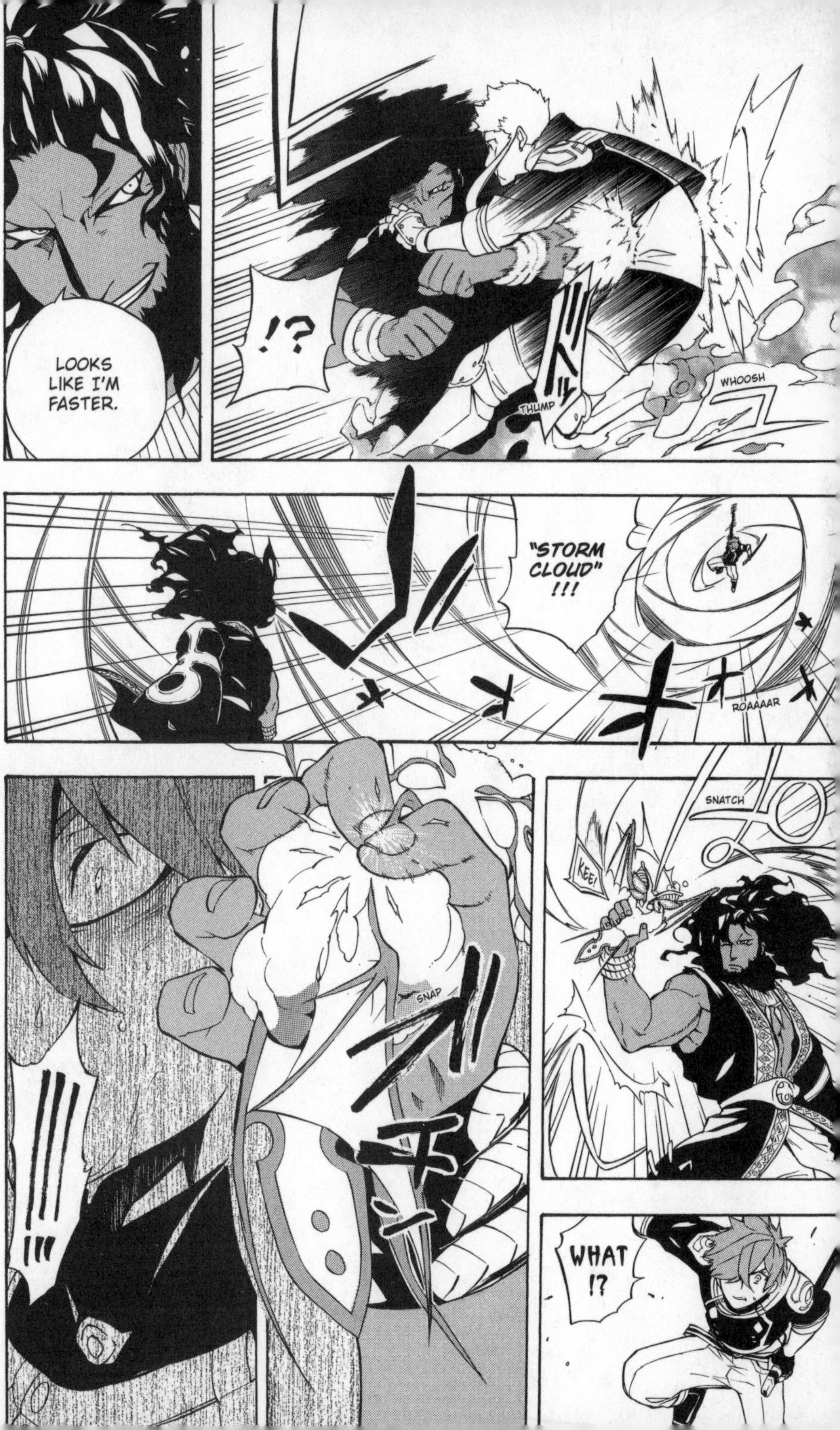
WHOOSH
!?
THUMP
LOOKS LIKE I'M FASTER.
"STORM CLOUD" !!!
ROAAAAR
SNATCH
KEE!
WHAT !?
SNAP
!!!

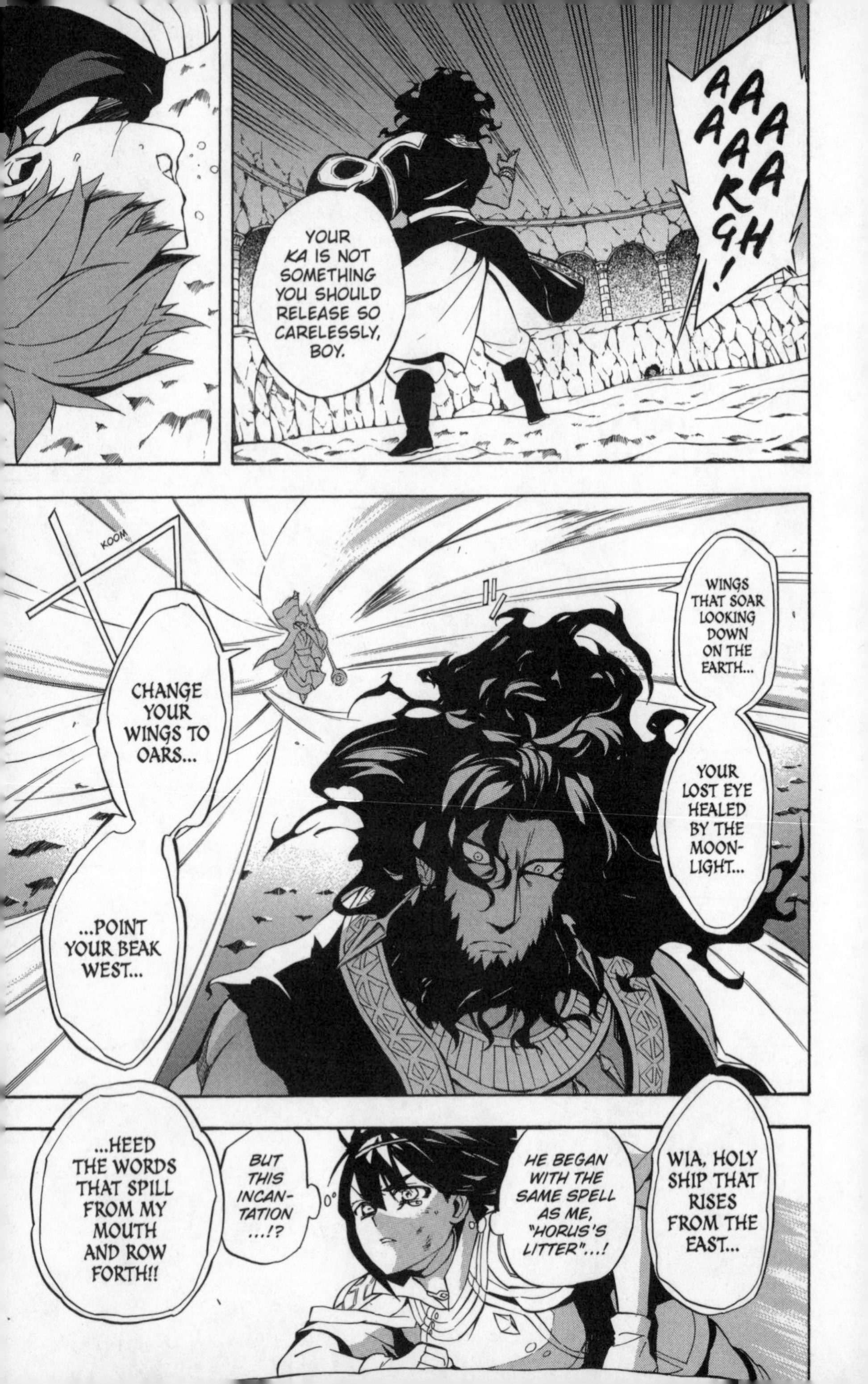
AAAAAAARGH!
YOUR *KA* IS NOT SOMETHING YOU SHOULD RELEASE SO CARELESSLY, BOY.
WINGS THAT SOAR LOOKING DOWN ON THE EARTH...
YOUR LOST EYE HEALED BY THE MOON-LIGHT...
KOOM
CHANGE YOUR WINGS TO OARS...
...POINT YOUR BEAK WEST...
WIA, HOLY SHIP THAT RISES FROM THE EAST...
HE BEGAN WITH THE SAME SPELL AS ME, "HORUS'S LITTER"...!
BUT THIS INCAN-TATION ...!?
...HEED THE WORDS THAT SPILL FROM MY MOUTH AND ROW FORTH!!

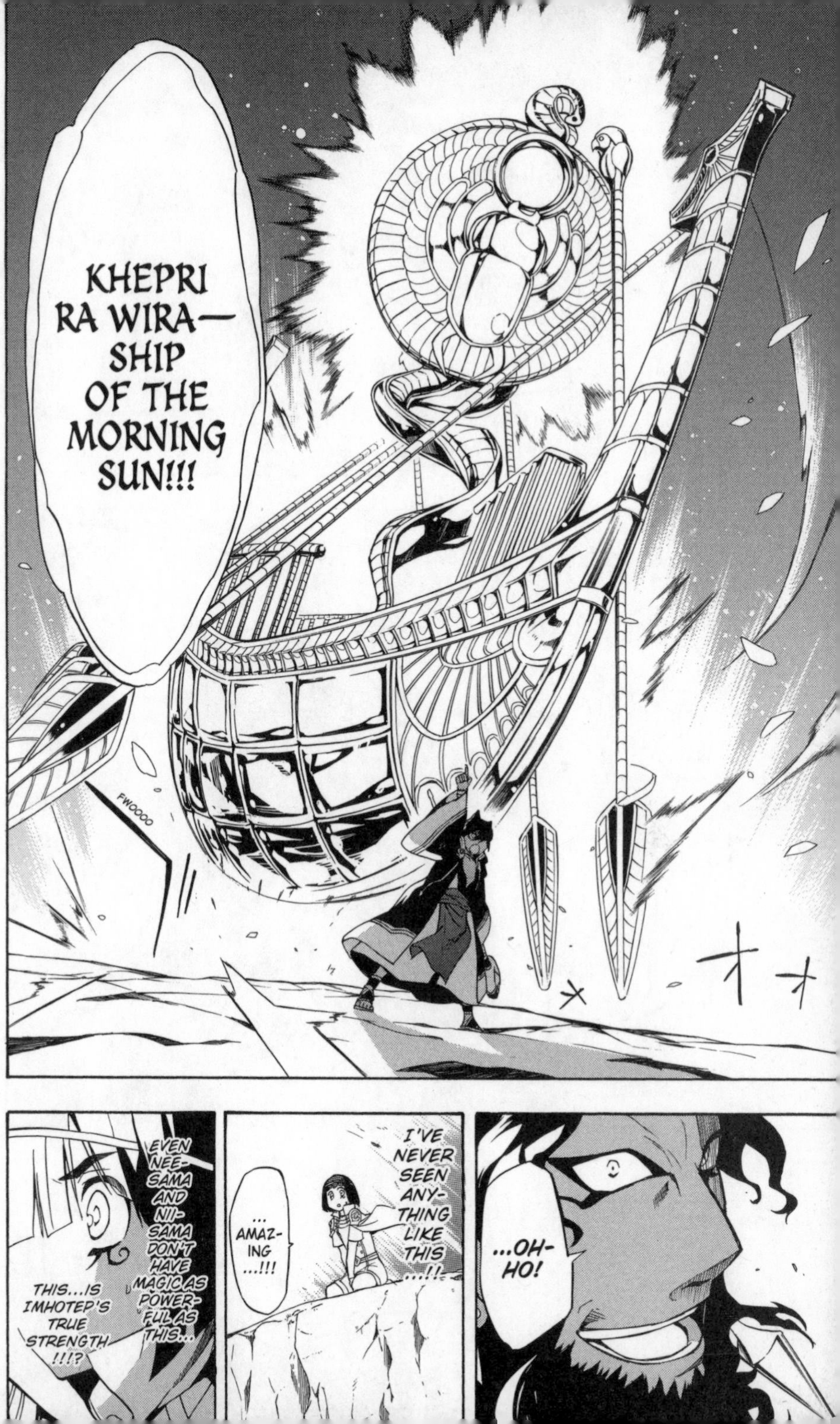
KHEPRI RA WIRA—SHIP OF THE MORNING SUN!!!
FWOOOO
...OH-HO!
I'VE NEVER SEEN ANYTHING LIKE THIS...!!
...AMAZING...!!!
EVEN NEE-SAMA AND NII-SAMA DON'T HAVE MAGIC AS POWERFUL AS THIS...
THIS...IS IMHOTEP'S TRUE STRENGTH!!!?

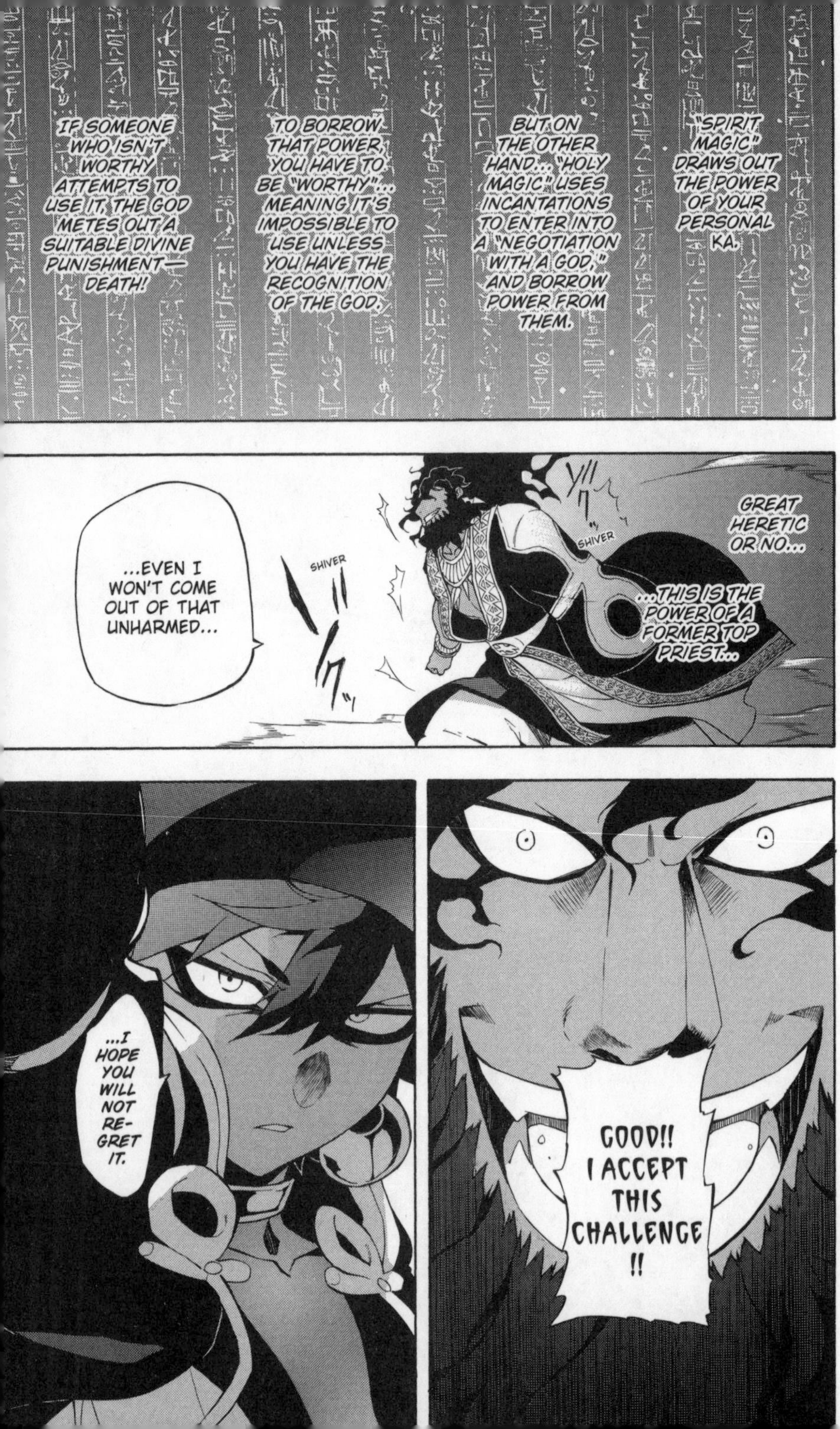
"SPIRIT MAGIC" DRAWS OUT THE POWER OF YOUR PERSONAL KA.
BUT ON THE OTHER HAND... "HOLY MAGIC" USES INCANTATIONS TO ENTER INTO A "NEGOTIATION WITH A GOD," AND BORROW POWER FROM THEM.
TO BORROW THAT POWER, YOU HAVE TO BE "WORTHY"... MEANING IT'S IMPOSSIBLE TO USE UNLESS YOU HAVE THE RECOGNITION OF THE GOD.
IF SOMEONE WHO ISN'T WORTHY ATTEMPTS TO USE IT, THE GOD METES OUT A SUITABLE DIVINE PUNISHMENT—DEATH!
GREAT HERETIC OR NO...
...THIS IS THE POWER OF A FORMER TOP PRIEST...
SHIVER
SHIVER
...EVEN I WON'T COME OUT OF THAT UNHARMED...
GOOD!! I ACCEPT THIS CHALLENGE !!
...I HOPE YOU WILL NOT RE-GRET IT.

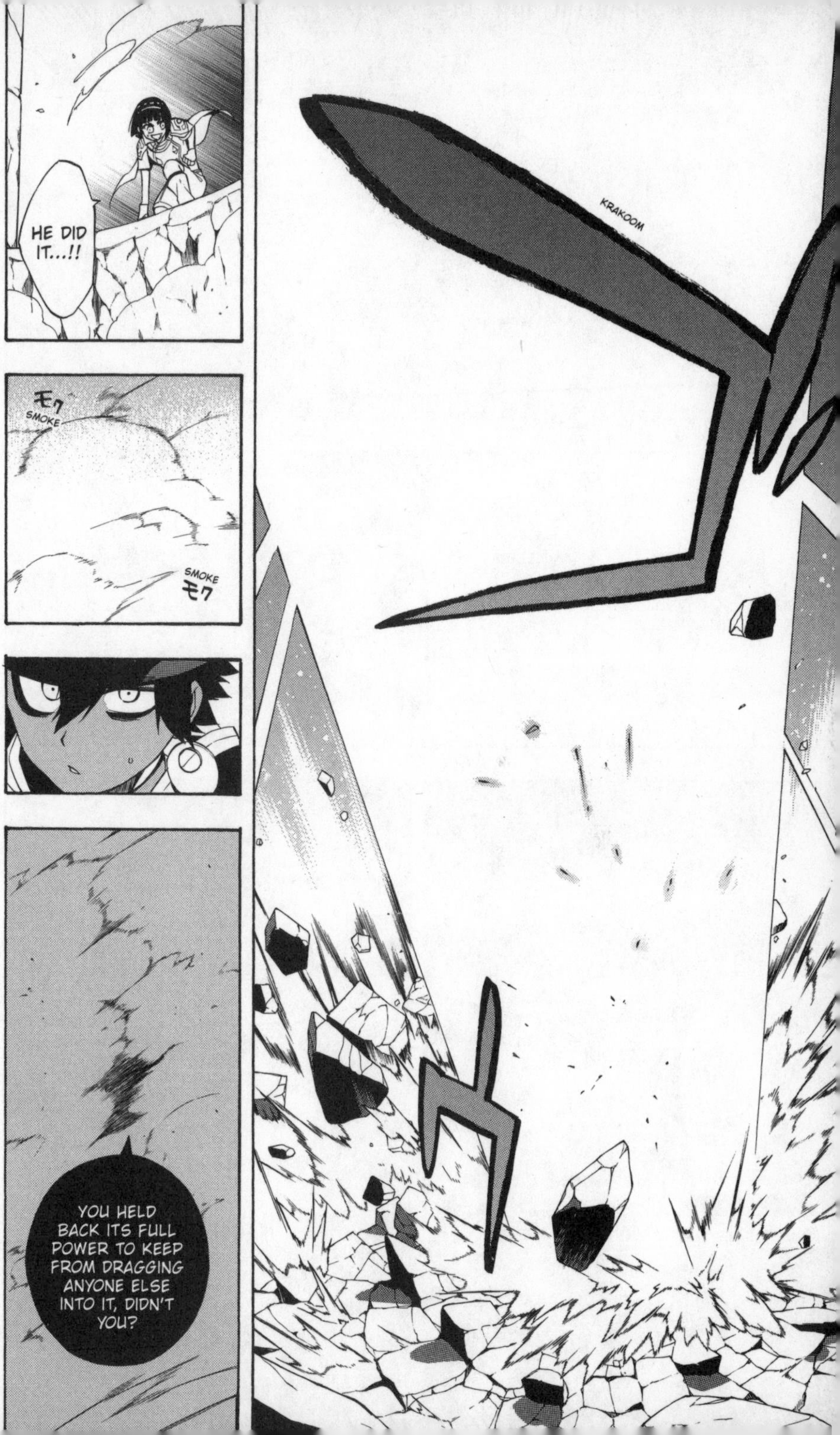
KRAKOOM
HE DID IT...!!
モク
SMOKE
SMOKE
モク
YOU HELD BACK ITS FULL POWER TO KEEP FROM DRAGGING ANYONE ELSE INTO IT, DIDN'T YOU?

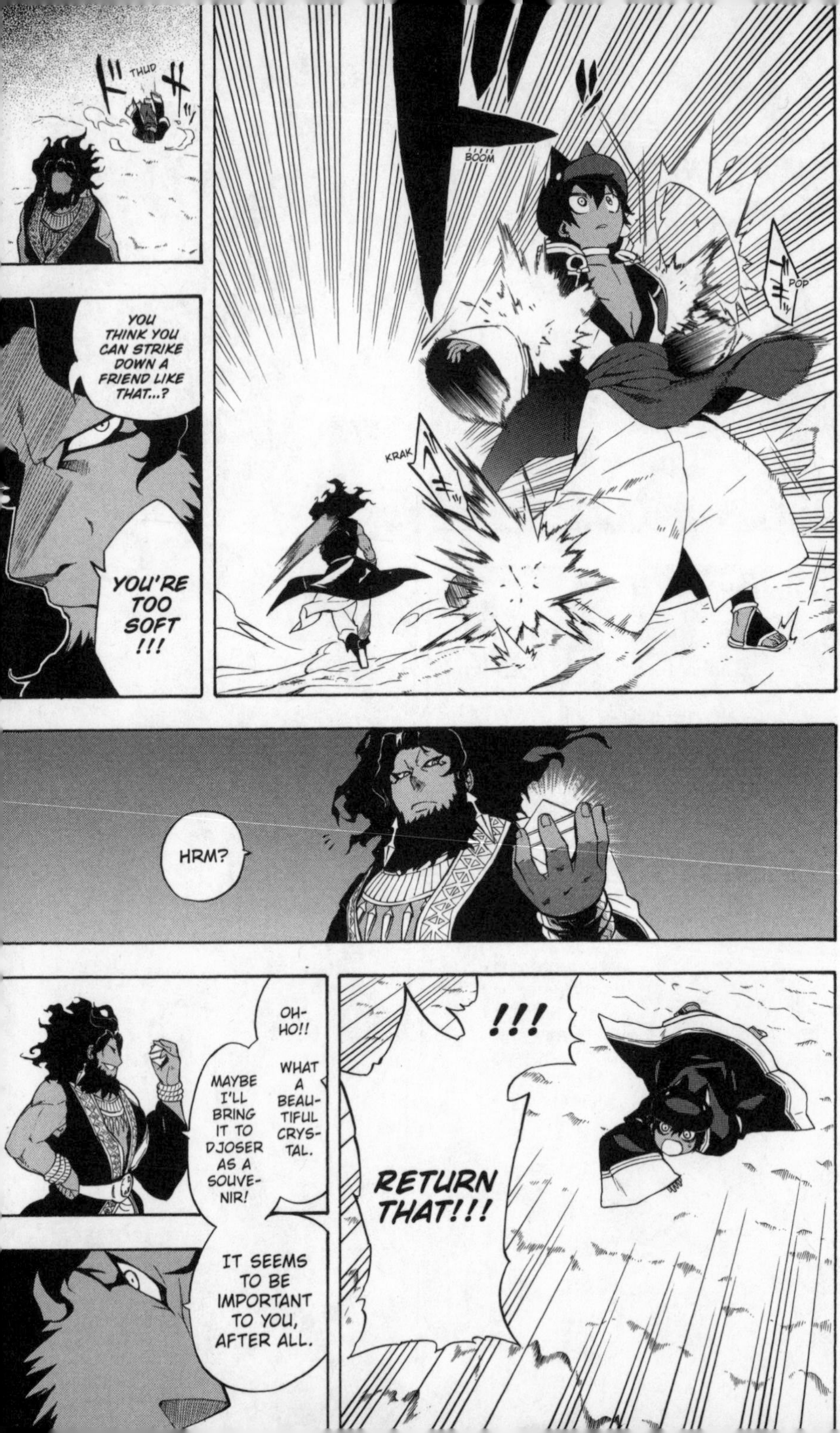
BOOM
POP
KRAK
THUD
YOU THINK YOU CAN STRIKE DOWN A FRIEND LIKE THAT...?
YOU'RE TOO SOFT!!!
HRM?
!!!
RETURN THAT!!!
OH-HO!! WHAT A BEAUTIFUL CRYSTAL.
MAYBE I'LL BRING IT TO DJOSER AS A SOUVENIR!
IT SEEMS TO BE IMPORTANT TO YOU, AFTER ALL.

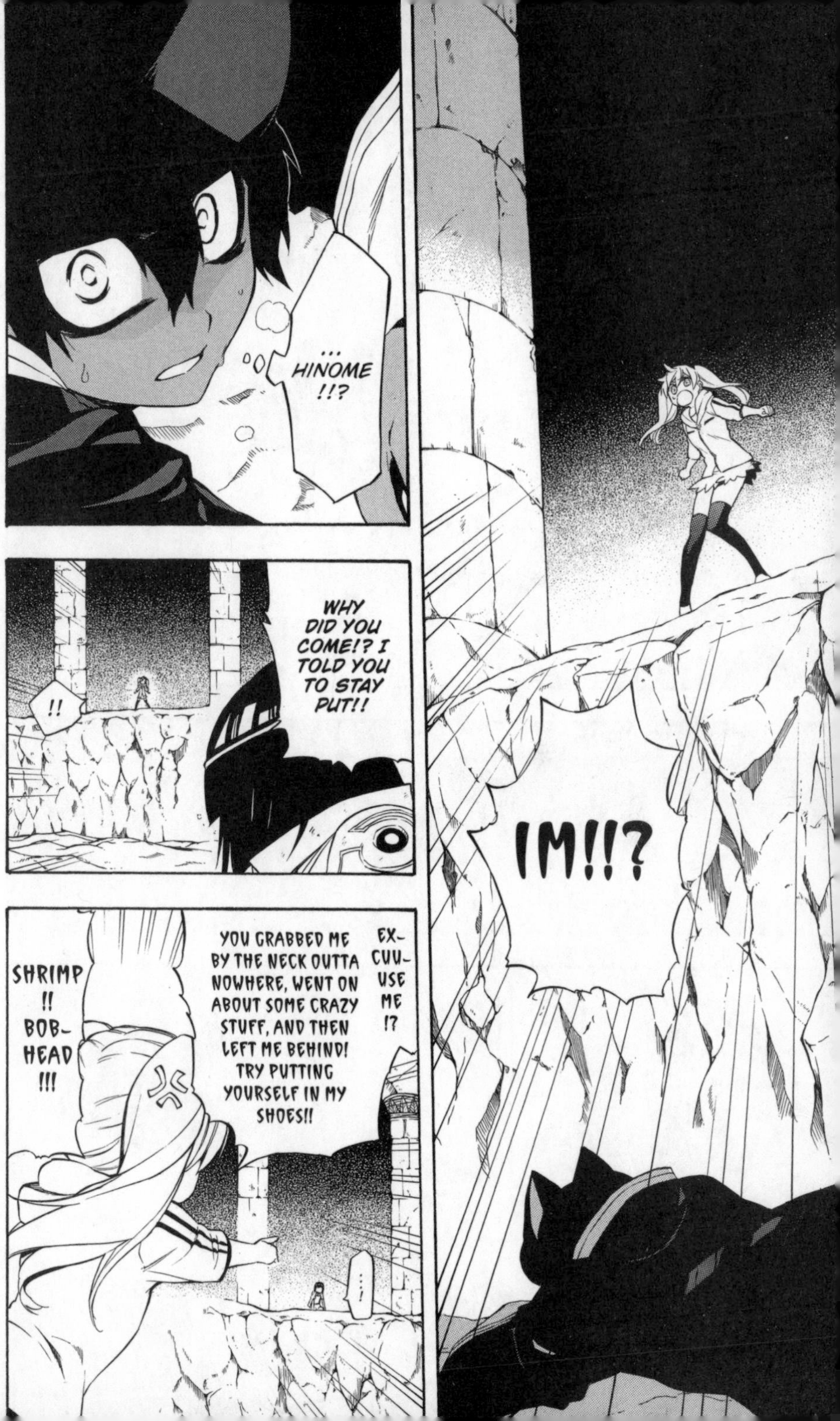
IM!!?
... HINOME !!?
WHY DID YOU COME!? I TOLD YOU TO STAY PUT!!
!!
EX-CUU-USE ME !?
YOU GRABBED ME BY THE NECK OUTTA NOWHERE, WENT ON ABOUT SOME CRAZY STUFF, AND THEN LEFT ME BEHIND! TRY PUTTING YOURSELF IN MY SHOES!!
SHRIMP !! BOB-HEAD !!!
...!

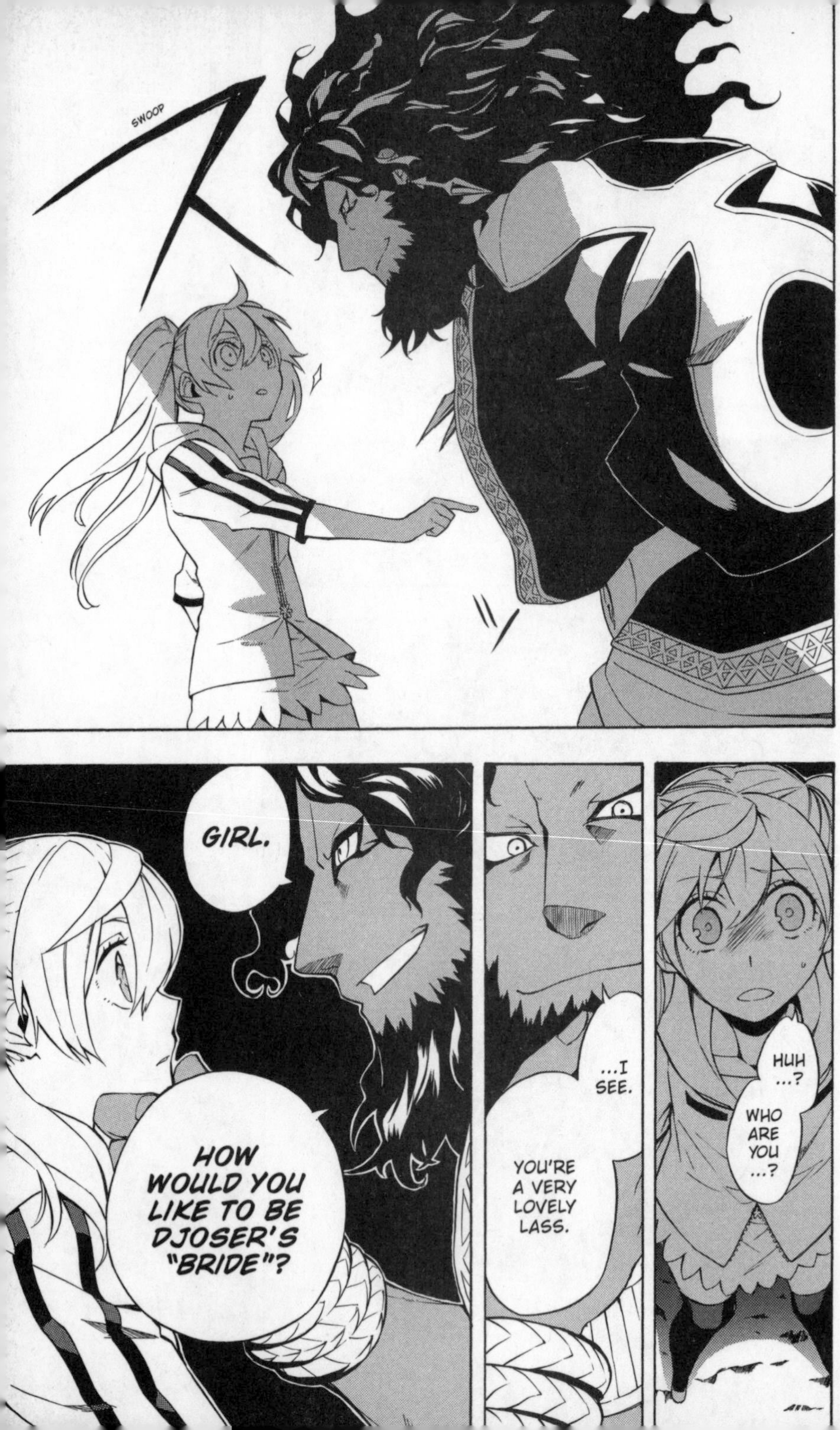
SWOOP
HUH ...?
WHO ARE YOU ...?
...I SEE.
YOU'RE A VERY LOVELY LASS.
GIRL.
HOW WOULD YOU LIKE TO BE DJOSER'S "BRIDE"?

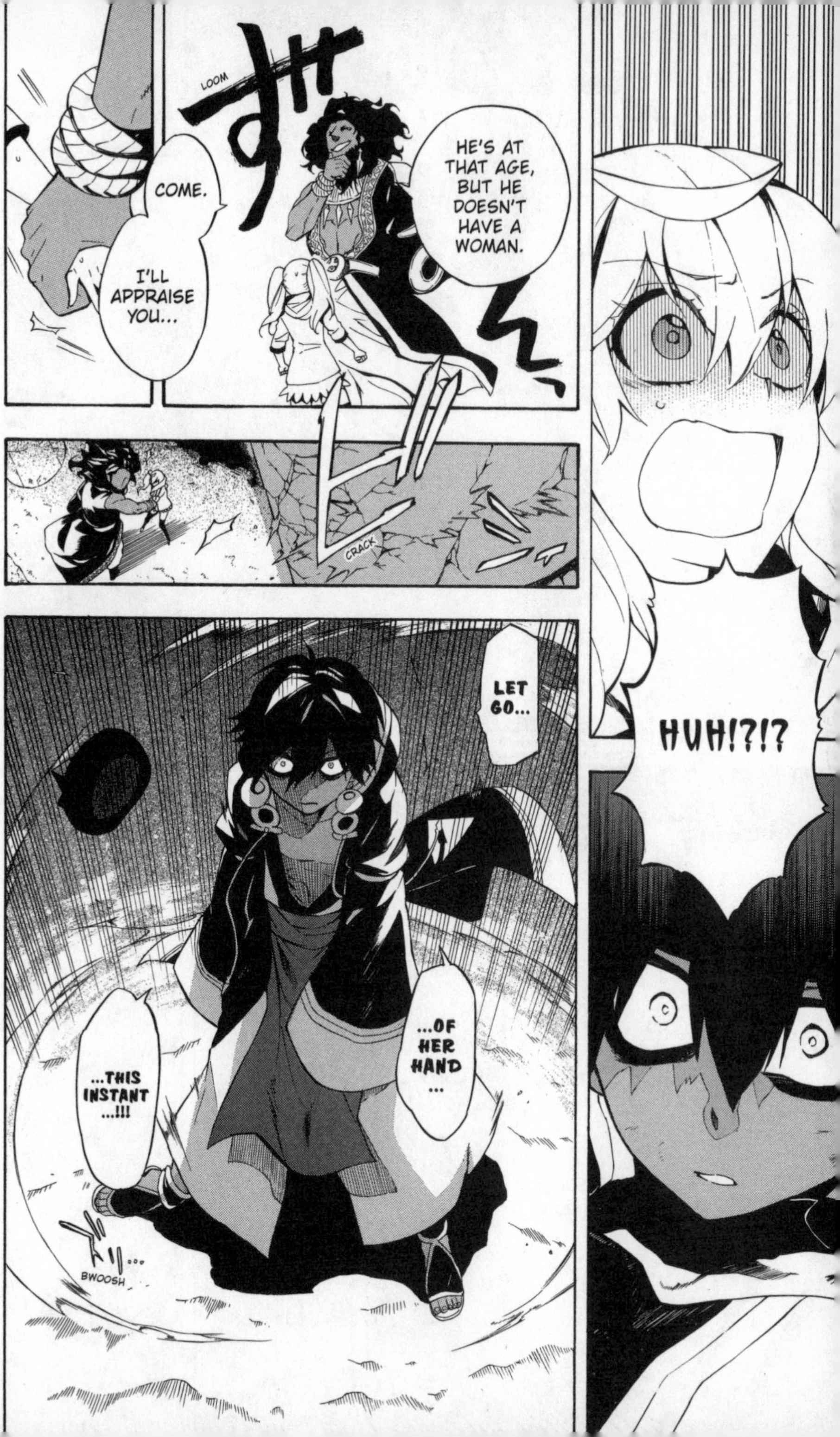
HUH!?!?
LOOM
HE'S AT THAT AGE, BUT HE DOESN'T HAVE A WOMAN.
COME.
I'LL APPRAISE YOU...
CRACK
LET GO...
...OF HER HAND...
...THIS INSTANT...!!!
BWOOSH

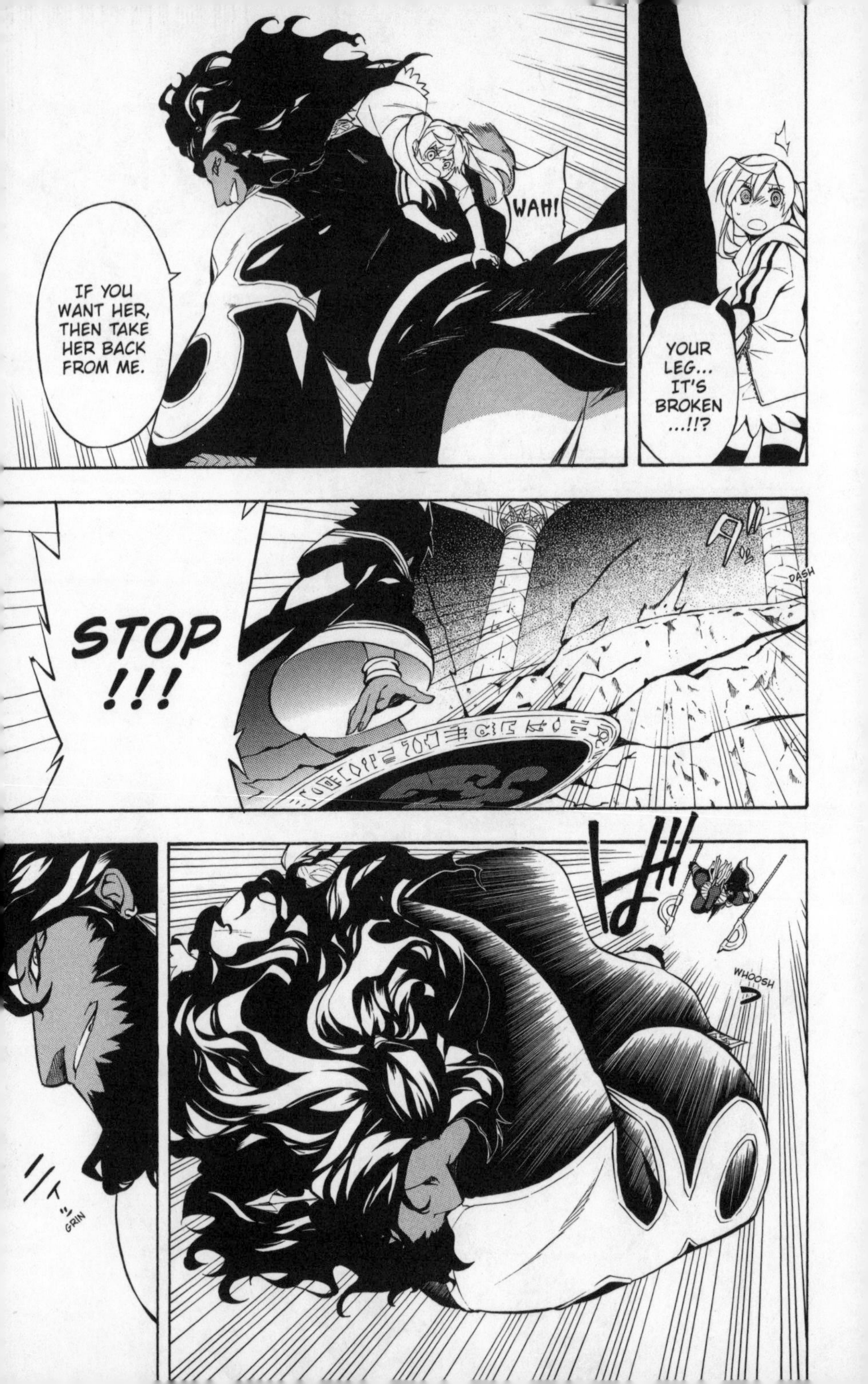
YOUR LEG... IT'S BROKEN ...!!?
WAH!
IF YOU WANT HER, THEN TAKE HER BACK FROM ME.
DASH
STOP !!!
WHOOSH
GRIN

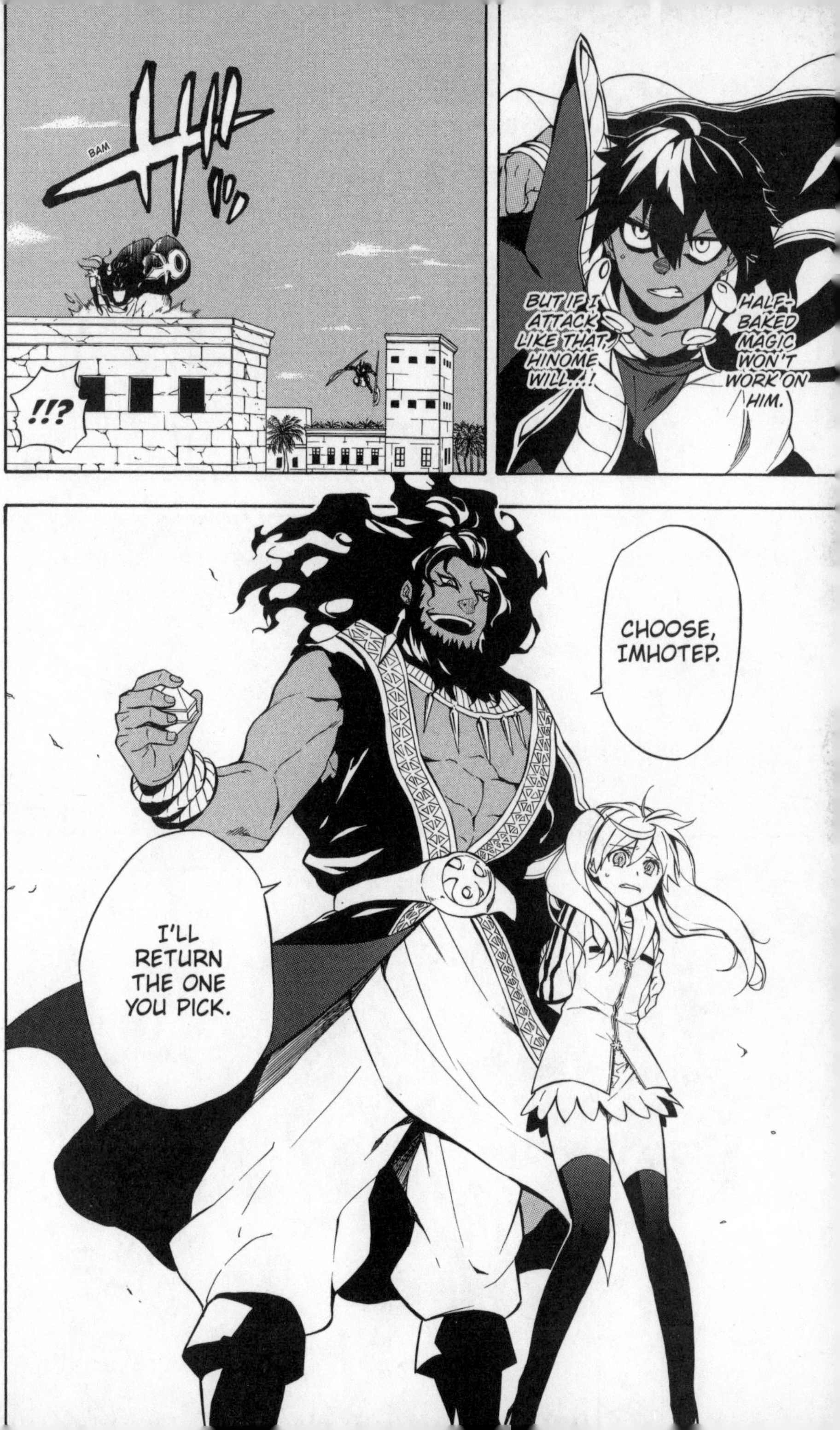
HALF-BAKED MAGIC WON'T WORK ON HIM.
BUT IF I ATTACK LIKE THAT, HINOME WILL...!
BAM
!!?
CHOOSE, IMHOTEP.
I'LL RETURN THE ONE YOU PICK.

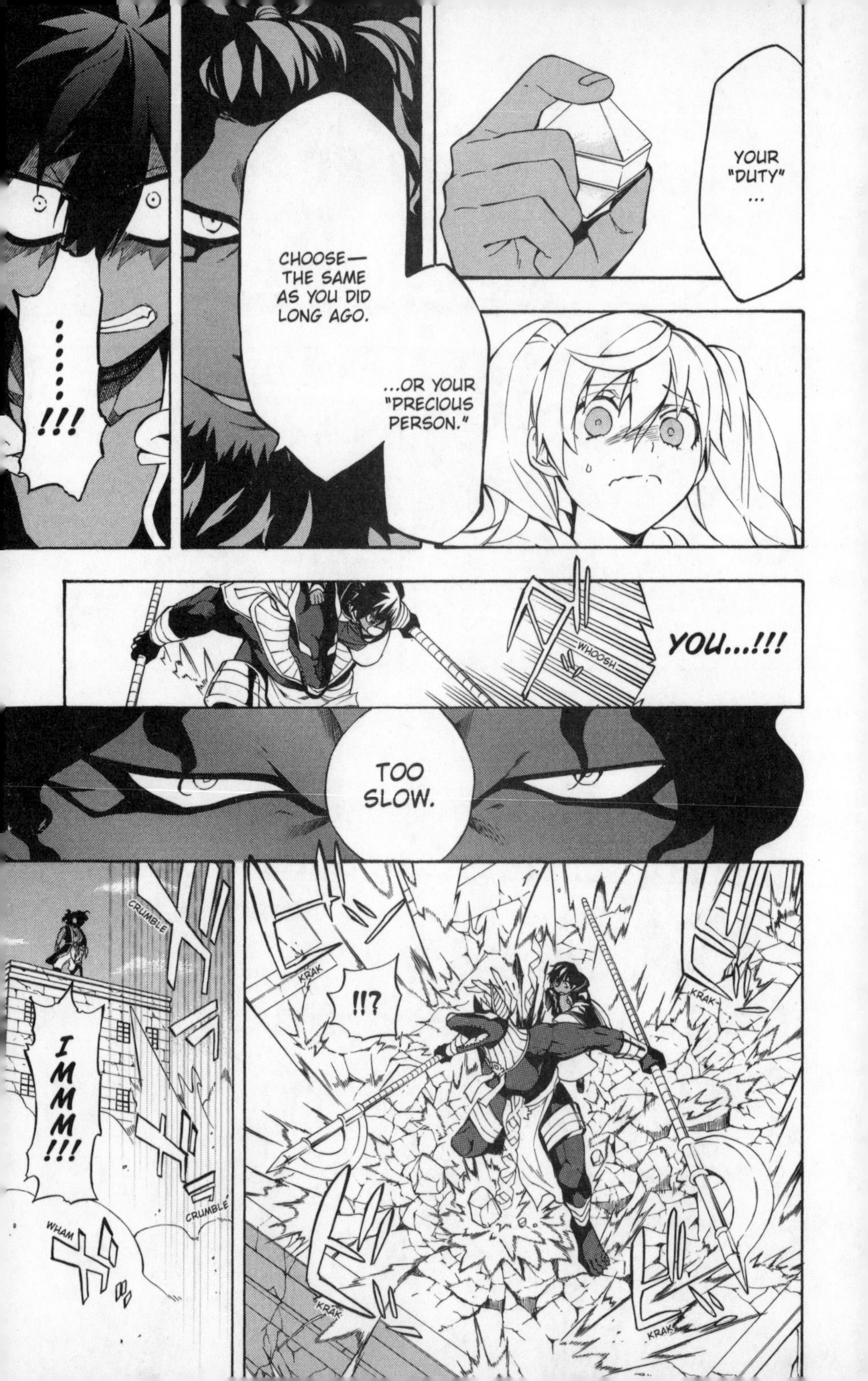
YOUR "DUTY" ...
...OR YOUR "PRECIOUS PERSON."
CHOOSE— THE SAME AS YOU DID LONG AGO.
......!!!
YOU...!!!
WHOOSH
TOO SLOW.
KRAK
!!?
KRAK
KRAK
KRAK
CRUMBLE
IMMMM!!!
CRUMBLE
WHAM

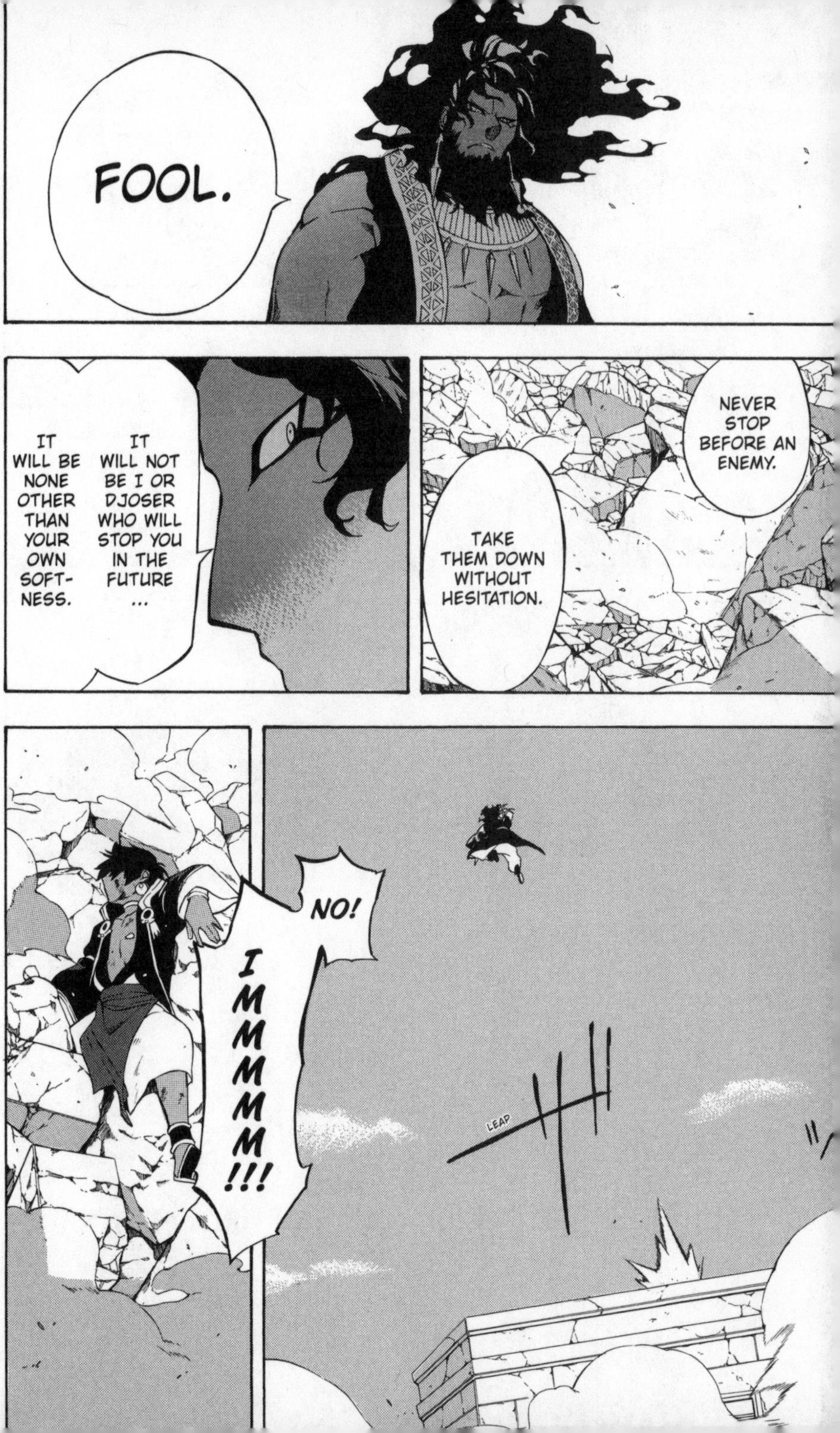
FOOL.
NEVER STOP BEFORE AN ENEMY.
TAKE THEM DOWN WITHOUT HESITATION.
IT WILL NOT BE I OR DJOSER WHO WILL STOP YOU IN THE FUTURE ...
IT WILL BE NONE OTHER THAN YOUR OWN SOFTNESS.
LEAP
NO!
IMMMMM!!!

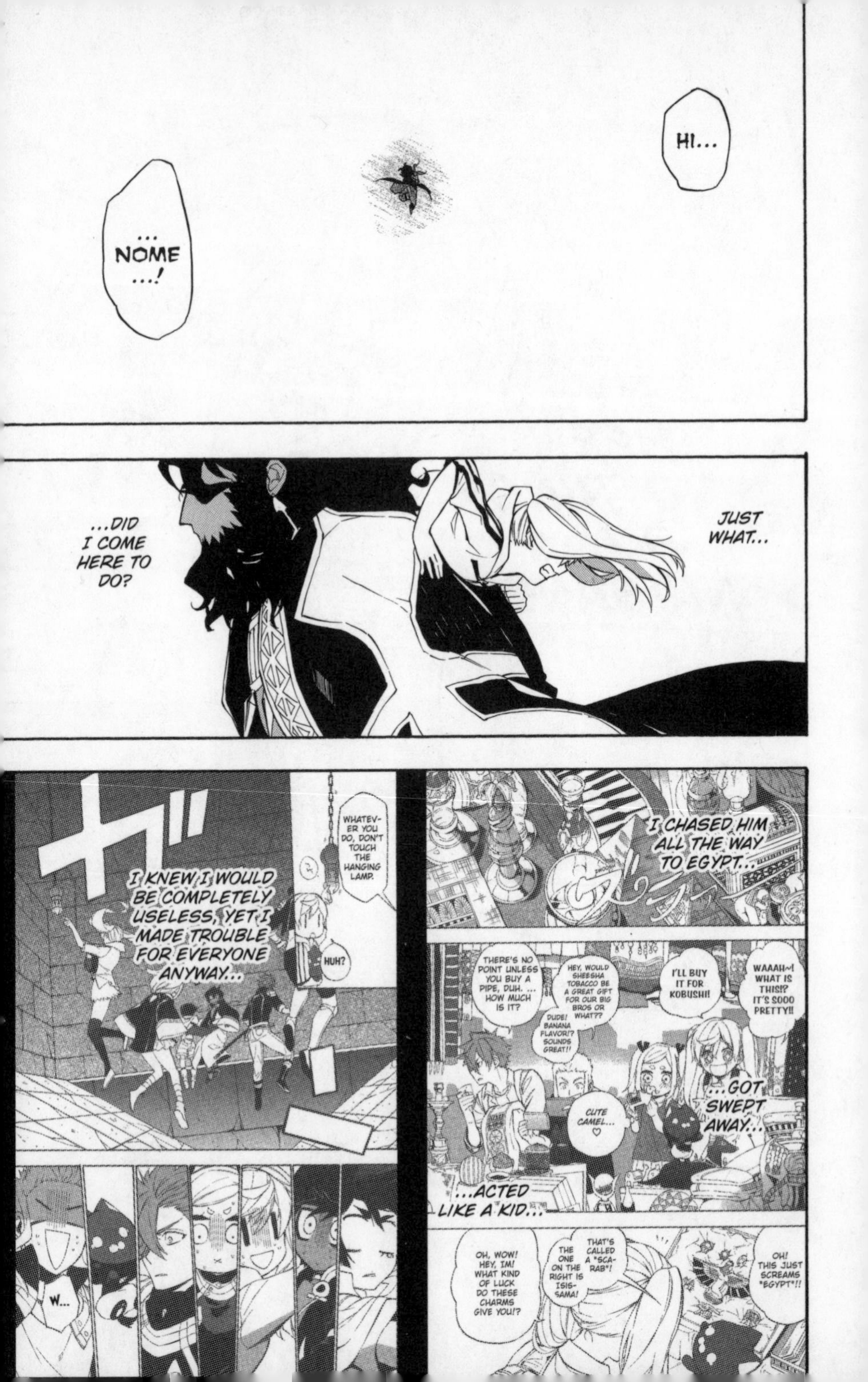

HI...
...NOME ...!
JUST WHAT...
...DID I COME HERE TO DO?
I CHASED HIM ALL THE WAY TO EGYPT...
WAAAH~! WHAT IS THIS!? IT'S SOOO PRETTY!!
I'LL BUY IT FOR KOBUSHI!
HEY, WOULD SHEESHA TOBACCO BE A GREAT GIFT FOR OUR BIG BROS OR WHAT??
THERE'S NO POINT UNLESS YOU BUY A PIPE, DUH. ... HOW MUCH IS IT?
DUDE! BANANA FLAVOR!? SOUNDS GREAT!!
...GOT SWEPT AWAY...
CUTE CAMEL... ♡
...ACTED LIKE A KID...
OH! THIS JUST SCREAMS "EGYPT"!!
THAT'S CALLED A "SCARAB"!
THE ONE ON THE RIGHT IS ISIS-SAMA!
OH, WOW! HEY, IM! WHAT KIND OF LUCK DO THESE CHARMS GIVE YOU!?
WHATEVER YOU DO, DON'T TOUCH THE HANGING LAMP.
HUH?
I KNEW I WOULD BE COMPLETELY USELESS, YET I MADE TROUBLE FOR EVERYONE ANYWAY...
W...

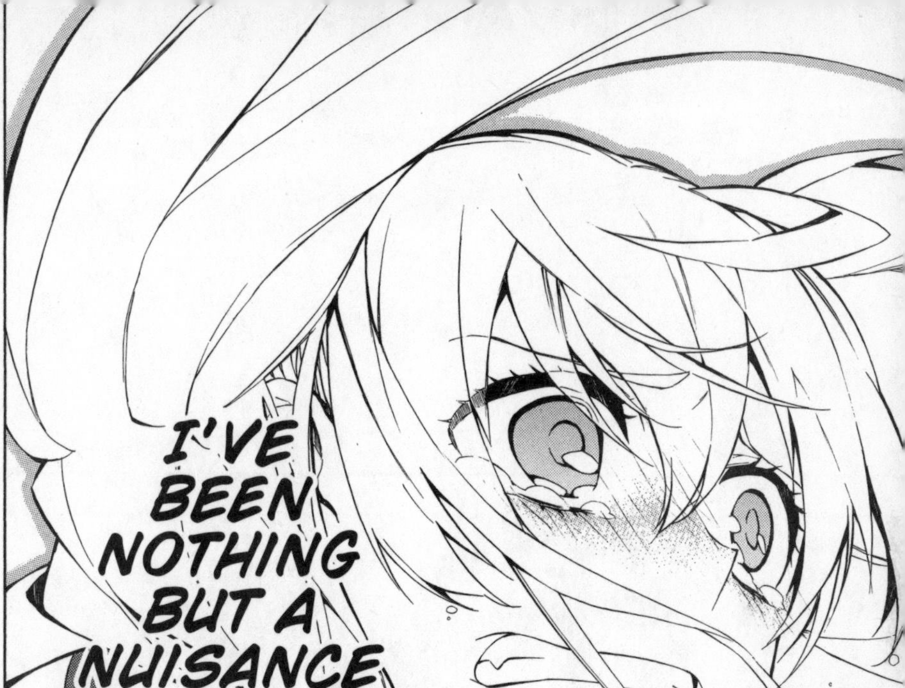
I'VE BEEN NOTHING BUT A NUISANCE TO IM...!
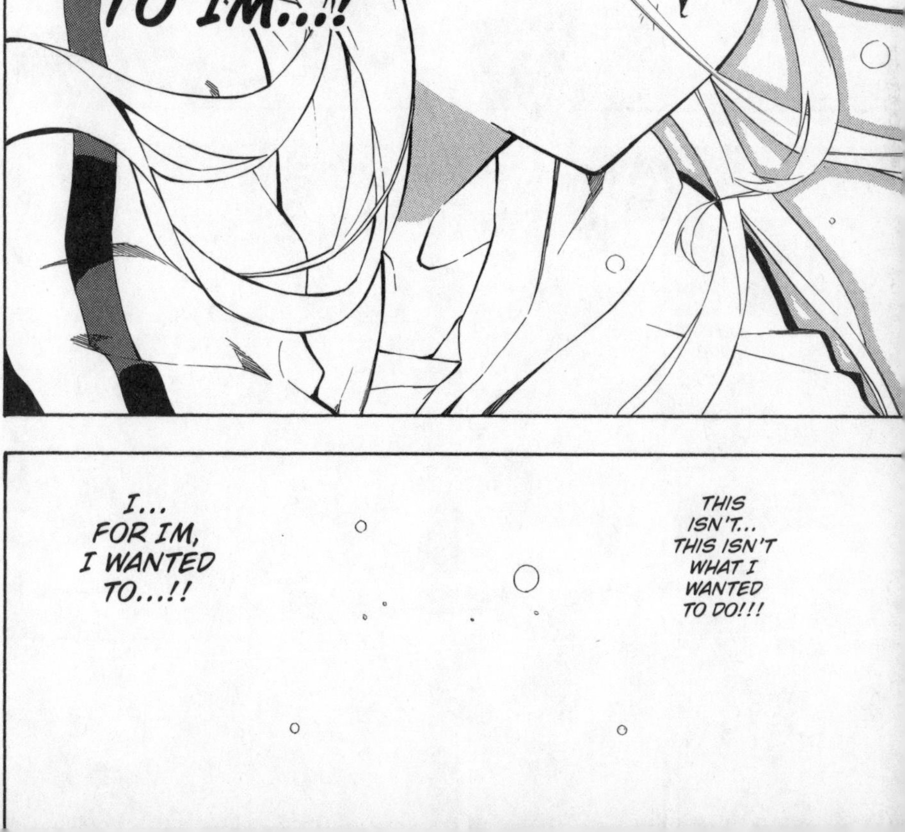
THIS ISN'T... THIS ISN'T WHAT I WANTED TO DO!!!
I... FOR IM, I WANTED TO...!!

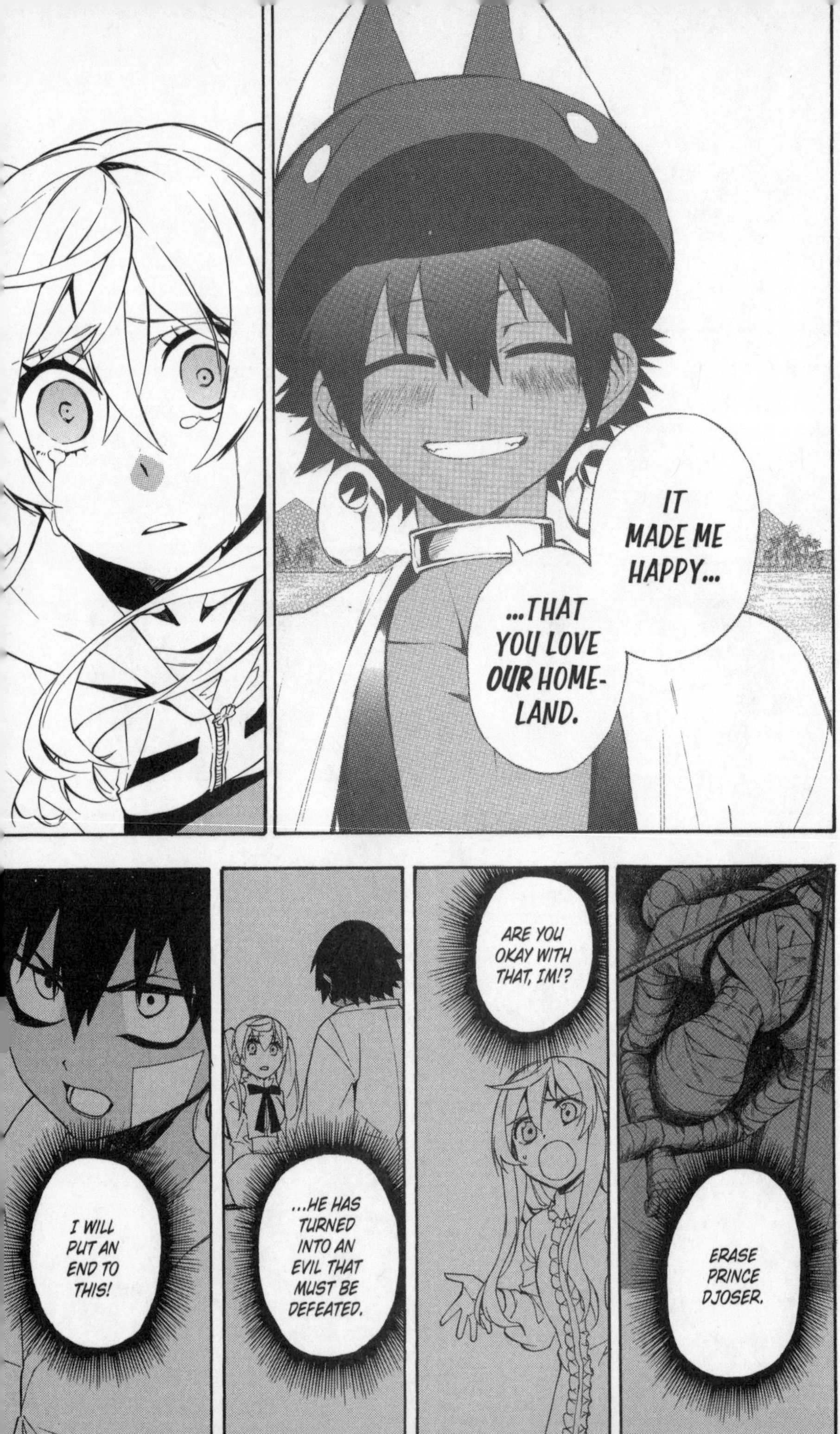
IT MADE ME HAPPY...
...THAT YOU LOVE **OUR** HOME-LAND.
ERASE PRINCE DJOSER.
ARE YOU OKAY WITH THAT, IM!?
...HE HAS TURNED INTO AN EVIL THAT MUST BE DEFEATED.
I WILL PUT AN END TO THIS!

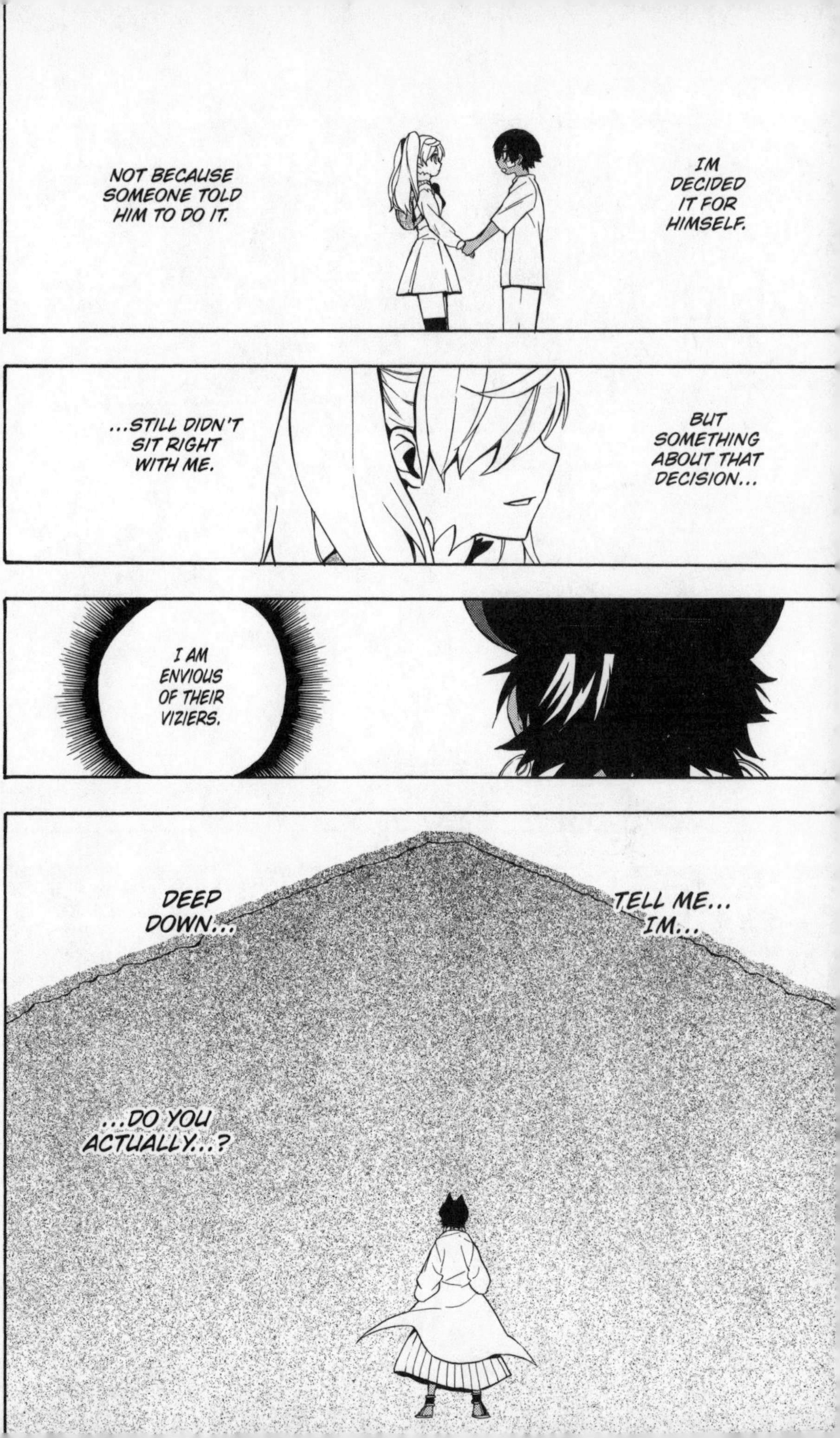
IM DECIDED IT FOR HIMSELF.
NOT BECAUSE SOMEONE TOLD HIM TO DO IT.
BUT SOMETHING ABOUT THAT DECISION...
...STILL DIDN'T SIT RIGHT WITH ME.
I AM ENVIOUS OF THEIR VIZIERS.
TELL ME... IM...
DEEP DOWN...
...DO YOU ACTUALLY...?

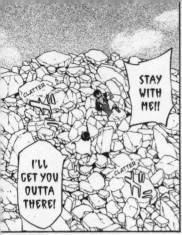

STAY WITH ME!!

I'LL GET YOU OUTTA THERE!

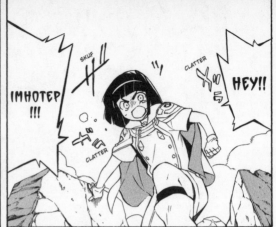

IMHOTEP!!!

SKUF

HEY!!

CLATTER

CLATTER

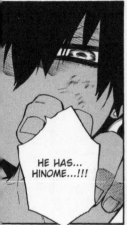

HE HAS... HINOME...!!!

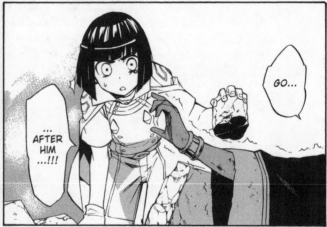

GO...

...AFTER HIM...!!!

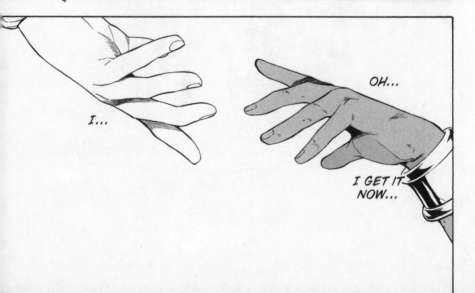

I...

OH...

I GET IT NOW...

*I WANT THEM
TO MAKE UP.*

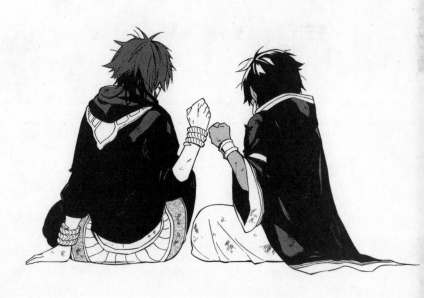

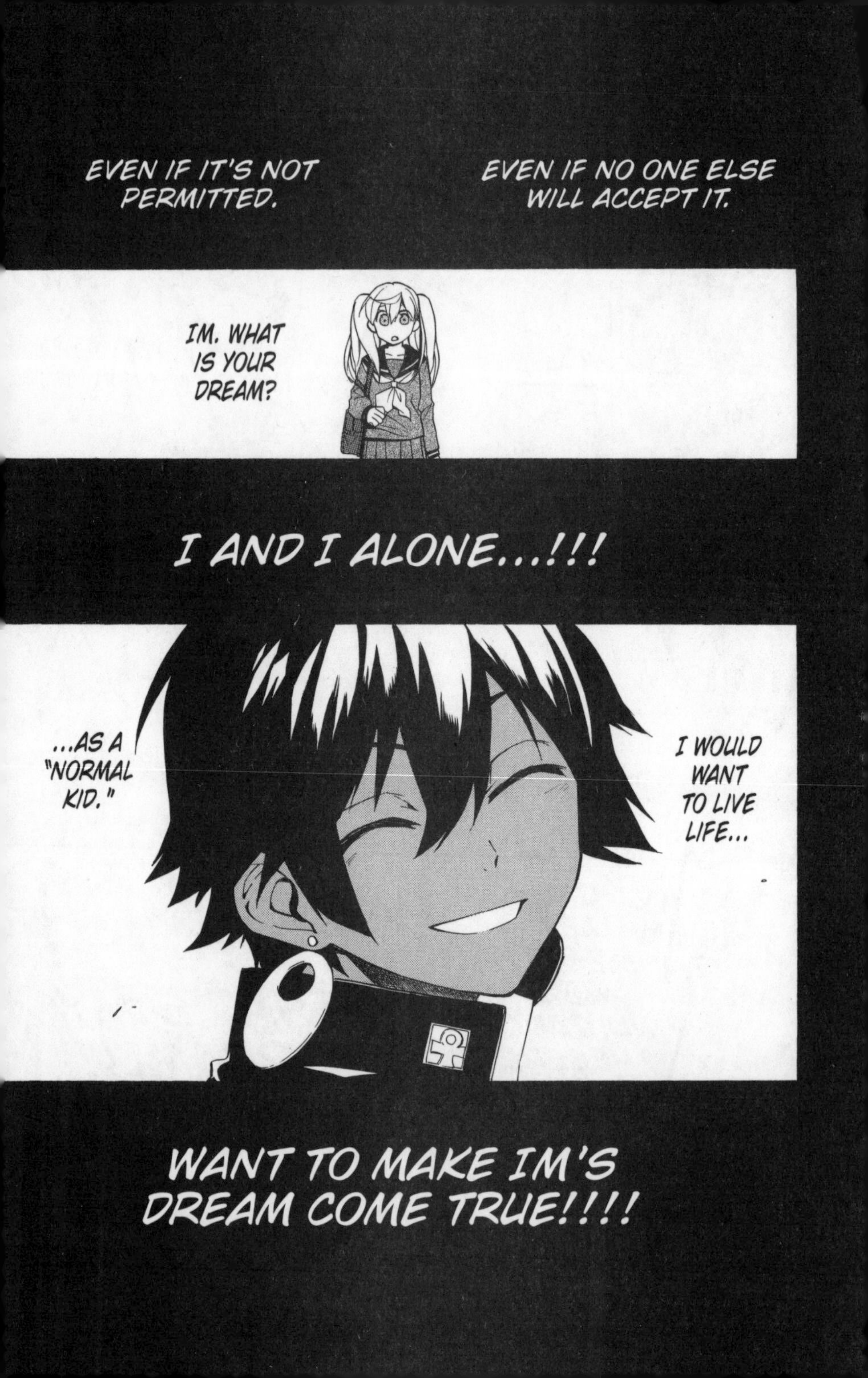
EVEN IF NO ONE ELSE WILL ACCEPT IT.
EVEN IF IT'S NOT PERMITTED.
IM. WHAT IS YOUR DREAM?
I AND I ALONE...!!!
I WOULD WANT TO LIVE LIFE...
...AS A "NORMAL KID."
WANT TO MAKE IM'S DREAM COME TRUE!!!!

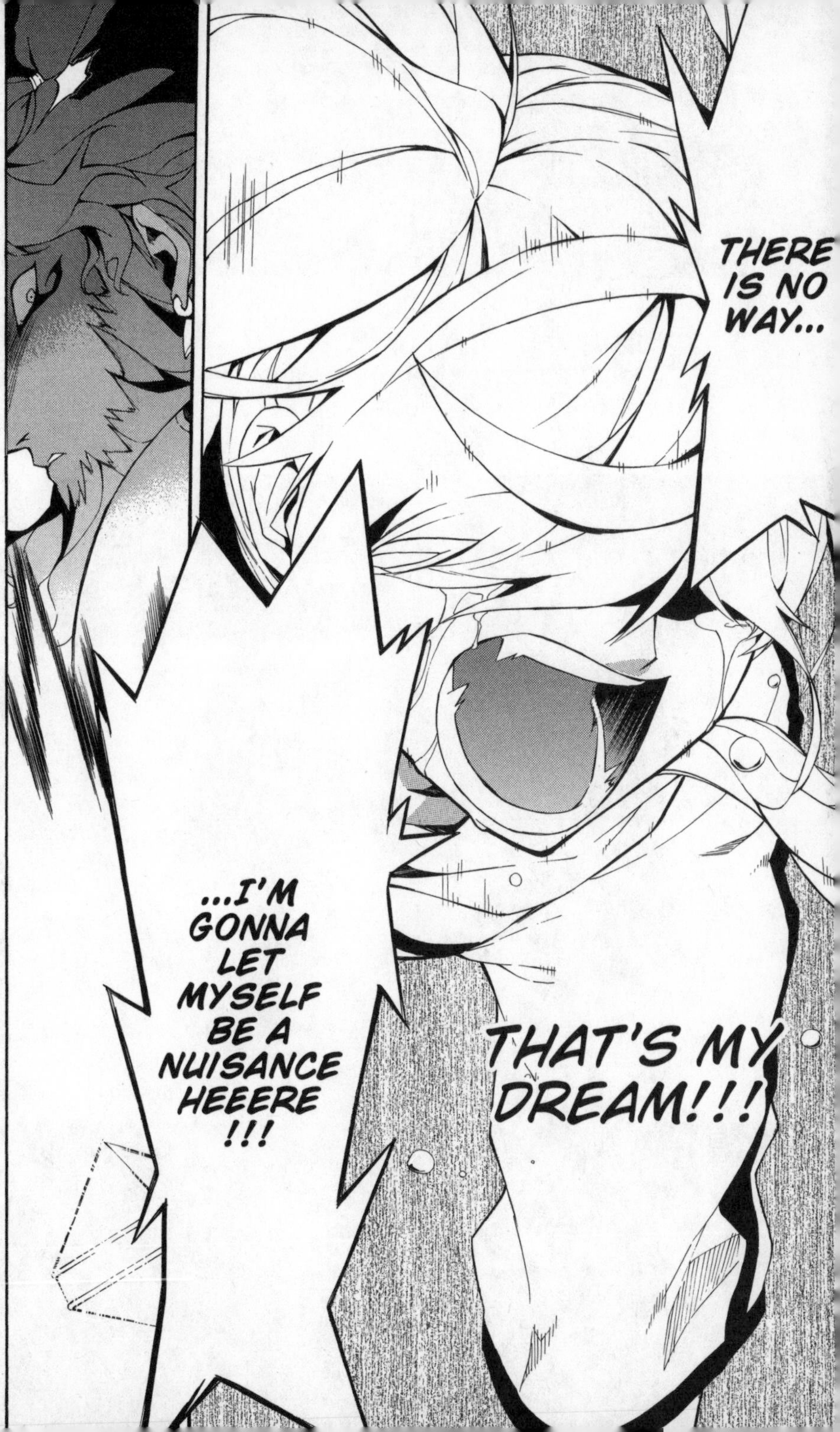
THERE IS NO WAY...
...I'M GONNA LET MYSELF BE A NUISANCE HEEERE!!!
THAT'S MY DREAM!!!

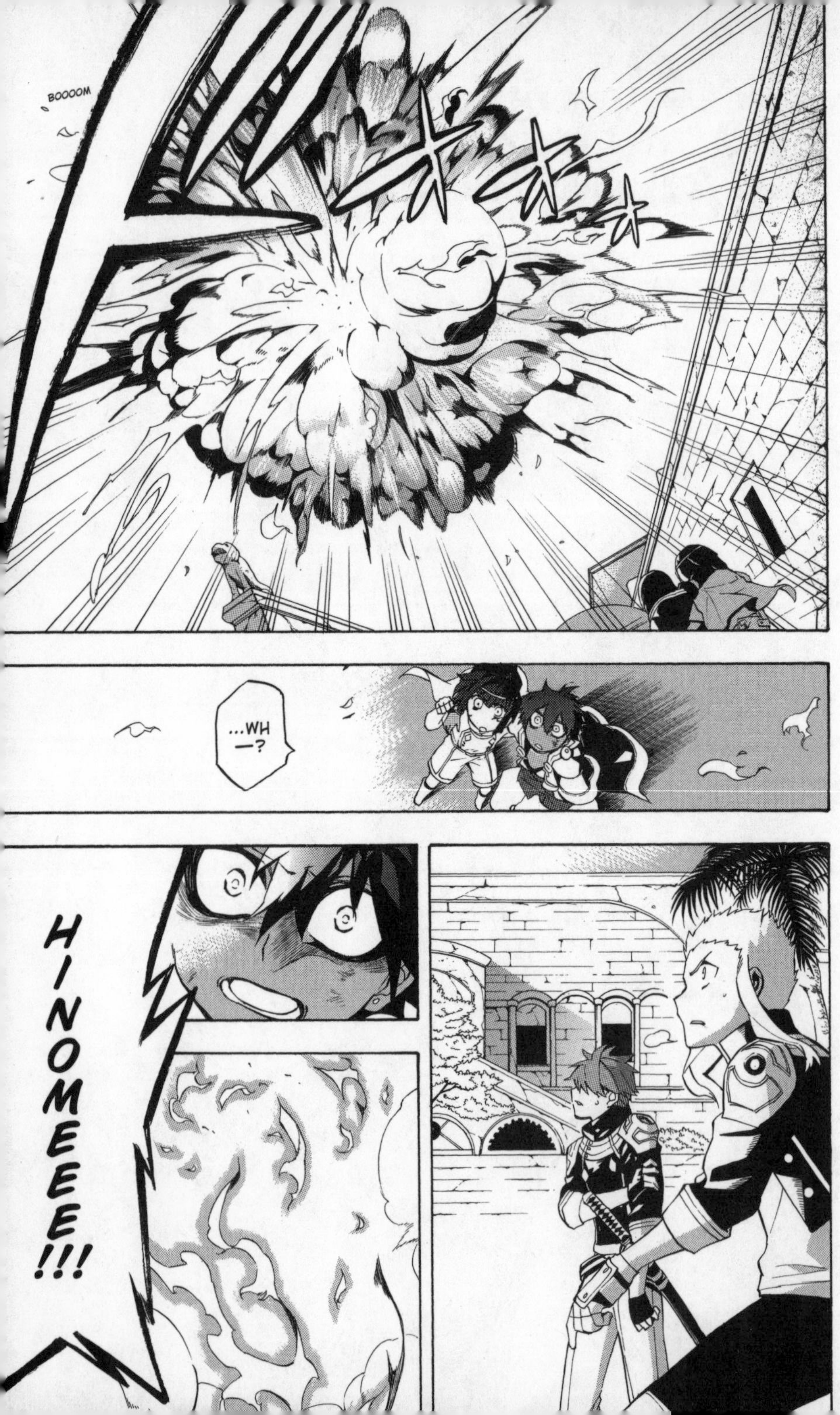
BOOOOM
...WH—?
HINOMEEEE!!!

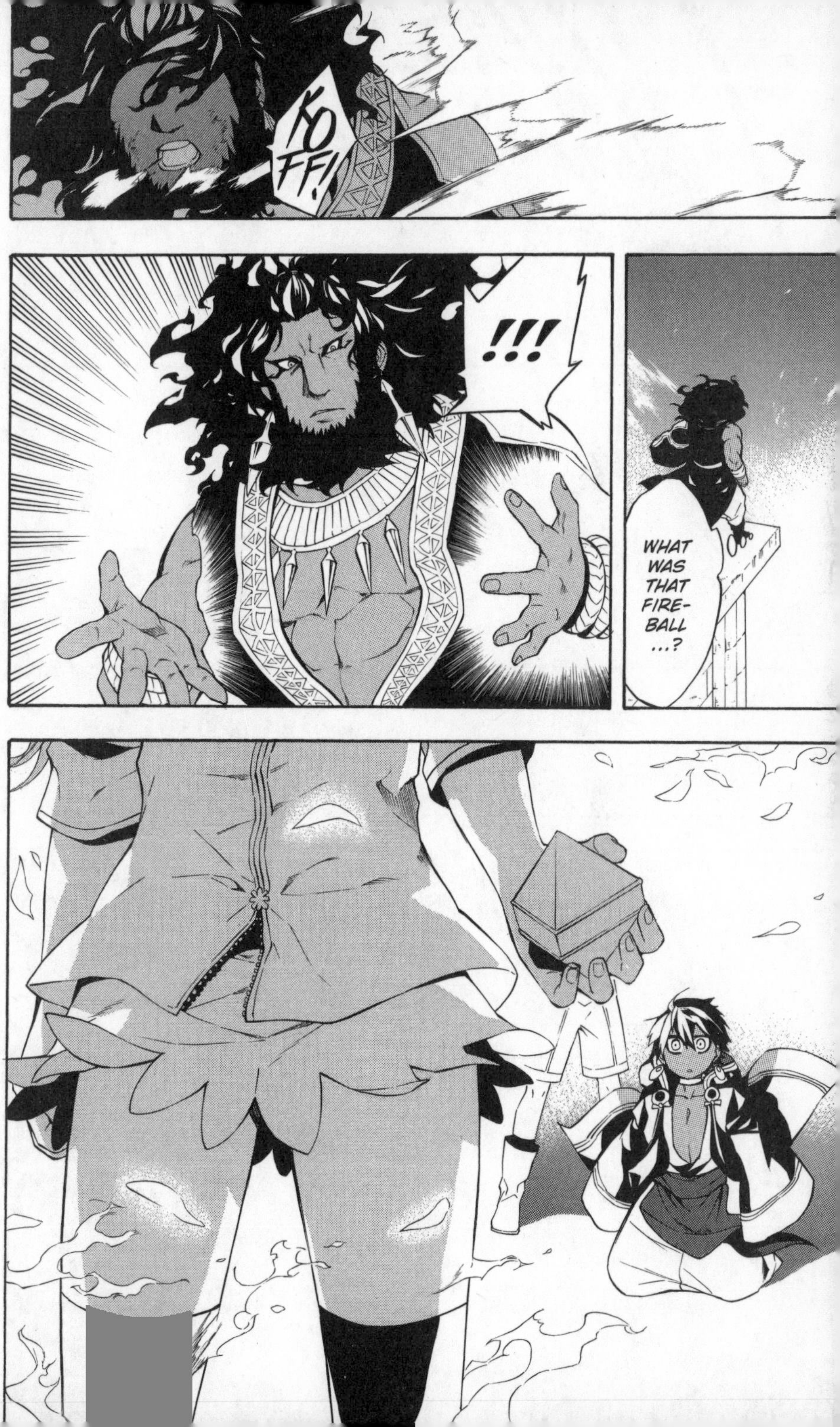
KOFF!
WHAT WAS THAT FIRE-BALL ...?
!!!

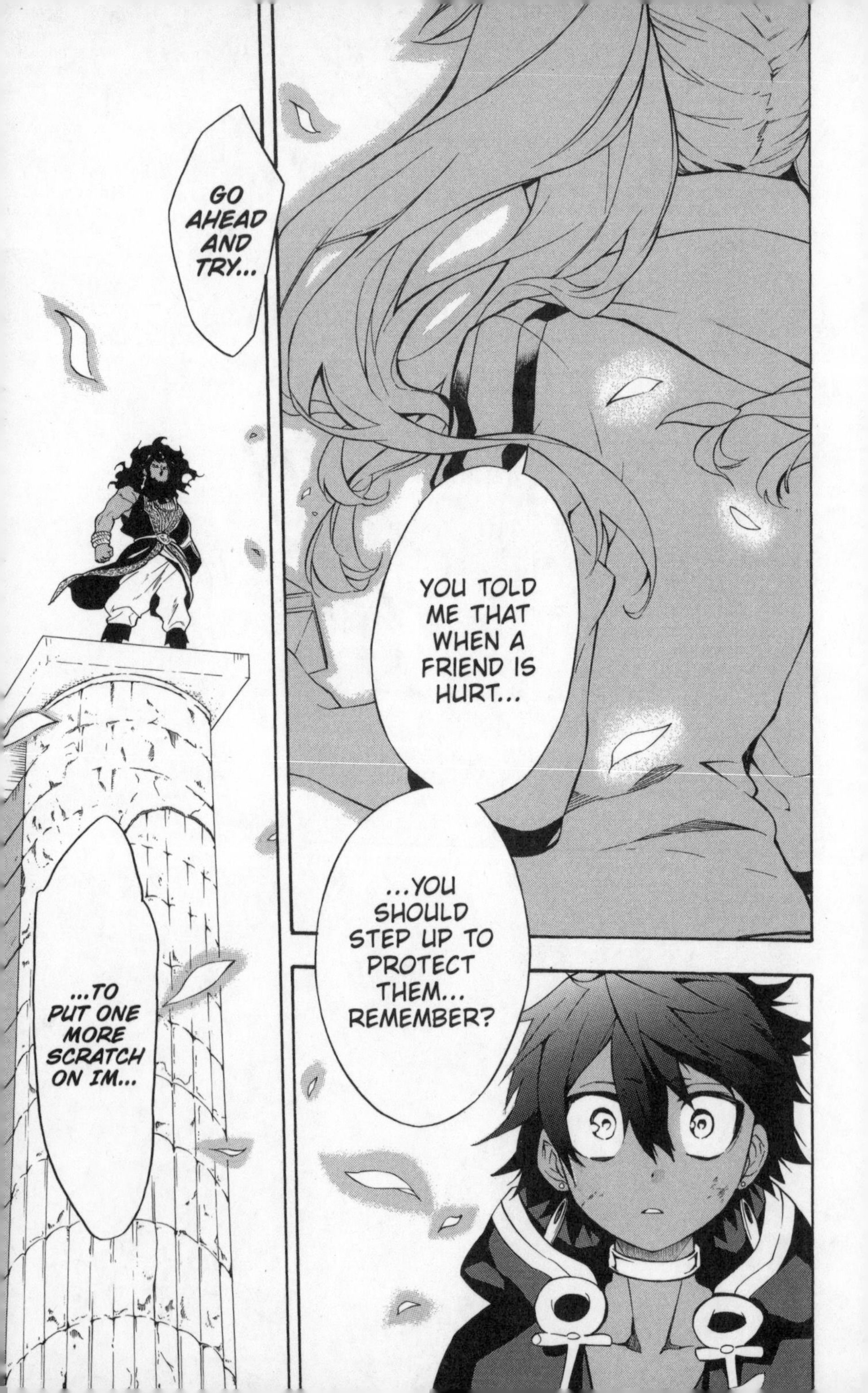
YOU TOLD ME THAT WHEN A FRIEND IS HURT...
...YOU SHOULD STEP UP TO PROTECT THEM... REMEMBER?
GO AHEAD AND TRY...
...TO PUT ONE MORE SCRATCH ON IM...

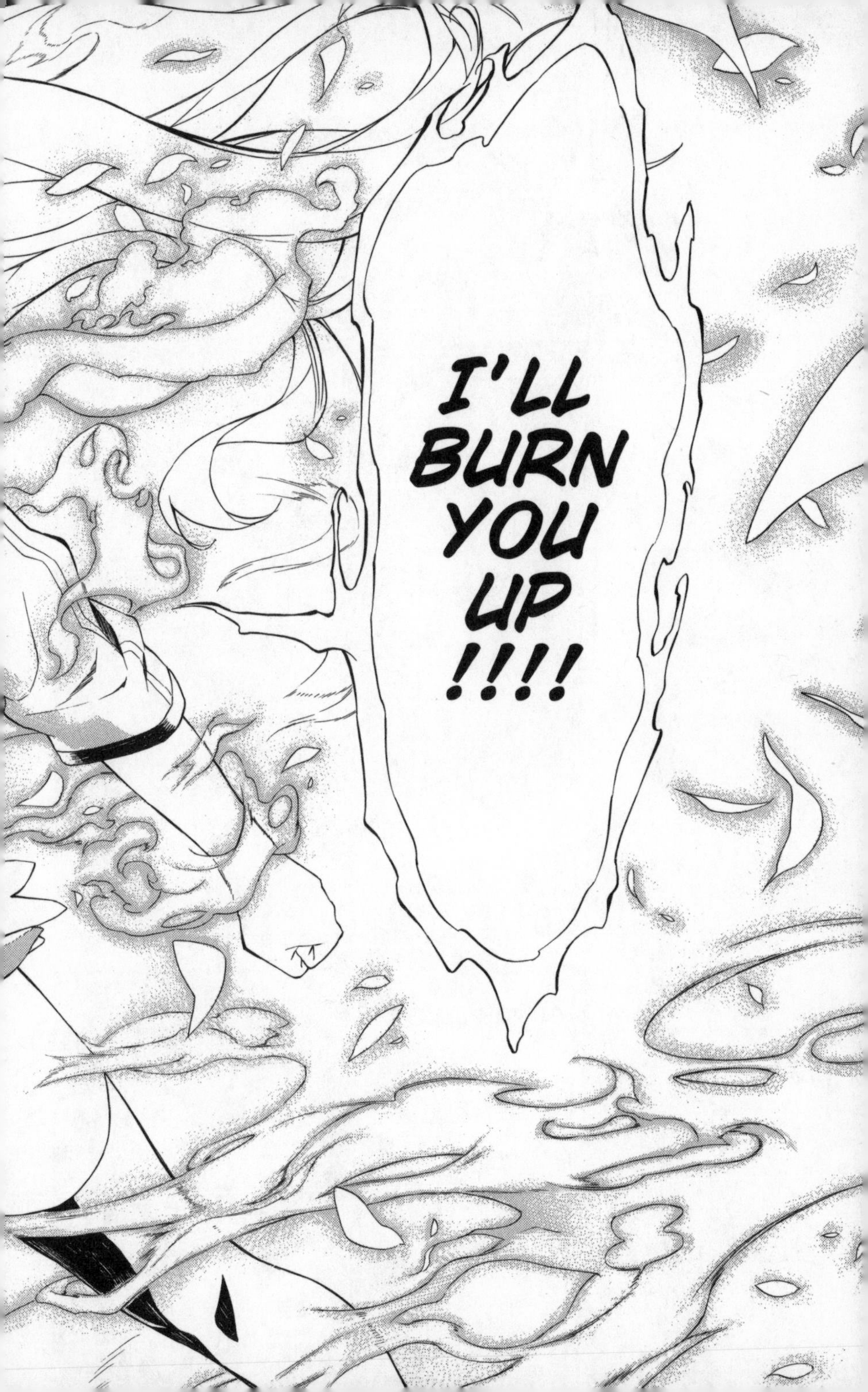
I'LL BURN YOU UP !!!!

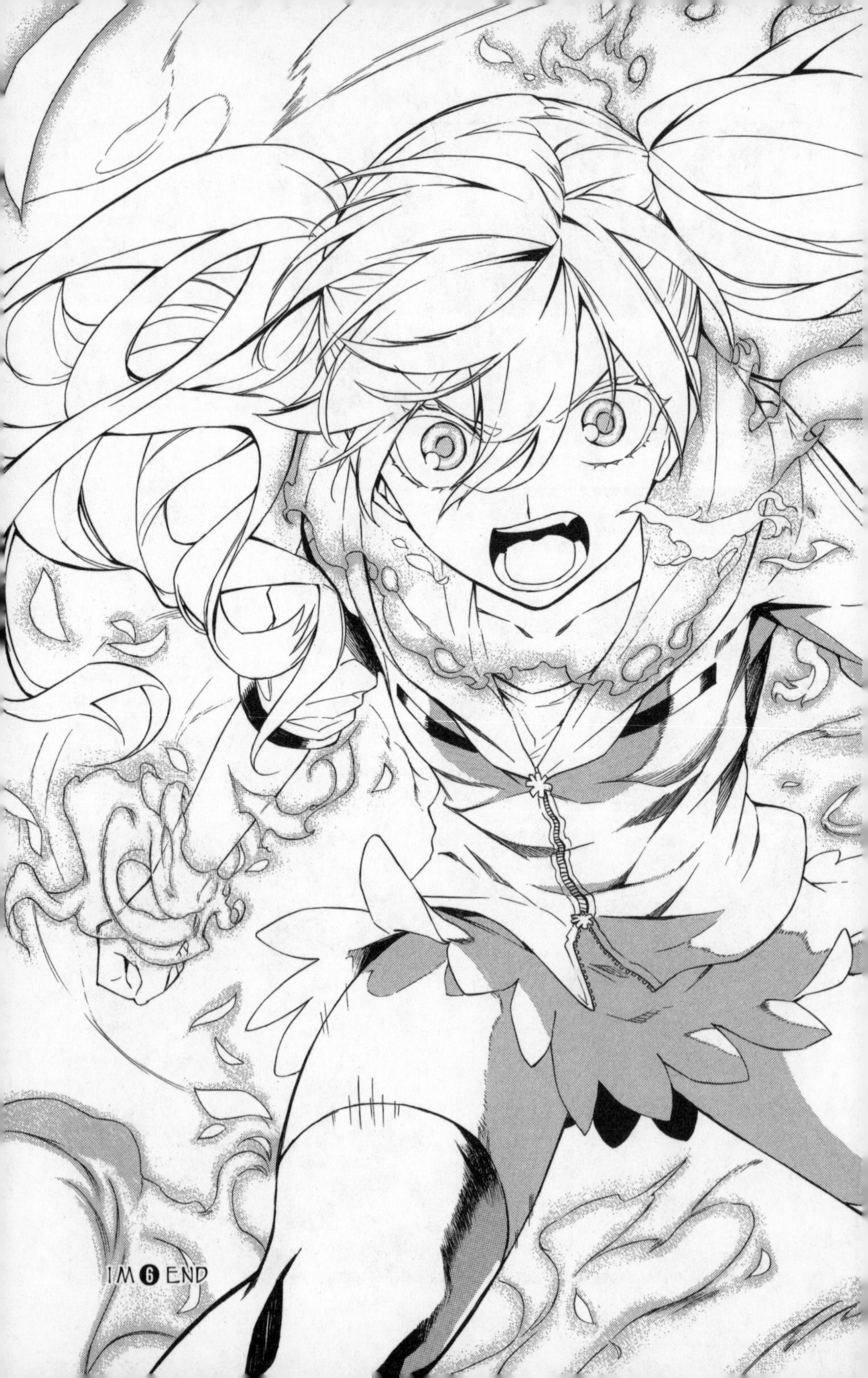
IM 6 END

BONUS STORY: "DESPAIR RAM-CHAN☆"

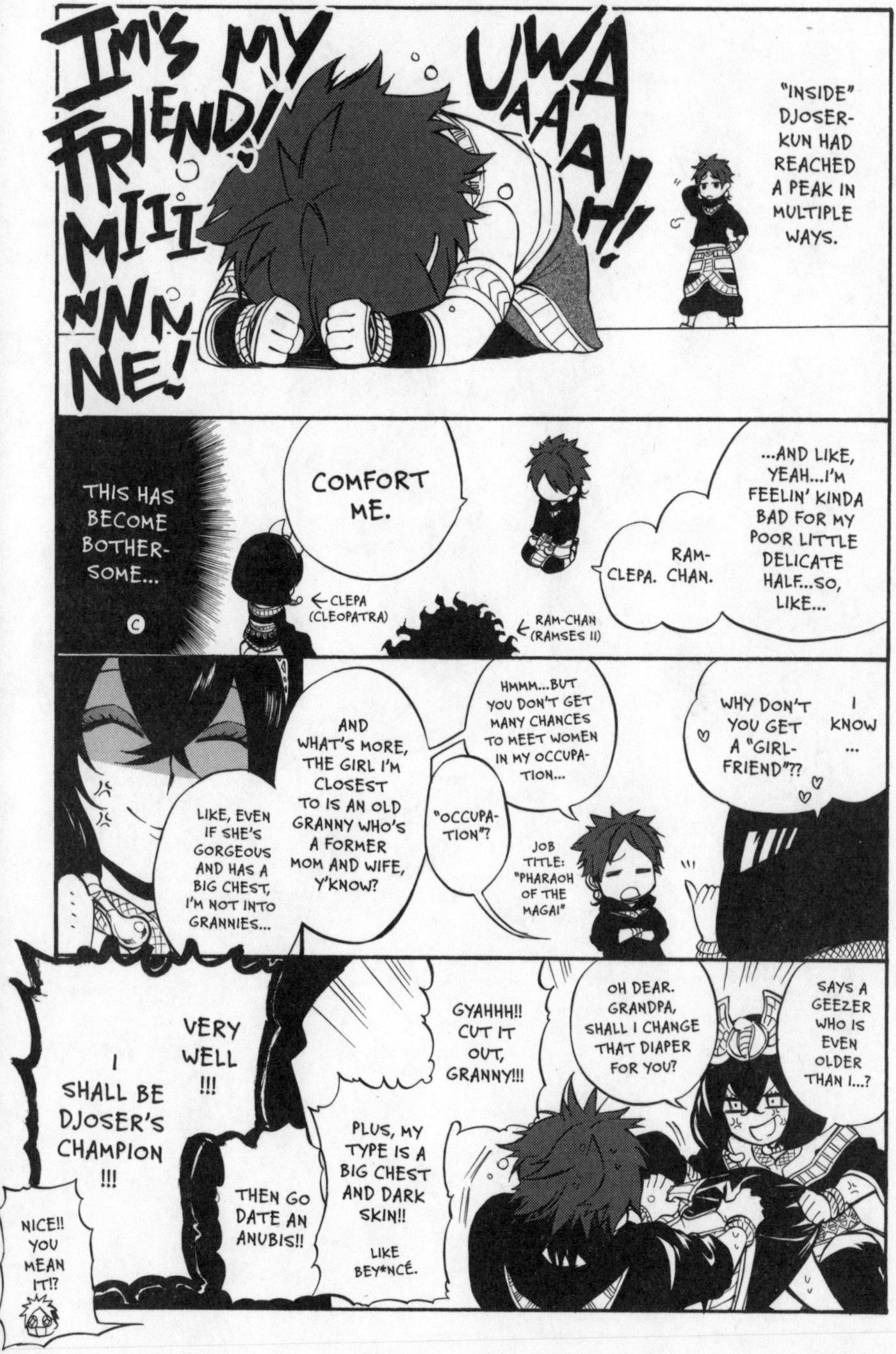
"INSIDE" DJOSER-KUN HAD REACHED A PEAK IN MULTIPLE WAYS.
UWAAAAAH!!
IM'S MY FRIEND! MIIINNNNE!
...AND LIKE, YEAH...I'M FEELIN' KINDA BAD FOR MY POOR LITTLE DELICATE HALF...SO, LIKE...
RAM-CHAN. CLEPA.
← RAM-CHAN (RAMSES II)
COMFORT ME.
← CLEPA (CLEOPATRA)
THIS HAS BECOME BOTHER-SOME...
I KNOW...
WHY DON'T YOU GET A "GIRL-FRIEND"??
HMMM...BUT YOU DON'T GET MANY CHANCES TO MEET WOMEN IN MY OCCUPA-TION...
JOB TITLE: "PHARAOH OF THE MAGAI"
"OCCUPA-TION"?
AND WHAT'S MORE, THE GIRL I'M CLOSEST TO IS AN OLD GRANNY WHO'S A FORMER MOM AND WIFE, Y'KNOW?
LIKE, EVEN IF SHE'S GORGEOUS AND HAS A BIG CHEST, I'M NOT INTO GRANNIES...
SAYS A GEEZER WHO IS EVEN OLDER THAN I...?
OH DEAR. GRANDPA, SHALL I CHANGE THAT DIAPER FOR YOU?
GYAHHH!! CUT IT OUT, GRANNY!!!
PLUS, MY TYPE IS A BIG CHEST AND DARK SKIN!!
LIKE BEY*NCÉ.
THEN GO DATE AN ANUBIS!!
VERY WELL!!!
I SHALL BE DJOSER'S CHAMPION!!!
NICE!! YOU MEAN IT!?

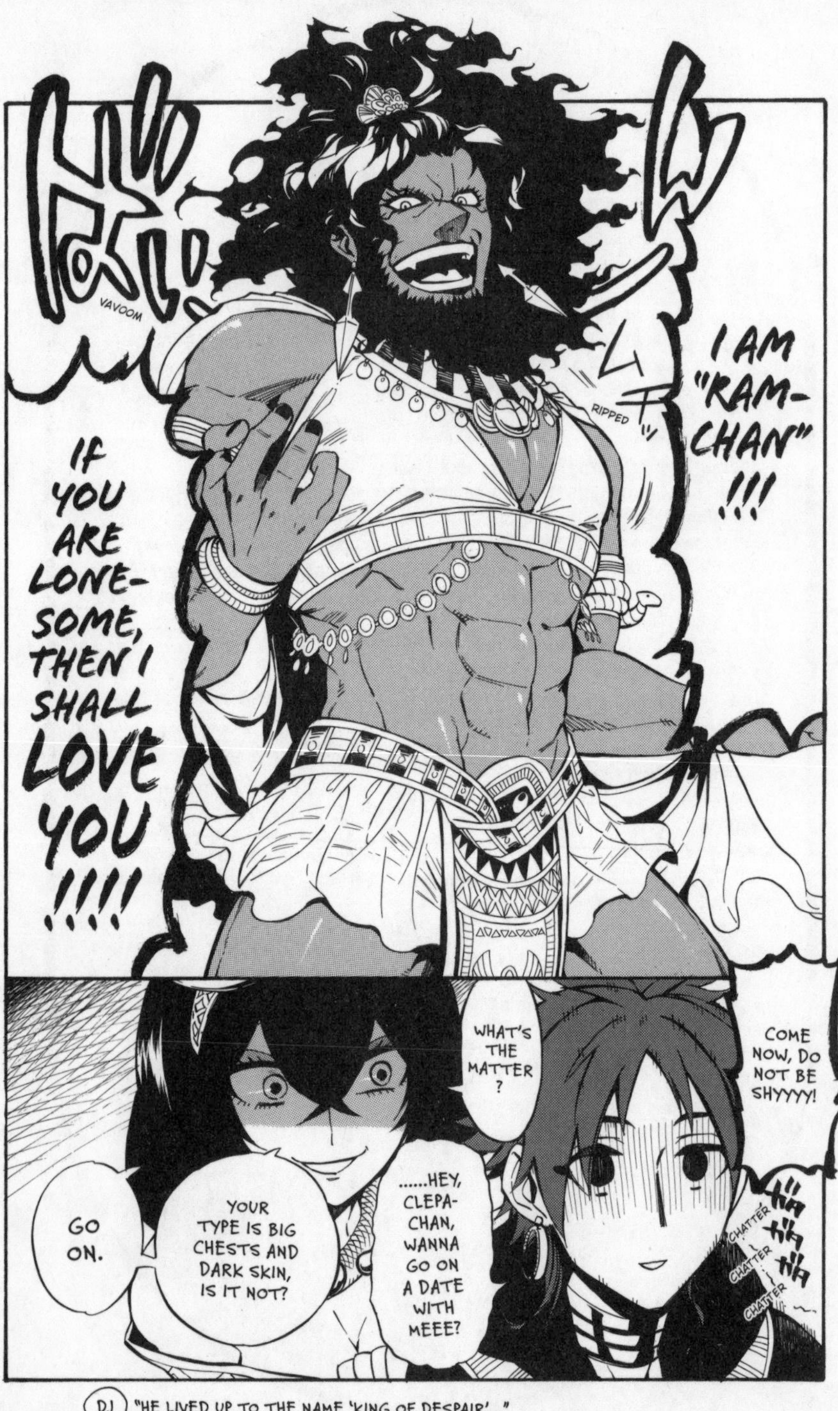
I AM "RAM-CHAN"!!!
RIPPED
VAVOOM
IF YOU ARE LONESOME, THEN I SHALL LOVE YOU!!!!
COME NOW, DO NOT BE SHYYYYY!
CHATTER CHATTER CHATTER
WHAT'S THE MATTER?
......HEY, CLEPA-CHAN, WANNA GO ON A DATE WITH MEEE?
YOUR TYPE IS BIG CHESTS AND DARK SKIN, IS IT NOT?
GO ON.

DJ "HE LIVED UP TO THE NAME 'KING OF DESPAIR'..."

TRANSLATION NOTES

Common Honorifics

no honorific: Indicates familiarity or closeness; if used without permission or reason, addressing someone in this manner would constitute an insult.

-san: The Japanese equivalent of Mr./Mrs./Miss. If a situation calls for politeness, this is the fail-safe honorific.

-sama: Conveys great respect; may also indicate the social status of the speaker is lower than that of the addressee.

-kun: Used most often when referring to boys, this honorific indicates affection or familiarity. Occasionally used by older men among their peers, but it may also be used by anyone referring to a person of lower standing.

-chan: An affectionate honorific indicating familiarity used mostly in reference to girls; also used in reference to cute persons or animals of either gender.

-sensei: A respectful term for teachers, artists, or high-level professionals.

-oniisan, *nii-san*, *aniki*, etc.: A term of endearment meaning "big brother" that may be more widely used to address any young man who is like a brother, regardless of whether he is related or not.

-oneesan, *nee-san*, *aneki*, etc.: The female counterpart of the above, nee-san means "big sister."

Page 16

Mochi is a sticky rice cake. They often have a filling, such as red bean paste, but these particular mochi are *ankoro mochi*, which have red bean paste on the outside instead.

Page 36

Gumi, meaning "group," refers to a gang of yakuza—and since Shirahana is Kobushi's last name, she might be having a "family thing" in more than one sense...

Page 44

Assalamu is a shortened form of the Arabic greeting *Assalamu alaykum*, or "peace be upon you."

Page 62
The **Field of Reeds**, also known as the "Field of Aaru," is the ancient Egyptian afterlife, a place of endless, fertile reed fields free of pain or suffering. The souls of the dead could enter it only if their hearts were judged to be lighter than an ostrich feather, with every sin they had committed in life increasing the weight. Those who failed this test had their hearts consumed by the crocodile demon Ammit and were consigned to Duat, the land of the dead.

Page 85
Tanuki, or "racoon dogs," are a real animal but also shapeshifting spirits in Japanese folklore. Tanuki tricksters are famously lazy.

Page 91
In Japanese, *ukaru* means to pass something, like an exam. For students studying for exams, it's a lucky word among other similar words. On the flip side, you shouldn't say words like *ochiru*, "to fail," around exam students!

Page 136
"Look on my works, ye mighty, and despair!" is a reference to the poem "Ozymandias," by Percy Bysshe Shelley. While the poem does have the very same Ramses II say these lines, the implication is a bit different from what we see in *Im*—only a few ruins remains of Ramses's "works," making them a warning against hubris since even the deeds of the greatest of kings will crumble to nothing in the face of time instead of a boast claiming "nobody will ever be as awesome as I was."

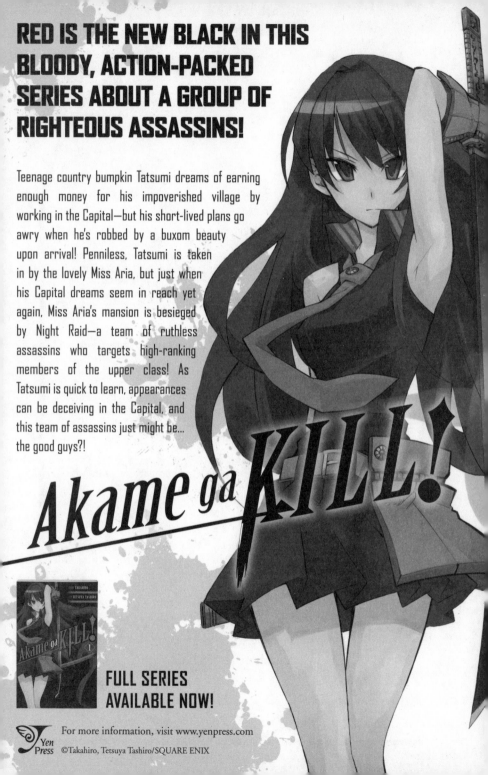

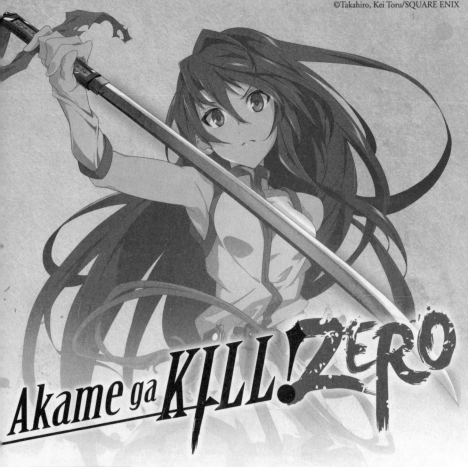
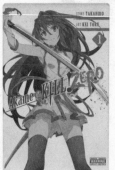

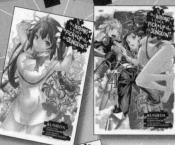
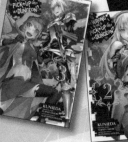
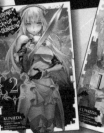
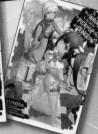
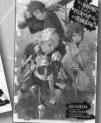
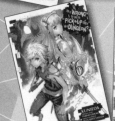
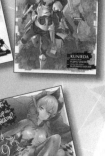
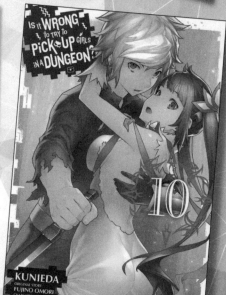

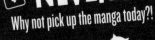

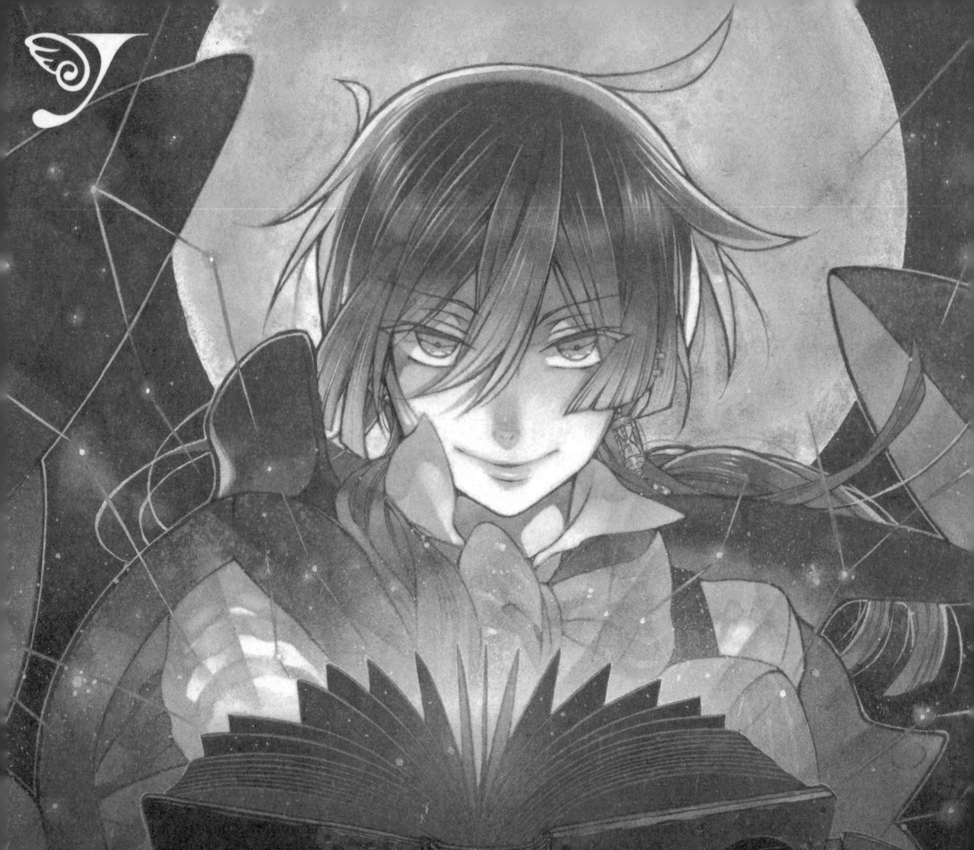

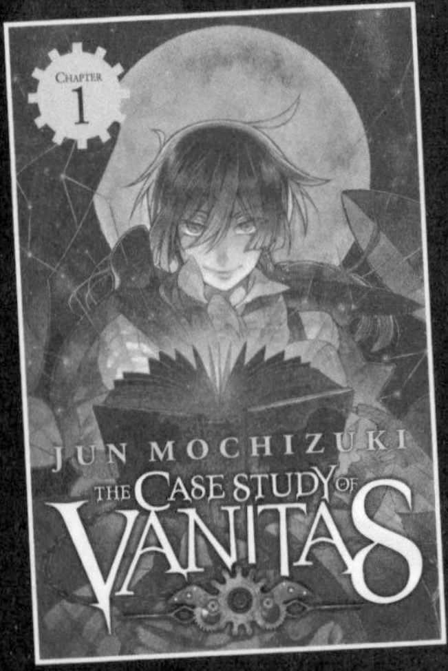
CHAPTER
1
JUN MOCHIZUKI
THE CASE STUDY OF
VANITAS

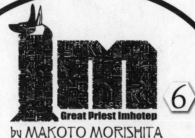

Great Priest Imhotep 6

by MAKOTO MORISHITA

Translation: Amanda Haley
Lettering: Rochelle Gancio

IM Vol. 6 ©2017 Makoto Morishita/SQUARE ENIX CO., LTD.
First published in Japan in 2017 by SQUARE ENIX CO., LTD. English translation rights arranged with SQUARE ENIX CO., LTD. and Yen Press, LLC through Tuttle-Mori Agency, Inc., Tokyo.

English translation ©2018 by SQUARE ENIX CO., LTD.

Yen Press
150 West 30th Street, 19th Floor
New York, NY 10001

Visit us at yenpress.com ‰ facebook.com/yenpress ⸙
twitter.com/yenpress ⸎ yenpress.tumblr.com 𝄪
instagram.com/yenpress

First Yen Press Print Edition: November 2020
Originally published as an ebook in April 2018 by Yen Press.

Yen Press is an imprint of Yen Press, LLC.
The Yen Press name and logo are trademarks of Yen Press, LLC.

Library of Congress Control Number: 2019953326

ISBN: 978-1-9753-1147-6 (paperback)

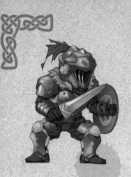

HE DOES NOT LET ANYONE ROLL THE DICE.

A young Priestess joins her first adventuring party, but blind to the dangers, they almost immediately find themselves in trouble. It's Goblin Slayer who comes to their rescue—a man who has dedicated his life to the extermination of all goblins by any means necessary. A dangerous, dirty, and thankless job, but he does it better than anyone. And when rumors of his feats begin to circulate, there's no telling who might come calling next...

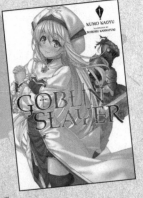

Light Novel V. 1-10 Available Now!

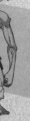

Check out the simul-pub manga chapters every month!

Yen Press   YEN ON

www.yenpress.com

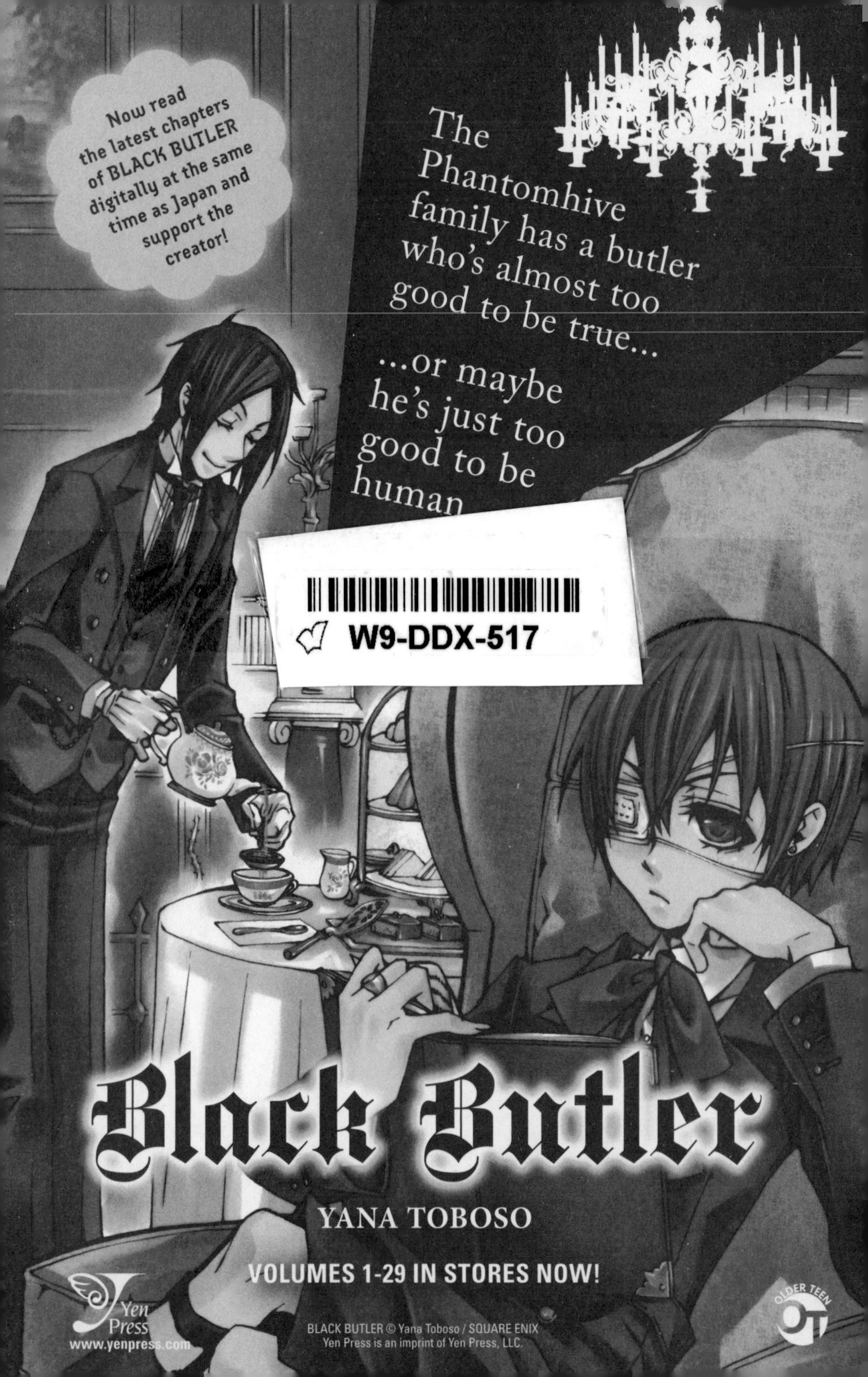
Now read the latest chapters of BLACK BUTLER digitally at the same time as Japan and support the creator!
The Phantomhive family has a butler who's almost too good to be true...
...or maybe he's just too good to be human.
Black Butler
YANA TOBOSO
VOLUMES 1-29 IN STORES NOW!
Yen Press
www.yenpress.com
BLACK BUTLER © Yana Toboso / SQUARE ENIX
Yen Press is an imprint of Yen Press, LLC.
OLDER TEEN
OT